Autism and Talent

Autism and Talent

Edited by

Professor Francesca Happé
Professor of Cognitive Neuroscience
Institute of Psychiatry
King's College London

Professor Uta Frith
Emeritus Professor of Cognitive Development
Institute of Cognitive Neuroscience
University College London

Originating from a Theme Issue first published in Philosophical
Transactions of the Royal Society B: Biological Sciences
http://publishing.royalsociety.org/philtransb

OXFORD
UNIVERSITY PRESS

Great Clarendon Street, Oxford OX2 6DP

Oxford University Press is a department of the University of Oxford.
It furthers the University's objective of excellence in research, scholarship,
and education by publishing worldwide in

Oxford New York

Auckland Cape Town Dar es Salaam Hong Kong Karachi
Kuala Lumpur Madrid Melbourne Mexico City Nairobi
New Delhi Shanghai Taipei Toronto

With offices in

Argentina Austria Brazil Chile Czech Republic France Greece
Guatemala Hungary Italy Japan Poland Portugal Singapore
South Korea Switzerland Thailand Turkey Ukraine Vietnam

Oxford is a registered trade mark of Oxford University Press
in the UK and in certain other countries

Published in the United States
by Oxford University Press Inc., New York

© The Royal Society, 2010

The moral rights of the author have been asserted

Database right Oxford University Press (maker)

First published by Oxford University Press 2010

All rights reserved. No part of this publication may be reproduced,
stored in a retrieval system, or transmitted, in any form or by any means,
without the prior permission in writing of Oxford University Press,
or as expressly permitted by law, or under terms agreed with the appropriate
reprographics rights organization. Enquiries concerning reproduction
outside the scope of the above should be sent to the Rights Department,
Oxford University Press, at the address above

You must not circulate this book in any other binding or cover
and you must impose the same condition on any acquirer

British Library Cataloguing in Publication Data

Data available

Library of Congress Cataloging in Publication Data

Data available

Typeset by Cepha Imaging Private Ltd, Bangalore, India
Printed in China
on acid-free paper by
C & C offset Printing Co., Ltd.

ISBN 978–0–19–956014–1

1 3 5 7 9 10 8 6 4 2

Contents

List of contributors	vii
Introduction: The beautiful otherness of the autistic mind *Francesca Happé and Uta Frith*	xi
1. The savant syndrome: an extraordinary condition. A synopsis: past, present, future *Darold A. Treffert*	1
2. Savant skills in autism: psychometric approaches and parental reports *Patricia Howlin, Susan Goode, Jane Hutton and Michael Rutter*	13
3. What aspects of autism predispose to talent? *Francesca Happé and Pedro Vital*	29
4. Talent in autism: hyper-systemizing, hyper-attention to detail and sensory hyper-sensitivity *Simon Baron-Cohen, Emma Ashwin, Chris Ashwin, Teresa Tavassoli and Bhismadev Chakrabarti*	41
5. Enhanced perception in savant syndrome: patterns, structure and creativity *Laurent Mottron, Michelle Dawson and Isabelle Soulières*	53
6. Perception and apperception in autism: rejecting the inverse assumption *Kate Plaisted Grant and Greg Davis*	65
7. Explaining and inducing savant skills: privileged access to lower level, less-processed information *Allan Snyder*	75
8. Talent in the taxi: a model system for exploring expertise *Katherine Woollett, Hugo J. Spiers and Eleanor A. Maguire*	89
9. Do calendrical savants use calculation to answer date questions? A functional magnetic resonance imaging study *Richard Cowan and Chris Frith*	105
10. A case study of a multiply talented savant with an autism spectrum disorder: neuropsychological functioning and brain morphometry *Gregory L. Wallace, Francesca Happé and Jay N. Giedd*	119

11. Radial cytoarchitecture and patterns of cortical connectivity in autism 135
 Manuel Casanova and Juan Trippe

12. How does visual thinking work in the mind of a person with autism? A personal account 141
 Temple Grandin

13. Assessing musical skills in autistic children who are not savants 151
 Pamela Heaton

14. Precocious realists: perceptual and cognitive characteristics associated with drawing talent in non-autistic children 161
 Jennifer E. Drake and Ellen Winner

15. Outsider Art and the autistic creator 181
 Roger Cardinal

16. Autistic autobiography 195
 Ian Hacking

17. Stereotypes of autism 209
 Douwe Draaisma

 Index 219

List of contributors

Chris Ashwin Autism Research Centre, Department of Psychiatry, University of Cambridge, Douglas House, 18b Trumpington Road, Cambridge CB2 8AH, UK

Emma Ashwin Autism Research Centre, Department of Psychiatry, University of Cambridge, Douglas House, 18b Trumpington Road, Cambridge CB2 8AH, UK

Simon Baron-Cohen Autism Research Centre, Department of Psychiatry, University of Cambridge, Douglas House, 18b Trumpington Road, Cambridge CB2 8AH, UK (sb205@cam.ac.uk)

Roger Cardinal Heath Field, Primrose Hill, Chartham Hatch, Canterbury, Kent CT4 7NS, UK (roger.cardinal@tiscali.co.uk)

Manuel Casanova Department of Psychiatry and Behavioral Sciences, University of Louisville, 500 South Preston Street, Building 55A, Suite 217, Louisville, KY 40292, USA (m0casa02@louisville.edu)

Bhismadev Chakrabarti Autism Research Centre, Department of Psychiatry, University of Cambridge, Douglas House, 18b Trumpington Road, Cambridge CB2 8AH, UK

Richard Cowan Psychology and Human Development, Institute of Education, University of London, 20 Bedford Way, London WC1H 0AL, UK (r.cowan@ioe.ac.uk)

Greg Davis Department of Experimental Psychology, University of Cambridge, Downing Site, Cambridge CB2 3EB, UK

Michelle Dawson Clinique spécialisée de l'autisme, Hôpital Riviére-des-Prairies, 7070 Boulevard Perras, Montréal, Québec, Canada H1E 1A4

Douwe Draaisma Heymans Institute, University of Groningen, PO Box 72, 9700 AB Groningen, The Netherlands (d.draaisma@rug.nl)

Jennifer E. Drake Department of Psychology, Boston College, Chestnut Hill, MA 02467, USA (drakejc@bc.edu)

Chris Frith Institute of Neurology, University College London, 12 Queen Square, London WC1N 3BG, UK

Jay N. Giedd Child Psychiatry Branch, National Institute of Mental Health, Bethesda, MD 20892, USA

Temple Grandin Department of Animal Sciences, Colorado State University, Fort Collins, CO 80523, USA (cheryl.miller@colostate.edu)

Kate Plaisted Grant Department of Experimental Psychology, University of Cambridge, Downing Site, Cambridge CB2 3EB, UK (kcp1000@cam.ac.uk)

Susan Goode Child and Mental Health Service, 3 Lennard Lodge, West Croydon, CRO 2UL UK

Ian Hacking Collége de France, 11, place Marcelin Berthelot, 75231 Paris Cedex 5, France (ian.hacking@college-de-france.fr)

Francesca Happé MRC Social, Genetic and Developmental Psychiatry Centre, Institute of Psychiatry, King's College London, De Crespigny Park, London SE5 8AF, UK (francesca.happé@kcl.ac.uk)

Pamela Heaton Department of Psychology, Goldsmiths College, University of London, New Cross, London SE14 6NW, UK (p.heaton@gold.ac.uk)

Patricia Howlin Department of Psychology, Institute of Psychiatry, King's College London, London SE5 8AF, UK (patricia.howlin@iop.kcl.ac.uk)

Jane Hutton Department of Psychological Medicine, King's College Hospital, London, SE5 9RS.

Eleanor A. Maguire Wellcome Trust Centre for Neuroimaging, Institute of Neurology, University College London, 12 Queen Square, London WC1N 3BG, UK (e.maguire@fil.ion.ucl.ac.uk)

Laurent Mottron Clinique spécialisée de l'autisme, Hôpital Riviére-des-Prairies, 7070 Boulevard Perras, Montréal, Québec, Canada H1E 1A4; Department of Psychiatry, Université de Montréal, Montréal, Québec, Canada H3T 1J4 (mottronl@istar.ca)

Michael Rutter MRC Social, Genetic and Developmental Psychiatry Centre, Institute of Psychiatry, King's College London, London, UK

Allan Snyder Centre for the Mind, University of Sydney, New South Wales 2006, Australia (allan@centreforthemind.com)

Isabelle Soulières Clinique spécialisée de l'autisme, Hôpital Riviére-des-Prairies, 7070 Boulevard Perras, Montréal, Québec, Canada H1E 1A4; Department of Psychiatry, Université de Montréal, Montréal, Québec, Canada H3T 1J4; Department of Psychiatry, Massachusetts General Hospital, Harvard Medical School, Boston, MA 02215, USA

Hugo J. Spiers Institute of Behavioural Neuroscience, Cognitive, Perceptual and Brain Sciences Research Department, University College London, 26 Bedford Way, London WC1H 0AP, UK

Teresa Tavassoli Autism Research Centre, Department of Psychiatry, University of Cambridge, Douglas House, 18b Trumpington Road, Cambridge CB2 8AH, UK

Darold A. Treffert University of Wisconsin Medical School, Madison, WI 53726, USA; Behavioral Health Department, St Agnes Hospital, 430 East Division Street, Fond du Lac, WI 54935, USA (daroldt@charter.net)

Juan Trippe Department of Psychiatry and Behavioral Sciences, University of Louisville, 500 South Preston Street, Building 55A, Suite 217, Louisville, KY 40292, USA

Pedro Vital MRC Social, Genetic and Developmental Psychiatry Centre, Institute of Psychiatry, King's College London, De Crespigny Park, London SE5 8AF, UK

Gregory L. Wallace Institute of Psychiatry, Social, Genetic, and Developmental Psychiatry Centre, King's College, University of London, London WC2R 2LS, UK Child Psychiatry Branch, National Institute of Mental Health, Bethesda, MD 20892, USA (gregwallace@mail.nih.gov)

Ellen Winner Department of Psychology, Boston College, Chestnut Hill, MA 02467, USA (winner@bc.edu)

Katherine Woollett Wellcome Trust Centre for Neuroimaging, Institute of Neurology, University College London, 12 Queen Square, London WC1N 3BG, UK

Introduction: The beautiful otherness of the autistic mind

Francesca Happé and Uta Frith

1. Introduction

Of all the features of autism, none is more widely admired than the remarkable talent found so frequently with this condition. Yet special talents are still less researched and less well understood than other features of autism. In popular accounts of autism, the existence of extraordinary talent in art, music, maths, calendar calculation or memory, often referred to as savant skills, has become a stock in trade. As a result of this fascination, it is now very likely that any eccentric scientist or artist, living or dead, will come under scrutiny for having traits of autism or Asperger syndrome. But are geniuses, such as Newton or Einstein, personifications of the association of autism and talent? In our view, this notion misrepresents both autism and talent. Nevertheless, the association of autism with special talent, sometimes at the highest level, cannot be denied and provides one of the most tantalizing mysteries of this condition.

Sacks (1985) was probably the first to raise popular awareness of people with severe brain abnormality who nonetheless showed extraordinary ability, in his famous account of 'the twins'. John and Michael, then 26, were living in an institution when Sacks met them. When a box of matches spilled on the floor, '111, they both cried simultaneously; and then, in a murmur, John said 37. Michael repeated this, John said it a third time and stopped. I counted the matches—it took me some time—and there were 111'. Amazingly, the twins could not only count the large number of matches within seconds, they were able to see the prime number 37 almost instantly, and saw it three times. While unable to communicate with John and Michael in the ordinary way, Sacks was able to engage with them by offering ever-larger prime numbers for their delight. Treffert (1989) described many more examples of staggering savant skills in his seminal book, *Extraordinary people*, in which he defined savantism as a rare condition that combines brilliance in one field with severe intellectual limitations in almost all others.

What can science tell us about autistic savants? Twenty years ago, O'Connor & Hermelin (1988) published an annotation on 'Low intelligence and special abilities'. These pioneering researchers had, for the first time, moved research on savant skills beyond the descriptive case study, through innovative experimental designs and the use of appropriate control groups. They thus paved the way for modern cognitive psychological studies of the conundrum: how can individuals with substantial impairments of intellect and social adaptation show skills that outstrip and baffle even the most intelligent 'neurotypical'?[1]

---

[1] A note on terminology: 'Neurotypical' is the term coined by people with autism spectrum conditions/disorders for those without such conditions. In this issue, we have left unedited authors' use of 'autistic' and 'with autism'. While the latter has been preferred in recent years by those working in the field, the former has been embraced in some recent writings by those on the autism spectrum.

The later 1980s and 1990s were dominated by social deficit accounts of autism spectrum disorders (ASD), fired by the breakthrough finding that individuals with ASD failed simple tests of theory of mind. However, the last decade has seen a return to interest in domain-general accounts, and particularly to interest in areas in which people with ASD show special ability rather than disability—a trend started by the concept of 'weak central coherence' (Frith 1989).

There has also been a return to interest in basic sensory processes in autism, also foreshadowed by Hermelin & O'Connor's (1964) early experiments on unusual processing of sensory input. Their initial hypothesis that children with autism favoured touch and smell over vision and hearing gave way to accounts centred on the nature of the resulting representations in the mind of the autistic child. Their notion that sensory information was stored more veridically, but less adaptively, due to lack of recoding for meaning, also prefigured the theories presented by some authors in this issue.

The papers in this issue reflect the content of a joint Royal Society and British Academy Discussion Meeting, held in September 2008. In line with the remit of these institutions, the range of contributions spans humanities and sciences, to debate questions such as: does autism predispose to talents, and if so why? Can talent result from neurocognitive deficits? What is the nature of autistic creativity versus 'neurotypical' creativity? In this way, the contents reach out beyond autism and raise questions about the basis of talent and creativity more generally.

2. The key puzzle: special skills are associated with autistic disorder

The history and origins of the savant concept are introduced by Treffert (2009), who vividly illustrates the phenomenon with case material. Treffert originally introduced and here discusses the distinction between savant skills at different levels of achievement. The very rare 'prodigious savants' are those whose abilities would be staggering in any context. 'Talented savants' and those with 'splinter skills' show striking abilities relative to their other skills and are relatively more common. While up to now the assumption has been that savantism only occurs in approximately 10 per cent of cases with ASD, Howlin and her colleagues (2009) provide evidence of much higher prevalence. In a large clinical cohort, almost 30 per cent show an outstanding skill either in terms of peak performance on intelligence subtests or parent-rated savant skills (in, for example, memory, music or calculation). The task, then, is to explain why people with ASD appear to show striking isolated talents at such a high rate, and much more often than any other group.

Several authors in this issue offer hypotheses for why autism should be associated with talent, with remarkable consensus that the ability to process local information plays a key role. Happé & Vital (Chapter 3) suggest that detail-focused attention and memory predispose to the development of talent, both in the general population and in autism. Baron-Cohen *et al.* (2009) suggest that superior sensory acuity across modalities underlies such detail focus, which in turn fosters the tendency to explore and master closed systems (e.g. the calendar). With the enhanced perceptual functioning theory, Mottron *et al.* (2009) propose that locally orientated processing and, specifically, detection of patterns in the environment, underlies the high incidence of savant skills in autism. Plaisted Grant & Davis (2009) also emphasize the qualitative differences in perceptual and cognitive processing in ASD, and make tentative links to underlying neural systems. These very different theorists share the view that an ability to attend to and process featural information plays an important part in predisposing to special skills of a savant sort. This view is upheld, for example, in a detailed case study of a prodigious mnemonist and calculator with Asperger syndrome and synaesthesia who shows a preference for local processing and an unusual pattern of brain activation while remembering digits (Bor *et al.* 2007).

3. But not everyone with talent is autistic

There is general agreement that savant skills can be found in people who are not autistic. An open question is whether such individuals share the cognitive characteristic of bias for superior featural processing. If 'eye for detail' is an important predisposing factor in talent, regardless of autism, this might perhaps help to redirect the trend for 'Asperger spotting' in geniuses current or long dead: instead this theory suggests that it is one or more of the cognitive biases/abilities characteristic of ASD, rather than the diagnosis itself, that is linked to special abilities and could usefully be identified in well-known individuals, from Newton to Bill Gates.

If savant skills can be found in individuals who do not meet the diagnostic criteria for ASD, an obvious question is whether the nature of skill is different in ASD and non-ASD savants. Drake & Winner (2009) in their paper on 'precocious realists' discuss commonalities between these young amazingly accurate drawers and artists with autism. They explore global and local processing in these children and find superior segmentation of parts and good visual memory, as in autism, but, unlike in autism, a distinct benefit from global coherence.

Cardinal (2009) discusses artists uninfluenced by current art theory or fashion and largely self-taught, who may be considered 'outsiders' for a variety of reasons. Common features across these non-autistic and autistic artists include self-motivation, self-teaching and extreme productivity. One of the thorny questions that savant art in particular raises is whether we admire the art works for their own sake or because they were produced by a savant. Would these works be worthy of the highest regard if we did not know who had produced them? As Cardinal (2009) points out: 'Outsider art earns its name not because of an association with a lurid case history or a sensational biography, but because it offers its audience a thrilling visual experience', the chance 'to savour the extreme experience of Otherness, in the form of a seductive exoticism that produces an inarticulate yet intense pleasure'. Indeed art and music, whether created by the autistic individual or by any other individual, act as 'a privileged medium of human contact'. This view resonates with Heaton's (2009) position, and her findings specifically that emotion communicated in music is apparently fully accessible to children with autism.

4. And not every person with ASD shows savant skills

The public fascination with savant skills may have the dangerous consequence that striking skills are expected of everyone on the autism spectrum. Draaisma (2009) explores the presentation of autism in fictional narrative, particularly in film, and concludes that savant skills are vastly overemphasized in this genre. For the parents of a lower-functioning child with autism who does not show a developed talent, the equation of autism with savant skills can be quite distressing. Hacking (2009) considers how the proliferation of autobiographies written by people on the autism spectrum may also inadvertently give a misleading picture of autism, since these writers are by their very nature exceptional in their ability to communicate their experience.

A key question is why some, maybe most, people with ASD do *not* develop savant skills. This puzzle is paralleled in the case of acquired skills following neurological damage or induced by repetitive trans-cranial magnetic stimulation (rTMS), as reported by Snyder (2009). Snyder's controversial theory proposes that it is only top-down inhibition that prevents us from being creative artists ourselves. People with autism, and neurotypicals when their left anterior temporal lobe is reversibly disabled with rTMS, can escape this inhibition. This means they have privileged access to raw forms of information, not normally accessible, that may give a new and more veridical perceptual insight, in contrast to expectation-biased interpretations. However, not every volunteer improves their savant-type skills under rTMS. Young *et al.* (2004), for example, found enhanced skills in memory, drawing, maths or calendar calculating as a result of rTMS, but only in 5 of 17 participants. What is different, cognitively or neurally, in this subgroup?

One possibility is that *all* people with autism have the potential to develop savant skills, and that chances of exposure and opportunity play a large part in determining outcome. Heaton (2009) reports data from musically untrained young people with autism and suggests that a substantial minority show potential to develop skills in music perception and performance. Better pitch and timbre discrimination appear to be widespread in ASD. Plaisted Grant & Davis (2009) make a plea for greater recognition of the value of autistic characteristics such as fine discrimination, which have currency in the workplace. While it is unlikely that every child with autism would become a maths, art or music savant, even with hours of training, we hypothesize that each could develop an identifiable special ability. For example, great facility with programming, rote memory for an area of interest, absolute pitch and superior ability to spot grammatical and typographical errors are often observed. Hyperlexia, and in some striking cases even learning to read fluently before developing speech, is moderately common in autism (Grigorenko *et al.* 2002)—and is well discussed in the contribution by Mottron *et al.* (2009). However, this is often not considered a savant skill because the absolute level of attainment does not exceed what ordinary older children eventually achieve. Similarly, distress at minute changes in the environment, insistence on taking exactly the same route to a destination or extreme reactions to apparently mild sensory stimuli are not viewed as 'talents', but might signal superior memory and discrimination. The challenge is to know how such abilities might be channelled into useful skills that could bring personal satisfaction or vocational success.

5. 10 000 hours of practice

It is sometimes said that genius is 99 per cent practice, and a target article by Howe *et al.* (1998) emphasized the overwhelming role of practice in expertise across a range of skills. However, many of the commentaries to this article argued for the role of innate talent, e.g. in predisposing cognitive or physical characteristics. In addition, individual differences in commitment, endurance, concentration and motivation are widely discussed in the literature on, for example, success in sports (e.g. Ericsson *et al.* 1993). The origins of these motivational characteristics are not well understood.

Modern conceptions of gene-environment interplay render obsolete any strict dichotomy between nature and nurture. However, it is impossible to resist asking, could we all be savants if only we put in the hours of practice? Woollett *et al.* (2009) show that navigation expertise rests on years of training and even then depends on constant practice. London taxi drivers who have internalized the complex street map of London show concomitant changes in the hippocampus. Interestingly, these changes reverse once practice ceases, following retirement. However, there is also another side to the argument. Approximately two-thirds of the candidates who begin the 3-year London black-cab training drop out and never acquire 'The Knowledge'. This large attrition rate may suggest that future taxi drivers who stay the course have a preexisting talent, and it is in the context of this self-selected sample that years of practice translate into the highest level of expertise. It seems very likely, then, that the same amount of practice will have dramatically different outcomes in different people.

Neuroimaging studies in this issue by Cowan & Frith (2009) and Wallace *et al.* (2009) also suggest that practice alters brain structure and/or function in savant calendar calculators. No evidence was found of abnormal or unexpected brain areas drawn into service, also supporting perhaps continuity with non-savant maths skills. This fits well with the assertion by Hermelin & O'Connor (1986), based on the patterns of behavioural data, that calendrical calculators have extracted rules and regularities of the calendar and are not simply using rote memory.

6. Wellsprings of talent

Can autism reveal some important truths about all creativity and genius? Among the contributors to this issue there is a strong consensus that one of the deep sources of exceptional skill is the obsessive drive to practice. But this is not all. According to Baron-Cohen there is also an obsessive need to classify and to make systems. In Chapter 15, Roger Cardinal presents an image of different species of crows by renowned savant Gregory Blackstock. This is typical of his art, which often consists of representing, in the form of a pictorial dictionary as it were, all the types of a category he knows. Other examples include turkeys, mackerel, collie dogs, carnivorous plants, hats, lighthouses, saws and knives. This type of work, which appears to reflect what Baron-Cohen has termed systemizing, exhaustively represents exemplars of a category side by side without concern for higher-level prototype.

Happé & Vital (Chapter 3) in this issue suggest that the preference for detail over prototype and generalisation underlies both talent and repetitive and restrictive behaviour in autism. Their analysis of twin data suggests a genetic basis for this association. Further exploration should shed light on whether talents in different domains spring from a common set of genetic/environmental factors. Do genetic factors predispose for talent in *any* area or for talent specifically in, say, music? Documenting the different or similar talents shown by identical twins will elucidate this question. It would also be of interest to establish whether relatives of savants—at least in cases of familial, versus de novo, autism (Abrahams & Geschwind 2008)—show special skills or cognitive characteristics that might predispose to talent.

Most of the accounts presented in this issue suggest that the predisposition to talent is to a large extent domain neutral. If this is the case, we would not be surprised to find that multiple talents develop in a single individual—time constraints allowing. Wallace *et al.* (2009) present one such case, and several more are known in the literature. Examples include: perfect pitch, calendar calculation and drawing all present in the case of Trehin (2006); perfect pitch, drawing and music in the case of Wiltshire (1989; Sacks 1995); and memory for numbers and learning languages in the case of Tammet (2006). Such cases would be very surprising if the basis for talent in, for example, calculation, were quite different from that for art or music.

Hardly anything is known as yet about the brain in autistic savants. The anatomical findings reviewed by Casanova and Trippe (2009) in their contribution to this issue suggest that minicolumnar peculiarities are seen in talented neurotypical scientists (Casanova *et al.* 2007), and are also found in ASD individuals, regardless of savant status. The evidence for atypical minicolumnar organization in autism fits well with the ideas on neural hyperconnectivity in local areas alongside hypoconnectivity over the longer range (e.g. Belmonte *et al.* 2004). A rather different approach focuses on rare single-gene disorders with a high prevalence of autism, with a recent suggestion that some molecular defects in autism may interfere with mechanisms of synaptic protein synthesis linked, theoretically, to both cognitive impairment and savant skills (Kelleher & Bear 2008).

7. The importance of fostering talent

A theme that emerged from the Discussion Meeting was the adaptive value of fostering special interests and talents. This might seem self-evident, but stands in contrast to the tendency to see narrow and obsessive interests as maladaptive and limiting. Heaton (2009) makes a strong case in her paper that learning to play music has benefits for both social integration and personal development for young people with autism. Her work suggests untapped potential special to ASD, which makes the task of teaching children with socio-communicative impairments particularly important. For such children, music lessons should not be considered a luxury. Untapped potential in art or maths remains to be documented, but anecdotally parents or carers often discover an existing talent entirely by accident.

It may well be that the most paradoxical talent shown by some autistic individuals is the ability to tell their own story. Grandin (2009), whose chapter (Chapter 12) discusses her own ability to think visually, is perhaps the most famous example. Hacking (2009) considers the paradox and the power of autobiographical accounts to shape our concept of autism. This, he points out, is not without danger. In particular, it is not clear to what extent we can generalize from the experiences reported by a number of high-functioning people with ASD to the experience of others who may never be able to speak for themselves. He gives the salutary warning that we really cannot know anything of what it is like 'inside the autistic mind'.

One outstanding message in Grandin's presentation at the meeting was the possibility of lifelong learning: 'I felt my brain switched on when I hit fifty'. This is discussed in her paper in this issue and raises the interesting possibility that developmental periods of exceptional brain plasticity may be extended in ASD. Lifelong learning may be of special importance in autism.

A striking feature of many talented people, whether autistic or not, is the precocious emergence of their skills. This in turn evokes a special environment, particularly in terms of the personal engagement of parents and teachers. The delight that parents feel in their child's achievement is at least as great in the case of autistic savants as neurotypical prodigies. Non-autistic maths, chess or sports prodigies also benefit from intense long-term professional coaching relationships, which deliver systematic expert feedback. By contrast, in many cases autistic talent emerges fully fledged without any systematic feedback by a trainer. In the case of calendar calculation, for instance, parents sometimes say they would not have wished to train this skill, and would have channelled their child's interest into a different direction, if only they could.

8. Future research directions

Paul Trehin (http://pagesperso-orange.fr/gilles.trehin.urville/accueil.html), whose comments and questions at the Discussion Meeting were enlightening, related the following anecdote about his son, Gilles, then aged 8: 'While coming back from New York City by train, in one of the cars one ceiling light was blinking, remaining longer dark than bright. As soon as our son arrived at home, he rushed to his bedroom to fetch a pencil and a page of paper to draw the ceiling of the train car with a dark ceiling light. It seems that, during early phases of talent observation at least, drawing is guided by a strong urge to draw, regardless of whether the drawing will be seen or not by someone else. There is no desire to communicate, the child draws for his own purpose, probably to fix a perception in space and time' (personal communication).

This anecdote highlights, as well as the remarkable focus on detail, the mystery of motivation in talent. Mottron *et al.* (2009) are unusual in considering explicitly the emotional aspects of savant skills. Winner (1996) coined the phrase the 'rage to learn' and argued that this is what characterizes exceptionally gifted children. For these children, learning, practice and performance are all rewarding in their own right and not a means to other rewards.

It seems to us that the single largest remaining puzzle is why repetitive practice in a narrow domain is so enormously rewarding for individuals who develop savant skills. On the one hand, we all enjoy doing things we are good at. However, most neurotypical individuals do not enjoy *getting to be good at* savant skills: when ordinary volunteers are instructed to learn calendar calculation, for example, it is notable that they stop as soon as they can.

Perhaps this contrast between meaningless repetition for the neurotypical trainee and enjoyable repetition for the ASD trainee savant can be understood through the notion of detail focus. Repetition is not repetition, for example, if you have expert levels of discrimination. Listening to different recordings of the same symphony might strike some as repetitive, but these sound entirely distinct to an expert. The child with autism who would happily spend hours spinning coins, or watching drops of water fall from his fingers, might be considered a connoisseur, seeing minute differences between events that others regard as pure repetition.

In the neuroscience of decision making, the tendencies 'to exploit' versus 'to explore' have been successfully contrasted in terms of computational models of learning (Daw *et al.* 2006). Why would you ever *not* order your usual dish at your favourite restaurant? Sameness is what people with ASD would prefer, even over decades, while for neurotypicals there is pleasure in novelty and boredom in repetition. In the natural environment, it makes sense for animals to stay and exploit a familiar and rewarding fruit tree, yet sooner or later a well-adapted animal needs to move on, and this will require exploring the unknown and finding reward in doing something different. In autism, the aversion to novelty suggests a different balance of reward value for exploiting versus exploring. Thus, reward-learning paradigms might open new avenues for investigation of savant skills. For example, is the ability to practice without boredom connected with a different balance of rewards from novelty and familiarity?

Understanding why the individual with savant skills chooses to 'practice' day and night may lead us to a better understanding of the apparently meaningless repetition and insistence on sameness seen throughout the autism spectrum. In this way, the study of savant skills could, perhaps, lead to a better appreciation of the beautiful otherness of the autistic mind.

We would like to thank our friends and colleagues for providing insightful reviews of the papers submitted for this special issue: Jan Atkinson, Simon Baron-Cohen, Matthew Belmonte, Sarah-Jayne Blakemore, Oliver Braddick, Anna Bonnel, Dermot Bowler, Neil Burgess, Tony Charman, Richard Cowan, Chris Frith, Claire Golomb, Ian Hacking, Patricia Howlin, Narinder Kapur, Laurent Mottron, Declan Murphy, Stephen Murray, Adam Ockelford, John Onians, Liz Pellicano, Josef Perner, Sue Sheppard, Neil Smith, Klaas-Enno Stephan, Darold Treffert, Tom Trusky, Greg Wallace, Vincent Walsh, Sarah White, Ellen Winner and Robyn Young.

January 2009

References

Abrahams, B. S. & Geschwind, D. H. 2008 Advances in autism genetics: on the threshold of a new neurobiology. *Nat. Rev. Genet.* **9**, 341–355. (doi:10.1038/nrg2346)

Baron-Cohen, S., Ashwin, E., Ashwin, C, Tavassoli, T. & Chakrabarti, B. 2009 Talent in autism: hyper-systemizing, hyper-attention to detail and sensory hypersensitivity. *Phil. Trans. R. Soc. B* **364**, 1377–1383. (doi:10.1098/rstb.2008.0337)

Belmonte, M. K., Allen, G., Beckel-Mitchener, A., Boulanger, L. M., Carper, R. A. & Webb, S. J. 2004 Autism and abnormal development of brain connectivity. *J. Neurosci.* **24**, 9228–9231. (doi:10.1523/JNEUROSCI.3340-04.2004)

Bor, D., Billington, J. & Baron-Cohen, S. 2007 Savant memory for digits in a case of synaesthesia and Asperger syndrome is related to hyperactivity in the lateral prefrontal cortex. *Neurocase* **13**, 311–319. (doi:10.1080/13554790701844945)

Cardinal, R. 2009 Outsider Art and the autistic creator. *Phil. Trans. R. Soc. B* **364**, 1459–1466. (doi:10.1098/rstb.2008.0325)

Casanova, M. R, Switala, A. E., Trippe, J. & Fitzgerald, M. 2007 Comparative minicolumnar morphometry of three distinguished scientists. *Autism* **11**, 557–569. (doi:10.1177/1362361307083261)

Casanova, M. & Trippe, J. 2009 Radial cytoarchitecture and patterns of cortical connectivity in autism. *Phil. Trans. R. Soc. B* **364**, 1433–1436. (doi:10.1098/rstb.2008.0331)

Cowan, R. & Frith, C. 2009 Do calendrical savants use calculation to answer date questions? A functional magnetic resonance imaging study. *Phil. Trans. R. Soc. B* **364**, 1417–1424. (doi:10.1098/rstb.2008.0323)

Daw, N. D., O'Doherty, J. P., Dayan, P., Seymour, B. & Dolan, R. J. 2006 Cortical substrates for exploratory decisions in humans. *Nature* **441**, 876–879. (doi:10.1038/nature04766)

Draaisma, D. 2009 Stereotypes of autism. *Phil. Trans. R. Soc. B* **364**, 1475–1480. (doi:10.1098/rstb.2008.0324)

Drake, J. E. & Winner, E. 2009 Precocious realists: perceptual and cognitive characteristics associated with drawing talent in non-autistic children. *Phil. Trans. R. Soc. B* **364**, 1449–1458. (doi:10.1098/rstb.2008.0295)

Ericsson, K. A., Krampe, R. T. & Tesch-Roemer, C. 1993 The role of deliberate practice in the acquisition of expert performance. *Psychol. Rev.* **100**, 363–406. (doi:10.1037/0033-295X.100.3.363)

Frith, U. 1989 *Autism: explaining the enigma*. Oxford, UK: Blackwell. Grandin, T. 2009 How does visual thinking work in the mind of a person with autism? A personal account. *Phil. Trans. R. Soc. B* **364**, 1437–1442. (doi:10.1098/rstb.2008.0297)

Grigorenko, E. L., Klin, A., Pauls, D. L., Senft, R., Hooper, C. & Volkmar, F. 2002 A descriptive study of hyperlexia in a clinically referred sample of children with developmental delays. *J. Autism Dev. Disord.* **32**, 3–12. (doi:10.1023/A:1017995805511)

Hacking, I. 2009 Autistic autobiography. *Phil. Trans. R. Soc. B* **364**, 1467–1473. (doi:10.1098/rstb.2008.0329)

Happé, F. & Vital, P. 2009 What aspects of autism predispose to talent? *Phil. Trans. R. Soc. B* **364**, 1369–1375. (doi:10.1098/rstb.2008.0332)

Heaton, P. 2009 Assessing musical skills in autistic children who are not savants. *Phil. Trans. R. Soc. B* **364**, 1443–1447. (doi:10.1098/rstb.2008.0327)

Hermelin, B. & O'Connor, N. 1964 Effects of sensory input and sensory dominance on severely disturbed, autistic children and on subnormal controls. *Br. J. Psychol.* **55**, 201–206.

Hermelin, B. & O'Connor, N. 1986 Idiot savant calendrical calculators: rules and regularities. *Psychol. Med.* **16**, 885–893.

Howe, M. J., Davidson, J. W & Sloboda, J. A. 1998 Innate talents: reality or myth? *Behav. Brain Sci.* **21**, 399–407. (doi:10.1017/S0140525X9800123X) [Discussion, pp. 407–442.]

Howlin, P., Goode, S., Hutton, J. & Rutter, M. 2009 Savant skills in autism: psychometric approaches and parental reports. *Phil. Trans. R. Soc. B* **364**, 1359–1367. (doi:10.1098/rstb.2008.0328)

Kelleher III, R. J. & Bear, M. F. 2008 The autistic neuron: troubled translation? *Cell* **135**, 401–406. (doi:10.1016/j.cell.2008.10.017)

Mottron, L., Dawson, M. & Soulières, I. 2009 Enhanced perception in savant syndrome: patterns, structure and creativity. *Phil. Trans. R. Soc. B* **364**, 1385–1391. (doi:10.1098/rstb.2008.0333)

O'Connor, N. & Hermelin, B. 1988 Low intelligence and special abilities. *J. Child Psychol. Psychiatry* **29**, 391–396. (doi:10.1111/j.l469-7610.1988.tb00732.x)

Plaisted Grant, K. & Davis, G. 2009 Perception and apperception in autism: rejecting the inverse assumption. *Phil. Trans. R. Soc. B* **364**, 1393–1398. (doi:10.1098/rstb.2009.0001)

Sacks, O. 1985 *The man who mistook his wife for a hat, and other clinical tales*. London, UK: Picador.

Sacks, O. 1995 *An anthropologist on Mars. Seven paradoxical tales*. London, UK: Picador.

Snyder, A. 2009 Explaining and inducing savant skills: privileged access to lower level, less-processed information. *Phil. Trans. R. Soc. B* **364**, 1399–1405. (doi:10.1098/rstb.2008.0290)

Tammet, D. 2006 *Born on a blue day: a memoir of Aspergers and an extraordinary mind*. London, UK: Hodder & Stoughton.

Treffert, D. A. 1989 *Extraordinary people: understanding savant syndrome*. New York, NY: Ballantine Books.

Treffert, D. A. 2009 The savant syndrome: an extraordinary condition. A synopsis: past, present, future. *Phil. Trans. R. Soc. B* **364**, 1351–1357. (doi:10.1098/rstb.2008.0326)

Trehin, G. 2006 *Urville*. London, UK: Jessica Kingsley.

Wallace, G. L., Happé, F. & Giedd, J. N. 2009 A case study of a multiply talented savant with an autism spectrum disorder: neuropsychological functioning and brain morphometry. *Phil. Trans. R. Soc. B* **364**, 1425–1432. (doi:10.1098/rstb.2008.0330)

Wiltshire, S. 1989 *Cities*. London, UK: Dent. Winner, E. 1996 *Gifted children: myths and realities*. New York, NY: Basic Books.

Woollett, K., Spiers, H. J. & Maguire, E. A. 2009 Talent in the taxi: a model system for exploring expertise. *Phil. Trans. R. Soc. B* **364**, 1407–1416. (doi:10.1098/rstb.2008.0288)

Young, R. L., Ridding, M. C. & Morrell, T. L. 2004 Switching skills on by turning off part of the brain. *Neurocase* **10**, 215–222. (doi:10.1080/13554790490495140)

1

The savant syndrome: an extraordinary condition. A synopsis: past, present, future

Darold A. Treffert

> Savant syndrome is a rare, but extraordinary, condition in which persons with serious mental disabilities, including autistic disorder, have some 'island of genius' which stands in marked, incongruous contrast to overall handicap. As many as one in 10 persons with autistic disorder have such remarkable abilities in varying degrees, although savant syndrome occurs in other developmental disabilities or in other types of central nervous system injury or disease as well. Whatever the particular savant skill, it is always linked to massive memory. This paper presents a brief review of the phenomenology of savant skills, the history of the concept and implications for education and future research.
>
> **Keywords:** savant syndrome; autism; memory; brain; education

1.1 Introduction

Without doubt, the best-known autistic savant is a fictional one, Raymond Babbitt, as portrayed by Dustin Hoffman in the 1988 movie *Rain man*. However, the original inspiration for the savant portrayed in *Rain man* was a now 57-year-old male who has memorized over 6000 books and has encyclopedic knowledge of geography, music, literature, history, sports and nine other areas of expertise (Peek & Hanson 2008). He can name all the US area codes and major city zip codes. He has also memorized the maps in the front of telephone books and can tell you precisely how to get from one US city to another, and then how to get around in that city street by street. He also has calendar-calculating abilities and, more recently, rather advanced musical talent has surfaced. Of unique interest is his ability to read extremely rapidly, simultaneously scanning one page with the left eye and the other page with the right eye. Magnetic resonance imaging (MRI) shows the absence of the corpus callosum along with other substantial central nervous system (CNS) damage.

The combination of blindness, mental handicap and musical genius is conspicuously over-represented throughout the reports of savant syndrome from earliest times. Prominent cases include Blind Tom who travelled internationally and became famous in the 1800s, Tredgold's case at the Salpetriere even earlier than that and a number of well-known present-day musical savants. Why that rare triad of musical genius, blindness and mental handicaps should occur so consistently in the already rare condition of savant syndrome deserves very careful study.

Reports of female savants continue to be relatively few. Selfe (1978) described the case of Nadia, which has triggered considerable debate about the possible 'trade-off' of special skills for language and social skills acquisition. Viscott (1969) documented in detail, including psychodynamic formulations, a female musical savant whom he followed for many years. Treffert (2006*a*) described a blind, autistic musical savant who, along with her musical ability, demonstrated very precise spatial location abilities and precise timekeeping skills without access to a clock face or other time instruments.

Detailed reports of these and many other savants dating from Down's original description of the disorder are contained in *Extraordinary people: understanding savant syndrome* (Treffert 2006*a*). Moreover, information about many of them, including some video clips, can be accessed on the savant syndrome website at www.savantsyndrome.com maintained by the Wisconsin Medical Society Foundation.

1.2 Where we have been

Savant syndrome, with its 'islands of genius', has a long history. The first account of savant syndrome in a scientific paper appeared in the German psychology journal, *Gnothi Sauton*, in 1783, describing the case of Jedediah Buxton, a lightning calculator with extraordinary memory (Mortiz 1783). Rush (1789), the father of American psychiatry, also provided one of the earliest reports when he described the lightning calculating ability of Thomas Fuller 'who could comprehend scarcely anything, either theoretical or practical, more complex than counting'. However, when Fuller was asked how many seconds a man had lived who was 70 years, 17 days and 12 hours old, he gave the correct answer of 2 210 500 800 in 90s, even correcting for the 17 leap years included (Scripture 1891).

However, the first specific description of savant syndrome took place in London in 1887 when Dr J. Langdon Down gave that year's prestigious Lettsomian Lecture at the invitation of the Medical Society of London. In that lecture, he reflected on his 30 years as a physician at the Earlswood Hospital and described 'an interesting class of cases for which the term 'idiot savants' has been given, and of which a considerable number have come under my observation'. He then presented 10 cases of persons with 'special faculties' that read exactly similar to cases now 121 years later. One of his patients had memorized *The rise and fall of the Roman Empire* verbatim and could recite it backwards or forwards. Other children drew with remarkable skill but 'had a comparative blank in all the other faculties of mind'. Still other children showed music ability, arithmetical genius or precise timekeeping skill, all of which, taken together, comprised a clinical picture of savant syndrome—special skills + phenomenal memory—which unfailingly reoccurs in case reports to this day.

In 1887, 'idiot' was an accepted classification for persons with an IQ below 25, and 'savant', or 'knowledgeable person', was derived from the French word *savoir* meaning 'to know'. Down joined those words together and coined the term idiot savant by which the condition was generally known over the next century. While descriptive, the term was actually a misnomer since almost all cases occur in persons with an IQ higher than 40. In the interest of accuracy and dignity, savant syndrome now has been substituted and is widely used. Savant syndrome is preferable to 'autistic savant' since only approximately

50 per cent of persons with savant syndrome have autistic spectrum disorder and the other 50 per cent have some other forms of CNS injury or disease.

Tredgold (1914), also from the Earlswood Hospital, wrote a very comprehensive account of savant syndrome in a chapter in his well-known textbook, *Mental deficiency*. This classic chapter, which was carried for many years into subsequent editions, described over 20 additional cases from a variety of clinicians. Hill (1978), provided a review of the literature between 1890 and 1978, including 60 reports involving over 100 savants. That same year, Rimland provided a summary of his data on 'special abilities' in 531 cases from a survey population of 5400 children with autism. Treffert (1988) provided an updated review, which contained more detail on all of those earlier cases and suggested that the name of the condition be changed to savant syndrome. In 1989, *Extraordinary people* was first published by Treffert, summarizing a century of cases, observations and research findings since Down's 1887 description of the disorder. In her book, *Bright splinters of the mind*, Hermelin (2001) summarized her findings based on 20 years of research by her and her co-workers. A comprehensive review article by Heaton & Wallace (2004) also provides an extensive bibliography on research to that date.

(a) Did Dr Down describe autism?

While Down is best known for having described Down's syndrome (trisomy 21) and savant syndrome in his 1887 lecture, he made an additional very astute observation about what he called 'developmental retardation'. Today, that condition is known as autistic disorder (Treffert 2006*b*). Reflecting on his 30 years of experience, he divided mental retardation into 'congenital' and 'accidental' categories. However, he mentioned, there was a third kind of mental retardation that occurred in children who did not have the usual 'physical aspects' of retardation. Some of these children had developed normally and then suddenly regressed and 'lost wonted brightness' and 'lost speech'. There was the suspension of 'normal intellectual growth'. These children lived 'in a world of their own', spoke 'in the third person', had 'rhythmical and automatic movements' and 'lessened responsiveness to all endearments of friends'.

Down called this 'developmental retardation' and described what are, without doubt, cases of both early-onset and late-onset (regressive) autism. That he should choose the term 'developmental' for this form of disorder is interesting indeed, because it was fully 93 years later that the term 'developmental disorders' was included, for the first time, in the DSM III (DSM-III, 1980), for the category in which autistic disorder was included. The fact that regressive or late-onset autism occurred, and was described so accurately by Down, more than a century ago is an important perspective to bear in mind in present-day discussions about the autism 'epidemic' and causes of regressive autism.

Of course, it was Kanner (1944) who described what he called 'early infantile autism'. Many of the same behaviours and traits Down commented on in his developmental retardation group of patients were similarly noted by Kanner in his description of his 10 original cases. Six of those individuals had special musical abilities and Kanner was struck as well by the overall heightened memory capacity of all 10 persons in that original group.

1.3 What we do know

After several centuries of reports and observations, we know that:

(a) The condition is rare but one in 10 autistic persons show some savant skills

In Rimland's (1978) survey of 5400 children with autism, 531 were reported by parents to have special abilities and a 10 per cent incidence of savant syndrome has become the generally accepted figure in autistic disorder. Hermelin (2001), however, estimated that figure to be as low as 'one or two in 200'. But the presence of savant syndrome is not limited to autism. In a survey of an institutionalized population with a diagnosis of mental retardation, the incidence of savant skills was 1:2000 (0.06%; Hill 1977). A more recent study surveyed 583 facilities, and found a prevalence rate of 1.4 per 1000, or approximately double the Hill estimate (Saloviita *et al.* 2000).

Whatever the exact figures, mental retardation and other forms of developmental disability are more common than autistic disorder, so a reasonable estimate might be that approximately 50 per cent of persons with savant syndrome have autistic disorder and the other 50 per cent have other forms of developmental disability, mental retardation or other CNS injury or disease. Thus, not all autistic persons have savant syndrome and not all persons with savant syndrome have autistic disorder.

(b) Males outnumber females in autism and savant syndrome

Males outnumber females by an approximate 6:1 ratio in savant syndrome compared with an approximate 4:1 ratio in autistic disorder. In explaining that finding, Geschwind & Galaburda (1987) in their work on cerebral lateralization pointed out that the left hemisphere normally completes its development later than the right hemisphere and is thus subjected to prenatal influences, some of which can be detrimental, for a longer period of time. In the male foetus particularly, circulating testosterone, which can reach very high levels, can slow growth and impair neuronal function in the more vulnerably exposed left hemisphere, with actual enlargement and shift of dominance favouring skills associated with the right hemisphere. A 'pathology of superiority' was postulated, with compensatory growth in the right brain as a result of impaired development or actual injury to the left brain.

This finding may account as well for the high male: female ratio in other disorders, including autism itself since left hemisphere dysfunction is often seen in autism (Treffert 2005, 2006*a*). Other conditions, such as dyslexia, delayed speech and stuttering, also have a male predominance in incidence, which may be a manifestation of the same left hemisphere growth interference in the prenatal period described above.

(c) Savant skills typically occur in an intriguingly narrow range of special abilities

Considering all the abilities in the human repertoire, it is interesting that savant skills generally narrow to five general categories: *music*, usually performance, most often piano, with perfect pitch, although composing in the absence of performing has been reported as has been playing multiple instruments (as many as 22); *art*, usually drawing, painting or sculpting; *calendar calculating* (curiously an obscure skill in most persons); *mathematics*, including lightning calculating or the ability to compute prime numbers, for example, in the absence of other simple arithmetic abilities; and *mechanical* or *spatial skills*, including the capacity to measure distances precisely without benefit of instruments, the ability to construct complex models or structures with painstaking accuracy or the mastery of map making and direction finding.

Other skills have been reported less often, including: prodigious language (poly-glot) facility; unusual sensory discrimination in smell, touch or vision including synaesthesia; perfect appreciation of passing time without benefit of a clock; and outstanding knowledge in specific fields such as neurophysiology, statistics or navigation. In Rimland's (1978) sample of 543 children with special skills, musical ability was the most frequently reported skill followed by memory, art, pseudo-verbal abilities, mathematics, maps and directions, coordination, calendar calculating and extrasensory perception. Hyperlexia, which is distinguished by precocity rather than age-independent level of skill, has also been frequently reported in autism (Grigorenko *et al.* 2002).

Generally, a single special skill exists but, in some instances, several skills exist simultaneously. Rimland & Fein (1988) noted that the incidence of multiple skills appeared to be higher in savants with autism than in savants with other developmental disabilities. Whatever the special skill, it is always associated with prodigious memory. Some observers list memory as a separate special skill; however, prodigious memory is an ability all savants possess cutting across all of the skill areas as a shared, integral part of the syndrome itself. Several investigators have shown that memory alone cannot fully account for savant abilities, particularly calendar calculating and musical skills (Nettlebeck & Young 1999; Hermelin 2001). Formal testing for eidetic imagery shows that phenomenon to be present in some, but certainly not all, savants and when present it may exist more as a marker of brain damage than being central to savant abilities (Bender *et al.* 1968; Giray & Barclay 1977).

(d) There is a spectrum of savant skills

The most common are *splinter skills*, which include obsessive preoccupation with, and memorization of, music and sports trivia, license plate numbers, maps, historical facts or obscure items such as vacuum cleaner motor sounds, for example. *Talented savants* are those cognitively impaired persons in whom the musical, artistic or other special abilities are more prominent and highly honed, usually within an area of single expertise and are very conspicuous when viewed in contrast to overall disability. *Prodigious savant* is a term reserved for those extraordinarily rare individuals for whom the special skill is so outstanding that it would be spectacular even if it were to occur in a non-impaired person. There are, from my experience, probably fewer than 100 *known* prodigious savants living worldwide at the present time who would meet that very high threshold of savant ability.

(e) The special skills are always accompanied by prodigious memory

Whatever the special abilities, a remarkable memory of a unique and uniform type welds the condition together. Terms such as automatic, mechanical, concrete and habit-like have been applied to this extraordinary memory. Down (1887) used the term 'verbal adhesion'; Critchley (1979) used the term 'exultation of memory' or 'memory without reckoning'; Tredgold (1914) used the term 'automatic'; and Barr (1898) characterized his patient with prodigious memory as 'an exaggerated form of habit'. Such unconscious memory suggests what Mishkin *et al.* (1984) referred to as non-conscious 'habit' formation rather than a 'semantic' memory system. They proposed two different neural circuits for these two different types of memory: a higher level corticolimbic circuit for semantic memory and a lower level cortico-striatal circuit for the more primitive habit memory, which is sometimes referred to as procedural or implicit memory. Savant memory is characteristically very deep, but exceedingly narrow, within the confines of the accompanying special skill.

(f) Savant syndrome can be congenital or it can be acquired

Most often savant skills emerge in childhood, superimposed on some underlying developmental disability present at birth. However, 'acquired' savant skills can also appear, when none were previously present, in neurotypical individuals following brain injury or disease later in infancy, childhood or adult life (Lythgoe *et al.* 2005; Treffert 2006*a*). Recent reports of savant-type abilities emerging in previously healthy elderly persons with frontotemporal dementia have been particularly intriguing (Miller *et al.* 1998, 2000; Hou *et al.* 2000). The prospect of dormant potential triggered, or released, by CNS injury existing within each person has far-reaching implications, as discussed elsewhere in this volume.

An important question is whether special skills are found in first-degree relatives of savants. Two studies, one with 25 savants and another with 51 subjects, showed relatives with special skills in *some* but certainly not all cases (Duckett 1976; Young 1995). Another study of 23 relatives of carefully studied savants found only one family member with special skills (LaFontaine 1974).

Young (1995) travelled to a number of countries and met with 51 savants and their families, completing the largest study performed on savants to date using uniform history taking and standardized psychological testing. Forty-one savants carried a diagnosis of autism and the remainder some other type of intellectual disability: 12 were rated as prodigious savants; 20 were rated as talented; and the remaining 19 had splinter skills. The savants in this series of cases had the following elements in common: neurological impairment with idiosyncratic and divergent intellectual ability; language and intellectual impairments consistent with autism; intense interest and preoccupation with particular areas of ability; rule-based, rigid and highly structured skills lacking critical aspects of creativity and cognitive flexibility; preserved neurological capacity to process information relating to the particular skills; a well-developed declarative memory; a family history of similar skills in some, but not all, cases but even in the absence of a history of a specific skill, there was a familial predisposition towards high achievement; and a climate of support, encouragement and reinforcement from families, case workers, teachers, caretakers and others.

(g) Savant skills do not fade or disappear; rather a pattern of replication to improvisation to creation is often seen

The case of Nadia, who lost her special art skills when exposed to traditional schooling, raised the prospect of a 'dreaded trade-off' of savant skills for acquisition of better language, communication and daily living skills (Selfe 1978). But experience has shown that such loss of special skills is the exception rather than the rule in savant syndrome. Instead, with continued use, the special abilities either persist at the same level or actually increase.

Now that I have had an opportunity to follow the unfolding of savant abilities in some individuals for nearly 30 years, I have seen a pattern of progression of savant abilities in a number of prodigious savants particularly that ends in the capacity to be creative. In the light of these observations, I would revise my original comments in my book *Extraordinary people* that savants certainly demonstrated remarkable talent, and stunning replication abilities, but were not very creative. I was wrong.

The pattern I have observed begins with spectacular, literal *replication* of things seen or heard. Leslie Lemke, for example, played back Tchaikovsky's first piano concerto flawlessly at age 14, having heard it for the first time as a theme song to a television movie. From there Leslie moved, over time, from literal *replication* (which he can still do) to *improvisation*, seemingly having become bored with *just* reproducing what he has heard. In recent years, Leslie has moved now to *creation* of entirely new songs that he composes, plays and sings. This pattern of *replication* to *improvisation* to *creation* has been demonstrated in other musical savants. A well-known Japanese musical savant's ability as a *composer* demonstrates decisively that savants can be creative; his 40 *original* pieces on two internationally popular CDs forcefully document that ability (Cameron 1998).

That same transition can be seen in artistic savants. For example, Stephen Wiltshire can certainly *replicate* in stunning fashion what he sees as demonstrated in a recent documentary film clip, when, after a 45 min helicopter ride over Rome, he completed, in a three-day drawing marathon, an impeccably accurate drawing, on a five and half yard canvas. It captures with precision the many square miles he has seen street by street, building by building and column by column. A blueprint of the coliseum, superimposed on his drawing, shows an astonishing accurate replication. That clip can be seen at www.savant-syndrome.com. However, Stephen can also *improvise* in his drawings, and he can also *create* scenes of his choosing. He has several art books published, and now has his own art gallery in London, which displays his various drawing styles (Wiltshire 1987, 1991).

There are other examples of this same replication to improvisation to creation pattern that space prohibits describing here. However, they are documented in *Extraordinary people* and on the savant syndrome website in detail.

(h) No single theory can explain all savants

Since Down's first description of savant syndrome, numerous theories have been put forth to explain this astonishing juxtaposition of ability and disability in the same person. Space precludes outlining those here but I do discuss them in detail in *Extraordinary people*. In the 'How do they do it?' chapter in that book, I outline in detail as well my speculation, based on observation, imaging and neuropsychological studies of a number of savants, that one mechanism in some savants, whether congenital or acquired, is left brain dysfunction with right brain compensation, a form of 'paradoxical functional facilitation' as described by Kapur (1996). Brink (1980) raised that possibility with a case in which left brain injury in a child gave rise to some mechanical and other savant skills. Miller's recent work with persons with fronto-temporal dementia (FTD) in whom savant skills surfaced, sometimes at a prodigious level, adds impetus to that speculation (Miller *et al*. 1998, 2000). Those studies led him to conclude that 'loss of function in the left anterior lobe may lead to facilitation of artistic or musical skills'. Hou *et al*. (2000) stated it this way: 'The anatomic substrate for the savant syndrome may involve loss of function in the left temporal lobe with enhanced function of the posterior neocortex'.

Other current theories, including genetic, cognitive and neural, will be explored in other contributions to this volume.

1.4 'Training the talent': successful educational approaches

Aetiologic considerations aside, what is the best approach to the savant and his or her special skills? Phillips framed the controversy in 1930 when he stated: 'The problem of treatment comes next...is it better to eliminate the defects or train the talent?' Experience has provided a clear answer—'train the talent'! And as one does so, some of the 'defect' subsides. The special talent, in fact, becomes a conduit towards normalization, using the unique savant skills to achieve better socialization, language acquisition and independence, all without the trade-off or loss of special abilities for those valuable gains in other areas of functioning. The special skills can be used as a way of engaging attention of the savant, and rather than seeing the special abilities as frivolous, they can be used as a form of expression with the goal of channelling those abilities more usefully.

Clark (2001) developed a savant skill curriculum using a combination of successful strategies currently employed in the education of gifted children (enrichment, acceleration and mentorship) and autism education (visual supports and social stories) in an attempt to channel and apply, usefully, the often nonfunctional obsessive savant and splinter skills of a group of students with autism. This special curriculum proved highly successful in the functional application of savant skills and an overall reduction in the level of autistic behaviours in many subjects. Improvements in behaviour, social skills and academic self-efficacy were reported, along with gain in the communication skills of some subjects.

Donnelly & Altman (1994) noted that increasing numbers of 'gifted students with autism' are now being included in gifted and talented classrooms with non-disabled gifted peers. Accompanying elements are an adult mentor in the field of their talent, individual counselling and small-group social skills training.

Some specialized schools are emerging as well. For example, Soundscape Centre in Surrey, England began operating in 2003 as the only specialized educational facility in the world uniquely dedicated to the needs and potential of persons with sight loss and special musical abilities, including musical savants. Orion Academy (www.orionacademy.org) in Moraga, California, USA specializes in providing a positive educational experience for high school students with Asperger's syndrome. Hope University (www.hopeu.com) in Anaheim, California is a fine arts facility for adults with developmental disabilities. Its mission is to 'train the talents and diminish the disability' through the use of fine arts therapy including visual arts, music, dance, drama and storytelling.

Dr Temple Grandin is well known as an international authority in her field of animal science. She is also well known for her books including *Thinking in pictures* (1995) and *Translating with animals* (2005). She is also autistic. Another recent book, *Developing talents: careers for individuals with Asperger syndrome and high-functioning autism* (Grandin & Duffy 2004), is an excellent, practical resource for discovering, nurturing and 'training the talent' so that many persons on the autistic spectrum can enjoy the important experience of work and 'the satisfaction of contributing to their families and their communities, of being independent and economically self-sufficient'. This book outlines methods of helping children 'develop their natural talents' using 'drawing, writing, building models, programming computers' and similar skills to help build a 'portfolio' of skills that can help in the search for a meaningful work experience.

The book helps persons on the autistic spectrum, and their family members, teachers, counsellors and others to better understand and develop the career planning process for these special persons with special skills.

1.5 Future directions

No model of brain function, including memory, will be complete until it can account for, and fully incorporate, the rare but spectacular condition of savant syndrome. In the past decade, particularly, much progress has been made towards explaining this jarring juxtaposition of ability and disability, but many unanswered questions remain. However, interest in this fascinating condition is accelerating, especially since the discovery of savant-type skills in previously unimpaired older persons with FTD and other acquired savant instances. This finding has far-reaching implications regarding buried potential in some or, perhaps, all of us.

Advanced technologies will help in those investigations. Computed tomography (CT) and MRI provide stunningly high-resolution images of all the brain architecture, surface and deep, permitting detailed inspection of brain *structure*. However, studies of brain *function*, such as positron emission tomography (PET), single photon emission CT (SPECT) or functional MRI, are much more informative regarding savant syndrome, and, indeed, autism itself, since these newer techniques provide information about the brain at work, rather than simply viewing brain architecture. An even more recent imaging technique is diffusion tensor imaging, based on measuring water flow within neurons, which provides graphic images of brain *connectivity* between the brain hemispheres, within the brain hemispheres and between upper cortical and lower brain stem structures. A related technique, diffusion tensor tracking, provides a direct visual view of the actual fibre tracks, or wiring, of the brain in great detail.

One of the drawbacks to savant functional imaging research, especially art and music performance skills, has been the necessary immobilization of the subject when doing the imaging. Near-infrared spectroscopy, which measures haemoglobin, uses an infrared cap which the patient can wear while 'at work' performing music or painting or drawing, for example. Also there have been many advances in electroencephalographic techniques, including magnetoencephalography, which provides a great deal of additional information beyond the usual electroencephalographic findings.

Detailed, standardized neuropsychological test results can then be correlated with the imaging findings in savants in sufficiently large samples to move away from what have been so many single subject, anecdotal reports. Control groups of non-impaired persons can be assembled to compare and contrast findings in both groups. Beyond that, since the interface between genius, prodigies and savants is an important, and in some ways a very narrow one, those persons should be included also in these multidisciplinary, multimodality, compare and contrast studies. Such studies can shed light on the debate regarding general intelligence versus separate intelligences. Some researchers suggest that savants provide a unique window into the creative process itself. From studies already completed, important information has already emerged regarding brain function, brain plasticity, CNS compensation, recruitment and repair.

Savant syndrome, both in the congenital and acquired types, provides compelling evidence of remarkable brain plasticity. Indeed, brain plasticity will be a central aspect of all neuroscience research in the decades ahead. Until fairly recently, there has been what Dodge (2007), in his book *The brain that changes itself*, calls 'neurologic nihilism'. This was a generally pessimistic view of the ability of neuronal tissue to regenerate and rewire itself in the face of injury or disease. The concept of one brain area being 'recruited' to take over the function of some other damaged area, paradoxical functional facilitation (Kapur 1996), is central to explaining savant syndrome. Some argue that the 'recruitment' of abilities is actually a 'release' phenomenon of already *existing*, but dormant, abilities as opposed to the compensatory development of *new* skills. In the case of right brain versus left brain capacity, some have referred to that substitution as a release 'from the tyranny' of the left, or dominant, hemisphere.

But there is more to savant syndrome than genes, circuitry and the brain's marvellous intricacy. As important as those matters are in terms of *scientific* interest, there is also much we can learn from savant syndrome from the *human* interest perspective provided by these remarkable people, and the equally remarkable and dedicated families, caretakers, teachers and therapists who surround them. For human potential consists of more than neurons and synapses. It also comprises, and is propelled along by, the vital forces of encouragement and reinforcement that flow from the unconditional love, belief, support and determination of those families and friends who not only care *for* the savant, but care *about* him or her as well.

At a 1964 meeting of the American Psychiatric Association, a discussant concluded, with respect to the 'calculating twins', that the importance of the savant 'lies in our inability to explain him; he stands as a landmark of our own ignorance and the phenomenon of the idiot savant exists as a challenge to our capabilities' (Horwitz et al. 1965). But savant syndrome is less now a 'landmark to our ignorance' than 44 years ago. More progress has been made in the past 15 years in better understanding and explaining savant syndrome than in the previous 100 years. Also, that important inquiry continues, with the prospect of propelling us along further than we have ever been in unravelling the mystery of these extraordinary people and their remarkable abilities. Moreover, in that process, we can also learn more about ourselves, explore the 'challenge to our capabilities' and uncover the hidden potential—the little Rain man—that resides, perhaps, within us all.

References

Barr, M. W. 1898 Some notes on echolalia, with the report of an extraordinary case. *J. Nerv. Merit. Dis.* **25**, 20–30. (doi:10.1097/00005053-189801000-00002)
Bender, M. B., Feldman, M. & Sobin, A. J. 1968 Palinopsia. *Bmin* **91**, 321–338. (doi:10.1093/brain/91.2.321)
Brink, T. 1980 Idiot savant with unusual mechanical ability. *Am. J. Psychiatry* **137**, 250–251.
Cameron, L. 1998 *The music of light: the extraordinary story of Hikari and Kenzaburo Oe.* New York, NY: Free Press.
Clark, T. 2001 The application of savant and splinter skills in the autistic population through curriculum design: a longitudinal multiple replication case study. PhD thesis. School of Education Studies, The University of New South Wales, Sydney, Australia.
Critchley, M. 1979 *The divine banquet of the brain.* New York, NY: Raven Press.

Dodge, N. 2007 *The brain that changes itself*. New York, NY: Penguin. Donnelly, J. A. & Altman, R. 1994 The autistic savant: recognizing and serving the gifted student with autism. *Roeper Rev.* **16**, 252–255.

Down, J. L. 1887 *On some mental affections of childhood and youth*. London, UK: Churchill.

DSM-III 1980 *Diagnostic and statistical manual of mental disorders*. Washington, DC: American Psychiatric Association.

Duckett, J. 1976 Idiot-savants: superspecialization in mentally retarded persons. Doctoral thesis, Department of Special Education, University of Texas in Austin.

Geschwind, N. & Galaburda, A. M. 1987 *Cerebral lateralization: biological mechanisms, associations, and pathology*. Cambridge, MA: MIT Press.

Giray, E. F. & Barclay, A. G. 1977 Eidetic imagery; longitudinal results in brain-damaged children. *Am. J. Ment. Defic.* **82**, 311–314.

Grandin, T 1995 *Thinking in pictures and other reports from my life with autism*. New York, NY: Vintage Books.

Grandin, T. 2005 *Animals in translation: using the mysteries of autism to decode animal behavior*. New York, NY: Scribner.

Grandin, T. & Duffy, K. 2004 *Developing talents: careers for individuals with Asperger syndrome and high functioning autism*. Shawnee Mission, KS: Autism Asperger Publishing Company.

Grigorenko, E. L., Klin, A., Pauls, D. L., Senft, R., Hooper, C. & Volkmar, F. 2002 A descriptive study of hyperlexia in a clinically referred sample of children with developmental delays. *J. Autism Dev. Disord.* **32**, 3–12. (doi:10.1023/A:1017995805511)

Heaton, P. & Wallace, G. L. 2004 Annotation: the savant syndrome. *Child Psychol. Psychiatr.* **45**, 899–911. (doi:10.1111/j.1469-7610.2004.t01-1-00284.x)

Hermelin, B. 2001 *Bright splinters of the mind*. London, UK: Jessica Kingsley Publishers.

Hill, A. L. 1977 Idiot savants: rate of incidence. *Percept. Mot. Skills* **44**, 161–162.

Hill, A. L. 1978 Savants: mentally retarded individuals with special skills. In *International review of research in mental retardation* (ed. N. Ellis), pp. 277–298. New York, NY: Academic Press.

Horwitz, W. A., Kestenbaum, C, Person, E. & Jarvik, L. 1965 Identical twins—'idiot savants'—calendar calculators. *Am. J. Psychiatry* **121**, 1075.

Hou, C., Miller, B., Cummings, J., Goldberg, M., Mychack, P., Bottino, B. & Benson, F. 2000 Artistic savants. *Neuropsychiatry Neuropsychol. Behav. Neurol.* **13**, 29–38.

Kanner, L. 1944 Infantile autism. *J. Pediatr.* **25**, 200–217.

Kapur, N. 1996 Paradoxical functional facilitation in brain-behavior research: a critical. *Rev. Brain* **119**, 1775–1790. (doi:10.1093/brain/119.5.1775)

LaFontaine, L. 1974 Divergent abilities in the idiot savant. Doctoral thesis, School of Education, Boston University in Boston.

Lythgoe, M., Pollak, T., Kalmas, M., de Hann, M. & Chong, W. K. 2005 Obsessive, prolific artistic output following subarachnoid hemorrhage. *Neurology* **64**, 397–398.

Miller, B. L., Cummings, J., Mishkin, F., Boone, K., Prince, F., Ponton, M. & Cotman, C. 1998 Emergence of artistic talent in fronto-temporal dementia. *Neurology* **51**, 978–982.

Miller, B. L., Boone, K., Cummings, L. R. & Mishkin, F. 2000 Functional correlates of musical and visual ability in frontotemporal dementia. *Br. J. Psychiatry* **176**, 458–463. (doi:10.1192/bjp.176.5.458)

Mishkin, M., Malamut, B. & Bachevalier, J. 1984 Memories and habits: two neural systems. In *Neurobiology of learning and memory* (eds G. Lynch, J. L. MacGaugh & N. M. Weinberger), pp. 65–77. New York, NY: Guilford Press.

Mortiz, K. P. 1783 *Gnothi Sauton oder Magazin der Erfahrungsseelenkunde als ein Lesebuch fur Gelehrte und Ungelehrte*. Berlin, Germany: Mylius.

Nettlebeck, T. & Young, R. 1999 Savant syndrome. *Int. Rev. Res. Ment. Retard.* **22**, 137–173. (doi:10.1016/S0074-7750(08)60133-0)

Peek, F. & Hanson, L. L. 2008 *The life and message of the real rain man*. New York, NY: Dude Publishing.

Phillips, A. 1930 Talented imbeciles. *Psychol. Clin.* **18**, 246–255.

Rimland, B. 1978 Savant capabilities of autistic children and their cognitive implications. In *Cognitive defects in the development of mental illness* (ed. G. Serban), pp. 43–65. New York, NY: Brunner/Mazel.

Rimland, B. & Fein, D. A. 1988 Special talents of autistic savants. In *The exceptional brain: neuropsychology of talent and special abilities* (eds L. K. Obler & D. A. Fine), pp. 474–492. New York, NY: Guilford Press.

Rush, B. 1789 Account of a wonderful talent for arithmetical calculation in an African slave, living in Virginia. *Am. Mus.* **5**, 62–63.

Saloviita, T., Ruusila, L. & Ruusila, U. 2000 Incidence of savant skills in Finland. *Percept. Mot. Skills* **91**, 120–122. (doi:10.2466/PMS.91.5.120-122)

Scripture, E. W. 1891 Arithmetical prodigies. *Am. J. Psychol.* **4**, 1–59. (doi:10.2307/1411838)

Selfe, L. 1978 *Nadia: a case of extraordinary drawing ability in an autistic child*. New York, NY: Academic Press.

Tredgold, A. F. 1914 *Mental deficiency*. New York, NY: William Wood.

Treffert, D. A. 1988 The idiot savant: a review of the syndrome. *Am. J. Psychiatry* **145**, 563–572.

Treffert, D. A. 2005 The savant syndrome in autistic disorder. In *Recent developments in autism research* (ed. M. F. Casanova), pp. 27–55. New York, NY: Nova Science Publishers.

Treffert, D. A. 2006a *Extraordinary people: understanding savant syndrome*. Omaha, NE: iUniverse, Inc. Treffert, D. A. 2006b Dr Down and 'developmental disorders'. *J. Autism Dev. Disord.* **36**, 965–966. (doi:10.1007/s10803-006-0183-1)

Viscott, D. S. 1969 A musical idiot savant. *Psychiatry* **32**, 494–515.

Wiltshire, S. 1987 *Drawings*. London, UK: J. M. Dent and Sons. Wiltshire, S. 1991 *Floating cities*. New York, NY: Summit Books.

Young, R. 1995 Savant syndrome: processes underlying extraordinary abilities. PhD thesis, University of Adelaide, Adelaide, South Australia.

2

Savant skills in autism: psychometric approaches and parental reports

Patricia Howlin, Susan Goode, Jane Hutton and Michael Rutter

> Most investigations of savant skills in autism are based on individual case reports. The present study investigated rates and types of savant skills in 137 individuals with autism (mean age 24 years). Intellectual ability ranged from severe intellectual impairment to superior functioning. Savant skills were judged from parental reports and specified as 'an outstanding skill/knowledge clearly above participant's general level of ability *and* above the population norm'. A comparable definition of exceptional cognitive skills was applied to Wechsler test scores—requiring a subtest score at least 1 standard deviation above general population norms and 2 standard deviations above the participant's own mean subtest score. Thirty-nine participants (28.5%) met criteria for either a savant skill or an exceptional cognitive skill: 15 for an outstanding cognitive skill (most commonly block design); 16 for a savant skill based on parental report (mostly mathematical/calculating abilities); 8 met criteria for both a cognitive and parental rated savant skill. One-third of males showed some form of outstanding ability compared with 19 per cent of females. No individual with a non-verbal IQ below 50 met criteria for a savant skill and, contrary to some earlier hypotheses, there was no indication that individuals with higher rates of stereotyped behaviours/interests were more likely to demonstrate savant skills.
>
> **Keywords:** autism; savant skills; adults with autism

2.1 Introduction

(a) What are 'savant skills'?

Reports of individuals who despite having severe intellectual impairments nevertheless show remarkable skills in a particular area can be traced back centuries (see Southall 1979; Smith 1983; Heaton & Wallace 2004). Down (1887) was the first to coin the term 'idiot savant' in his description of 10 individuals who exhibited outstanding abilities in specific areas but whose level of general ability was so poor that they were unable to live independently. Subsequently, the American Association on Mental Deficiency (AAMD; Grossman 1983) defined 'savants' as 'persons with obvious mental retardation who are capable of performing in sharply circumscribed areas (e.g. arithmetic, calendar calculating) at a remarkably high level'. Miller (1998) argued that the term savant should be used for those individuals who show (i) normatively superior performance in an area *and* (ii) a discrepancy between their performance in that area and their general level of functioning. Miller (1999) also noted that very few savants for whom assessment details were available had IQ scores below 50, and many had at least some subtest scores within the normal range. Treffert (1989) differentiated 'prodigious' savants (i.e. individuals possessing an exceptional ability in relation to both their overall level of functioning *and* the general population) from 'talented' savants (individuals showing an outstanding skill in comparison with their overall level of functioning). There is a parallel literature on the marked intra-individual discrepancies in the cognitive profiles of many individuals with autism (Joseph *et al.* 2002; Kuschner *et al.* 2007). Typically, cognitive peaks involve visuospatial skills (notably block design and object assembly) or rote memory; scores tend to be lowest on tests involving verbal abstraction or comprehension. Curiously, there has been no systematic comparison between these isolated exceptional cognitive skills and savant skills as usually conceptualized. That comparison constituted a key aim of our study.

(b) Savant skills in individuals with neurodevelopmental disorders

Savant skills are reported much more frequently in males than in females (ratio approximately 3:1), and have been identified in a wide range of neurological and neurodevelopmental disorders (Miller 1998; Treffert 2000). Specific skills, in relation to overall levels of function but not population norms, have also been reported in genetic conditions such as Smith-Magenis syndrome (computing and memory; I. A. Horn 1999, unpublished thesis; C. Webber 1999, unpublished thesis), Prader-Willi syndrome (memory and visuospatial skills; Milner *et al.* 2005) and Williams syndrome (music and memory; Howlin *et al.* 1998; Levitin *et al.* 2004). However, the condition in which both prodigious and talented savants are most frequently reported is autism/autism spectrum disorder (ASD).

(c) Specific areas of savant skill

Early anecdotal accounts of savants and more recent experimental studies (see Young 1995; Miller 1998; Heaton & Wallace 2004 for reviews) indicate that savant skills fall within a fairly circumscribed range. The most commonly reported are mathematical skills (calendrical calculations, lightening arithmetic and prime number calculations), music (especially the ability to replay complex sequences after only one exposure), art (complex scenes with accurate perspective either created or replicated following a single brief viewing) and memory for dates, places, routes or facts. Less frequently reported are 'pseudo-verbal' skills (hyperlexia or facility with foreign languages), coordination skills and mechanical aptitude (Tredgold 1952; Rimland 1978).

(d) Savant skills in autism

In Kanner's (1971) follow-up of his original 11 cases, six individuals were described as having an outstanding skill, mainly in the areas of music and rote memory. Two of the four cases described in detail by Asperger (1944, translated by Frith 1991) had outstanding calculating skills; another had exceptional spelling skills. Rimland (1978), in a postal survey of 5400 parents of children with autism, found that 531 (9.8%) were reported to have savant skills. Of those with reported skills, the most common were music (53%), memory (40%), mathematical/calculating skills (25%) and art (19%); 53 per cent had multiple special abilities (Rimland & Fein 1988). Bolte & Poustka (2004), in a study of 254 individuals with autism, identified 33 (13%) with at least one special skill as assessed on the Autism Diagnostic Interview—Revised (ADI-R; Le Couteur *et al.* 2003).

Exceptional memory was the most frequently reported and 29 individuals had multiple savant skills. Treffert (2000) concluded that approximately 50 per cent of individuals with savant skills described in the literature appeared to meet criteria for autism/ASD—a prevalence much higher than the less than 1 per cent figure he estimates for savant skills in other syndromes. Miller (1998) also noted that out of the total of 45 individuals described in his review, 22 had autism or showed symptoms highly suggestive of this diagnosis. Similarly, O'Connor & Hermelin (1987) reported that 50 per cent of the individuals with savant skills in their experimental studies had autism.

(e) Association with cognitive levels and presence of stereotyped and ritualistic behaviours

Although early studies by O'Connor & Hermelin (1984, 1987; Hermelin & O'Connor 1986, 1990) used the traditional definition of idiot savant (i.e. special skills in individuals with severe cognitive impairment), some of their participants (and *all* of those with outstanding mnemonic skills) had IQ scores within the normal range. In a later study, O'Connor & Hermelin (1991) noted that the mean IQ of savants with autism was considerably higher than that of non-savants (nonverbal IQ 72 versus 52; verbal IQ equivalent 70 versus 59). Miller (1999), in a review of studies providing more detailed IQ information, reported that the mean overall IQ/IQ estimate for the savants with autism was 71 (range 40–99), mean verbal IQ 77 (range 52–114) and mean non-verbal IQ 75 (range 47–92). Thus, although savant syndrome can occur in individuals with autism of very low IQ, in the majority of reported cases cognitive ability falls within the mild learning disability range or above.

O'Connor & Hermelin (1988, 1991) suggested that a tendency to repetitive behaviour and/or preoccupations with a restricted area of interest were crucial features of individuals with savant syndrome. They also found that 'autistic savants' showed a particular interest in one specific topic (names, buttons, birthdates, etc.) and in the repetitive ordering of possessions.

(f) Summary

Although there have been many single case or small group studies of individuals with autism who possess savant abilities or exceptional cognitive skills, there have been few systematic, large-scale investigations in this area. Inconsistencies in definition and wide variation in diagnostic ascertainment, ages and ability levels of the cases reported also give rise to problems, and there is little valid information on rates of savant skills in ASDs.

2.2 Present study

(a) Aims

The aim of the present study was to investigate the nature and frequency of savant skills in a large sample of individuals with autism who had been initially diagnosed as children. The specific issues investigated were as follows.

(i) What are the types and frequency of savant skills or exceptional cognitive skills in individuals with a confirmed diagnosis of autism?

(ii) What is the degree of association between the two?
(iii) Are savant skills associated with overall levels of cognitive ability?
(iv) Do rates of such skills differ between males and females?
(v) What is the relationship between savant or exceptional cognitive skills and the presence of repetitive, restricted and stereotyped behaviours?

(b) Sample

The total sample comprised 137 individuals, first diagnosed with autism at the Maudsley Hospital, London between 1950 and 1985, who have subsequently been involved in an ongoing, longitudinal follow-up study (Howlin *et al.* 2004; Hutton *et al.* 2008; see appendix A for process of sample identification). All initial diagnostic and cognitive assessments were conducted when individuals were aged 3–16 years. No participants had experienced any prolonged period in institutional care; all were Caucasian and singletons. Follow-up cognitive data were collected when participants were aged, on average, 24 years. Parental report data on savant skills were obtained approximately 10 years later, at a subsequent follow-up (mean age 34 years).

Inclusion criteria for the present study were as follows.

— Lifetime diagnosis of autism confirmed on Autism Diagnostic Interview (ADI; Le Couteur *et al.* 1989).
— Initial IQ ≥ 30 (this cut-off was chosen owing to the difficulties of making a reliable diagnosis of autism when IQ < 30).
— Aged ≥11 at follow-up (as savant skills may not be evident in early childhood).
— No evidence of a specific medical disorder possibly related to autism (e.g. tuberous sclerosis, phenyl-ketonuria, infant spasms, neurofibromatosis) or evidence of major physical or sensory impairment. (This criterion derived from the original follow-up studies.)

(c) Diagnostic and cognitive assessments

(i) Autism diagnosis

Diagnosis at follow-up (mean age 24 years) was reconfirmed using the ADI (Le Couteur *et al.* 1989). This was the precursor to the current ADI-R (Le Couteur *et al.* 2003), and although the two versions are very similar, there are some differences in the items included. The ADI-R provides a lifetime diagnostic algorithm for autism (based on scores in the domains of reciprocal interaction, language/communication and restricted, repetitive and stereotyped behaviours). To meet ADI-R criteria for autism, individuals must score above cut-off on each of the three domains, and have shown features of autism by 3 years.

(ii) Psychometric tests

Cognitive and language measures were completed for all participants. The exact battery of tests used depended on individual age and developmental level.

Non-verbal ability

Eighty-seven individuals were able to obtain a score on the Wechsler Performance Scale (Wechsler Intelligence Scale for Children, 1974 or Wechsler Adult Intelligence Scale

Revised, 1984, as appropriate; PIQ mean = 79.7, s.d. 18.4, range 42–133). For the remainder, nonverbal IQ calculations were based on the Raven's matrices standard, coloured or board forms (Raven 1976) ($n = 23$), the Leiter (1980) ($n = 18$) or Merrill-Palmer Scales (Stutsman 1948) ($n = 9$). The mean performance IQ (based on any test) of the total sample was 69.9 (s.d. 23.1, range 28–135).

Verbal ability
Eighty-two participants scored on the Wechsler Verbal Scale (Mean VIQ 77.5, s.d. 20.4, range 44–134); for 53 individuals a verbal IQ was derived from their scores on the British Picture Vocabulary Test; two individuals were not able to score on any language scale. Mean verbal IQ/or ratio IQ estimate (based on any test) was 52.9 (s.d. 34.6, range 7–134).

(iii) Ratings of preoccupations, unusual interests and repetitive behaviours
To investigate the possible relationship of savant and exceptional cognitive skills with unusual interests, rituals and/or repetitive behaviours, a rating was derived from five items included in the repetitive, restricted and stereotyped behaviours domain of the ADI (unusual preoccupations, compulsions/rituals, resistance to change, unusual attachments to objects, unusual sensory interests). (Range of scores for each item 0–3; maximum possible total score = 15.)[1]

(d) Statistical analysis
Parametric analyses were used for comparisons where data permitted. Probability tests were two-tailed and, as multiple comparisons were conducted, the significance level for p was set at less than 0.01.

2.3 Frequency and nature of exceptional skills in autism

(a) Exceptional cognitive skills

(i) Definition
An exceptional cognitive skill was defined as *any* subtest score greater than or equal to 1 standard deviation above the population mean on the Wechsler IQ test *and* greater than or equal to 2 standard deviations (based on population norms) above the participant's mean subtest score. (Mean score for each subtest = 10, s.d. = approx. 3.0, depending on the specific subtest.)

(ii) Participants
Cognitive assessments were completed for all participants (100 males and 37 females) when aged between 11 and 48 years (mean 24.1 years, s.d. 8.6 years).

---

[1] Note that these domain items differ slightly from those in the current ADI-R, which now also includes circumscribed interests.

(iii) Results
Eighty-seven individuals (64% of total sample) were able to obtain a performance, verbal or full-scale IQ score on the adult or child versions of the Wechsler IQ test. Of these, 23 (17% of total sample) met the above criteria for an exceptional cognitive skill.

Table 2.1 provides details of individuals meeting cognitive skills criteria. The most common *single* area of special skill was block design (BD, $n = 9$); followed by digit span (DS, $n = 5$), arithmetic ($n = 4$) and object assembly (OA, $n = 1$). In addition, three individuals met criteria on two subtests (BD and OA) and one on three subtests (BD, OA and DS).

(b) Parental reports of savant skills

(i) Definition
Savant skill was defined according to the definition of Miller (1998), i.e. a skill exceptional both in terms of population norms and above the individual's overall level of ability.

(ii) Source of information
Data on special skills were derived principally from a postal questionnaire sent to parents and focusing on outcome since the cognitive assessment conducted approximately

Table 2.1 Details of 23 individuals meeting criteria for one or more exceptional cognitive skill. (Arranged in order of full-scale IQ score (three individuals able to complete PIQ only) arith, arithmetic; BD, block design; DS, digit span; OA, object assembly; CC, calendrical calculator.)

M/F	Age (years)	Wechsler FSIQ	PIQ	VIQ	Mean subtest score	Score of subtest (s) meeting 'exceptional' cognitive criteria	Parent-reported savant skills (blank = no parent-reported skill)
F	16	64	66	44	4.0	15 BD	
M	49	72	88	59	4.2	14 BD	
M	36	72	92	59	4.9	13 BD	
F	26	73	87	64	5.7	13 BD 13 OA	
M	33	76	66	86	6.5	19 DS	CC
M	34	78	82	78	6.7	14 DS	
M	22	83	98	76	7.0	13 BD	
M	26	84	100	76	7.0	14 BD	
M	24	85	108	75	7.7	16 BD	
M	30	87	85	92	8.2	16 DS	maths/memory
M	45	88	89	89	7.0	13 arith	CC/music/maths
M	49	88	111	74	7.6	15 BD 13 OA	
F	30	90	94	91	8.0	15 DS	
M	49	94	102	89	8.5	15 OA	CC
M	48	95	80	109	8.9	16 arith	CC
M	32	96	111	87	9.2	19 BD	
M	46	98	85	111	9.6	17 arith	CC/memory
M	28	110	98	118	10.5	17 arith	
M	28	124	122	118	9.7	18 DS 19 BD 15 OA	
M	48	130	116	131	12.2	19 DS	CC
F	14		80		7.0	13 BD	
M	33		92		7.2	15 BD	
M	28		108		9.3	19 BD 18 OA	maths

10 years earlier. The questionnaire asked specifically about the current presence of any outstanding skills and talents 'at a level that would be unusual even for normal people' (Hutton et al. 2008). Examples of the kinds of skill of interest were provided and parents were requested to give details of any special skills noted.

(iii) Reliability of researcher ratings of parental questionnaire data
In total, 90 questionnaires were returned. All written information on special skills provided by parents was transcribed (removing details of name and sex) and each example blind-coded by PH and MR using the ratings below.

— 0, no outstanding skills/knowledge in relation to overall level of ability.
— 1, isolated skill/knowledge commented on by parents but unlikely to be above population norms.
— 2, outstanding skill/knowledge definitely above the subject's general level of ability *and* above the population normal level.
— 7, possible outstanding skill but not enough information to be certain.

A code of 2 was set as the criterion for a *savant* skill.

Inter-rater reliability was calculated using weighted kappas (Cohen 1968). Parents' descriptions indicated that 45 individuals had some form of special skill. Of these, 21 individuals were rated as meeting the necessary criteria (i.e. coding of 2) by one or both coders (17 by both and 4 by one rater only); $\kappa = 0.8$ (high agreement). (Agreement on three other cases was based on information from detailed case-note reports.) Any disagreement between the two raters was due mainly to the very circumscribed nature of some skills (e.g. having perfect pitch and ability to identify any musical chords, but no other musical skills; ability to memorize the names of classmates from 20 years ago). Following consensus discussion, all examples coded as 2 by at least one rater were included as meeting criterion; three individuals coded as scoring 7 by both raters were excluded (e.g. one individual who had a form of synaesthesia; others with good but not exceptional artistic skills). (Examples of savant skills meeting criteria are provided in appendix B.)

Parents reported unusual memory skills more often than categorized here as savant. We decided to exclude personal memories of a kind that did not allow any valid assessment of the extent to which they might be above population norms. Those included did provide such information (see appendix B). Because we adopted very strict criteria, it is likely that the true number of individuals with unusual memory skills was greater than included here. For similar reasons, we did not rate as savant skills that were obtained unusually early (e.g. precocious reading).

Special skills were categorized into five principal areas: visuospatial; computational (including calendrical calculators); memory; music; and art. Inter-rater agreement on these categories (based on written transcripts for the 21 individuals meeting criteria) was 100 per cent.

(iv) Participants
Of the original 137 participants in the cognitive study, two individuals had died, two asked not to be contacted again and five could not be traced. Questionnaire data were obtained for 90 of the remaining 128 individuals and additional information on special skills was available for three participants from written information collected from parents by PH or MR on previous occasions. Thus, detailed parental information was obtained

for 73 per cent of available participants. The average age at which the parental questionnaire data were obtained was 34.2 years (s.d. 7.8 years, range 21.0–55.0 years).

(v) Results

Among the 93 individuals for whom data were available, 24 were identified as having one or more savant skills (total = 26%). There were 14 calendrical calculators (one also showed exceptional memory and another also showed skills in computation and music). There were four others with computational skills (in one case combined with memory and in another case with music). Visuospatial skills (i.e. directions or highly accurate drawing) were reported in three individuals. One individual had a musical talent, one an exceptional memory skill and one had skills in both memory and art.

(c) Relationship between exceptional cognitive savant skills and skills identified by parental report

Of the 93 individuals for whom parental questionnaire and cognitive data were available, 16 (17.2%) met criteria for a parent-rated skill, 15 (16.8%) had an exceptional cognitive skill and 8 (8.6%) met criteria for both.

All participants who met criteria for both unusual cognitive skill *and* parent-reported savant skill were male and, in each case, the parent-reported skill involved either mathematical or calendrical calculating abilities (table 2.1). For six out of these eight individuals, the exceptional area of cognitive ability identified on the Wechsler test also involved either the arithmetic or digit span subtests (one individual with exceptional mathematical ability was non-verbal and thus could not attempt the Wechsler arithmetic subtest).

2.4 Relationship between special skills and intellectual ability

The IQ levels of individuals meeting criteria for any area of savant skill were compared with those of individuals with no savant skills (Table 2.2). Individuals with exceptional cognitive skills had significantly higher full, performance and verbal scores than the non-cognitive skill group ($p < 0.001$ for each comparison). Since, by definition, exceptional cognitive skills were required to involve one or more subtest scores above the population norm, this difference was not unexpected. However, there were also highly significant differences between the FSIQ, PIQ and VIQ scores of the parentally rated savant/non-savant groups ($p \leq 0.009$ for each comparison). Far more individuals in the non-savant group obtained IQ scores of less than 60 (on any test) than in the savant group. Moreover, among those with parent-rated special skills, all but two individuals were able to achieve an IQ score on the Wechsler tests and all the remainder obtained Wechsler full-scale, performance and verbal scale IQ scores above 60. The profile of Wechsler subtest scores was very similar in both groups, although, again, the means of the savant group were consistently higher.

2.5 Sex differences

The total sample for whom parental and/or cognitive data were available comprised 100 males and 37 females. Overall, many more males showed some form of savant skill (32M:7F). The M: F ratio for cognitive skill was 19:4 and for parent-rated skill was 21:3

Table 2.2 IQ scores of individuals with or without special areas of skill.

Area of skill	Group	N tested Wechsler FS IQ[a]; mean (s.d.) [range]	N tested PIQ; mean (s.d.) [range]	N tested VIQ/IQ estimate; mean (s.d.) [range]
exceptional cognitive	skill	N = 20; 89.4 (16.9) [64–130]	N = 23; 96.7 (14.7) [76–135]	N = 23; 77.4 (22.4) [14[b]–131]
	no skill	N = 62; 73.7 (17.9) [39–126]	N = 114; 64.4 (20.6) [28–133]	N = 114; 47.9 (33.2) [7[b]–134]
parent-rated savant	skill	N = 22; 88.1 (20.1) [63–130]	N = 24; 86.4 (20.3) [53–135]	N = 24; 84.7 (30.4) [15[b]–134]
	no skill	N = 40; 74.9 (17.5) [44–124]	N = 69; 69.1 (22.2) [29–122]	N = 69; 50.1 (32.5) [7[b]–118]
savant and exceptional cognitive skill		N = 7; 95.4 (16.8) [76–130]	N = 8; 96.0 (20.4) [76–135]	N = 8; 90.4 (33.8) [16[b]–134]

[a] FSIQ based on Wechsler tests only. PIQ and VIQ estimates are based on a number of different tests (see text) and include all participants with parental data.
[b] Low verbal IQ scores based on ratio IQ estimate (language age/chronological age × 100).

(eight males were assessed as having both cognitive and parent-rated skills). None of these ratios differed significantly from the M: F ratio for the total group (Yates corrected χ^2 $p \geq 0.20$ for each comparison) but the small number of females in the sample necessarily limits the statistical power for detecting a sex difference. It is also notable that no female was rated as having both exceptional cognitive and parent-rated skills. There was no difference in scores on any of the IQ measures ($p > 0.14$ for each comparison) between males and females with either savant or unusual cognitive skills.

2.6 Relationship between savant skills and stereotyped and repetitive behaviours/interests

Data on repetitive/stereotyped behaviours and special interests had been collected when diagnostic status was reconfirmed, by means of the ADI, during the cognitive follow-up stage of the study. ADI data were available for 93 participants. Scores from the five ADI items relating to repetitive/stereotyped behaviours and interests (unusual preoccupations, compulsions/rituals, resistance to change, unusual attachments to objects and unusual sensory interests) were summed to create a total 'stereotyped/special interests' score (range of scores for each item 0–3; maximum possible total score = 15). There was no difference in the overall scores of those individual rated as not/having skills (either cognitive or parent-reported; mean score for those with a skill = 6.9, s.d. 3.0; mean for the remainder 7.1; s.d. 3.0, $t = 1.09$, $p = 0.28$). On the individual items included in the repetitive/stereotyped behaviours domain, there were no differences in the numbers of individuals in the non-versus any-skill groups reported as having severe problems (ratings of 2–3) in any area ($\chi^2 > 0.05$ for each comparison). These findings suggest that the severity of stereotyped or repetitive patterns of behaviour/interest was not associated with special savant or unusual cognitive skills, although it should be noted that the original version of the ADI did not include circumscribed interests, which might possibly be related to savant skills. Also, of course, the diagnosis of autism required the presence of repetitive behaviours/interests, so it was only variations and their extent that could be examined.

2.7 Discussion

In total, 39 participants (28.5%) met criteria for a savant skill. Cognitively, 23 individuals (17% of total sample) met criteria for one or more exceptional area of skill on the Wechsler tests. Combining the two, 37 per cent of the sample showed either savant skills or unusual cognitive skills or both—a far higher proportion than previously reported. Moreover, for reasons already noted, this estimate of 28.5 per cent for savant skills is likely to be an underestimate. It may be concluded that unusual talents are found in at least a third of individuals with autism. Theoretical models of autism and animal models will both have to account for the frequency of unusual talents as well as the presence of important deficits.

The subtest on which participants were most likely to meet the specified criteria for an area of unusual cognitive skill was block design followed by digit span, object assembly and arithmetic. On the basis of parental report, 24 individuals (26% of those for whom data were available) were rated as having a savant skill, mostly involving mathematical/calculating abilities. Generally, there was only modest overlap between individuals with savant skills based on parental report and those who had specific cognitive areas of ability. Thus, of 93 individuals for whom cognitive and parental questionnaire data were available, only eight (11.6%) met criteria for an outstanding skill on both measures. Nevertheless, that overlap is greater than the 4.8 per cent expected by chance and, among these eight individuals, the area of special skill identified by both cognitive testing and parental report was similar. All the eight individuals were reported by parents as having talents related to numerical skills (mathematics or calendrical calculations) and in all but two cases the additional cognitive area identified was either arithmetic or digit span (one of the eight individuals was non-verbal and thus could not attempt either of these subtests).

As indicated in earlier reviews (Miller 1998), there was a sex difference (albeit statistically non-significant) in the prevalence of savant skills. Almost one-third (32%) of males showed some form of savant or special cognitive skill compared with 19 per cent of females.

(a) Theoretical implications

From a theoretical perspective, two rather different questions arise. First, why is the rate of savant skills among individuals with autism so high (see Heaton & Wallace 2004)? On our findings, at least a quarter, but probably over a third, of individuals with autism show unusual skills or talents that are both above population norms and above their own overall level of cognitive functioning. Adequate studies comparing autism with other neurodevelopmental disorders have yet to be undertaken, but the rate of such unusual talents or skills seems particularly high in autism. Why? Second, within the realm of special talents, why (in autism) do these particularly involve computational skills, and is their basis the same as that underlying, say memory or artistic skills? There is plenty of speculation on both these questions but very little in the way of systematic testing of alternative mechanisms. Such research is much needed.

Contrary to suggestions that the presence of savant skills is associated with ritualistic behaviours or special interests (e.g. O'Connor & Hermelin 1991), there was no evidence in the present study that those individuals with either exceptional cognitive or parent-rated skills had higher rates of repetitive or stereotyped behaviours/interests than those who did not. Thus, although *all* participants showed abnormalities in this domain, the severity of such behaviours was not related to savant abilities.

Finally, the fact that savant skills are not unique to autism, but are reported in a number of other syndromes with very different cognitive and behavioural phenotypes (e.g. Prader-Willi, Smith-Magenis and Williams syndromes), also requires further exploration. However, to date, the very different assessment methods and varying definitions used make it impossible to draw reliable conclusions about the relative rates and types of savant skills in other disorders. This is clearly an area in which better standardized measures and ascertainment criteria are crucial if comparative studies on syndrome-specific savant skills are to progress.

Methodological differences between studies also limit conclusions concerning the overall rates of savant skills in ASD. Lack of clear diagnostic criteria, inadequate definition of savant skills, the age of the cohort studied (savant skills may be less apparent in younger children) and the sex ratio (cohorts with a higher preponderance of males may well contain greater numbers of savants) all contribute to different estimates of prevalence. Questions also remain about the most effective way of collecting valid information on savant skills. Cognitive data, although the most objective, are also the most circumscribed; parental reports, while more detailed, are frequently highly subjective. Detailed observational and experimental studies such as those of Hermelin (2001) are feasible only for individual case studies or small case series. Moreover, definitions of what constitutes a skill that is truly exceptional in terms of population norms are also variable and highly unusual characteristics may not necessarily be equivalent to special skills. One individual in the present study, for example, had synaesthesia, seeing people, objects and numbers in colours, in a way that was often distressing for him. In our view, this did not meet criteria for a savant skill but drawing distinct boundaries between this and other savant abilities clearly presents difficulties.

Although the study is not without methodological problems—in particular, the fact that cognitive and parental data were collected at different times and parental information was available for a smaller proportion (73%) of the total sample—the findings are considered valid for a number of reasons. Sample size was relatively large; standardized diagnostic criteria for autism were met in all cases; criteria for savant skills were clearly defined; data were derived from two separate sources (cognitive assessment and parental information); the parental questionnaires used provided detailed descriptions of savant-type skills; and inter-rater reliability was high. The results suggest that the rates of savant skills in autism are substantial, particularly among males, and although these estimates are higher than reported by other researchers, in other ways our findings parallel those of previous studies (e.g. Bolte & Poustka 2004). Thus, females seem less likely than males to develop savant skills, and in both this study and that of Bolte & Poustka (2004), the average non-verbal IQ of the savant group was over 80, consistently higher than that of the non-savant group. Indeed, in our study, no individual with a non-verbal IQ below 50 was judged as having any special talents. These data offer no support to claims that savant skills occur most frequently in individuals with autism who are intellectually impaired.

Despite the fact that savant abilities reported in the literature cover a relatively circumscribed range, the underlying cognitive mechanisms appear to vary widely. The ability to make rapid calendrical calculations (which is clearly *not* simply a feat of memory; Heavey *et al.* 1999; Iavarone *et al.* 2007), to calculate prime numbers, to remember dates/places/events from many years in the past or recite a long list of digits backwards may all require very different cognitive skills. Similarly, a high level of expertise in art or music is very different from being able to score highly on tests of block design or object assembly. It is possible that an overarching explanation may exist for why certain individuals go on to develop *any* area of exceptional skill, but understanding why these skills encompass such different areas and what the underlying basis of such skills is may require a rather different, research-based theoretical approach than adopted thus far.

Finally, there is the issue of how innate talents can be developed to form the basis of truly *functional* skills. In the present study, only five individuals with exceptional abilities (four related to maths and one related to visuospatial ability) had succeeded in using these skills to find permanent employment. For the majority, the isolated skill remained just that, leading neither to employment nor greater social integration. The practical challenge now is to determine how individuals with special skills can be assisted, from childhood onwards, to develop their talents in ways that are of direct practical value (in terms of educational and occupational achievements), thereby enhancing their opportunities for social inclusion as adults.

References

Asperger, H. 1991 Autistic psychopathy in childhood. In *Autism and Asperger syndrome* (ed. U. Frith), pp. 37–92. Cambridge, UK: Cambridge University Press. (Original work published 1944.)

Bölte, S. & Poustka, F. 2004 Comparing the profiles of savant and non-savant individuals with autistic disorder. *Intelligence* **32**, 121–131. (doi:10.1016/j.intell.2003.11.002)

Cohen, J. 1968 Weighted kappa; nominal scale agreement with provision for scaled disagreement or partial credit. *Psychol. Bull.* **70**, 213–220. (doi:10.1037/h0026256)

Down, J. L. 1887 *On some of the mental affections of childhood and youth*. London, UK: Churchill.

Grossman, H. 1983 *Classification in mental retardation*. Washington, DC: The American Association on Mental Deficiency.

Heaton, P. & Wallace, G. 2004 Annotation: the savant syndrome. *J. Child Psychol. Psychiatry* **45**, 899–911. (doi:10.1111/j.1469-7610.2004.t01-1-00284.x)

Heavey, L., Pring, L. & Hermelin, B. 1999 A date to remember: the nature of memory in savant calendrical calculators. *Psychol. Med.* **2**, 145–160. (doi:10.1017/S0033291798007776)

Hermelin, B. 2001 *Bright splinters of the mind: a personal story of research with autistic savants*. London, UK: Kingsley.

Hermelin, B. & O'Connor, N. 1986 Idiot savant calendrical calculators: rules and regularities. *Psychol. Med.* **16**, 885–893.

Hermelin, B. & O'Connor, N. 1990 Factors and primes: a specific numerical ability. *Psychol. Med.* **20**, 163–169.

Howlin, P., Davies, M. & Udwin, O. 1998 Cognitive functioning in adults with Williams syndrome. *J. Child Psychol. Psychiatry* **39**, 183–189. (doi:10.1017/S0021963097001789)

Howlin, P., Goode, S., Hutton, J. & Rutter, M. 2004 Adult outcome for children with autism. *J. Child Adolesc. Psychiatry* **45**, 212–229. (doi:10.1111/j.1469-7610.2004.00215.x)

Hutton, J., Goode, S., Murphy, M., Le Couteur, A. & Rutter, M. 2008 New-onset psychiatric disorders in individuals with autism. *Autism: Int. J. Res. Pract.* **12**, 373–390. (doi:10.1177/1362361308091650)

Iavarone, A., Patruno, M., Galeone, F., Chieffi, S. & Carlomagno, S. 2007 Brief report: error pattern in an autistic savant calendar calculator. *J. Autism Dev. Disord.* **37**, 775–779. (doi:10.1007/sl0803-006-0190-2)

Joseph, R., Tager-Flusberg, H. & Lord, C. 2002 Cognitive profiles and social-communicative functioning in children with autism spectrum disorder. *J. Child Psychol. Psychiatry* **43**, 807–822. (doi:10.1111/1469-7610.00092)

Kanner, L. 1971 Follow-up study of eleven autistic children originally reported in 1943. *J. Autism Child Schizophr.* **1**, 119-145. (doi:10.1007/BF01537953)

Kuschner, E., Bennetto, L. & Yost, K. 2007 Patterns of nonverbal cognitive functioning in young children with autism spectrum disorders. *J. Autism Dev. Disord.* **37**, 95–807. (doi:10.1007/s10803-006-0209-8)

Le Couteur, A., Rutter, M., Lord, C, Rios, P., Robertson, S., Holdgrafer, M. & McLennan, J. 1989 Autism Diagnostic Interview: a semi-structured interview for parents and caregivers of autistic persons. *J. Autism Dev. Disord.* **19**, 363–387. (doi:10.1007/BF02212936)

Le Couteur, A., Lord, C. & Rutter, M. 2003 *Autism diagnostic interview-revised*. Los Angeles, CA: Western Psychological Services.

Leiter, R. G. 1980 *Leiter international performance scale: instruction manual*. Chicago, IL: Stoetling.

Levitin, D. J., Cole, K., Chiles, M., Lai, Z., Lincoln, A. & Bellugi, U. 2004 Characterizing the musical phenotype in individuals with Williams syndrome. *Child Neuropsychol.* **10**, 223–247. (doi:10.1080/09297040490909288)

Miller, L. 1998 Defining the savant syndrome. *J. Dev. Phys. Disabil.* **10**, 73–85. (doi:10.1023/A:1022813601762)

Miller, L. 1999 The savant syndrome: intellectual impairment and exceptional skills. *Psychol. Bull.* **125**, 31–46. (doi:10.1037/0033-2909.125.1.31)

Milner, K. et al. 2005 Prader-Willi syndrome: intellectual abilities and behavioural features by genetic subtype. *J. Child Psychol. Psychiatry* **46**, 1089–1096. (doi:10.1111/j.1469-7610.2005.01520.x)

O'Connor, N. & Hermelin, B. 1984 Idiot savant calendrical calculators: maths or memory? *Psychol. Med.* **14**, 801–806.

O'Connor, N. & Hermelin, B. 1987 Visual and graphic abilities of the idiot savant artist. *Psychol. Med.* **17**, 79–90.

O'Connor, N. & Hermelin, B. 1988 Annotation: low intelligence and special abilities. *J. Child Psychol. Psychiatry* **29**, 391–396. (doi:10.1111/j.1469-7610.1988.tb00732.x)

O'Connor, N. & Hermelin, B. 1991 Talents and preoccupations in idiots-savants. *Psychol. Med.* **21**, 959–964.

Raven, J. 1976 *Standard progressive matrices*. London, UK: H. K. Lewis.

Rimland, B. 1978 Savant capabilities of autistic children and their cognitive implications. In *Cognitive defects in the development of mental illness* (ed. G. Serban), pp. 43–65. New York, NY: Bruner-Mazel.

Rimland, B. & Fein, D. 1988 Special talents and autistic savants. In *The exceptional brain: neuropsychology of talent and special abilities* (eds L. K. Obler & D. Fein), pp. 374–492. New York, NY: Guilford.

Smith, S. B. 1983 *The great mental calculators*. New York, NY: Columbia University Press.

Southall, G. 1979 *Blind Tom: the post Civil War enslavement of a black musical genius*. Minneapolis, MN: Challenge Productions.

Stutsman, R. 1948 *Merrill Palmer scale of mental tests*. Los Angeles, CA: Western Psychological Services.

Tredgold, A. 1952 *Mental deficiency*. Baltimore, MD: Williams & Wilkins.

Treffert, D. 1989 *Extraordinary people: understanding 'Idiot Savants'*. New York, NY: Harper & Row.

Treffert, D. 2000 *Extraordinary people: understanding savant syndrome*. New York, NY: Ballantine Books.

Wechsler, D. 1974 *Wechsler intelligence scale for children-revised*. New York, NY: Psychological Corporation.
Wechsler, D. 1984 *Wechsler adult intelligence scale-revised*. New York, NY: Psychological Corporation.
Young, R. L. 1995 Savant syndrome: processes underlying extraordinary abilities. PhD dissertation, University of Adelaide, Adelaide, South Australia.

Appendix A

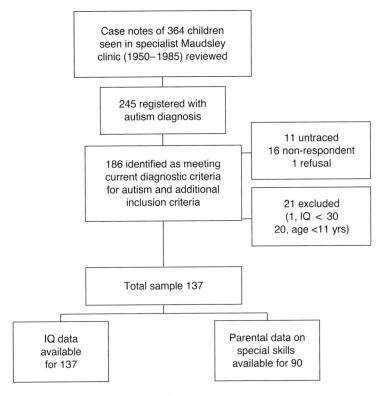

Figure 2.1 Sample identification.

Appendix B

Table 2.3 Examples of savant skills reported on parental questionnaire.

computation	arithmetical calculations have become increasingly possible; easily able to multiply two numbers in the millions together in head; can tell the elevation of both the Sun and the Moon at any time on any date without reference to any book; has written a computer program about this
calendar calculations	when very young obsessed with 'time'; learned to read digital/analogue/roman dials preschool; could tell folk when their birthday would occur (day of the week/what day of the week they were born on); can work out the day of a particular date in the future; however, soon gets fed up of being asked so is rarely tested on this ability
memory	has memorized a 100-year calendar; can tell you what day, say Christmas, occurs, over that 100 years; I bought the calendar *ca* 15 years ago and he just memorized all the pages; can tell you the name of any tunes he knows as soon as he hears the opening bars; we think he has outstanding memory ability but because he is reluctant to use speech, it is difficult to gauge how good it is; some examples: a few years ago, he was bought a book which was read to him; this year we read it to him again after over a year—if we stopped he would finish the rest of the sentence quite accurately; a second example is that he is able to give the names (both first and surnames) of his classmates at school 20 years earlier
visuospatial	successful in painting portraits of friends, friends' children and selling them; has exceptional talent for dealing with children; attends art classes at college of further education every week—an excellent tutor has succeeded in encouraging him to do the most outstanding abstract paintings which he has exhibited at the college; they bought one to use on their brochure; did not show this talent as a child or adolescent
music	has perfect pitch and is able to identify chords in pieces of music with ease
multiple skills: computation, music and memory	very talented in mathematics—evident since teens; Also has a very good memory of events that happened over the past number of years, i.e. knows the dates, days of the year when household appliances purchased; helps other people to fill in their CVs with dates for schools, jobs, etc; also quite talented in art as well as music; taught self to play the clarinet and guitar
calendar calculations, computation and music	calendar calculations, perfect pitch and music in general; arithmetic—always interested and good at this (for past 2 years has had several researchers visiting him testing him for calendar work, arithmetic and music)

3

What aspects of autism predispose to talent?

Francesca Happé and Pedro Vital

In this paper, we explore the question, why are striking special skills so much more common in autism spectrum conditions (ASC) than in other groups? Current cognitive accounts of ASC are briefly reviewed in relation to special skills. Difficulties in 'theory of mind' may contribute to originality in ASC, since individuals who do not automatically 'read other minds' may be better able to think outside prevailing fashions and popular theories. However, originality alone does not confer talent. Executive dysfunction has been suggested as the 'releasing' mechanism for special skills in ASC, but other groups with executive difficulties do not show raised incidence of talents. Detail-focused processing bias ('weak coherence', 'enhanced perceptual functioning') appears to be the most promising predisposing characteristic, or 'starting engine', for talent development. In support of this notion, we summarize data from a population-based twin study in which parents reported on their 8-year-olds' talents and their ASC-like traits. Across the whole sample, ASC-like traits, and specifically 'restricted and repetitive behaviours and interests' related to detail focus, were more pronounced in children reported to have talents outstripping older children. We suggest that detail-focused cognitive style predisposes to talent in savant domains in, and beyond, autism spectrum disorders.

Keywords: autism; savant skills; central coherence; theory of mind; genetic

3.1 Introduction

Special skills, such as lightning multiplication, identification of prime numbers, calendar calculation, perfect-perspective drawing, absolute pitch, instant reproduction of newly heard music and extraordinary memory for facts, are far more common in autism spectrum conditions (ASC: autism, Asperger's syndrome, atypical autism or PDD-NOS) than in any other group examined to date (see Treffert 2009). While robust epidemiological data are lacking, estimates from surveys of parents and carers (Rimland 1978) suggest that around one in 10 individuals with ASC have a talent out of line with their other abilities (but see Howlin *et al.* (2009), for an even higher estimate), compared with perhaps 0.6–0.1 per cent among those with other developmental or intellectual disabilities (Hill 1977; Saloviita *et al.* 2000). The reason for this association between special abilities and ASC remains unclear. In this paper, we briefly review three current cognitive accounts of ASC, and consider their explanatory power in relation to special skills. We then present some data from our own research with a large population-based twin sample examining relationships between ASC-like traits and talent. We begin, however, with a brief word about the unitary or fractionable nature of the core behavioural and cognitive features of ASD.

3.2 The 'fractionable triad'?

Autism and Asperger's syndrome (together referred to here under the umbrella term 'ASC') are diagnosed on the basis of qualitative impairments in social interaction and communication, with restricted and repetitive behaviours and interests (RRBIs). All three aspects of what has been termed the autistic (after Wing & Gould's (1979) triad of social, communication and imagination impairments) must co-occur for the diagnosis to be made. However, elsewhere, we (and others; e.g. Wing & Wing 1971; Bishop 1989; Goodman 1989; Mandy & Skuse 2008) have argued that the three parts of the diagnostic triad are in fact fractionable (see Happé et al. 2006; Happé & Ronald 2008). Very briefly, in population samples, it appears that individual differences in social interaction, communication and RRBIs correlate only moderately (Ronald et al. 2006a), that isolated impairments in just one (or two) part(s) of the triad can be found (e.g. in relatives of those with ASC; Piven et al. 1997; Pickles et al. 2000) and that largely non-overlapping genetic effects appear to operate on different parts of the triad (e.g. Ronald et al. 2006a,b; for a counter-view, see Constantino et al. 2004). While we recognize that this 'fractionable triad' view is still a working hypothesis, we take it as a starting point for the present paper: we ask not why ASC is linked to talent, but what (potentially dissociable) *aspect(s)* of ASC predispose to talent.

3.3 Current cognitive accounts of ASC: 'starting engines' for talent?

(a) Mind-blindness

There is now good agreement that at the heart of ASC lies a difficulty in recognizing and representing mental states (Frith 2003), reflected in abnormal brain functioning (e.g. Happé et al. 1996). While there are a number of alternative accounts of the nature of the primary social deficit (e.g. reduced salience of social stimuli; Klin et al. 2003), the fact that most people with ASC find it difficult to put themselves in another's shoes, or 'mind read', has been successful in explaining much of the pattern of impaired and intact social and communicative behaviour in ASC, as well as inspiring practical efforts in early diagnosis and intervention (for a review, see Baron-Cohen et al. 2000).

Can impaired recognition of mental states help explain the association between ASC and talent? Three possibilities seem worth considering. First, it might be argued that individuals with ASC free up both mental and time resources that so-called 'neurotypicals' use on tracking and remembering social content,[1] and that these may contribute to talent development. The idea of cortical 'rededication' underlying talent in ASC was suggested by Waterhouse (1988). For example, Grelotti et al. (2005) reported the case of a young boy with ASC who did not activate the fusiform gyrus in response to faces, but did so in response to Digimon cartoon characters—on which he was an expert. If reallocation of neural and cognitive resources from social to other (savant-skill relevant) processing explains the association between ASC and talent, we might predict an inverse

---

[1] Indeed, it is interesting to ask whether the neurotypical talent for, for example, remembering and recognizing hundreds of thousands of faces, might be considered a savant skill, were it not species-typical.

correlation between social interest and savant talent within ASC, and perhaps within the general population. Despite the stereotype of the eccentric genius or artist with no understanding of those around her/him, there is little evidence to date in support of this idea, and none to suggest a causal direction (but see Baron-Cohen (2002), for a discussion of systemizing-empathizing). Of course, those with exceptional talent may find it harder to find similar peers with whom to make close friendships, or may have to spend time in practice that limits socializing hours.

Second, difficulty tracking the mental states of others may contribute to the *originality* expressed in a developing talent. It is notable that typically developing (TD) children lose aspects of originality in, for example, their art as a result of acquiring stereotyped forms from their peers (think, for example, of rays drawn on a sun or birds drawn as 'ticks'). Without doubt, the obligatory and automatic recognition of others' mental states, and the desire to be viewed by others as part of the in-group, place blinkers on most TD young people. People with ASC, on the other hand, may be oblivious to what others think, what is considered the fashionable or correct mode of thought or how others perceive them or their work. Thus, individuals with ASC are, perhaps, more able than TD individuals to think their own thoughts, regardless of what others think. This contributes to originality, in the sense of a unique world view. However, originality of this type does not guarantee talent—an idea may be merely outre without being an advance on traditional thinking. Thus, Kanner and Asperger both highlight the unusual ideas of the young people they describe in their first accounts of ASC—some of these being interesting and potentially insightful, some bizarre and maladaptive. Kanner describes, for example, Donald; 'When asked to subtract 4 from 10, he answered "I'll draw a hexagon" (Kanner 1943, p. 222). Another of Kanner's original cases, Alfred, is described as follows: 'He once stopped and asked, very much perplexed, why there was 'The Johns Hopkins Hospital' printed on the history sheets: 'Why do they have to say that?' This, to him, was a real problem of major importance, calling for a great deal of thought and discussion. Since the histories were taken at the hospital, why should it be necessary to have the name on every sheet, though the person writing on it knew where he was writing?' (Kanner 1943, p. 235).

Third, mind-blindness for one's *own* mind may be relevant to talent development. The possibility that difficulty in representing mental states in ASC also affects the ability to reflect on one's own inner states has been suggested elsewhere (Frith & Happé 1999; Happé 2003; Williams & Happé in press). If people with autism are less self-aware in some ways, this might be advantageous for those skills best developed through implicit learning. To take a light-hearted example, it is said that the best way to disadvantage your golfing opponents is to ask them exactly how they achieve their perfect swing! Some tasks, such as extracting the regularities in an artificial grammar, are better achieved through implicit learning and are disrupted by attempts at explicit rule identification (e.g. Reber 1976; Fletcher *et al.* 2005). Interestingly, level of implicit learning (unlike explicit learning) is unrelated to IQ, and unimpaired in intellectually disabled groups (for a review, see Underwood (1996)). Also relevant to difficulty 'reading own mind', perhaps, is the notion of 'flow' (Csikszentmihályi 1990)—which, though non-scientific, describes a familiar state of reduced self-awareness and altered sense of the passage of time during periods of intense engagement with a task or process. If at least some people with ASC have reduced awareness of own inner states, it may be easier for them to enter a state of flow—which is thought to be inherently reinforcing and rewarding (Csikszentmihályi & Lefevre 1989) and might be especially so for individuals with ASC (in whom anxiety and depression are common; Kim *et al.* 2000).

Mind-blindness, then, may contribute an original world view and might foster skill development, but is unlikely, we would suggest, to act as the starting engine for talent.

(b) Executive dysfunction

The umbrella term executive function covers some areas of top-down control that are strikingly impaired in ASC. People with ASC show difficulties planning ahead, shifting from old patterns and generating new responses to adapt to novel demands in standard tests (see Hill (2004*a*,*b*) for a review), and in everyday life these difficulties significantly limit adaptation and independence in even the highly intelligent. Again, the popular stereotype would suggest a link between special talent and lack of common sense—the brilliant professor who cannot manage his everyday household needs. Is executive dysfunction a predisposing factor for talent?

Snyder has suggested that reduced frontal function may release special skills—a fascinating and bold proposal examined in Chapter 7 (see also Snyder *et al*. 2003, 2006). On this account, executive dysfunction in ASC paradoxically facilitates development of savant skills. However, executive dysfunction occurs in many other clinical groups (e.g. attention deficit hyperactivity disorder; Pennington & Ozonoff 1996), not characterized by a raised incidence of special skills. Good data on the relationship between executive function performance and talent are lacking. Reduced cognitive flexibility is perhaps the executive dysfunction most consistently associated with ASC (Liss *et al*. 2001), and might be considered to be related to obsessive pursuit of narrow interests. However, some authors have suggested that some executive skills, such as working memory, may be *superior* in savant versus non-savant groups with ASC (Bolte & Poustka 2004; but see Heavey 1997). From the small group studies to date, it appears that, for example, generativity is much better in the domain of talent (e.g. drawing) than in other areas (e.g. verbal fluency) or in non-savant individuals with ASC (Ryder 2003). However, large group and developmental studies would be needed to establish a causal role for individual differences in executive functions in talent development.

(c) Detail-focused cognitive style

Unlike the executive dysfunction and theory of mind accounts of autism, the suggestion that ASC is characterized in part by a different cognitive style has aimed from the outset to explain islets of ability typical of this condition (Frith 1989, 2003). Central coherence refers to the tendency in TD individuals to process incoming information in context for meaning, preserving gist and gestalt form at the expense of detail and featural information. People with ASC, the theory suggests, have instead a processing bias towards detail and featural information, and tend to succumb less to contextual and gestalt effects. Among the earliest demonstrations of so-called weak coherence were superior ability in block design and embedded figures tests by ASC groups compared with CA/IQ-matched control groups (see Happé & Frith (2006) for a review). A link between detail focus and well-developed talents in areas such as maths, music and art has been suggested in relation to weak central coherence (e.g. Happé 1999), 'enhanced perceptual functioning' (Mottron *et al*. 2006) and systemizing accounts of ASC (Baron-Cohen 2002). Since the latter accounts are elegantly discussed in Chapters 4, 5 and 6, the weak coherence account will be discussed in what follows (although for many of the predictions, these accounts, with their agreement on superior local processing, may not differ).

How might a tendency to process featural rather than configural information predispose to the development of specific talents? The suggestion is that attention to detail and tendency towards exemplar-based memory, rather than prototype extraction, is the starting engine for talent in the savant domains. Take the example of musical talent; musical savants appear universally to have absolute pitch, which is a great advantage in (at least some aspects of) musical memory and performance. Absolute pitch, it has been argued, is easy for young children to acquire in the first three or four years of life because, at this stage, music is processed with more attention to the exact notes and less attention to the relationships between the notes, i.e. the melody (Takeuchi & Hulse 1993). People with ASC show much better performance, regardless of age, on tests of memory for pitch, and absolute pitch seems to be more common in ASC than in comparable groups (see Heaton (Chapter 13), for a review). The argument is that detail-focused processing bias, which in ASC lasts throughout life, makes it easy for individuals with ASC to establish pitch-label representations that are stable and enduring.

In the domain of art, the ability to attend to details, to break the gestalt into parts, is probably helpful in achieving realistic-looking drawings. A trick used in teaching accurate drawing to TD students is to copy pictures turned upside down: inversion disproportionately disrupts configural processing. Pring *et al.* (1995) reported that block design skill, which may result from ability to see the parts within the to-be-copied design, was notable in children with artistic abilities and in children with autism. In the area of calendar calculation, too, Heavey has suggested that the starting point may be the discovery of small day-date regularities (Heavey *et al.* 1999).

The relationship between bias towards/superior local processing and reduced global processing has been re-examined in recent accounts of 'weak coherence' (see Happé & Booth (2008) for a discussion). The assumption of trade-off has been questioned, and, instead, the suggestion made that weak coherence may reflect two somewhat independent and dissociable features seen in some but not all individuals with ASC; bias towards/superior local processing, and bias away from/reduced global processing (Booth 2006). If this suggestion is confirmed, a testable hypothesis is that the individuals with ASC most likely to develop talents are those that show superior local processing without any impairment of global processing.

It is intriguing to wonder whether the top-down influences that usually suppress savant skills, in Snyder's account, relate to global processing biases—which require inhibition (from TMS or brain lesion) in TD individuals if featural information is to be processed. If so, individual differences in strength of global processing bias might predict which individuals show improvement of skill under TMS, or 'release' of talent in dementia or brain injury. In ASC, on the other hand, there may be no default bias towards global processing—hence no 'talent-suppressing' top-down influences, in terms of Snyder's account.

3.4 Exploring the relationship between aspects of autism and talent

O'Connor and Hermelin, the founders of the modern interest in special skills in autism (and other developmentally disabled groups) asked the important question; what is alike among savants? Their answer, briefly, was that a strong tendency towards repetitive behaviour and preoccupation characterized those with savant skills regardless of their diagnosis (O'Connor & Hermelin 1991). The subsequent broadening of diagnostic criteria probably means that many individuals then considered 'non-autistic' would now fall within the autism spectrum. However, it remains of interest that non-social ASC-like traits, rather than social-communicative difficulties, were highlighted in this early work. Young's work with a large number of savants with and without ASC also led her to conclude that a common characteristic of these individuals was an almost obsessional preoccupation with a restricted area of interest (Young 1995).

A rather different study compared personality and cognitive traits of musicians with and without absolute pitch. Brown et al. (2003) found that their 13 musicians with absolute pitch showed a significant peak in block design, were rated more often by interviewers as eccentric, and showed (non-significantly) worse social-communicative skills and more rigid/aloof/hypersensitive personality (at a level found in the broader autism phenotype) when compared with 33 musicians without absolute pitch. Block design skill has been taken as a marker of weak coherence, and an intriguing question is whether talent in the general population is related to non-social aspects of ASC, and specifically to detail-focused cognitive style.

(a) What aspects of autistic-like traits are associated with talent in the general population?

In our recent work, we have had the chance to explore what aspects of autism might predispose to talent, by examining the relationship between parent-reported ASC-like traits and parent-reported special abilities in a large sample of twins, then aged 8 (see Vital et al. (2009), for full details). The Twins Early Development Study (TEDS) is a longitudinal population-based study of twins born in England and Wales between 1994 and 1996 (for details see Oliver & Plomin 2007). We had relevant data, from postal measures at age 8, for 12 852 children participating in TEDS. Owing to the problems of non-independence of data points when considering twins, one twin from each twin pair was randomly selected for our analyses, with a final n of 6426. For these children, we could examine the relationship between parent-rated ASC-like traits as measured by the Childhood Asperger Screening Test (CAST; Scott et al. 2002) and special abilities, tapped by three simple questions to parents: (i) does (your child) display a striking skill, compared with her/his general ability level, (ii) does she/he display a striking skill, when compared with other children of her or his age, and (iii) does she/he display a special gift, when compared with children even much older? For each question, parents could tick a box to indicate skill in one or more of the following areas: maths, music, art, or memory. Because parents tended to be generous in their ratings (16% of children were reported to have a talent in response to question (iii)), we concentrated our analysis on the highest level of talent—skills considered to outstrip even those of much older children.

The results showed that ASC-like traits (as reported by parents using the CAST) were significantly more pronounced in children who were said to have special skills than in children not so rated. The overall elevated CAST score was particularly due to higher ratings on the 'RRBI' items ($d = 0.6$), while for social and communication items the significant effects were of small magnitude ($d = 0.2$). Relationships between CAST and reported special skills were not confounded by IQ effects; IQ was positively related to reports of special skills but negatively related to CAST ratings.

Ratings of RRBI were significantly higher regardless of area of talent, with effect sizes for music, maths, art and memory skill groups ranging from 0.4 to 0.9. By contrast, social skills/difficulty appeared to relate to specific area of talent. Children said to have special skills in music or art did not show significantly more social difficulty than children without such talents. Children skilled in maths or memory, on the other hand, showed slight, but significant, disadvantage in parent-rated social skills ($d = 0.2 – 0.3$).

We explored the relationship between parent ratings of special skills and ratings of ASC-like traits in the non-social domain further, by dividing the RRBI items into the subtypes given in the current diagnostic criteria (DSM-IV TR; APA 2000). Regression analyses suggested that the items that most differentiated children said to show 'special gifts' from those not so rated had to do with detail focus (noticing and remembering details others miss; $d = 0.7$) and to a lesser extent items to do with insistence on sameness or repetitive special interests ($d = 0.2$ in each case). This association between talent and eye/memory for detail remained even if children with special gifts in memory were excluded from the analyses.

These group results were unchanged whether we included or excluded the approximately 1 per cent of children meeting diagnostic criteria for autism, Asperger's syndrome or atypical autism (on the Development and Well-Being Assessment, DAWBA; Goodman et al. 2000). Not reported in Vital et al. (2009), but of interest in the present context, is the relationship between symptoms and special skills *within* this ASC subgroup. Interestingly, while social and communication impairments were somewhat ($d = 0.1$) reduced in the ASC children said to have special skills, RRBIs were raised in the special skills ASC group ($d = 0.4$) compared with ASC children without such skills (figure 3.1). While causal direction remains to be tested, these data might suggest that, even at the extreme, eye for detail predisposes to special skills, as well as that special skills may aid social adaptation in ASC.

Lastly, comparison of correlations between identical and fraternal twins across the full sample of more than 6000 twin pairs suggests that the association between ASC-like

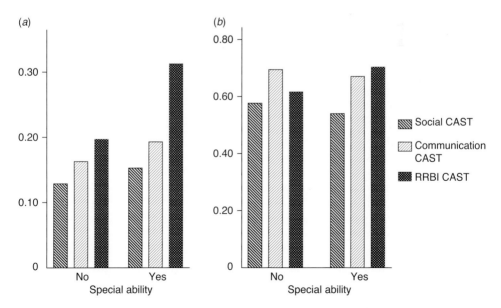

Figure 3.1 ASC-like trait scores (proportional, max = 1) as a function of special ability in (*a*) non-ASC ($n > 6330$) and (*b*) ASC ($n = 81$) groups. *Note.* The range shown on the y-axes for (*a,b*) are not equivalent.

traits in the non-social domain (RRBIs) and reported special skills (a phenotypic correlation of 0.37 for males and 0.52 for females) is in large part due to shared genetic effects (Vital *et al.* in preparation). The bivariate heritability, or the proportion of the phenotypic correlation accounted for by genetic factors, was 61 per cent for males and 78 per cent for females. This suggests that genetic factors play the central role in the co-occurrence of special abilities and RRBIs: approximately half of the genetic influences on individual differences in special abilities also appear to influence variation in RRBIs. Put simplistically, some genetic factors that predispose to ASC-like traits (and specifically RRBIs) also predispose to talent. We have previously shown, in a small sample of families, that around a half of fathers and a third of mothers of boys with ASC show detail-focused cognitive style across a battery of experimental tasks (Happé *et al.* 2001), and that this relates to self-reported 'eye for detail' (Briskman *et al.* 2001); we would predict that these traits will also be associated with increased rates of talent in the relatives of those with ASC.

3.5 Conclusions

In this paper, we have suggested that it is not autism *per se* that predisposes to talent, but rather the detail-focused cognitive style (weak coherence) that is characteristic of, but not confined to, ASC. Attention to detail, exemplar-based memory encoding, veridical (not context-distorted) representation is proposed to be the starting engine for talent. An interesting question for future research is whether individuals with ASC who develop talents are distinguished from those who do not do so by a more pronounced detail focus, by intact global processing (alongside local bias), or by aspects of personality or personal history for which we do not yet have good measures.

One implication of the fractionable triad proposal is that core components of ASC need not be unique to ASC—since it is the *combination* of cognitive deficits and assets that defines ASC uniquely. Because of this, it seems no problem, on our account, if special abilities and savant skills can be found in non-ASC groups. Our prediction would be that where savant-like talents are found, these will be linked to detail-focused cognitive style, regardless of diagnostic group. Because this cognitive style is extremely common in ASC, the incidence of savant skills and talents is raised.

We have summarized preliminary evidence of behavioural and genetic association between parent-reported special abilities and eye for detail in a large twin sample. We predict that family studies will show a raised incidence of talent among the relatives of those with ASC, and specifically among relatives sharing their detail-focused cognitive style. Unlike many other authors, we do not find implausible the notion of a single starting engine for the varied array of talents seen in savants; data from our twin sample showed largely similar patterns across reported maths, music, art and memory skills.

We have also suggested that mind-blindness, while not the starting engine, may act to enhance talent. Reduced social influence and concern over others' views, as well as time devoted to talent rather than socializing, are obvious contributors to this. A more novel suggestion is that reduced self-awareness may contribute to implicit learning of certain regularities, and aid achievement of flow states in ASC. The combination of detail focus as starting engine and reduced mentalizing as 'fuel' may give a special flavour, independence and true originality to talent in ASC that is hard to find in other groups.

The authors would like to thank all the participants and families who have taken part in TEDS throughout the years it has been running, as well as to all those on the TEDS team involved in the collection and management of the TEDS dataset. TEDS is supported by a programme grant from the UK Medical Research Council (G0500079). F.H.'s work was supported by MRC grant G0500870. P.V. was supported by a UK MRC doctoral studentship. Thanks are also due to the four reviewers who provided very helpful comments on an earlier draft.

References

American Psychiatric Association 2000 *Diagnostic and statistical manual of mental disorders*, 4th edn. Washington, DC: American Psychiatric Association.

Baron-Cohen, S. 2002 The extreme male brain theory of autism. *Trends Cogn. Sci.* **6**, 248–254. (doi:10.1016/ S1364-6613(02)01904-6)

Baron-Cohen, S., Tager-Flusberg, H. & Cohen, D. J. 2000 *Understanding other minds: perspectives from developmental cognitive neurosdence*, 2nd edn. Oxford, UK: Oxford University Press.

Bishop, D. V. 1989 Autism, Asperger's syndrome and semantic-pragmatic disorder: where are the boundaries? *Br. J. Disord. Commun.* **24**, 107–121. (doi:10.3109/13682828909011951)

Bölte, S. & Poustka, F. 2004 Comparing the intelligence profiles of savant and nonsavant individuals with autistic disorder. *Intelligence* **32**, 121–131. (doi:10.1016/j.intell.2003.11.002)

Booth, R. D. L. 2006 Local-global processing and cognitive style in autism spectrum disorders and typical development. PhD thesis, King's College, University of London, London, UK.

Briskman, J., Happé, F. & Frith, U. 2001 Exploring the cognitive phenotype of autism: weak 'central coherence' in parents and siblings of children with autism. II. Real-life skills and preferences. *J. Child Psychol. Psychiatry* **42**, 309–316. (doi:10.1111/1469-7610.00724)

Brown, W. A. *et al.* 2003 Autism-related language, personality, and cognition in people with absolute pitch: results of a preliminary study. *J. Autism Dev. Disord.* **33**, 163–167. (doi:10.1023/A:1022987309913)

Constantino, J. N., Gruber, C. P., Davis, S., Hayes, S., Passanante, N. & Przybeck, T. 2004 The factor structure of autistic traits. *J. Child Psychol. Psychiatry* **45**, 719–726. (doi:10.1111/j.1469-7610.2004.00266.x)

Csíkszentmihályi, M. 1990 *Flow: the psychology of optimal experience*. New York, NY: Harper and Row.

Csíkszentmihályi, M. & Lefevre, J. 1989 Optimal experience in work and leisure. *J. Pers. Soc. Psychol.* **56**, 815–822. (doi:10.1037/0022-3514.56.5.815)

Fletcher, P. C, Zafiris, O., Frith, C. D., Honey, R. A., Corlett, P. R., Zilles, K. & Fink, G. R. 2005 On the benefits of not trying: brain activity and connectivity reflecting the interactions of explicit and implicit sequence learning. *Cerebral Cortex* **15**, 1002–1015. (doi:10.1093/cercor/bhh201)

Frith, U. 1989 *Autism: explaining the enigma*. Oxford, UK: Blackwell.

Frith, U. 2003 *Autism: explaining the enigma*, 2nd edn. Oxford, UK: Blackwell.

Frith, U. & Happé, F. 1999 Theory of mind and self consciousness: what is it like to be autistic? *Mind Lang.* **14**, 1–22.

Goodman, R. 1989 Infantile autism: a syndrome of multiple primary deficits? *J. Autism Dev. Disord.* **19**, 409–424. (doi:10.1007/BF02212939)

Goodman, R., Ford, T., Richards, H., Gatward, R. & Meltzer, H. 2000 The development and well-being assessment: description and initial validation of an integrated assessment of child and adolescent psycho-pathology. *J. Child Psychol. Psychiatry* **41**, 645–655. (doi:10.1111/j.1469-7610.2000.tb02345.x)

Grelotti, D. J., Klin, A. J., Gauthier, I., Skudlarski, P., Cohne, D. J., Gore, J. C, Volkmar, F. R. & Schultz, R. T. 2005 fMRI activation of the fusiform gyrus and amygdala to cartoon characters but not to faces in a boy with autism. *Neuropsychologia* **43**, 373–385. (doi:10.1016/j.neuropsychologia.2004.06.015)

Happé, F. 1999 Autism: cognitive deficit or cognitive style? *Trends Cogn. Sci.* **3**, 216–222. (doi:10.1016/S1364-6613(99)01318-2)

Happé, F. 2003 Theory of mind and the self. In *The self: from soul to brain* (eds J. LeDoux, J. Debiec & H. Moss). *Ann. N YAcad. Sci.* **1001**, 134–144. See www.annalsnyas.org.

Happé, F. G. E. & Booth, R. D. L. 2008 The power of the positive: revisiting weak central coherence in autism spectrum disorders. *Q. J. Exp. Psychol.* **61**, 50–63. (doi:10.1080/17470210701508731)

Happé, F. & Frith, U. 2006 The weak coherence account: detail-focused cognitive style in autism spectrum disorders. *J. Autism Dev. Disord.* **36**, 5–25. (doi:10.1007/si 0803-005-0039-0)

Happé, F. & Ronald, A. 2008 The 'fractionable autism triad': a review of evidence from behavioural, genetic, cognitive and neural research. *Neuropsychol. Rev.* **18**, 287–304. (doi:10.1007/s11065-008-9076-8)

Happé, F., Ehlers, S., Fletcher, P., Frith, U., Johansson, M., Gillberg, C, Dolan, R., Frackowiak, R. & Frith, C. 1996 'Theory of mind' in the brain. Evidence from a PET scan study of Asperger syndrome. *Neuroreport* **8**, 197–201. (doi:10.1097/00001756-199612200-00040)

Happé, F., Briskman, J. & Frith, U. 2001 Exploring the cognitive phenotype of autism: weak 'central coherence' in parents and siblings of children with autism. I. Experimental tests. *J. Child Psychol. Psychiatry* **42**, 299–307. (doi:10.1111/1469-7610.00723)

Happé, F., Ronald, A. & Plomin, R. 2006 Time to give up on a single explanation for autism. *Nat. Neurosd.* **9**, 1218–1220. (doi:10.1038/nn1770)

Heaton, P. 2009 Assessing musical skills in autistic children who are not savants. *Phil. Trans. R. Soc. B* **364**, 1443–1447. (doi:10.1098/rstb.2008.0327)

Heavey, L. J. 1997 Memory in the calendar calculating savant. PhD thesis, Goldsmith's College, University of London, London, UK.

Heavey, L., Pring, L. & Hermelin, B. 1999 A date to remember: the nature of memory in savant calendrical calculators. *Psychol. Med.* **29**, 145–160. (doi:10.1017/S0033291798007776)

Hill, A. L. 1977 Idiot savants: rate of incidence. *Percept. Mot. Skills* **44**, 161–162.

Hill, E. L. 2004a Evaluating the theory of executive dysfunction in autism. *Dev. Rev.* **24**, 189–233. (doi:10.1016/j.dr.2004.01.001)

Hill, E. L. 2004b Executive dysfunction in autism. *Trends Cogn. Sci.* **81**, 26–32. (doi:10.1016/j.tics.2003.11.003)

Howlin, P., Goode, S., Hutton, J. & Rutter, M. 2009 Savant skills in autism: psychometric approaches and parental reports. *Phil. Trans. R. Soc. B* **364**, 1359–1367. (doi:10.1098/rstb.2008.0328)

Kanner, L. 1943 Autistic disturbances of affective contact. *Nerv. Child* **2**, 217–250.

Kim, J. A., Szatmari, P., Bryson, S. E., Streiner, D. L. & Wilson, F. J. 2000 The prevalence of anxiety and mood problems among children with autism and Asperger Syndrome. *Autism* **4**, 117–132. (doi:10.1177/1362361300004002002)

Klin, A., Jones, W., Schultz, R. & Volkmar, F. 2003 The enactive mind, or from actions to cognition: lessons from autism. *Phil. Trans. R. Soc. Lond. B* **358**, 345–360. (doi:10.1098/rstb.2002.1202)

Liss, M., Fein, D., Allen, D., Dunn, M., Feinstein, C, Morris, R., Waterhouse, L. & Rapin, I. 2001 Executive functioning in high-functioning children with autism. *J. ChUd Psychol. Psychiatry* **42**, 261–270. (doi:10.1111/1469-7610.00717)

Mandy, W. P. & Skuse, D. H. 2008 What is the association between the social-communication element of autism and repetitive interests, behaviours and activities? *J. Child Psychol. Psychiatry* **49**, 795–808. (doi:10.1111/j.1469-7610.2008.01911.x)

Mottron, L., Dawson, M., Soulieres, I., Hubert, B. & Burack, J. 2006 Enhanced perceptual functioning in autism: an update, and eight principles of autistic perception. *J. Autism Dev. Disord.* **36**, 27–43. (doi:10.1007/s10803-005-0040-7)

O'Connor, N. & Hermelin, B. 1991 Talents and preoccupations in idiot-savants. *Psychol. Med.* **21**, 959–964.

Oliver, B. R. & Plomin, R. 2007 Twins Early Development Study (TEDS): a multivariate, longitudinal genetic investigation of language, cognition and behaviour problems from childhood through adolescence. *Twin Res. Hum. Genet.* **10**, 96–105. (doi:10.1375/twin.10.1.96)

Pennington, B. F. & Ozonoff, S. 1996 Executive functions and developmental psychopathology. *J. Child Psychol. Psychiatry* **37**, 51–87. (doi:10.1111/j.1469-7610.1996.tb01380.x)

Pickles, A., Starr, E., Kazak, S., Bolton, P., Papanikolaou, K., Bailey, A., Goodman, R. & Rutter, M. 2000 Broader expression of the autism broader phenotype: findings from extended pedigrees. *J. Child Psychol. Psychiatry* **41**, 491–502. (doi:10.1111/1469-7610.00634)

Piven, J., Palmer, P., Jacobi, D., Childress, D. & Arndt, S. 1997 Broader autism phenotype: evidence from a family history-study of multiple-incidence autism families. *Am. J. Psychiatry* **154**, 185–190.

Pring, L., Hermelin, B. & Heavey, L. 1995 Savants, segments, art and autism. *J. Child Psychol. Psychiatry Allied Disciplines* **36**, 1065–1076. (doi:10.1111/j.1469-7610.1995.tb01351.x)

Reber, A. S. 1976 Implicit learning of synthetic languages: the role of instructional set. *J. Exp. Psychol. Hum. Learn. Memory* **2**, 88–94. (doi:10.1037/0278-7393.2.1.88)

Rimland, B. 1978 Savant capabilities of autistic children and their cognitive implications. In *Cognitive defects in the development of mental illness* (ed. G. Serban), pp. 44–63. New York, NY: Brunner/Mazel.

Ronald, A., Happé, R, Price, T. S., Baron-Cohen, S. & Plomin, R. 2006b Phenotypic and genetic overlap between autistic traits at the extreme of the general population. *J. Am. Acad. Child Adolesc. Psychiatry* **45**, 1206–1234. (doi:10.1097/01.chi.0000230165.54117.41)

Ryder, N. 2003 The generative ability of artistically gifted savants. PhD thesis, Goldsmith's College, University of London, London, UK.

Saloviita, T., Ruusila, L. & Ruusila, U. 2000 Incidence of savant syndrome in Finland. *Percept. Mot. Skills* **91**, 120–122. (doi:10.2466/PMS.91.5.120-122)

Scott, F. J., Baron-Cohen, S., Bolton, P. & Brayne, C. 2002 The CAST (Childhood Asperger Syndrome Test): preliminary development of a UK screen for mainstream primary-school aged children. *Autism* **6**, 9–31. (doi:10.1177/1362361302006001003)

Snyder, A. 2009 Explaining and inducing savant skills: privileged access to lower level, less-processed information. *Phil. Trans. R. Soc. B* **364**, 1399–1405. (doi:10.1098/rstb.2008.0290)

Snyder, A. W., Mulcahy, E., Taylor, J. L., Mitchell, D. J., Sachdev, P. & Gandevia, S. C. 2003 Savant-like skills exposed in normal people by suppressing the left fronto-temporal lobe. *J. Integr. Neurosci.* **2**, 149–158. (doi:10.1142/S0219635203000287)

Snyder, A., Bahramali, H., Hawker, T. & Mitchell, D. J. 2006 Savant-like numerosity skills revealed in normal people by magnetic pulses. *Perception* **35**, 837–845. (doi:10.1068/p5539)

Takeuchi, A. H. & Hulse, S. H. 1993 Absolute pitch. *Psychol. Bull.* **113**, 345–361. (doi:10.1037/0033-2909.113.2.345)

Treffert, D. A. 2009 The savant syndrome: an extraordinary condition. A synopsis: past, present, future. *Phil. Trans. R. Soc. B* **364**, 1351–1357. (doi:10.1098/rstb.2008.0326)

Underwood, G. 1996 *Implicit cognition*. Oxford, UK: Oxford University Press.

Vital, P., Ronald, A., Rijsdijk, F., Wallace, G., Happé, F. & Plomin, R. In preparation. A behavioural-genetic investigation of the aetiology of special ability and its association with autistic-like traits.

Vital, P., Ronald, A., Wallace, G. & Happé, F. 2009 Relationship between special abilities and autistic-like traits in a large population-based sample of 8-year-olds. *J. Child Psychol. Psychiatry* **50**, 1093–1101.

Waterhouse, L. 1988 Speculations on the neuroanatomical substrate of special talents. In *The exceptional brain: neuropsychology of talent and special abilities* (eds L. K. Obler & D. Fein), pp. 493–512. New York, NY: Guilford.

Williams, D. & Happé, F. In press. 'What did I say?' versus 'What did I think?': attributing false beliefs to self amongst children with and without autism. *J. Autism Dev. Disord.* (doi:10.1007/S10803-009-0695-6)

Wing, L. & Gould, J. 1979 Severe impairments of social interaction and associated abnormalities in children: epidemiology and classification. *J. Autism Child. Schizophr.* **9**, 11–29. (doi:10.1007/BF01531288)

Wing, L. & Wing, J. K. 1971 Multiple impairments in early childhood autism. *J. Autism Childhood Schizophr.* **1**, 256–266. (doi:10.1007/BF01557347)

Young, R. 1995 Savant syndrome: processes underlying extraordinary abilities. PhD thesis, University of Adelaide, Adelaide, South Australia.

4

Talent in autism: hyper-systemizing, hyper-attention to detail and sensory hyper-sensitivity

Simon Baron-Cohen, Emma Ashwin, Chris Ashwin, Teresa Tavassoli and Bhismadev Chakrabarti

We argue that *hyper-systemizing* predisposes individuals to show talent, and review evidence that hyper-systemizing is part of the cognitive style of people with autism spectrum conditions (ASC). We then clarify the hyper-systemizing theory, contrasting it to the weak central coherence (WCC) and executive dysfunction (ED) theories. The ED theory has difficulty explaining the existence of talent in ASC. While both hyper-systemizing and WCC theories postulate *excellent attention to detail*, by itself excellent attention to detail will not produce talent. By contrast, the hyper-systemizing theory argues that the excellent attention to detail is directed towards detecting 'if p, then q' rules (or [input-operation-output] reasoning). Such law-based pattern recognition systems can produce talent in systemizable domains. Finally, we argue that the excellent attention to detail in ASC is itself a consequence of *sensory hypersensitivity*. We conclude that the origins of the association between autism and talent begin at the sensory level, include excellent attention to detail and end with hyper-systemizing.

Keywords: autism; Asperger syndrome; savant

4.1 Introduction

Savantism is found more commonly in autism spectrum conditions (ASC) than in any other neurological group (see Howlin 2009), and the majority of those with savantism have an ASC (Hermelin 2002). This 'comorbidity' (or to use the more neutral term 'coocurrency', since comorbidity is a strange term to use when one of the characteristics is not a disability) shows us that these two profiles are associated well above chance. This forces us to ask: why the link between talent and autism?

In this paper, we argue that while savantism (defined as prodigious talent) is only seen in a subgroup of people with ASC, a universal feature of the autistic brain is *excellent attention to detail* (Shah & Frith 1993; Jolliffe & Baron-Cohen 1997; O'Riordan et al. 2001). Furthermore, we argue that excellent attention to detail exists in ASC because of evolutionary forces positively selecting brains for *strong systemizing*, a highly adaptive human ability (Baron-Cohen 2008).

Strong systemizing requires excellent attention to detail, and in our view the latter is in the service of the former. Attention occurs at an early level of cognition, while systemizing is a fairly high-level aspect of cognition. Next, we argue that one can trace excellent attention to detail to its basis in *sensory hypersensitivity* in ASC. Finally, in this paper, we review an experiment from our laboratory in vision, which points to sensory hypersensitivity in ASC, and briefly describe our research programme exploring this in other modalities (olfaction, hearing and touch). But first, what is systemizing?

4.2 Systemizing

Talent in autism comes in many forms, but a common characteristic is that the individual becomes an expert in *recognizing repeating patterns* in stimuli. We call this systemizing, defined as the drive to analyse or construct systems. These might be any kind of system. What defines a system is that it follows *rules,* and when we systemize we are trying to identify the rules that govern the system, in order to predict how that system will behave (Baron-Cohen 2006). These are some of the major kinds of system:

— *collectible* systems (e.g. distinguishing between types of stones or wood);
— *mechanical* systems (e.g. a video recorder or a window lock);
— *numerical* systems (e.g. a train timetable or a calendar);
— *abstract* systems (e.g. the syntax of a language or musical notation);
— *natural* systems (e.g. the weather patterns or tidal wave patterns);
— *social* systems (e.g. a management hierarchy or a dance routine with a dance partner); and
— *motoric* systems (e.g. throwing a Frisbee or bouncing on a trampoline).

In all these cases, one systemizes by noting regularities (or structure) and rules. The rules tend to be derived by noting if p and q are *associated* in a systematic way. The general formulation of what happens during systemizing is one looks for laws of the form 'if p, then q'. If it is Friday, then we eat fish. If we multiply 3 by itself, then we get 9. If we turn the switch to the down position, then the light comes on. When we think about the kinds of domains in which savants typically excel, it is those domains that are highly systemizable.

Examples might be from numbers (e.g. spotting if a number is a prime number), calendrical calculation (e.g. telling which day of the week a given date will fall), drawing (e.g. analysing space into geometric shapes and the laws of perspective, and perfecting an artistic technique), music (e.g. analysing the sequence of notes in a melody, or the lawful regularities or structure in a piece), memory (e.g. recalling long sequences of digits or lists of information) or even learning foreign languages (e.g. learning vocabulary or the laws of grammar). In each of these domains, there is the opportunity to repeat behaviour in order to check if one gets the very same outcome every time. Multiplying 3 by itself *always* delivers 9, the key change in this specific musical piece *always* occurs in the 13th bar, throwing the ball at this particular angle and with this particular force *always* results in it landing in the hoop.

4.3 Systemizing the Rubik's cube

Let us take a single-case example of savantism: a non-conversational child with autism who can solve the Rubik's Cube 'problem' in 1 min and 7 s. This is a nice example because it illustrates several things. First, that the child's non-verbal ability with the Rubik's Cube is at a much higher level than either his communication or social skills, or indeed what one would expect of his age. Second, it prompts us to ask: what are the processes involved in solving the Rubik's Cube? At a minimum, it involves analysing or memorizing the sequence of moves to produce the correct outcome. It is a series of 'if p, then q' steps. This child with autism appeared to have 'discovered' the layer-by-layer method to solve the $3 \times 3 \times 3$ Rubik's Cube problem, which at best takes a minimum of 22 moves. (Note that he was not as fast as the current 2008 World Champion Erik Akkersdijk who in the Czech Open championship solved the Rubik's Cube in 7.08 s!).

4.4 Systemizing in autism spectrum conditions

What is the evidence for intact or even unusually strong systemizing in ASC? First, such children perform above the level that one would expect on a physics test (Baron-Cohen *et al.* 2001). Children with Asperger's syndrome as young as 8–11 years old scored higher than a comparison group who were older (typical teenagers). Second, using the Systemizing Quotient (SQ), people with high-functioning autism or AS score higher on the SQ compared with general population controls (Baron-Cohen *et al.* 2003). Third, children with classic autism perform better than controls on the picture-sequencing test where the stories can be sequenced using physical-causal concepts (Baron-Cohen *et al.* 1986). They also score above average on a test of how to figure out how a Polaroid camera works, even though they have difficulties figuring out people's thoughts and feelings (Baron-Cohen *et al.* 1985; Perner *et al.* 1989). The Polaroid camera test was used as a mechanical equivalent to the false belief test, since, in the former, all one has to do is infer what will be represented in a photograph given the 'line of sight' between the camera and an object, whereas, in the latter, one has to infer what belief (i.e. mental representation) a person will hold given what they saw and therefore know about.

Strong systemizing is a way of explaining the non-social features of autism: narrow interests; repetitive behaviour; and resistance to change/need for sameness. This is because when one systemizes, it is best to keep everything constant, and to only vary one thing at a time. That way, one can see what might be causing what, and with repetition one can verify that one gets the very same pattern or sequence (if p, then q) every time, rendering the world predictable. One issue is whether hyper-systemizing only applies to the *high*-functioning individuals with ASC. While their obsessions (with computers or maths, for example) could be seen in terms of strong systemizing (Baron-Cohen *et al.* 1999), when we think of a child with Zozu-functioning autism, many of the classic behaviours can be seen as a reflection of their strong systemizing. Some examples are listed in Box 4.1.

4.5 Systemizing and weak central coherence

As with the weak central coherence (WCC) theory (Frith 1989; and discussed in this issue, Happé & Vital 2009), the hyper-systemizing theory is about a different cognitive style (Chapter 3). Similar to that theory, it also posits *excellent attention to detail* (in perception and memory), since when one systemizes one has to pay attention to the tiny details. This is because each tiny detail in a system might have a functional role leading to new information of the form 'if p, then q'. Excellent attention to detail in autism has been repeatedly demonstrated (Shah & Frith 1983, 1993; Jolliffe & Baron-Cohen 2001; O'Riordan *et al.* 2001; Mottron *et al.* 2003).

Box 4.1 Systemizing in classic autism and/or Asperger's syndrome.

Type of systemizing	Classic autism	Asperger's syndrome
sensory systemizing	tapping surfaces or letting sand run through one's fingers	insisting on the same foods each day
motoric systemizing	spinning round and round, or rocking back and forth	learning knitting patterns or a tennis technique
collectible systemizing	collecting leaves or football stickers	making lists and catalogues
numerical systemizing	obsessions with calendars or train timetables	solving maths problems
motion systemizing	watching washing machines spin round and round	analysing exactly when a specific event occurs in a repeating cycle
spatial systemizing	obsessions with routes	developing drawing techniques
environmental systemizing	insisting on toy bricks being lined up in an invariant order	insisting that nothing is moved from its usual position in the room
social systemizing	saying the first half of a phrase or sentence and waiting for the other person to complete it	insisting on playing the same game whenever a child comes to play
natural systemizing	asking over and over again what the weather will be today	learning the Latin names of every plant and their optimal growing conditions
mechanical systemizing	learning to operate the VCR	fixing bicycles or taking apart gadgets and reassembling them
vocal/auditory/verbal systemizing	echoing sounds	collecting words and word meanings
systemizing action sequences	watching the same video over and over again	analysing dance techniques

One difference between these two theories is that the WCC theory sees people with ASC as drawn to detailed information (sometimes called a local processing bias) either for *negative* reasons (an inability to integrate was postulated in the original version of this theory) or because of stronger local processing (in the later version of this theory). By contrast, the hyper-systemizing theory sees this same quality (excellent attention to detail) as being highly purposeful: it exists in order to understand a system. Attention to detail is occurring for *positive* reasons: in the service of achieving an ultimate understanding of a system (however small and specific that system might be).

We can return to the Rubik's Cube problem to see the difference between these two theories more clearly. At one level, the Rubik's Cube is a three-dimensional Block Design Test but where the cubes are all connected. Recall that the Block Design Test is the subtest on Weschler IQ tests on which people with autism perform at their best (Shah & Frith 1993; Happé 1996). The Rubik's Cube contains 21 movable connected cubes (since the five central cubes do not move) with different coloured faces in the $3 \times 3 \times 3$ version. According to the WCC theory, the reason why people with autism show superior performance on the Block Design Test is that their good local processing enables them to 'see' each individual cube even if the design to be copied is not 'pre-segmented' (Shah & Frith 1983). It is clear how good local processing would lead to faster 'analysis' of the whole (design) into constituent parts (the individual cubes), but to solve the Rubik's Cube (or the Block Design problem), more than just good local processing is needed. A strength in 'if p, then q'-type reasoning is also required. On the classic Block Design subtest, one needs to *mentally or manually* rotate the cube to produce the relevant output. That is, one needs to *perform an operation* on the input to produce the relevant output. The same is true (but with more cubes and therefore more complexity) in the Rubik's Cube problem: 'If the red cube with the green side is positioned on the top layer on the right side and I rotate the top layer anticlockwise by 90 degrees, then this will complete the top layer as all one colour'.

In earlier formulations of systemizing, the key cognitive process was held to be in terms of [input-operation-output] processing (Baron-Cohen 2006). In mathematics, if the input = 3, and the operation = cubing, then the output = 27. In the Rubik's Cube notional example above, the input = [the red cube with the green side is positioned on the top layer on the right side], the operation = [rotate the top layer anticlockwise by 90 degrees] and the output = [complete the top layer as all one colour]. Note that WCC makes no mention of the key part of this, that is, *noting the consequences of an operation.* Simply seeing the parts in greater detail would not by itself lead to *understand the operations* (the moves) needed to solve the Rubik's Cube.

Another difference between the WCC theory and the hyper-systemizing theory is that the latter (but not the former) predicts that over time, the person may achieve an excellent understanding of a whole system, given the opportunity to observe and control all the variables (all the 'if p, then q' rules) in that system. WCC would predict that even given all the time in the world, the individual will be forever lost in the detail. The existence of talented mathematicians with AS such as Richard Borcherds is proof that such individuals can *integrate* the details into a true understanding of the system (Baron-Cohen 2003). In the rule 'if *p,* then *q',* the terms 'if and 'then' are how the details become integrated, albeit one small step at a time. The idea at the neurological level that ASC involves an abundance of local short-range connectivity (Belmonte *etal.* 2004) may explain this cognitive style of identifying one specific link between two details.

4.6 Hyper-systemizing: implications for education

Teachers, whether of children with autism or adults with Asperger's syndrome, need to take into account that hyper-systemizing will affect not only how people with ASC learn but also how they should be assessed. IQ test items, essays and exam questions designed for individuals who are 'neurotypical' may lead to the person with ASC scoring zero when their knowledge is actually greater, deeper and more extensive than that of most people. What can appear as a slow processing style may be because of the massively greater quantity of information that is being processed.

A man with Asperger's syndrome reported recently that 'I see all information in terms of links. All information has a link to something and I pay attention to these links. If I am asked a question in an exam I have great difficulty in completing my answer within the allocated 45 min for that essay, because every fact I include has thousands of links to other facts, and I feel my answer would be incorrect if I didn't report all of the linked facts. The examiner thinks he or she has set a nice circumscribed question to answer, but for someone with autism or Asperger's syndrome, no topic is circumscribed. There is ever more detail with ever more links between the details'.

When asked about the concept of apple, for example, he could not give a short summary answer such as 'an apple is a piece of fruit' (i.e. referring to the prototypical level 'apple' as linked to the superordinate level 'fruit') but had to continue by also trying to link it to the 7500 different species of apple (the subordinate-level concepts), listing many of each type and the differences in terms of the history of each species, how they are cultivated, what they taste and look like, etc. When asked about the concept of beetle, he could not just give a summary answer such as 'a beetle is an insect' but had to mention as many of the 350 000 species of beetle that he knew existed.

This cognitive style is understandable in terms of the hyper-systemizing theory because a concept is a system. A concept is a way of using an 'if p, then q' rule to define what to include as members of a category (e.g. if it has scales and gills, then it is a fish). Furthermore, concepts exist within a classification system, which are rules for how categories are related to one another. So, the question 'what is a beetle?' is trivial for a neurotypical individual who simply answers in terms of a crude, imprecise and fuzzy category: 'it is an insect'. It may, however, require a very long, exhaustive answer from someone with ASC: beetles are members of the category of animal (kingdom), arthropods (phylum), insects (class), pterygota (subclass), neoptera (infraclass), endopterygota (super-order), coleoptera (order), and could be in one of four suborders (adephaga, archostemata, mycophaga and polyphaga), each of which has an infraorder, a superfamily and a family. Even the previous sentence would for this man with Asperger's syndrome be a gross violation of the true answer to the question because so much potentially important factual information has been left out. But for the hyper-systemizer, getting these details correct matters, because the concept—and the classification system linking concepts—is *a system for predicting* how this specific entity (this specific beetle) will behave or will differ from all other entities.

4.7 Hyper-systemizing theory versus executive dysfunction theory

The executive dysfunction (ED) theory (Rumsey & Hamberger 1988; Ozonoff *et al.* 1991; Russell 1997) is the other major theory that has attempted to explain the non-social features of ASC, and particularly the repetitive behaviour and narrow interests that characterize ASC. According to this theory, aspects of executive function (action control) involved in flexible switching of attention and planning are impaired, leading to perseveration. The ED theory, similar to the WCC theory, has difficulty in explaining instances of good understanding of a whole system, such as calendrical calculation, since within the well-defined system (calendar) attention can switch very flexibly. The ED theory also predicts perseveration (so-called 'obsessions') but does not explain why in autism and Asperger's syndrome these should centre on systems (Baron-Cohen & Wheelwright 1999). Finally, the ED theory simply re-describes repetitive behaviour as an instance of ED without seeing what might be positive about the behaviour.

So, when the low-functioning person with classic autism has shaken a piece of string thousands of times close to his eyes, while the ED theory sees this as perseveration arising from some neural dysfunction which would normally enable the individual to shift attention, the hyper-systemizing theory sees the same behaviour as a sign that the individual 'understands' the physics (i.e. recognizes the patterns) behind the movement of that piece of string. He may be able to make it move in exactly the same way every time. Or to take another example, when he makes a long, rapid sequence of sounds, he may 'know' exactly that acoustic pattern, and get some pleasure from the confirmation that the sequence is the same every time. Much as a mathematician might feel an ultimate sense of pleasure at the 'golden ratio' $((a+b)/a = a/b)$ and that this always comes out as 1.61803399, so the child—even with low-functioning autism—who produces the same outcome every time with their repetitive behaviour, appears to derive some emotional pleasure at the predictability of the world. This may be what is clinically described as 'stimming' (Wing 1997). Autism was originally described as involving 'resistance to change' and 'need for sameness' (Kanner 1943), and here we see that important clinical observation may be the hallmark of strong systemizing. It will be important for future neuroimaging studies to test if the reward systems in the brain (e.g. the dopaminergic or cannabinoid systems) are active during such repetitive behaviour.

If we return to the Rubik's Cube example, the ED theory would predict that an inability to 'plan' should make solving a Rubik's Cube impossible for a savant with autism. By contrast, as we saw earlier, the hyper-systemizing theory has no difficulty in explaining such talent.

4.8 Sensory hyper-sensitivity

Rather than assuming that the strong systemizing in ASC is ultimately reducible to excellent attention to detail, in this section we pursue the idea that the excellent attention to detail is itself reducible to sensory hypersensitivity. Mottron & Burack (2001) postulated the 'enhanced perceptual functioning' model of ASC, characterized by superior low-level perceptual processing. To what extent is this a feature of basic sensory physiology?

Studies using questionnaires such as the Sensory Profile Questionnaire have revealed sensory abnormalities in over 90 per cent of children with ASC (Leekam *et al.* 2001; Kern *et al.* 2006; Tomchek & Dunn 2007). In *vision,* Bertone *et al.* (2003) found that individuals with ASC are more accurate at detecting the orientation of first-order gratings (simple, luminance-defined) but less accurate at identifying second-order gratings (complex, texture-defined). In the *auditory* modality, superior pitch processing has been found in ASC (Mottron *et al.* 1999; Bonnel *et al.* 2003; Heaton *et al.* 2008). In a case study, Mottron *et al.* (1999) reported exceptional absolute judgement and production of pitch. Bonnel *et al.* (2003) found superior pitch discrimination and processing abilities in individuals with high-functioning autism. O'Riordan & Passetti (2006) also reported superior auditory discrimination ability in children with ASC, and Jarvinen-Pasley *et al.* (2002) showed superior perceptual processing of speech in children with autism. Ashwin *et al.* (2009) reported superior visual acuity in adults with ASC using the Freiburg Visual Acuity and Contrast Test.

In the *tactile* modality, Blakemore *et al.* (2006) showed hypersensitivity to vibrotactile stimulation to a frequency of 200 Hz but not for 30 Hz. In addition, the ASC group rated suprathreshold tactile stimulation as significantly more tickly and intense than did the control group. Tommerdahl *et al.* (2007) reported participants with ASC outperformed controls in tactile acuity after short adaptation to a vibrotactile stimulus period of 0.5 s. (Note that this hypersensitivity is not always observed. On a tactile discrimination task, O'Riordan & Passetti (2006) found no differences in children with autism compared with controls.) Cascio *et al.* (2008) investigated tactile sensation and reported increased sensitivity to vibrations and thermal pain in ASC, while detection to light touch and warmth/cold was similar in both groups.

Only two previous studies have been reported investigating olfaction in ASC, and unlike the research into the other senses which consistently find hypersensitivity, both of these studies reported *deficits* in identifying odours despite intact odour detection (Suzuki et al. 2003; Bennetto et al. 2007). Looking more closely at the two previous studies into olfaction in ASC, both required participants to explicitly identify the odour from a choice of responses, and methodology likely to involve both executive function and memory. For example, the study by Bennetto and colleagues required participants to decide which of four possible responses an odour matched. A simpler task might provide a purer test of low-level olfactory discrimination in ASC.

Results from these experiments demonstrated greater sensory perception in ASC across multiple modalities. In the context of the earlier discussion of hyper-systemizing and excellent attention to detail, we surmise that these sensory differences in functioning may be affecting information processing at an early stage (in terms of both sensation/cognition and development) in ways that could both cause distress but also predispose to unusual talent. These results of hypersensitivity confirm previous findings and mirror anecdotal reports of individuals with ASC (Grandin 1996). For example, Temple Grandin writes that 'overly sensitive skin can be a big problem.Shampooing actually hurt my skin.To be lightly touched appeared to make my nervous system whimper, as if the nerve ends were curling up'. In terms of increased sensitivity to certain types of auditory stimuli (high frequencies), there are anecdotal reports that individuals with autism tend to avoid certain sounds. Grandin states 'I can shut out my hearing and withdraw from most noise, but certain frequencies cannot be shut out... High pitched, shrill noises are the worst'. Mottron et al. (1999) reported the case of a woman with autism who was hypersensitive to frequencies from 1 to 5 kHz at 13 years of age, and to 4 kHz at 18 years.

Enhanced sensitivity may be specific to certain stimuli in all modalities. In vision, Bertone et al. (2003) pointed out the importance of specific stimuli in investigating visual differences in ASC. In touch, Blakemore et al. (2006) reported hypersensitivity for higher frequency (200 Hz) vibrotactile stimulation, but not for lower (30 Hz). Pinpointing the precise stimuli in which enhanced sensitivity occur in ASC will be important for future research. To our knowledge, the highest frequency that has been used to investigate hearing in ASC is 8 kHz (Bonnel et al. 2003). Our ongoing study investigates very high frequencies, up to 18 kHz (Tavassoli et al. submitted). The reported hypersensitivity through frequencies above 16 kHz is especially important since some environmental sounds operate at or above this range of frequencies. Grandin reported 'Some of the sounds that are most disturbing to autistic children are the high-pitched, shrill noises made by electrical drills, blenders, saws, and vacuum cleaners'.

Hypersensitivity could result from a processing difference at various sensory levels including the density or sensitivity of sensory receptors, inhibitory and exhibitory neurotransmitter imbalance or speed of neural processing. Belmonte et al. (2004) suggested *local range neural overconnectivity* in posterior, sensory parts of the cerebral cortex is responsible for the sensory 'magnification' in people with ASC. While our laboratory and others have tested sensory profiles in ASC using functional magnetic resonance imaging (fMRI) (Gomot et al. 2006, 2008), the combination of imaging and genetic approaches to study sensory perception in fMRI may lead towards a more complete picture. We conclude that the search for the association between autism and talent should start with the sensory hypersensitivity, which gives rise to the excellent attention to detail, and which is a prerequisite for hyper-systemizing.

T.T. was supported by the Pinsent Darwin Trust and Autism Speaks UK during the period of this work. E.A., C.A., B.C. and S.B.-C. were supported by the MRC UK. Parts of this paper are reproduced with permission from Ashwin *et al.* (2008) and Baron-Cohen (2008).

References

Ashwin, E., Ashwin, C, Rhydderch, D., Howells, J. & Baron-Cohen, S. 2009 Eagle-eyed visual acuity: an experimental investigation of enhanced perception in autism. *Biol. Psychiatry* **65**, 17–21. (doi:10.1016/j.biopsych.2008.06.012)
Ashwin, C, Ashwin, E., Tavassoli, T., Howells, J., Rhydderch, D. & Baron-Cohen, S. Submitted. Olfactory hypersensitivity in autism spectrum conditions.
Baron-Cohen, S. 2003 *The essential difference: men, women and the extreme male brain*. London, UK: Penguin.
Baron-Cohen, S. 2006 The hyper-systemizing, assortative mating theory of autism. *Prog. Neuropsychopharmacol. Biol. Psychiatry* **30**, 865–872. (doi:10.1016/j.pnpbp. 2006.01.010)
Baron-Cohen, S. 2008 Autism, hypersystemizing, and truth. *Q. J. Exp. Psychol.* **61**, 64–75. (doi:10.1080/17470210701508749)
Baron-Cohen, S. & Wheelwright, S. 1999 'Obsessions' in children with autism or Asperger syndrome. Content analysis in terms of core domains of cognition. *Br. J. Psychiatry* **175**, 484–490. (doi:10.1192/bjp.175.5.484)
Baron-Cohen, S., Leslie, A. M. & Frith, U. 1985 Does the autistic child have a 'theory of mind'? *Cognition* **21**, 37–46. (doi:10.1016/0010-0277(85)90022-8)
Baron-Cohen, S., Leslie, A. M. & Frith, U. 1986 Mechanical, behavioural and intentional understanding of picture stories in autistic children. *Br. J. Dev. Psychol.* **4**, 113–125.
Baron-Cohen, S., Wheelwright, S., Stone, V. & Rutherford, M. 1999 A mathematician, a physicist, and a computer scientist with Asperger syndrome: performance on folk psychology and folk physics test. *Neurocase* **5**, 475–483. (doi:10.1080/13554799908402743)
Baron-Cohen, S., Wheelwright, S., Scahill, V., Lawson, J. & Spong, A. 2001 Are intuitive physics and intuitive psychology independent? *J. Dev. Learn. Disord.* **5**, 47–78.
Baron-Cohen, S., Richler, J., Bisarya, D., Gurunathan, N. & Wheelwright, S. 2003 The systemising quotient: an investigation of adults with Asperger syndrome or high-functioning autism, and normal sex differences. *Phil. Trans. R. Soc. Lond.* B **358**, 361–374. (doi:10.1098/rstb. 2002.1206)
Belmonte, M. K., Allen, G., Beckel-Mitchener, A., Boulanger, L. M., Carper, R. A. & Webb, S. J. 2004 Autism and abnormal development of brain connectivity. *J. Neurosci.* **24**, 9228–9231. (doi:10.1523/jneurosci.3340-04.2004)
Bennetto, L., Kuschner, E. S. & Hyman, S. L. 2007 Olfaction and taste processing in autism. *Biol. Psychiatry* **62**, 1015–1021. (doi:10.1016/j.biopsych.2007.04.019)
Bertone, A., Mottron, L., Jelenic, P. & Faubert, J. 2003 Motion perception in autism: a 'complex' issue. *J. Cogn. Neurosci.* **15**, 218–225. (doi:10.1162/089892903321208150)
Blakemore, S. J., Tavassoli, T, Calo, S., Thomas, R. M., Catmur, C, Frith, U. & Haggard, P. 2006 Tactile sensitivity in Asperger syndrome. *Brain Cogn.* **61**, 5–13. (doi:10.1016/j.bandc.2005.12.013)
Bonnel, A., Mottron, L., Peretz, I., Trudel, M., Gallun, E. & Bonnel, A.-M. 2003 Enhanced pitch sensitivity in individuals with autism: a signal detection analysis. *J. Cogn. Neurosci.* **15**, 226–235. (doi:10.1162/0898929 03321208169)
Cascio, C.j McGlone, F., Folger, S., Tannan, V., Baranek, G., Pelphrey, K. A. & Essick, G. 2008 Tactile perception in adults with autism: a multidimensional psychophysical study. *J. Autism Dev. Disord.* **38**, 127–137. (doi:10.1007/ S10803-007-0370-8)
Frith, U. 1989 *Autism: explaining the enigma*. Oxford, UK: Basil Blackwell.
Gomot, M., Bernard, F. A., Davis, M. H., Belmonte, M. K., Ashwin, C, Bullmore, E. T. & Baron-Cohen, S. 2006 Change detection in children with autism: an auditory event-related fMRI study. *Neuroimage* **29**, 475–495. (doi:10.1016/j.neuroimage.2005.07.027)

Gomot, M.j Belmonte, M. K., Bullmore, E. T, Bernard, F. A. & Baron-Cohen, S. 2008 Brain hyper-reactivity to auditory novel targets in children with high-functioning autism. *Brain* **131**, 2479–2488. (doi:10.1093/brain/awn172)

Grandin, T. 1996 My experiences with visual thinking, sensory problems and communication difficulties. The Center for the Study of Autism. See http://www.autism.org/.

Happé, F. 1996 *Autism*. London, UK: UCL Press.

Happé, F. & Vital, P. 2009 What aspects of autism predispose to talent? *Phil. Trans. R. Soc. B* **364**, 1369–1375. (doi:10.1098/rstb.2008.0332)

Heaton, P., Davis, R. E. & Happé, F. G. 2008 Research note: exceptional absolute pitch perception for spoken words in an able adult with autism. *Neuropsychologia* **46**, 2095–2098. (doi:10.1016/j.neuropsychologia.2008.02.006)

Hermelin, B. 2002 *Bright splinters of the mind: a personal story of research with autistic savants.* London, UK: Jessica Kingsley.

Howlin, P., Goode, S., Hutton, J. & Rutter, M. 2009 Savant skills in autism: psychometric approaches and parental reports. *Phil. Trans. R. Soc. B* **364**, 1359–1367. (doi:10.1098/rstb.2008.0328)

Järvinen-Pasley, A., Wallace, G. L., Ramus, F., Happé, F. & Heaton, P. 2002 Enhanced perceptual processing of speech in autism. *Dev. Sci.* **11**, 109–121. (doi:10.1111/j.1467-7687.2007.00644.x)

Jolliffe, T. & Baron-Cohen, S. 1997 Are people with autism or Asperger's syndrome faster than normal on the Embedded Figures Task? *J. Child Psychol. Psychiatry* **38**, 527–534. (doi:10.1111/j.1469-7610.1997.tb01539.x)

Jolliffe, T. & Baron-Cohen, S. 2001 A test of central coherence theory: can adults with high functioning autism or Asperger syndrome integrate fragments of an object. *Cogn. Neuropsychiatry* **6**, 193–216. (doi:10.1080/13546800042000124)

Kanner, L. 1943 Autistic disturbance of affective contact. *Nerv. Child* **2**, 217–250.

Kern, J. K., Trivedi, M. H., Garver, C. R., Grannemann, B. D., Andrews, A. A., Savla, J. S., Johnson, D. G., Mehta, J. A. & Schroeder, J. L. 2006 The pattern of sensory processing abnormalities in autism. *Autism* **10**, 480–494. (doi:10.1177/1362361306066564)

Leekam, S. R., Neito, C, Libby, S. J., Wing, L. & Gould, J. 2001 Describing the sensory abnormalities of children and adults with autism. *J. Autism Dev. Disord.* **37**, 894–910. (doi:10.1007/s10803-006-0218-7)

Mottron, L. & Burack, J. A. 2001 *Enhanced perceptual functioning in the development of autism.* Mahwah, NJ: Erlbaum.

Mottron, L., Burack, J. A., Stauder, J. E. & Robaey, P. 1999 Perceptual processing among high-functioning persons with autism. *J. Child Psychol. Psychiatry* **40**, 203–211. (doi:10.1111/1469-7610.00433)

Mottron, L., Burack, J. A., Iarocci, G., Belleville, S. & Enns, J. T. 2003 Locally orientated perception with intact global processing among adolescents with high-functioning autism: evidence from multiple paradigms. *J. Child Psychol. Psychiatry* **44**, 904–913. (doi:10.1111/1469-7610.00174)

O'Riordan, M. & Passetti, F. 2006 Discrimination in autism within different sensory modalities. *J. Autism Dev. Disord.* **36**, 665–675. (doi:10.1007/s10803-006-0106-1)

O'Riordan, M., Plaisted, K., Driver, J. & Baron-Cohen, S. 2001 Superior visual search in autism. *J. Exp. Psychol. Hum. Percept. Perform.* **27**, 719–730. (doi:10.1037/0096-1523.27.3.719)

Ozonoff, S., Pennington, B. & Rogers, S. 1991 Executive function deficits in high-functioning autistic children: relationship to theory of mind. *J. Child Psychol. Psychiatry* **32**, 1081–1106. (doi:10.1111/j.1469-7610.1991.tb00351.x)

Perner, J., Frith, U., Leslie, A. M. & Leekam, S. 1989 Exploration of the autistic child's theory of mind: knowledge, belief, and communication. *Child Dev.* **60**, 689–700. (doi:10.2307/1130734)

Rumsey, J. & Hamberger, S. 1988 Neuropsychological findings in high functioning men with infantile autism, residual state. *J. Clin. Exp. Neuropsychol.* **10**, 201–221. (doi:10.1080/01688638808408236)

Russell, J. 1997 How executive disorders can bring about an inadequate theory of mind. In *Autism as an executive disorder* (ed. J. Russell), pp. 256–304. Oxford, UK: Oxford University Press.

Shah, A. & Frith, U. 1983 An islet of ability in autism: a research note. *J. Child Psychol. Psychiatry* **24**, 613–620. (doi:10.1111/j.1469-7610.1983.tb00137.x)

Shah, A. & Frith, U. 1993 Why do autistic individuals show superior performance on the block design test? *J. Child Psychol. Psychiatry* **34**, 1351–1364. (doi:10.1111/j.1469-7610.1993.tb02095.x)

Suzuki, Y., Critchley, H. D., Rowe, A., Howlin, P. & Murphy, D. G. 2003 Impaired olfactory identification in Asperger's syndrome. *J. Neuropsychiatry Clin. Neurosd.* **15**, 105–107. (doi:10.1176/appi.neuropsych.15.1.105)

Tavassoli, T., Ashwin, E., Ashwin, C, Chakrabarti, B. & Baron-Cohen, S. Submitted. Multimodal hypersensitivity in individuals with autism spectrum conditions.

Tomchek, S. D. & Dunn, W 2007 Sensory processing in children with and without autism: a comparative study using the short sensory profile. *Am. J. Occup. Ther.* **61**, 190–200.

Tommerdahl, M., Tannan, V., Cascio, C. J., Baranek, G. T. & Whitsel, B. L. 2007 Vibrotactile adaptation fails to enhance spatial localization in adults with autism. *Brain Res.* **1154**, 116–123. (doi:10.1016/j.brainres.2007.04.032)

Wing, L. 1997 *The autistic spectrum.* Oxford, UK: Pergamon.

5

Enhanced perception in savant syndrome: patterns, structure and creativity

Laurent Mottron, Michelle Dawson and Isabelle Soulières

According to the enhanced perceptual functioning (EPF) model, autistic perception is characterized by: enhanced low-level operations; locally oriented processing as a default setting; greater activation of perceptual areas during a range of visuospatial, language, working memory or reasoning tasks; autonomy towards higher processes; and superior involvement in intelligence. EPF has been useful in accounting for autistic relative peaks of ability in the visual and auditory modalities. However, the role played by atypical perceptual mechanisms in the emergence and character of savant abilities remains underdeveloped. We now propose that enhanced detection of patterns, including similarity within and among patterns, is one of the mechanisms responsible for operations on human codes, a type of material with which savants show particular facility. This mechanism would favour an orientation towards material possessing the highest level of internal structure, through the implicit detection of within- and between-code isomorphisms. A second mechanism, related to but exceeding the existing concept of redintegration, involves completion, or filling-in, of missing information in memorized or perceived units or structures. In the context of autistics' enhanced perception, the nature and extent of these two mechanisms, and their possible contribution to the creativity evident in savant performance, are explored.

Keywords: autism; savant syndrome; perception; creativity; pattern recognition; redintegration

5.1 Enhanced perception: from autism to savant syndrome

Autism is characterized by enhanced perceptual processing (Happè & Frith 2006; Mottron *et al.* 2006a). The superiority of autistics in low-level cognitive operations (e.g. discrimination) is a widely replicated finding in both the visual and auditory modalities (Dakin & Frith 2005; Samson *et al.* 2006). At least at the group level, this advantage can be observed in most operations involving perceptual material. For example, superior discriminative performance co-occurs in the same autistic individuals with enhanced abilities in a variety of target detection tasks involving mnemonic, attentional or visuospatial operations (Caron *et al.* 2006). In the auditory modality, superior pitch discrimination, labelling and memory also co-occur (Bonnel *et al.* 2003; Heaton 2003). Mechanisms involved in these perceptual skill superiorities are not yet fully understood, but a more extensive and atypical involvement of primary and associative perceptual areas during perceptual tasks (Gaffrey *et al.* 2007; Manjaly *et al.* 2007; Milne *et al.* 2009), atypical lateral inhibition in both modalities (Bertone *et al.* 2005; Vandenbroucke *et al.* 2008) and functional autonomy of perceptual operations from top-down processing influences (Caron *et al.* 2006) are complementary and promising physiological explanations.

The collection of empirical findings and associated putative partial mechanisms related to autistic perception has been combined under the label of enhanced perceptual functioning (EPF), a behavioural and physiological model that has recently been updated in the form of a short list of principles (Mottron *et al.* 2006*a*). These principles can be considered variously as descriptive and/or explicative. For example, one principle is that top-down influences on perceptual systems are optional in autism and mandatory in non-autistics. This assertion may act not only as a unifying description for the dominant and extended role of perception in autistic strengths, but also as an explanatory mechanism for the autonomy of perception with respect to various higher level cognitive processes. The wide variety of atypical mechanisms involved in EPF principles suggests that autistic cognitive atypicalities are more accurately described as an entirely different processing system, rather than as a collection of negative cascade effects resulting from one or many major impairments (excesses or deficits) impeding typical processing and development.

The extensive support for EPF in autism is strongly suggestive that perception as a whole should be viewed as an integral part of the mechanisms of savant abilities, in as much as these unexpectedly strong skills are intrinsic manifestations of autistic behaviour, learning and intelligence. However, it is not yet clear to what extent basic perceptual mechanisms are associated with autistic ability peaks and *a fortiori* with savant abilities. Multiple intervening variables (e.g. nature, age and intensity of exposure to relevant material) may intercede between superior low-level processing and superior visual and auditory cognitive abilities, impeding any affirmation that, for example, enhanced visual discrimination directly produces visuospatial ability peaks, or that enhanced auditory discrimination produces superior musical ability in savant or non-savant autistics.

The key role of atypical perception in savant syndrome is not an entirely new story (see Heaton & Wallace 2004, for a review). For example, Treffert (1989) proposed that eidetic memory may be important in savant syndrome, but this view is contradicted by the transformations that savants consistently perform on their material of expertise. While Snyder & Mitchell (1999) elaborated on a privileged access to typical low-level perceptual processes, these authors do not explain why savant syndrome is so prevalent in autism or why particular abilities (e.g. calendar calculation) are disproportionately represented. Neither do they specify the details of the low-level operations responsible for savant performance. The aim of this paper is therefore to further explore the role of these aspects of perception and memory in the materials and cognitive operations commonly encountered in the investigations of savant syndrome.

5.2 Savant abilities entail structured material

Materials involved in savant syndrome consist mainly of human codes (e.g. written language for hyperlexia and list memorizers, music for savant performers and composers, numeration for savant mathematical and calendar calculators, and complex three-dimensional graphic representations for savant artists). Human codes share the property of being structured and predominantly non-arbitrary. Emphasizing the role of pattern recognition is therefore in strong contrast with the idea that unstructured, eidetic-type, memory is a major mechanism underlying savant ability. A structured sequence (as opposed to noise) can be phenomenally defined by the recurrence of a finite list of elementary constituents (letters or ideograms, phonemes, digits, notes and geons). These constituents are spatio-temporally stable, in the sense that the shape of a letter, for example, remains roughly equivalent across its various occurrences. The constituents are also relatively simple forms, generally presented in homogeneous series (letters with letters or digits with digits).

The units composing most human codes are embedded in a hierarchy of recurrent patterns of increasing scale. In the case of written language, a finite series of letters forms a larger number of words, and these words are arranged in phrases and sentences with syntactic regularities. Each level contains elements that are intrinsically more similar within that level than they are across levels. Resemblance within letters defines the alphabet, resemblance among words defines lexicon and redundancy in the arrangement of words defines syntax. A similar structural regularity characterizes music (Jackendoff 1987), and could be used to encode the complexities of the three-dimensional perceptual world (Biederman 1987). Phenomenal resemblance or isomorphism is therefore at the centre of what describes a code, and the structured material composing human codes can be described as embedded organizations of isomorphisms, each class of isomorphism defining a particular level (e.g. phonological, lexical). We contend that the phenomenal redundancy of human perceptual and cognitive codes, in as much as they are processed by autistic perceptual mechanisms, grounds the key role these codes play in autistic strong interests and savant abilities.

5.3 Pattern detection in savant cognition

Structure being defined by the presence of repeating basic patterns, one possibility would be that pattern detection mechanisms are especially active in autism. This would explain the unique relationship between what phenomenally defines a structure, and perceptual mechanisms in autism. By especially active, we mean essential in achieving a high level of performance, guiding behaviour, detecting smaller or larger scale units, and being more independent from the influence of non-perceptual cognitive processes. Following this hypothesis, the detection of perceptual similarity between spatio-temporal recurrences of a pattern, whatever its scale, could result in the creation of a lexicon of units—and provide the perceptual root of savant ability. More generally, the detection of regions of the world possessing a high density of similarity among perceptual patterns would orient savants towards their principal materials of interest, i.e. towards commonly available human codes. For example, letters and digits presented in printed material belong to a finite list of visual patterns sharing overall shape and features, with multiple recurrences in the world, and are associated by largely non-arbitrary rules maximizing their salience as stimuli. In calendar calculation, the target information is commonly presented in the form of matrices where digits and letters occupy consistent places in the structure. Three-dimensional geometrical regularities (e.g. geons) are presented and available as two-dimensional representations structured and ruled by linear perspective, while pitches may be presented as locations on keyboards.

The same mechanism that detects intrinsic similarity among simultaneously presented units, or between presented and memorized units, could also detect higher scale isomorphisms by analysing the recurrent structures formed by redundant arrangement of these units, as well as their extrinsic similarities, i.e. recurrent figure-ground relationships between these structures and their context of occurrence. An enhanced role for pattern detection would therefore parsimoniously account both for the heightened interest in codes (characterized by their high level of structural redundancy), and for the detection of within-code, large-scale isomorphisms such as arithmetical structure, calendar structure, syntax and three-dimensional perspective rules.

At a still higher scale level, we propose that many savant abilities involve a one-to-one mapping process between two isomorphic series of elements, a veridical mapping between different codes involving the detection of structural similarity between the two series of units (e.g. written code/oral code). Accordingly, a significant proportion of savant ability involves between-code mapping: hyperlexia maps graphic and oral codes; absolute pitch maps pitch labels or keyboard locations and pitches of the chromatic scale; calendar calculation maps days of the week with dates; and prime number detection maps series of numbers with their factor composition. In all cases, the mastering of these mappings is implicit, both in the way they are learned, and in the frequent difficulty or impossibility that savants have in verbalizing the strategies used to produce answers relying on these mappings.

A beneficial consequence of enhanced pattern detection is that it allows stabilizing associations between labels and precise values within continuous dimensions, which non-autistics are poorly able to memorize. In a significant number of savant abilities, the equivalent ability in non-autistics is only poorly or rarely, if at all, represented. This may be because one series of representations cannot be anchored on the other, as in the example of relative rather than absolute pitch. For pitch perception, non-autistics are able to easily discriminate two distinct pitches as well as to maintain an absolute pitch value in short-term memory, but the pitch is generally lost in long-term memory. Similarly, the three-dimensional regularities of the real world are easily manipulated in three-dimensional visual perception but cannot be maintained even in short-term memory and *a fortiori* cannot be accessed through high-level processes. Recently, we have described prodigious abilities in weight estimation (Mottron *et al.* submitted), which are achieved through the stabilization of a veridical mapping mechanism. GT, who estimates the weight of objects below 500 g with a precision within approximately 5 per cent, proceeds by mentally comparing each object to a 35 g reference unit (the weight of a cereal bar).

Pattern recognition cannot be dissociated from grouping processes. Accordingly, pattern detection could be defined as the capacity to detect organization in the phenomenal aspects of the world. This may be done within the perceptual field, by the detection of relative properties of a series of features (e.g. proximity), or between two series of features (e.g. symmetry and similarity). It has been proposed that in autistics, some mechanisms involved in detecting relational feature properties such as grouping are less efficient (Dakin & Frith 2005). However, as demonstrated in Caron *et al.* (2006), grouping process are, at least under some experimental conditions, intact or even superior, but not mandatory in autism. Likewise, locally oriented graphic construction, resulting from the non-mandatory nature of grouping principles, produces a global figure that respects the relative proportions of each of its elements—demonstrating the integrity of these principles, as has been repeatedly demonstrated in autistic graphic arts (Selfe 1983). Similarly, musical performance in savants encompasses both superior local perception (absolute pitch) and the ability to perceive, perform, transpose, improvise on and enhance global aspects of musical structure (Sloboda *et al.* 1985; Hermelin *et al.* 1987, 1989; Miller 1989; Young & Nettlebeck 1995). Finally, autistics' more independent cognitive processes result in regularities within and among patterns being detected, manipulated and generated at the scale of very large structures (e.g. the 28- or 400-year regularity in calendar calculation)—while still retaining their perceptual nature.

5.4 Pattern completion at a different scale

We have proposed elsewhere (Mottron *et al.* 2006a) that the concept of redintegration, as applied to pattern completion tasks, may play an important role in the enhanced cognitive operations characterizing savant syndrome. Redintegration in its current use (Schweickert 1993) consists in completing a cue identical to a part of a larger configuration previously encountered. This completion is multidirectional, such that any part of a configuration can prompt recall of its missing parts. In the case of words, the recalled parts have been encountered as such and the cue and response form a unit in long-term memory. This concept is therefore close to that of pattern completion or of multidirectional cued recall, i.e. the ability to recognize an incomplete figure, a well-documented function of implicit memory (e.g. Toth *et al.* 1994). Its application to autistic production is related to the task support hypothesis first put forward by Bowler *et al.* (1997), in which cues perceptually identical to a part of the remembered material disproportionably aid autistics during recall. Redintegration-related mechanisms could describe savant abilities that are characterized by providing an answer to a closed question (e.g.: what day of the week was…; what is the square root of…; can you sing a C flat…), as well as bidirectional access to some calendar information, which allows the autistic savant DBC to answer with the same facility questions such as 'what are the months beginning by a Friday?' and 'what day of the week was the 30th of April, 1998?' (Mottron *et al.* 2006b). In addition, with some latitude, this account may help explain the ability of savant artists to complete three-dimensional representations starting from any part of a figure, if one considers the state of the drawing at time 1 as a cue for its completion at time 2 (e.g. Mottron & Belleville 1994, fig. 2).

However, a more general concept of pattern or information completion is required in order to encompass the creative scope of savant performance, which clearly exceeds memory and the limitations of redintegration in non-autistics. In addition, autistics' atypical perception would result in pattern or information completion occurring both at a more local level, as well as within structures much larger, than those used to demonstrate the equivalent mechanism in non-autistics. A greater independence among encoded levels of information would also be involved. For example, a non-autistic expert musician with absolute pitch is far more limited than DP, an autistic savant musician, in disembedding and reproducing (that is, completing or filling-in the pattern of) the individual notes in large chords (Pring 2008). Pattern or information completion may also act in combination with typical, conscious cognitive processes. In the case of a response to a question such as 'is this a prime number?', the limited concept of redintegration would be unable to account for factorization of never-encountered numbers or the detection of primes within very large numbers. It is therefore conceivable that the rapid decomposition of the target number into multiple subcomponents can return it to a state of memorized equivalence (e.g. $4 \times 3 = 12$) where pattern completion can occur. A similar mechanism could participate in the production of future dates, as in the case of the autistic calendar calculator Donny (Thioux *et al.* 2006) who exhibited a distance effect for future dates, implying the use of some kind of computational procedure.

5.5 Savant creativity: a different relationship to structure

Savant performance cannot be reduced to uniquely efficient rote memory skills (see Miller 1999, for a review), and encompasses not only the ability for strict recall, requiring pattern completion, but also the ability to produce creative, new material within the constraints of a previously integrated structure, i.e. the process of pattern generation. This creative, flexible, albeit structure-guided, aspect of savant productions has been clearly described (e.g. Pring 2008). It is analogous to what Miller (1999, p. 33) reported on error analyses in musical memory: 'savants were more likely to impose structure in their renditions of musical fragments when it was absent in the original, producing renditions that, if anything, were less 'literal' than those of the comparison participants'. Pattern generation is also intrinsic to the account provided by Waterhouse (1988).

The question of how to produce creative results using perceptual mechanisms, including those considered low-level in non-autistics, is at the very centre of the debate on the relationship between the nature of the human factor referred to as intelligence and the specific cognitive and physiological mechanisms of savant syndrome (maths or memory, O'Connor & Hermelin 1984; rules or regularities, Hermelin & O'Connor 1986; implicit or explicit, O'Connor 1989; rhyme or reason, Nettlebeck 1999). It also echoes the questions raised by recent evidence of major discrepancies in the measurement of autistic intelligence according to the instruments used (Dawson *et al.* 2007).

A combination of multiple pattern completions at various scales could explain how a perceptual mechanism, apparently unable to produce novelty and abstraction in non-autistics, contributes in a unique way to autistic creativity. The atypically independent cognitive processes characteristic of autism allow for the parallel, non-strategic integration of patterns across multiple levels and scales, without information being lost owing to the automatic hierarchies governing information processing and limiting the role of perception in non-autistics.

An interest in internal structure may also explain a specific, and new, interest for domains never before encountered. For example, a savant artist newly presented with the structure of visual tones learned this technique more rapidly and proficiently than typical students (Pring *et al.* 1997). In addition, the initial choice of domain of so-called restricted interest demonstrates the versatility of the autistic brain, in the sense that it represents spontaneous orientation towards, and mastering of, a new domain without external prompts or instruction. How many such domains are chosen would then depend on the free availability of the kinds, amounts and arrangements of information which define the structure of the domain, according to aspects of information that autistics process well. Generalization also occurs under these circumstances, for example, to materials that share with the initial material similar formal properties, i.e. those that allow 'veridical mapping' with the existing ability. In Pring & Hermelin (2002), a savant calendar calculator with absolute pitch displayed initial facility with basic number-letter associations, and was able to quickly learn new associations and provide novel manipulations of these letter-number correspondences.

The apparently 'restricted' aspects of restricted interests are at least partly related to pattern detection, in that there are positive emotions in the presence of material presenting a high level of internal structure, and a seeking out of material related in form and structure to what has already been encountered and memorized. Limitation of generalization may also be explained by the constraints inherent in the role of similarity in pattern detection, which would prevent an extension of isomorphisms to classes of elements that are excessively dissimilar to those composing the initial form. In any case, there is no reason why autistic perceptual experts would be any less firm, diligent or enthusiastic in their specific preferences for materials and domains than their non-autistic expert counterparts. However, it must also be acknowledged that the information autistics require in order to choose and generalize any given interest is likely to be atypical in many respects (in that this may not be the information that non-autistics would require), and may not be freely or at all available. In addition, the atypical ways in which autistics and savants learn well have attracted little interest and are as yet poorly studied and understood, such that we remain ignorant as to the best ways in which to teach these individuals (Dawson *et al.* 2008). Therefore, a failure to provide autistics or savants with the kinds of information and opportunities from which they can learn well must also be considered as explaining apparent limitations in the interests and abilities of savant and non-savant autistics (see also Heaton 2009).

5.6 Structure, emotion and expertise

While reliable information about the earliest development or manifestations of savant abilities in an individual is very sparse, biographies of some savants suggest a sequence starting with uninstructed, sometimes apparently passive, but intent and attentive (e.g. Horwitz *et al.* 1965; Selfe 1977; Sacks 1995) orientation to and study of their materials of interest. In keeping with our proposal about how savants perceive and integrate patterns, materials that spontaneously attract interest may be at any scale or level within a structure, including those that appear unsuitable for the individual's apparent developmental level. For example, Paul, a 4-year-old autistic boy (with a presumed mental age of 17 months), who was found to have outstanding literacy, exceeding that of typical 9-year olds, intently studied newspapers starting before his second birthday (Atkin & Lorch 2006). It should not be surprising that in savants, the consistent or reliable availability of structured or formatted information and materials can influence the extent of the resulting ability. For example, the types of words easily memorized by NM, proper names, in addition to being redundant in Quebec, share a highly similar structural presentation in the context where NM learned them, including phone books, obituaries and grave markers (Mottron *et al.* 1996, 1998). However, a fuller account of why there is the initial attraction to and preference for materials with a high degree of intrinsic organization, and for specific kinds of such structured materials in any particular individual, is necessary.

Positive emotions are reported in connection with the performance of savant abilities (e.g. Selfe 1977; Sloboda *et al.* 1985; Miller 1989). Therefore, it is possible that a chance encounter with structured material gives birth to an autistic special interest, which then serves as the emotional anchor of the codes involved in savant abilities, associated with both positive emotions and a growing behavioural orientation towards similar patterns (Mercier *et al.* 2000). Brain structures involved in the processing of emotional content can be activated during attention to objects of special interest in autistics (Grelotti *et al.* 2005). So-called repetitive play in autism, associated with positive emotions, consists of grouping objects or information encompassing, as in the codes described above, series of similar or equivalent attributes. In addition, in our clinical experience, we observe that repetitive autistic movements are often associated with positive emotions.

One possibility worth further investigation would be that patterns in structured materials, in themselves, may trigger positive emotions in autism and that arbitrary alterations to these patterns may produce negative emotions—a cognitive account of the insistence on sameness with which autistics have been characterized from the outset (Kanner 1943). Individuals who excel in detecting, integrating and completing patterns at multiple levels and scales, as we propose is the case with savants, would have a commensurate sensitivity to anomalies within the full array of perceived similarities and regularities (e.g. O'Connell 1974). In Hermelin & O'Connor (1990), an autistic savant (with apparently very limited language skills) known for his numerical abilities, including factorization, but who had never been asked to identify prime numbers, instantly expressed—without words—his perfect understanding of this concept when first presented with a prime number. The superior ability of autistics to detect anomalies—departures from pattern or similarity— has accordingly been reported (e.g. Plaisted *et al.* 1998; Baron-Cohen 2005).

Overexposure to material highly loaded with internal structure plausibly favours implicit learning and storage of information units based on their perceptual similarity, and more generally, of expertise effects. Savants benefit from expertise effects to the same extent as non-autistic experts (Miller 1999). Among expertise effects is the recognition of units at a more specific level compared with non-experts and the suppression of negative interference effects among members of the same category. Reduced interference has been demonstrated between lists of proper names in a savant memorizer (Mottron *et al.* 1998). Another expertise effect is the 'frequency effect', the relative ease with which memorization and manipulation of units, to which an individual has been massively exposed, can be accomplished (Segui *et al.* 1982). For example, Heavey *et al.* (1999) found that calendar calculators recalled more calendar-related items than controls matched for age, verbal IQ and diagnosis, but exhibited unremarkable short- or long-term recall of more general material unrelated to calendars. These two aspects of expertise would favour the emergence and the stabilization of macrounits (e.g. written code in a specific language, or set of pitches arranged by harmonic rules), which are perceptually the spatio-temporal conjunctions of recognizable patterns related by isomorphisms. Conversely, pattern detection may be unremarkable or even diminished in the case of arbitrarily presented unfamiliar material (Frith 1970).

Identifying savant syndrome as aptitude, material availability and expertise, combined with an autistic brain characterized by EPF, is also informative on the relationship between savant syndrome and peaks of ability in non-savant autistics. Perceptual peaks are largely measured using materials with which the participant has not been trained, whereas savant syndrome encompasses the effects of a life spent pursuing the processing of specific information and materials. We therefore forward the possibility that the range and extent of autistic abilities may be revealed only following access to specific kinds, quantities and arrangements of information. However, we do not expect savant abilities to differ from non-savant autistic peaks of ability in their basic mechanisms. According to this understanding of differences between savant and non-savant autistics, the fact that not all autistics are savants is no more surprising than the fact that not all non-autistics are experts.

5.7 Behavioural and brain imaging support for enhanced perception in savant syndrome

The proposals in this paper lack sufficient empirical support from savant studies, but are consistent with the well-established role of enhanced perception in autistic cognitive abilities. This is evident in a large variety of tasks studied in non-savant autistics, ranging from visuospatial peaks of ability such as the hidden figure task (Manjaly *et al.* 2007) to high-order tasks such as the N-back task (Koshino *et al.* 2005). In the latter study, the authors report that whereas non-autistics exposed to series of letters that can be either linguistically or perceptually processed exhibit activation of left frontal regions, consistent with the occurrence of mandatory linguistic processing, autistics exhibit mainly extrastriate activation, consistent with their optional use of a more perceptual mechanism. The ability to engage perception in this task did not disadvantage the autistics who performed as well as their controls, and were more flexible in rapidly adjusting to different N-back conditions. Nor does the optional ability of autistics to perceive letters as images hamper their ability to comprehend sentences, a task in which a group of autistics performed dramatically faster than typical individuals (Just *et al.* 2004).

Similarly, hyperlexic children display 'acute visual registration mechanisms for written language' (Goldberg & Rothermel 1984, p. 759; see also, Cobrinik 1982), but this superior perceptual ability does not impinge on their skill in reading visually distorted words or pseudowords (Goldberg & Rothermel 1984; Atkin & Lorch 2006); and these children are not impeded, as are typical children, by the notorious complexity and difficult orthography of written English (Seymour *et al.* 2003). An extrastriate pattern of activation has also been observed in a 9-year-old boy with limitations in oral skills in the presence of decoding skills 6 years in advance of his chronological age (he began his interest for printed material at 13 months). He showed greater activity than reading age-matched controls in the right posterior inferior temporal sulcus, an extrastriate region belonging to the right ventral stream known to be important in visual form recognition. This area is activated in early stages of reading acquisition, but its activity disappears with age. Interestingly, these areas were activated in addition to typical left hemisphere phonological decoding systems (Turkeltaub *et al.* 2004), which is indicative of an important role for perception in exceptional reading ability in autistics.

Future research should explore the role of enhanced perception across the development of expertise, as well as in the entire range of exceptional abilities in savants and autistics. Particular consideration should be given to domains in which, given the opportunity, these individuals perform with proficiency, flexibility and creativity.

This work was supported by grant MOP-84243 from the Canadian Institutes for Health Research to L.M. We thank Sylvie Belleville, Fransesca Happé, Pamela Heaton, Richard Schweickert and Thomas Zeffiro for their helpful comments on the earlier versions of this manuscript.

References

Atkin, K. & Lorch, M. P. 2006 Hyperlexia in a 4-year old boy with autistic spectrum disorder. *J. Neurolinguistics* **19**, 253–269. (doi:10.1016/j.jneuroling.2005.11.006)

Baron-Cohen, S. 2005 Enhanced attention to detail and hyper-systemizing in autism. *Curr. Psychol. Cogn.* **23**, 59–64.

Bertone, A., Mottron, L., Jelenic, P. & Faubert, J. 2005 Enhanced and diminished visuospatial information processing in autism depends on stimulus complexity. *Brain* **128**, 2430–2431. (doi:10.1093/brain/awh561)

Biederman, I. 1987 Recognition-by-components: a theory of human image understanding. *Psychol. Rev.* **94**, 115–147. (doi:10.1037/0033-295X.94.2.115)

Bonnel, A., Mottron, L., Peretz, I., Trudel, M., Gallun, E. & Bonnel, A. M. 2003 Enhanced pitch sensitivity in individuals with autism: a signal detection analysis. *J. Cogn. Neurosci.* **15**, 226–235. (doi:10.1162/08989290 3321208169)

Bowler, D. M., Matthews, N. J. & Gardiner, J. M. 1997 Asperger's syndrome and memory: similarity to autism but not amnesia. *Neuropsychologia* **35**, 65–70. (doi:10.1016/S0028-3932(96)00054-l)

Caron, M. J., Mottron, L., Berthiaume, C. & Dawson, M. 2006 Cognitive mechanisms, specificity and neural underpinnings of visuospatial peaks in autism. *Brain* **129**, 1789–1802. (doi:10.1093/brain/awl072)

Cobrinik, L. 1982 The performance of hyperlexic children on an 'incomplete words' task. *Neuropsychologia* **20**, 569–577. (doi:10.1016/0028-3932(82)90030-6)

Dakin, S. & Frith, U. 2005 Vagaries of visual perception in autism. *Neuron* **48**, 497–507. (doi:10.1016/j.neuron.2005.10.018)

Dawson, M., Soulieres, I., Gernsbacher, M. A. & Mottron, L. 2007 The level and nature of autistic intelligence. *Psychol. Sci.* **18**, 657–662. (doi:10.1111/j.1467-9280. 2007.01954.x)

Dawson, M., Mottron, L. & Gernsbacher, M. A. 2008 Learning in autism. In *Learning and memory: a comprehensive reference,* vol. 2 (eds J. Byrne & H. L. Roediger) *Cognitive psychology,* pp. 759–772. Oxford, UK: Elsevier.

Frith, U. 1970 Studies in pattern detection in normal and autistic children. I. Immediate recall of auditory sequences. *J. Abnorm. Psychol.* **76**, 413–420. (doi:10.1037/h0020133)

Gaffrey, M. S., Kleinhans, N. M., Haist, F., Akshoomoff, N., Campbell, A., Courchesne, E. & Milller, R. A. 2007 Atypical participation of visual cortex during word processing in autism: an fMRI study of semantic decision. *Neuropsychologia* **45**, 1672–1684. (doi:10.1016/j.neuropsychologia.2007.01.008)

Goldberg, T. E. & Rothermel Jr, R. D. 1984 Hyperlexic children reading. *Brain* **107**, 759–785. (doi:10.1093/brain/107.3.759)

Grelotti, D. J., Klin, A. J., Gauthier, I., Skudlarski, P., Cohen, D. J., Gore, J. C, Volkmar, F. R. & Schultz, R. T. 2005 fMRI activation of the fusiform gyrus and amygdala to cartoon characters but not to faces in a boy with autism. *Neuropsychologia* **43**, 373–385. (doi:10.1016/j.neuropsychologia.2004.06.015)

Happé, F. G. & Frith, U. 2006 The weak coherence account: detailed-focused cognitive style in autism spectrum disorders. *J. Autism Dev. Disord.* **36**, 5–25. (doi:10.1007/si 0803-005-0039-0)

Heaton, P. 2003 Pitch memory, labelling and disembedding in autism. *J. Child Psychol. Psychiatry* **44**, 543–551. (doi:10.1111/1469-7610.00143)

Heaton, P. 2009 Assessing musical skills in autistic children who are not savants. *Phil. Trans. R. Soc. B* **364**, 1443–1447. (doi:10.1098/rstb.2008.0327)

Heaton, P. & Wallace, G. L. 2004 Annotation: the savant syndrome. *J. Child Psychol. Psychiatry* **45**, 899–911.(doi:10.1111/j.l469-7610.2004.t01-l-00284.x)

Heavey, L., Pring, L. & Hermelin, B. 1999 A date to remember: the nature of memory in savant calendrical calculators. *Psychol. Med.* **29**, 145–160. (doi:10.1017/S0033291798007776)

Hermelin, B. & O'Connor, N. 1986 Idiot savant calendrical calculators: rules and regularities. *Psychol. Med.* **16**, 885–893.

Hermelin, B. & O'Connor, N. 1990 Factors and primes: a specific numerical ability. *Pscychol. Med.* **20**, 163–169.

Hermelin, B., O'Connor, N. & Lee, S. 1987 Musical inventiveness of five idiots-savants. *Psychol. Med.* **17**, 685–694.

Hermelin, B., O'Connor, N., Lee, S. & Treffert, D. 1989 Intelligence and musical improvisation. *Psychol. Med.* **19**, 447–457.

Horwitz, W. A., Kestenbaum, C., Peson, E. & Jarvik, L. 1965 Identical twin—'idiot-savant'—calendar calculators. *Am. J. Psychiatry* **121**, 1075–1079.
Jackendoff, R. S. 1987 *Consciousness and the computational mind.* Cambridge, MA: MIT Press.
Just, M. A., Cherkassy, V. L., Keller, T. A. & Minshew, N. J. 2004 Cortical activation and synchronization during sentence comprehension in high-functioning autism: evidence of underconnectivity. *Brain* **27**, 1811–1821. (doi:10.1093/brain/awhl99)
Kanner, L. 1943 Autistic disturbances of affective contact. *Nerv. Child* **2**, 217–250.
Koshino, H., Carpenter, P. A., Minshew, N. J., Cherkassy, V. L., Keller, T. A. & Just, M. A. 2005 Functional connectivity in an fMRI working memory task in high-functioning autism. *Neuroimage* **24**, 810–821. (doi:10. 1016/j.neuroimage.2004.09.028)
Manjaly, Z. M. et al. 2007 Neurophysiological correlates of relatively enhanced local visual search in autistic adolescents. *Neuroimage* **35**, 283–291. (doi:10.1016/j.neuro-image.2006.11.036)
Mercier, C., Mottron, L. & Belleville, S. 2000 A psychological study on restricted interests in high-functioning persons with pervasive developmental-disorders. *Autism* **4**, 406–25. (doi:10.1177/13 62361300004004006)
Miller, L. K. 1989 *Musical savants: exceptional skill in the mentally retarded.* Hillsdale, NJ: Erlbaum.
Miller, L. K. 1999 The savant syndrome: intellectual impairment and exceptional skill. *Psychol. Bull.* **125**, 31–46. (doi:10.1037/0033-2909.125.1.31)
Milne, E., Scope, A., Pascalis, O., Buckley, D. & Makeig, S. 2009 Independent component analysis reveals atypical electroencephalographic activity during visual perception in individuals with autism. *Biol. Psychiatry* **65**, 22–30. (doi:10.1016/j.biopsych.2008.07.017)
Mottron, L. & Belleville, S. 1994 L'apport de la neuro-psychologie cognitive à l'étude de l' autisme. *J. Psychiatry Neurosci.* **19**, 95–102.
Mottron, L., Belleville, S. & Stip, E. 1996 Proper name hypermnesia in an autistic subject. *Brain Lang.* **53**, 326–350. (doi:10.1006/brln.1996.0052)
Mottron, L., Belleville, S., Stip, E. & Morasse, K. 1998 Atypical memory performance in an autistic savant. *Memory* **6**, 593–607. (doi:10.1080/741943372)
Mottron, L., Dawson, M., Soulieres, I., Hubert, B. & Burack, J. A. 2006a Enhanced perceptual functioning in autism: an update, and eight principles of autistic perception. *J. Autism Dev. Disord.* **36**, 27–43. (doi:10.1007/sl0803-005-0040-7)
Mottron, L., Lemmens, K., Gagnon, L. & Seron, X. 2006b Non-algorithmic access to calendar information in a calendar calculator with autism. *J. Autism Dev. Disord.* **36**, 239–247. (doi:10.1007/s 10803-005-0059-9)
Mottron, L., Hubert, B., Rouleau, N., Gagnon, L., Tremblay, P. & Seron, X. Submitted. First empirical report of superior estimation abilities in two 'savant' children with pervasive developmental disorders. *Cogn. Neuropsychol.*
Nettlebeck, T. 1999 Savant syndrome—rhyme without reason. In *The development of intelligence* (ed. M. Anderson), pp. 247–273. Hove, UK: Psychology Press.
O'Connell, T. S. 1974 The musical life of an autistic boy. *J. Autism Child Schizophr.* **4**, 223–229. (doi:10.1007/ BF02115228)
O'Connor, N. 1989 The performance of the 'idiot savant': implicit or explicit. *Br. J. Disord. Commun.* **24**, 1–20. (doi:10.3109/13682828909011943)
O'Connor, N. & Hermelin, B. 1984 Idiot savant calendrical calculators: maths or memory? *Psycol. Med.* **14**, 801–806.
Plaisted, K., O'Riordan, M. & Baron-Cohen, S. 1998 Enhanced discrimination of novel, highly-similar stimuli by adults with autism during a perceptual learning task. *J. Child Psychol. Psychiatry* **39**, 765–775. (doi:10.1017/ S0021963098002601)
Pring, L. 2008 Memory characteristics in individuals with savant skills. In *Memory in autism: theory and evidence* (eds J. Boucher & D. Bowler), pp. 210–230. Cambridge, UK: Cambridge University Press.
Pring, L. & Hermelin, B. 2002 Numbers and letters: exploring an autistic savant's unpracticed ability. *Neurocase* **8**, 330–337.

Pring, L., Hermelin, B., Buhler, M. & Walker, I. 1997 Native savant talent and acquired skill. *Autism* **1**, 199–214. (doi:10.1177/1362361397012006)

Sacks, O. 1995 *An anthropologist on Mars.* London, UK: Picador.

Samson, F., Mottron, L., Jemel, B., Belin, P. & Ciocca, V. 2006 Can spectro-temporal complexity explain the autistic pattern of performance on auditory tasks? *J. Autism Dev. Disord.* **36**, 65–76. (doi:10.1007/s10803-005-0043-4)

Schweickert, R. 1993 A multinomial processing tree model for degradation and redintegration in immediate recall. *Mem. Cognit.* **21**, 168–175.

Segui, J., Mehler, J., Frauenfelder, U. & Morton, J. 1982 The word frequency effect and lexical access. *Neuropsychologia* **20**, 615–627. (doi:10.1016/0028-3932(82)90061-6)

Selfe, N. 1977 *Nadia: a case of extraordinary drawing ability in an autistic child.* London, UK: Academic Press.

Selfe, N. 1983 *Normal and anomalous representational drawing ability in children.* London, UK: Methuen.

Seymour, P. H., Aro, M. & Erskine, J. M. 2003 Foundation literacy acquisition in European orthographies. *Br. J. Psychol.* **94**, 143–174. (doi:10.1348/000712603321661859)

Sloboda, J., Hermelin, B. & O'Connor, N. 1985 An exceptional musical memory. *Music Percept.* **3**, 155–170.

Snyder, A. W. & Mitchell, D. J. 1999 Is integer arithmetic fundamental to mental processing?: the mind's secret arithmetic. *Proc. R. Soc. B* **266**, 587–592. (doi:10.1098/rspb.1999.0676)

Thioux, M., Stark, D. E., Klaiman, C. & Schultz, R. T. 2006 The day of the week when you were born in 700 ms: calendar computation in an autistic savant. *J. Exp. Psychol. Hum. Percept. Perform.* **32**, 1155–1168. (doi:10.1037/0096-1523.32.5.1155)

Toth, J. P., Reingold, E. M. & Jacogy, L. L. 1994 Toward a redefinition of implicit memory: process dissociations following elaborative processing and self-generation. *J. Exp. Psychol. Learn. Mem. Cogn.* **20**, 290–303. (doi:10.1037/0278-7393.20.2.290)

Treffert, D. 1989 *Extraordinary people: understanding 'idiot savants'.* New York, NY: Harper, Row.

Turkeltaub, P. E., Flowers, D. L., Verbalis, A., Miranda, M., Gareau, L. & Eden, G. F. 2004 The neural basis of hyperlexic reading: an FMRI case study. *Neuron* **41**, 11–25. (doi:10.1016/S0896-6273(03)00803-1)

Vandenbroucke, M. W., Scholte, H. S., van Engeland, H., Lamme, V. A. & Kemner, C. 2008 A neural substrate for atypical low-level visual processing in autism spectrum disorder. *Brain* **131**, 1013–1024. (doi:10.1093/brain/awm321)

Waterhouse, L. 1988 Speculations on the neuroanatomical substrate of special talents. In *The exceptional brain: neuropsychology of talent and special abilities* (eds L. K. Obler & D. Fein), pp. 493–512. New York, NY: Guilford.

Young, R. L. & Nettlebeck, T. 1995 The abilities of a musical savant and his family. *J. Autism Dev. Disord.* **25**, 231–248. (doi:10.1007/BF02179286)

6

Perception and apperception in autism: rejecting the inverse assumption

Kate Plaisted Grant and Greg Davis

> In addition to those with savant skills, many individuals with autism spectrum conditions (ASCs) show superior perceptual and attentional skills relative to the general population. These superior skills and savant abilities raise important theoretical questions, including whether they develop as compensations for other underdeveloped cognitive mechanisms, and whether one skill is inversely related to another weakness via a common underlying neurocognitive mechanism. We discuss studies of perception and visual processing that show that this inverse hypothesis rarely holds true. Instead, they suggest that enhanced performance is not always accompanied by a complementary deficit and that there are undeniable difficulties in some aspects of perception that are not related to compensating strengths. Our discussion emphasizes the qualitative differences in perceptual processing revealed in these studies between individuals with and without ASCs. We argue that this research is important not only in furthering our understanding of the nature of the qualitative differences in perceptual processing in ASCs, but can also be used to highlight to society at large the exceptional skills and talent that individuals with ASCs are able to contribute in domains such as engineering, computing and mathematics that are highly valued in industry.
>
> **Keywords:** enhanced perceptual processing; gestalt; grouping; intelligence

6.1 Theories of superior abilities

The phenomenal talents of some savant individuals with autism spectrum conditions (ASCs) have attracted enormous media attention, because many are in domains highly prized by Western societies, such as art and music, and others go beyond what most neurotypical individuals can achieve, such as calendrical calculation. In whatever domain the skills are displayed, society reacts with astonishment and delight towards performances and exhibitions of these talents. But for those researchers who assess perception and attention in individuals with ASCs in experimental studies, the exceptional performance demonstrated by the participants with ASCs compared with neuro-typical control participants is no less thrilling. For example, some years ago, we reported a series of studies examining visual search in ASCs, in which we asked children to detect targets hidden among distractors as quickly and as accurately as possible (Plaisted *et al.* 1998*a*). Although we reported the graphical representations and statistical analyses that demonstrated the superior rapidity of visual search in children with ASCs compared with neurotypical children, we did not, in the context of those formal experimental papers, report our experience of astonishment and admiration while watching the children with ASCs complete the tasks with such remarkable skilful speed.

Other studies have shown superior abilities compared with neurotypicals in studies of block design and embedded figures (Shah & Frith 1983, 1993), memory for pitch (Heaton *et al.* 1998; Heaton 2003), attentional focus (Townsend & Courchesne 1994), local processing (Plaisted *et al.* 1999; Mottron *et al.* 2003) and discrimination (Plaisted *et al.* 1998*b*).

What psychological processes might underpin these exceptional skills? Could there be a single underlying process that can explain all the savant skills and the exceptional performance seen in some tests in psychological studies? Probably not. Yet, there is a surprising conceptual similarity between a class of theory that has been put forward to explain savant skills in art, music and calculation and those that have been proposed to explain the exceptional performance in perceptual and attentional tasks in experimental studies. Each of these theories, although different in specific detail, propose that these abilities result from low-level processing mechanisms that operate exceptionally well to compensate for deficits in higher level mechanisms. All broadly predict inverse relationships between performance on tasks that primarily marshal lower level processes and complementary tasks that heavily rely on higher level processes.

For example, in a prominent theory of savant skills, Snyder proposes that these exceptional skills result from privileged access to lower level processes responsible for supporting drawing, calculation and so on. This privileged access is a consequence of compromise to other brain areas responsible for conceptual holistic processing. This raises the astonishing possibility that even neurotypicals possess latent savant abilities, but that these are prevented from expression as a consequence of the masking of the lower level processes by the operation of higher order conceptual processes (Snyder *et al.* 2003). There are direct parallels between this theory of savant skills and those theories that have been debated in the literature concerning superior performance on tests of visual perception and attention. For example, the reduced generalization hypothesis proposes that individuals with ASC have a reduced perception of similarity, resulting in enhanced abilities to discriminate, on the one hand, and a reduced ability to categorize, on the other hand (Plaisted 2000, 2001). Similarly, Mottron and colleagues (e.g. Mottron & Burack 2001) have proposed a model of enhanced perceptual functioning, suggesting that the superior skills of individuals with autism arise as a consequence of overdeveloped perceptual functioning. According to the theory, this overdevelopment occurs as a consequence of under-development of higher level cognitive processes (although in a later version of the theory, Mottron *et al.* (2006) emphasize a difference in the *relation* between lower and higher level processing in ASCs, the latter being optional for individuals with ASCs but mandatory for neurotypicals). Perhaps the best known, and certainly the seminal theory in this area of research, is the weak central coherence theory (Frith 1989). In its original form, this proposed that the exceptional part-based processing seen in performance on tasks such as block design and embedded figures results from deficits in integration processes that serve to draw information together as a meaningful whole.

6.2 Experimental studies of perceptual grouping

Experiments designed to 'drill down' to identify the mechanisms suggested by these inverse theories have provided little evidence to support them. Taking the weak central coherence hypothesis as an example, a range of experimental approaches to identifying deficits in integration processes leading to deficits in global-level processing have revealed intact integration instead. For example, several studies have used hierarchical stimuli (e.g. a large global letter constructed from small letters) to tap grouping processes, finding that individuals with ASCs process the global level with the same efficiency as neurotypical individuals (Mottron & Belleville 1993; Ozonoff *et al.* 1994). In the light of such findings, Happé and colleagues (Happé & Frith 2006; Happé & Booth 2008) have argued that the local superiority bias is independent of global processing operations in ASCs.

This is not to say, however, that grouping processes in individuals with ASCs are the same as those in neurotypicals. Instead, individuals with ASCs demonstrate a much more complex and subtle pattern of perceptual and cognitive processing. For example, when given a choice between processing the global or the local level, individuals with autism choose to prioritize the local level (Plaisted *et al.* 1999). Furthermore, in recent studies of gestalt grouping, it has been found that individuals with ASCs show selective grouping abilities and biases in comparison with neurotypicals. For example, Brosnan *et al.* (2004) found that children with ASCs tended not to process gestalt stimuli based on nature relationships (such as grouping white dots and black dots displayed in the same array in two separate groups). They concluded that individuals with ASCs may show selective deficits in grouping by principles such as similarity rather than grouping based on place relationships, such as is required when processing hierarchical stimuli.

However, a recent study using different methodologies complicates the picture of grouping processes in ASCs still further. We have recently suggested that the methodology employed by previous studies does not always allow for performance to be based on the initial perceptual representation and does not therefore adequately tap the nature of the gestalt experienced by individuals with ASCs (Falter 2007). For example, many studies employ tasks that require participants to identify or detect the presence of a stimulus at the global level, or draw the stimulus, all of which introduce a substantial delay between percept and action to exacerbate the distorting influence of cognitive, attentional and motoric factors on perception. The studies do not necessarily therefore provide the most sensitive and accurate reflection of the nature of the initial gestalt representation in individuals with ASCs.

Accordingly, we employed a procedure that has recently been successfully employed in neurotypical adults to measure grouping processes without explicitly asking observers to introspect on these processes (Feldman 2007). This procedure relies on the well-documented tendency of observers to pay attention to shapes that are grouped together, rather than shapes that are not grouped. Typically, when observers are asked to make a judgement concerning two 'features' (in our study, to say whether two oriented lines had the same or different orientations), they do so more rapidly and/or accurately when these features appear on two grouped objects than when they appear on two ungrouped objects (e.g. Duncan 1984). This effect of grouping can therefore be used to assess an observer's grouping processes, even though the observer does not need to report whether they saw grouping in the display, or not.

In our task (Falter *et al.* in preparation), we presented a row of circles, some coloured blue and others red. Adjacent circles could be of the same colour (such that we expected them to be perceptually grouped together owing to the established perceptual principle that neurotypicals 'group by similarity') or different colours (such that they should be less well grouped). We also varied how near dots were to each other (nearer dots should, we expected, be perceptually grouped together as neurotypicals have been shown to 'group by proximity'). Pairs of oriented lines were then presented on adjacent circles in each trial

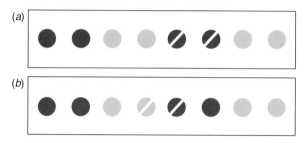

Figure 6.1 Examples of stimuli used in grouping experiments. Note that circles in actual displays were red and blue (indicated by light and dark greys, respectively). The observer's task was to determine as quickly and accurately as possible whether the two bars were of the same or different orientations. Stimuli in (*a*), but not (*b*), are considered grouped by similarity for neurotypical observers.

and the observer's task was simply to determine whether these lines had the same orientation or different orientations. These could either appear on circles we expected to be grouped (figure 6.1*a*) or circles we expected not to be grouped (figure 6.1*b* and accompanying legend). Each array of circles could be horizontally oriented (as illustrated in figure 6.1) or vertically oriented (as was the case for the results provided in figure 6.2).

We compared patterns of performance on these tasks in 46 children with ASCs and 46 neurotypical children. The children were matched for chronological age (mean 12.9 years, range 8–16) and general mental functioning as assessed by the Standard Progressive Raven's Matrices (Raven *et al.* 1998; mean raw score 43). We found that children with ASCs showed robust grouping by proximity (i.e. grouping together circles that were near to each other) at least to the same extent as neurotypicals.

However, the most interesting results arose in displays where circles of the same colour versus different colours were equidistant, such that only similarity, not proximity, was

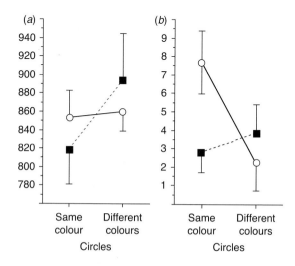

Figure 6.2 (*a*) Reaction time and (*b*) accuracy data for the neurotypical children (filled squares) and children with ASCs (open circles).

available as a cue for grouping. Here, as expected, neurotypical children exhibited more efficient responses in terms of faster reaction times (RTs; figure 6.2a) and the same trend in errors (figure 6.2b) when the two oriented lines appeared on circles of the same colour than when the lines appeared on circles of different colours, showing that these had been perceptually grouped together. However, the ASC children showed no such pattern in RTs (figure 6.2a) and robustly the opposite pattern in terms of their error rates (figure 6.2b), in that they more efficiently (accurately) compared the line segments' orientations when they appeared on circles of different colours than when they appeared on circles of the same colour.

This finding could not be explained by appealing to a possible tendency for ASD individuals to ignore colour information when grouping elements in a scene; such a tendency would have predicted no effect of the circles' colours on their performance. Nor, indeed, was there any bias among the errors made by ASC children that might suggest a role for response competition ('Stroop') effects in this result—they did not, for example, find it particularly difficult to say that the two lines' orientations were different when they appeared on circles of the same colour. Rather, it was clear that the ASC children had processed the circles' colours, and these had affected their grouping of the scene, but in a manner that was qualitatively different from grouping in neurotypicals. Our ASC children appeared to have grouped together circles of different colours rather than of the same colour.

This short review of studies of global-level processing in ASCs thus provides little evidence for the proposal that the enhanced local and part-based processing often observed in individuals with ASCs results from deficits in higher level global processing. Instead, a far more complex profile of perceptual processing emerges that cannot be captured by theoretical models that propose straightforward inverse relationships.

6.3 Difficulties in perception

A general assumption made by the inverse theories is that lower level processing is enhanced in ASCs, and thus responsible for their superior performance on many tasks compared with individuals without ASCs. However, a recent line of research has revealed that at least some perceptual processes are *adversely* affected in ASCs. Several studies have now shown that individuals with ASCs show higher thresholds for the perception of motion coherence (e.g. Spencer *et al.* 2000; Milne *et al.* 2002; Pellicano *et al.* 2005). Two proposals have been advanced for this relative insensitivity to motion coherence. One is that higher levels of the dorsal visual stream, typically responsible for the integration of motion signals, are adversely affected in ASCs. The other is that motion integration difficulties result from deficits in early perceptual processes that drive the dorsal visual stream, in particular the magnocellular pathway. Insofar as inverse theories predict deficits in higher level processes and enhanced processing in lower level systems, then they propose that the difficulties in motion coherence observed in ASCs result from abnormalities in areas higher in the dorsal visual stream, such as area MT/V5.

We are currently assessing this assumption in a series of studies examining visual dorsal stream processing in ASCs. The emerging evidence suggests that, far from there being deficits at higher levels of processing in the dorsal visual stream, the causal deficit originates even before vision information reaches the visual cortex, in low levels of perceptual processing by magnocells in the thalamus.

For example, in one of our first experiments, we presented participants with a task designed to target selectively the information processed by magnocells or parvocells (Greenaway 2005). Effective targeting of one or other of these two types of cell using behavioural psychophysical measures is notoriously difficult, owing to the often rather opaque relationship between individual cell responses and the visual system's overall response, the presence of a third broad class of cell in the LGN ('koniocells') and heterogeneity of response within each class of cell. Indeed, many previous studies of human observers have employed stimuli that should be preferred by individual magnocells, yet as Skottun (2000) has demonstrated, such studies have not effectively measured either magnocellular or parvocellular function.

An elegant procedure that comes closest to targeting magnocellular functions is that developed by Pokorny & Smith (1997). It relies on the presence of robust differences in response to 'luminance contrast' between magnocells and parvocells. Luminance contrast is a measure of the magnitude of differences in light coming from different parts of a stimulus. At low contrast levels (faint stimuli), magnocells respond much more robustly than parvocells, but this response soon reaches a maximum. Parvocells' responses to low contrast stimuli are poor, but continue to increase as the contrast of the stimulus is increased. These two response properties give rise to two patterns of findings. Magnocells are more sensitive than parvocells to single low contrast stimuli, whereas parvocells are more sensitive than parvocells to *differences between* higher contrast stimuli.

Pokorny & Smith's (1997) procedure exploits this pattern of responses. On each trial, a 'pedestal' of four squares is presented. After looking at the pedestal for a while, one of the squares becomes momentarily slightly darker or lighter (figure 6.3b). Because only one aspect of the display has changed, magnocells are very good at detecting even very faint changes in these stimuli (better than parvocells or indeed koniocells), so performance on this condition should be governed by how efficiently a person's magnocells are functioning. Accordingly, for our current purposes, we refer to this type of trial as the 'magnocell condition'.

In a second type of trial, the pedestal of four squares, one of which is slightly lighter or darker than the others, is presented simultaneously on a grey background (figure 6.3a). The observer must detect which of the squares is slightly darker or brighter than the others. Now, because all stimuli are presented at once, the task is effectively to distinguish between different levels of light in the four squares (rather than simply to detect a single light change). Accordingly, parvocells should govern performance under these conditions rather than magnocells.

We compared 17 children with ASCs and 17 neurotypical children, matched for chronological age (mean 12 years, range 9–14) and general mental functioning (mean raw Raven's matrices score 40). Each child's threshold was measured using a two-down, one-up staircase procedure (i.e. two correct responses led to a decrease in luminance increment and one incorrect response led to an increase in luminance increment). The task continued until 10 reversals had been reached, and the threshold was calculated by taking the mean of the last eight reversals.

Independent *t*-tests revealed that while the thresholds of the groups did not differ on the parvocell condition ($t(32) = 1.1, p = 0.281$), they did differ on the magnocell condition ($t(32) = 3.7, p = 0.001$). Thus, in comparison with the typically developing children, the

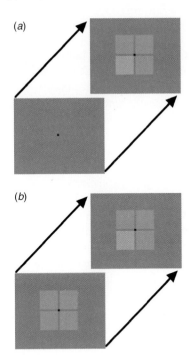

Figure 6.3 Typical display sequences for the study of (*a*) magnocellular and (*b*) parvocellular function.

children with ASCs exhibited clear deficits in the magnocell condition but no deficit or benefit in the parvocell condition. This finding, on the face of it, seems similar to findings of magnocellular dysfunction in other developmental disorders, such as dyslexia (e.g. Cornelissen *et al.* 1995). However, a debate exists as to whether there are such deficits in other developmental disorders, because it is possible that the stimulus parameters chosen in previous studies may not be sensitive enough to adequately target magnocellular processing separately from parvocellular processing. We are currently extending this study examining magnocellular processing in ASCs using flicker stimuli that target magnocellular processing far more precisely than flicker stimuli used in previous studies (e.g. Pellicano & Gibson 2008; see Skottun (2000) and Plaisted & Davis (2005) for discussions of the importance of appropriate stimulus selection in assessments of magnocellular dysfunction in discriminating developmental disorders). Further comparative research, using the kinds of procedure used here, is now urgently required to establish the degree of similarity of perceptual abnormalities between developmental disorders (Braddick *et al.* 2003).

For our current purposes, however, this study demonstrates a perceptual difficulty that has no obvious benefit, and clearly does not compensate for lack of development of any higher order process in a straightforward inverse manner. Thus, although there are clear demonstrations of some superior processes that lead to highly skilled performance, there are other damaged processes that are deleterious to the individual and which require amelioration.

6.4 The need for encouragement, education and training

This short review of studies of perception in individuals with ASCs demonstrates quite clearly that the superior performance seen in ASCs cannot be explained by a model proposing enhanced perceptual processing and defective higher level processing. Instead, the pattern of results is complex: sometimes the perceptual processes are quite different, and cannot be classified as either superior or inferior compared with those used by neurotypicals. In the case of grouping studies, individuals with ASCs parse the visual scene in different ways, resulting in a bias towards grouping by proximity and away from grouping by similarity. In other cases, perception is atypical in ways that do not enhance perceptual performance, and individuals with ASCs perform poorly compared with neurotypicals, as studies in motion processing and magnocellular processing have revealed.

This review has important implications not only for research on the psychological, neurological and genetic bases of ASCs, but also for an understanding of the contribution that individuals with ASCs can make to business and industry. At the present time, savant skills in drawing, painting and music appear to be among those most highly prized by society. Yet, an understanding of the differences in perception in ASCs should lead to an appreciation that these differences result in high-level skills and expertise in areas such as computing, engineering and mathematics. Research such as that described here makes this important point: savant abilities are relatively rare, but the skills observed in individuals with ASCs in many studies are common among the population with ASCs. These skills need as much training and encouragement as is given to any individual with talent in detailed processing, mathematics, engineering, design and so on. With such dedicated training, society, business and industry will reap the great benefits of the unusual minds of individuals with ASCs.

References

Braddick, O., Atkinson, J. & Wattam-Bell, J. 2003 Normal and anomalous development of visual motion processing: motion coherence and 'dorsal-stream vulnerability'. *Neuropsychologia* **41**, 1769–1784. (doi:10.1016/S0028-3932(03)00178-7)

Brosnan, M. J., Scott, F. J., Fox, S. & Pye, J. 2004 Gestalt processing in autism: failure to process perceptual relationships and the implications for contextual understanding. *J. ChildPsychol. Psychiatry* **45**, 459–469. (doi:10.1111/j.1469-7610.2004.00237.x)

Cornelissen, P., Richardson, A., Mason, A., Fowler, S. & Stein, J. 1995 Contrast sensitivity and coherent motion detection measured at photopic luminance levels in dyslexics and controls. *Vision Res.* **35**, 1483–1494. (doi:10.1016/0042-6989(95)98728-R)

Duncan, J. 1984 Selective attention and the organization of visual information. *J. Exp. Psychol. Gen.* **113**, 501–517. (doi:10.1037/0096-3445.113.4.501)

Falter, C. M. 2007 The influence of testosterone on cognition in typical development and autism spectrum disorders. PhD thesis, University of Cambridge, Cambridge, UK.

Falter, C, Plaisted Grant, K. & Davis, G. In preparation. Object-based attention benefits reveal selective abnormalities of visual integration in autism.

Feldman, J. 2007 Formation of visual objects in the early computation of spatial relations. *Percept. Psychophys.* **69**, 816–827.

Frith, U. 1989 *Autism: explaining the enigma,* 2nd edn. 2003 Oxford, UK: Basil Blackwell.

Greenaway, R. 2005 Factors underlying attentional abnormalities in autism. PhD thesis, University of Cambridge, Cambridge, UK.

Happé, F. & Booth, R. 2008 The power of the positive: revisiting weak coherence in autism spectrum disorders. *Q. J. Exp. Psychol.* **61**, 50–63. (doi:10.1080/174702 10701508731)

Happé, F. & Frith, U. 2006 The weak central coherence account: detail focused cognitive style in autism spectrum disorders. *J. Autism Dev. Disord.* **36**, 5–25. (doi:10.1007/si0803-005-0039-0)

Heaton, P. 2003 Pitch memory, labeling and disembedding in autism. *J. Child Psychol. Psychiatry* **42**, 543–551. (doi:10.1111/1469-7610.00143)

Heaton, P., Hermelin, B. & Pring, L. 1998 Autism and pitch processing: a precursor for savant musical ability. *Music Percept.* **15**, 291–305.

Milne, E., Swettenham, J., Hansen, P., Campbell, R., Jeffries, H. & Plaisted, K. 2002 High motion coherence thresholds in children with autism. *J. Child Psychol. Psychiatry Allied Discip.* **43**, 255–263. (doi:10.1111/1469-7610.00018)

Mottron, L. & Belleville, S. 1993 A study of perceptual analysis in a high-level autistic subject with exceptional graphic abilities. *Brain Cogn.* **23**, 279–309. (doi:10.1006/ brcg.1993.1060)

Mottron, L. & Burack, J. 2001 Enhanced perceptual functioning in the development of autism. In *The development of autism: perspectives from theory and research* (eds J. A. Burack, T Charman, N. Yirmiya & P. R. Zelazo), Mahwah, NJ: Lawrence Erlbaum Associates.

Mottron, L., Burack, J. A., Iarocci, G., Belleville, S. & Enns, J. T 2003 Locally oriented perception with intact global processing among adolescents with high-functioning autism: evidence from multiple paradigms. *J. Child Psychol. Psychiatry Allied Discip.* **44**, 904–913. (doi:10.1111/ 1469-7610.00174)

Mottron, L., Dawson, M., Soulieres, I., Hubert, B. & Burack, J. 2006 Enhancedperceptual functioning in autism: an update, and eight principles of autistic perception. *J. Autism Dev. Disord.* **36**, 27–43. (doi:10.1007/s10803-005-0040-7)

Ozonoff, S., Strayer, D. L., McMahon, W. M. & Filloux, F. 1994 Executive function abilities in autism and Tourette syndrome: an information processing approach. *J. Child Psychol. Psychiatry Allied Discip.* **35**, 1015–1032. (doi:10.1111/j.1469-7610.1994.tb01807.x)

Pellicano, E. & Gibson, L. 2008 Investigating the functional integrity of the dorsal visual pathway in autism and dyslexia. *Neuropsychologia* **46**, 2593–2596. (doi:10.1016/j.neuropsychologia. 2008.04.008)

Pellicano, E., Gibson, L., Maybery, M., Durkin, K. & Badcock, D. 2005 Abnormal global processing along the dorsal visual pathway in autism: a possible mechanism for weak visuospatial coherence? *Neuropsychologia* **43**, 1044–1053. (doi:10.1016/j.neuropsychologia.2004.10.003)

Plaisted, K. C. 2000 Aspects of autism that theory of mind cannot easily explain. In *Understanding other minds: perspectives from autism and cognitive neurosdence* (eds S. Baron-Cohen & H. Tager-Flusberg), 2nd edn. Oxford, UK: Oxford University Press.

Plaisted, K. C. 2001 Reduced generalisation in autism: an alternative to weak central coherence. In *Development and Autism: perspectives from theory and research* (eds J. A.Burack, A. Charman, N. Yirmiya & P. R. Zelazo). Mahwah, NJ: Lawrence Erlbaum Associates.

Plaisted, K. C. & Davis, G. 2005 Examining magno-cellular processing in autism. *Curr. Psychol. Cogn.* **23**, 172–180.

Plaisted, K. C., O'Riordan, M. A. F. & Baron-Cohen, S.1998a Enhanced visual search for a conjunctive target in autism: a research note. *J. Child Psychol. Psychiatry* **39**, 777–783. (doi:10.1017/ S0021963098002613)

Plaisted, K. C., O'Riordan, M. A. F. & Baron-Cohen, S. 1998b Enhanced discrimination of novel highly similar stimuli by adults with autism during a perceptual learning task. *J. Child Psychol. Psychiatry* **39**, 765–775. (doi:10.1017/S0021963098002601)

Plaisted, K. C., Swettenham, J. & Rees, L. 1999 Children with autism show local precedence in a divided attention task and global precedence in a selective attention task. *J. Child Psychol. Psychiatry* **40**, 733–742. (doi:10.1111/1469-7610.00489)

Pokorny, J. & Smith, V. 1997 Psychophysical signatures associated with magnocellular and parvocellular pathway contrast gain. *J. Opt. Soc. Am. A* **14**, 2477. (doi:10.1364/JOSAA.14.002477)

Raven, J., Raven, J. C. & Court, J. H. 1998 *Raven manual: section 3. Standard progressive matrices.* Oxford, UK: Oxford Psychologists Press.

Shah, A. & Frith, U. 1983 An islet of ability in autistic children: a research note. *J. Child Psychol. Psychiatry Allied Disdp.* **24**, 613–620. (doi:10.1111/j.1469-7610.1983.tb00137.x)

Shah, A. & Frith, U. 1993 Why do autistic individuals show superior performance on the block design task? *J. Child Psychol. Psychiatry Allied Disdp.* **34**, 1351–1364. (doi:10.Hll/j.1469-7610.1993.tb02095.x)

Skottun, B. 2000 The magnocellular deficit theory of dyslexia: the evidence from contrast sensitivity. *Vision Res.* **40**, 111–127. (doi:10.1016/S0042-6989(99)00170-4)

Snyder, A. W., Mulcahy, E., Taylor, J. L., Mitchell, D. J., Sachdev, P. & Gandevia, S. C. 2003 Savant-like skills exposed in normal people by suppressing the left fronto-temporal lobe. *J. Integr. Neurosd.* **2**, 149–158. (doi:10.1142/S0219635203000287)

Spencer, J., O'Brien, J., Riggs, K., Braddick, O., Atkinson, J. & Wattam-Bell, J. 2000 Motion processing in autism: evidence for a dorsal stream deficiency. *Neuroreport* **11**, 2765–2767. (doi:10.1097/00001756-200008210-00031)

Townsend, J. & Courchesne, E. 1994 Parietal damage and narrow 'spotlight' spatial attention. *J. Cogn. Neurosd.* **6**, 220–232. (doi:10.1162/jocn.1994.6.3.220)

7

Explaining and inducing savant skills: privileged access to lower level, less-processed information

Allan Snyder

I argue that savant skills are latent in us all. My hypothesis is that savants have privileged access to lower level, less-processed information, before it is packaged into holistic concepts and meaningful labels. Owing to a failure in top-down inhibition, they can tap into information that exists in all of our brains, but is normally beyond conscious awareness. This suggests why savant skills might arise spontaneously in otherwise normal people, and why such skills might be artificially induced by low-frequency repetitive transcranial magnetic stimulation. It also suggests why autistic savants are atypically literal with a tendency to concentrate more on the parts than on the whole and why this offers advantages for particular classes of problem solving, such as those that necessitate breaking cognitive mindsets. A strategy of building from the parts to the whole could form the basis for the so-called autistic genius. Unlike the healthy mind, which has inbuilt expectations of the world (internal order), the autistic mind must simplify the world by adopting strict routines (external order).

Keywords: autism; Asperger syndrome; savant skills; exceptional talent; privileged access; transcranial magnetic stimulation

7.1 Introduction

My intention here is to propose an explanation for savant skills and to explore the possibility of artificially inducing such skills in healthy, normal individuals. This gives insights into the architecture of the healthy mind, especially why certain abilities are deliberately inhibited from conscious awareness. I suggest that the savant condition occurs as a failure of this top-down inhibition process. To set the stage, I argue in §7.2 that savant skills are latent in us all.

The savant syndrome is a rare condition in which persons with autistic disorder or other mental disabilities have extraordinary skills that stand in stark contrast to their overall handicap. Savant skills are typically confined to five areas: art, music, calendar calculating, mathematics and mechanical/spatial skills (Treffert 2005). These skills are accompanied by an exceptional ability to recall meaningless detail—memory without understanding (Sacks 2007) and a high incidence of absolute pitch (AP) and synaesthesia.

Snyder & Mitchell (1999) argued that all savant skills, including AP and synaesthesia, reside within everyone, but that they are not normally accessible to conscious awareness. Owing to some atypical brain function, savants have *privileged access* to raw, less-processed information—information in some interim state before it is packaged into holistic labels. This privileged access facilitates a distinct literal cognitive style in which a person thinks in detail, working from the parts to the whole (De Clercq 2003). Savant skills are a form of reproduction. Savants access or read off something that exists in all of our brains, but is normally inaccessible through introspection (Snyder & Mitchell 1999). The precise neuroanatomical mechanism for gaining this privileged access is not yet resolved. It may be associated with an atypical hemispheric imbalance wherein concept networks are bypassed or inhibited.

Accordingly, it was predicted (Snyder, in Carter 1999) and subsequently shown (Snyder *et al.* 2003, 2006; Young *et al.* 2004; Gallate *et al.* 2009) that savant-like skills can sometimes be artificially induced in normal healthy individuals by inhibiting part of the brain—the left anterior temporal lobe (LATL). This is consistent with the notion that autistic savants have some atypical left brain dysfunction or inhibition together with right brain compensation (Miller *et al.* 1998; Treffert 2005; Sacks 2007). In addition, this explanation would appear to fit with contemporary views on hemispheric competition and how disinhibiting the non-dominant hemisphere can artificially offset such competition (Hilgetag *et al.* 2001). It possibly also explains the right-hemispheric bias sometimes associated with autism and other pathologies (§7.4, below). In other words, everyone has the raw information for savant skills, but it requires a form of cortical disinhibition or atypical hemispheric imbalance to be accessed. As I discuss below, there are various factors that could facilitate this disinhibition.

Apart from attempting to demonstrate that savant skills exist in everyone, there is an additional reason for attempting to artificially induce the savant-like state. Savant skills are normally not creative, being largely imitative. Nonetheless, by being atypically literal, with a tendency to concentrate more on the parts than on the whole, a person sees the world in a less-biased light. Such a cognitive strategy offers advantages for particular classes of problem solving, such as those that necessitate breaking cognitive illusions. A strategy of building from the parts to the whole could form the basis for the so-called autistic genius (Snyder 2004), and provide hints for avenues to artificially enhance creativity as has been discussed elsewhere (Snyder *et al.* 2004).

7.2 Savant skills latent in everyone?

We have argued that savants have privileged access to lower level, less-processed information, before it is packaged into holistic concepts and labels—savants tap into or read off information that exists in all of our brains; but this information is normally beyond conscious awareness owing to top-down inhibition (Snyder & Mitchell 1999; Snyder *et al.* 2004).

This is supported by powerful arguments: those who have protracted experience with savants say that their 'gift springs so to speak from the ground, unbidden, apparently untrained and at the age of somewhere between 5 and 8 years of age. There is often no family history of the talent' and it 'is apparently not improved by practice' (O'Connor 1989, p. 4). 'The core ability behind the skill emerges spontaneously and does not improve qualitatively with time even though it might become better articulated' (O'Connor 1989). In addition, the talents are largely imitative.

If these skills are not latent, it would appear highly coincidental that such a peculiar subset of abilities should be so compelling to a significant fraction of savants across all cultures and also that many of these same savants simultaneously have several savant skills (Rimland & Fein 1988), each of which are similarly peculiar and restricted. Furthermore, autistic savant skills are known to recede or be lost altogether with maturity (Selfe 1977; Barnes & Earnshaw 1995; Treffert 2006).

Savants cannot normally give insights into how they perform their skill and are uncontaminated by learnt algorithms. It just comes to them. They just see it. With maturity, the occasionally offered insights are suspect, possibly being contaminated by the acquisition of concepts concerning the particular skill. Yet, I have labelled one savant, Daniel Tammet, a Rosetta stone (Johnson 2005).

By far, the most compelling argument for savant skills residing equally within everyone is that they can emerge 'suddenly and spontaneously' (Miller *et al.* 2000, p. 86) in individuals who had no prior history for them, either in interest, ability or talent (Treffert 2006; Sacks 2007, pp. 157 and 313). Striking examples include skills in art, music (Sacks 2007), mathematics (Treffert 2006, p. 85), calendar calculating (LaFay 1987; Osborne 2003) and possibly AP (Zatorre 1989, see p. 573). The same appears to hold for synaesthesia (Sacks 2007, p. 180), as theory suggested (Snyder & Mitchell 1999), which is reported frequently by autistic savants (Heaton *et al.* 1998; Sacks 2007; Tammet 2007, 2009). Furthermore, these acquired savant skills have been known to diminish with recovery from illness (Sacks 2007, p. 315).

Acquired savants arise from a variety of causes (Treffert 2006) including left frontotemporal dementia (Miller *et al.* 1998), physical injury to the left temporal lobe (LaFay 1987; J. Hirsch & A. Snyder 2005, personal communication), left hemispheric strokes (Sacks 2007, p. 315), severe illness to the central nervous system (Treffert 2006) and even when under the influence of hallucinogens (Humphrey 2002; Sacks 2007, p. 181).

7.3 Inducing savant skills artificially

Taken together, the above facts argue persuasively that savant skills reside within us all and that they can be rapidly switched on and off by natural causes. But, can they be induced temporarily by artificial means?

'Although we do not normally have access to lower levels of information as do savants, is there nonetheless some artificial means to promote this access' (Snyder & Mitchell 1999), say, by inhibiting part of the brain with magnetic pulses to inhibit top-down inhibition? (see Snyder's suggestion in Carter 1999).

There are now several accounts of artificially induced savant-like skills, in drawing, proofreading, numerosity and false memory reduction, all by inhibiting the LATL with repetitive transcranial magnetic stimulation (rTMS; Snyder *et al.* 2003, 2006; Young *et al.* 2004; Gallate *et al.* 2009).

Low-frequency rTMS temporarily inhibits neural activity in a localized area of the cerebral cortex, thereby creating 'virtual lesions' (Hilgetag *et al.* 1999; Walsh & Cowey 2000; Hoffman & Cavus 2002; Steven & Pascual-Leone 2006). As discussed below in §7.4, the LATL is implicated in the savant syndrome for both autistic savants as well as savants who emerge late in life as a result of frontotemporal lobe dementia (Miller *et al.* 1998, 2000; Hou *et al.* 2000).

(a) Induced drawing skills

We cannot draw naturalistic scenes unless we are taught tricks (Gombrich 1960). This is surprising because our brains obviously possess all of the necessary visual information required to draw, but we are apparently unable to consciously access it for the purpose of drawing (Snyder & Thomas 1997; Snyder & Mitchell 1999). Unlike artistic savants

(Selfe 1977; Wiltshire 1987; Miller *et al.* 1998), we tend to be more aware of the meaningful whole than its constituent parts.

Snyder *et al.* (2003) directed low-frequency rTMS for 15 min over the LATL of 11, right-handed, healthy participants. The participants were given 1 min to draw a dog, horse or face from memory, before, during, immediately after and 45 min after rTMS treatment.

Magnetic stimulation caused a major change in the schema of the drawings of 4 out of 11 participants. Two of these also underwent sham (inactive) stimulation either the week before or after the real test. The changes in drawing style were observed *only* following active stimulation and not after sham stimulation. In some cases, the drawings returned to 'normal' 45 min after rTMS ceased. Young *et al.* (2004) also reported rTMS-enhanced drawing skills.

Several participants reported greater awareness of detail in their surrounds after active rTMS. One participant published his experience, stating that he 'could hardly recognize the drawings as his own even though he had watched himself render each image'. (Osborne 2003, p. 38).

(b) Induced proofreading skills

It is easy to miss errors of writing in a familiar passage. Presumably, our propensity to impose meaning inhibits our awareness for the details that comprise the meaning (Bartlett 1932). So, in an attempt to artificially induce autistic-like literalness, Snyder *et al.* (2003) had the above 11 participants undergo a test for proofreading following the same rTMS protocol. Without rTMS, participants almost always missed a duplicated word, such as 'the' in familiar proverbs, even after multiple exposures.

Two participants displayed a noticeable improvement in their ability to recognize duplicated words in text following stimulation. They did comparatively well during and/or immediately after stimulation and comparatively poorly both before and 45 min after. Importantly, these two participants also displayed pronounced style changes in their drawings during and after real stimulation but not after placebo stimulation. None of the participants improved at proofreading with placebo stimulation.

In conclusion, low-frequency rTMS of the left frontotemporal lobe caused major changes in the schema of drawings for 4 out of 11 participants, 2 of whom significantly improved at proofreading.

(c) Induced numerosity

It is not possible to accurately estimate a large number of objects without counting them successively. A small number, three or four, can be accessed (Jevons 1871). Yet, there have been reports over time about the ability of autistic savants to accurately guess large numbers of objects (Scripture 1891; Sacks 1986; Treffert 2006). For instance, Sacks (1986) observed autistic twins who instantly guessed the exact number of match sticks that had just fallen on the floor, saying in unison '111'. Such reports motivated Snyder *et al.* (2006) to induce savant-like numerosity abilities in 12 right-handed participants.

Low-frequency rTMS was applied to the LATL for 15 min (Snyder *et al.* 2006). Participants were presented with between 50 and 150 discrete elements on a monitor with rTMS and sham stimulation. Each session involved 60 trials, that is 20 opportunities to guess the number of elements before, immediately after and 1 hour after rTMS.

Explaining and inducing savant skills 79

Figure 7.1 TMS set-up for the numerosity experiment.

The exposure time was 1.5 s: too short for anyone to count the number of elements, but sufficiently long to resemble exposure times in real-life situations (figure 7.1).

Out of 12 participants, 10 improved their ability to accurately guess the number of discrete elements immediately following magnetic pulse stimulation. Out of these 10 participants, 8 became worse 1 hour later, as the effects of the magnetic pulses receded. None of those eight participants exhibited that pattern during the sham session. The probability of as many as 8 out of 12 people doing the best just after rTMS and not just after the sham by chance alone is less than 1 in 1000 ($p = 0.001$; figure 7.2).

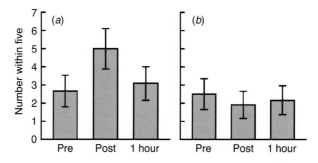

Figure 7.2 Mean ability across all participants to make guesses within the bulls-eye criterion of 5 with (*a*) TMS and (*b*) sham. Shows numerosity performance before (pre), immediately after (post) and 1 hour after rTMS. Error bars represent 95% confidence intervals and 99% of estimates were multiples of five (from Snyder *et al.* 2004).

(i) Why does becoming more literal enhance numerosity?
We argue that the estimation of number by normal people is performed on information after it has been processed into meaningful patterns. The meaning we unconsciously assign to these patterns interferes with our accuracy of estimation, whereas savants, by virtue of being literal, have less interference.

This is consistent with the fact that the accuracy of estimating numbers of elements depends on their arrangement (Ginsburg 1976, 1991; Dehaene 1997)—'perceived numerosity depends more on higher level cognitive factors. than on lower level perceptual or sensory factors'. (Krueger 1984, p. 540).

This insight has an important generalization. The healthy brain makes hypotheses in order to extract meaning from the sensory input, hypotheses derived from prior experience (Gregory 1970, 2004; Snyder & Barlow 1988; Snyder *et al.* 2004). So judgements in general are likely to be performed on this hypothesized content, not on the actual raw sensory input. This suggests the possibility of artificially reducing certain types of false memories and prejudice by making a person more literal, as well as enhancing creativity (Snyder *et al.* 2004).

(d) Reducing false memories

It is well known that our memories are not literal representations of the past. Instead, 'facts' are unconsciously constructed to fit our schemata (Loftus 2003; Schacter & Addis 2007). Yet, certain pathologies, including autism and anterior temporal lobe (ATL) dementia (Beversdorf *et al.* 2000; Simons *et al.* 2005; Hillier *et al.* 2007), can lead to literal recall and thus greater resistance to false memories.

This inspired Gallate *et al.* (2009) to reduce false memories by temporarily inhibiting the LATL in 14 normal participants, using low-frequency magnetic pulse stimulation. The false memory paradigm of Roediger & McDermott (1995) was adopted, with stimulation applied between the study and test phases of the task.

After stimulation, participants had 36 per cent fewer false memories and intact veridical memory, a result that is comparable with the improvement that people with autism and semantic dementia show over normal individuals.

7.4 The role of the left anterior temporal lobe in the savant syndrome

Why did we apply rTMS to the LATL? The savant syndrome is often associated with some form of left brain dysfunction together with right brain compensation, leading to a predilection for literal, non-symbolic skills (Sacks 2007, pp. 314–315; Treffert 2005, 2006). This is consistent with the role of the left hemisphere in hypothesis formation: the left, but not the right, hemisphere tends to search for patterns, and match them to prior experience (Wolford *et al.* 2000). Furthermore, most savants are autistic and autism has sometimes been associated with a right-hemispheric bias (Herbert *et al.* 2005; Koshino *et al.* 2005) and a left hemisphere dysfunction (Wilson *et al.* 2007).

The LATL has been specifically implicated in the savant syndrome, both for an autistic savant as well as for individuals who become savants at the onset of frontotemporal dementia (FTD; Miller *et al.* 1998, 2000; Hou *et al.* 2000). Patients with FTD displayed autistic savant-like artistic skills where none existed, along with other autistic traits such as preoccupation with visual details and a loss of semantic memory. Miller *et al.* (1998) conclude that, 'loss of function in the LATL may lead to "paradoxical functional facilitation" of artistic and musical skills'.

Compelling evidence also exists for the ATL as the critical substrate for semantic representation, encompassing the memory and meaning of all types of verbal and non-verbal stimuli—words, pictures, objects and faces (Pobric *et al.* 2007). The LATL is especially vital for semantic processing, implicated as the region responsible for conceptual knowledge, labels and categories (Miller *et al.* 1998; Mummery *et al.* 2000; Thompson *et al.* 2003; Gainotti 2007; Noppeney *et al.* 2007; Olson *et al.* 2007).

When the LATL is damaged, patients lose their semantic memory and their ability to name or label objects, while retaining the ability to recall object details (Mummery *et al.* 2000; Gainotti 2007). Oliveri *et al.* (2004) found that participants were less accurate in interpreting the meaning of opaque idioms (they became more literal) after rTMS to the left temporal lobe. Finally, the core features of semantic dementia have been induced by inhibiting the LATL with rTMS. Inhibition of LATL in normal participants can temporarily lead to semantic impairment in picture and word comprehension tasks, mimicking symptoms of semantic dementia—'with impairment to the ATL, core semantic representations become degraded and patients are unable to activate all of the information associated with a concept' (Pobric *et al.* 2007, p. 20 139).

7.5 Why rTMS improves a person's savant-like ability?

It is interesting to speculate on how rTMS, or damage to the LATL, could give rise to savant-like skills. One theory is that, in the normal brain, the conceptual networks (concerned with meaning and labels) tend to inhibit networks concerned with detail (Snyder *et al.* 2004). By inhibiting these networks, we may facilitate conscious access to literal details, leading to savant-like skills.

By obscuring the meaning of something, we become more aware of the details that comprise it. It is easier to draw a face if its meaning is suppressed, for example, by turning the face upside down (Edwards 1989). Inhibiting concept networks could disinhibit networks that are receptive to novel detail, as foreshadowed by Kapur (1996), Miller *et al.* (2000) and Hilgetag *et al.* (2001). Both hemispheres contribute to semantic memory, but the right hemisphere appears to have a greater role in novel meanings (Goldberg 2005; Goel *et al.* 2007; Sacks 2007, p. 155; Pobric *et al.* 2008).

The possibility that cortical areas responsible for concepts could inhibit those concerned with detail is consistent with top-down processing (Summerfield *et al.* 2006; Furl *et al.* 2007) and with evidence about hemispheric competition (Kapur 1996; Miller *et al.* 2000; Sacks 2007, p. 155), as is also the possibility of reversing the inhibition by suppressing the dominant cortical area with rTMS (Oliveri *et al.* 1999, 2004; Hilgetag *et al.* 2001; Theoretetal. 2003; Sack *et al.* 2005). In particular, Hilgetag *et al.* (2001) concluded that 'competition between different brain structures might, thus, be a general principle of brain function (Walsh *et al.* 1998) and may explain the paradoxical behavioural enhancement or recovery observed after various brain lesions' (Kapur 1996; Hilgetag *et al.* 1999).

7.6 Discussion

I have argued that the extraordinary skills of savants are latent in us all and that they can be induced artificially owing to the inhibiting influence of low-frequency rTMS, that is, by turning off part of the brain, not by exciting it. My hypothesis is that savant skills are facilitated by privileged access to raw, less-processed sensory information, information that exists in all brains but is inaccessible owing to top-down inhibition. Thus, autistic savants tend to see a more literal, less filtered view of the world. Their 'skill' or performance does not depend on active learning, but simply on an effortless 'reading off' of this less-processed information.

Sensory hypersensitivity and enhanced perception of details (Minshew & Hobson 2008) are a direct consequence of privileged access. AP is another. Although we all have the necessary frequency analysers, AP cannot be learned and yet it is common among savants. The same goes for naturalistic drawing skills, for recall of seemingly meaningless details and for other savant performance (Snyder & Mitchell 1999).

Finally, it should be said that our 'privileged access' hypothesis remains to be proven. The empirical evidence so far, while consistent with the hypothesis, is preliminary and requires independent researchers to replicate the findings. In this regard, there are many factors that could frustrate attempts to artificially induce savant skills with low-frequency rTMS (e.g. see Robertson *et al.* 2003). This could in part explain why savant skills are not induced uniformly in everyone. Furthermore, networks in addition to those of the LATL may be implicated.

Why are savant skills suppressed in normal individuals? And, why is it that all autistic individuals are not savants?

(a) Why are savant skills normally suppressed?

If we all have latent savant skills, why are they not normally accessible? Perhaps they are deliberately inhibited as a principle of economy—object attributes are inhibited from conscious awareness once a label (concept) is formed (Snyder *et al.* 2004). After all, it is the object label or its symbolic identification that is of ultimate importance and not the actual attributes derived by the brain to formulate the label (Snyder & Barlow 1998; Snyder & Mitchell 1999). There is no need to be consciously aware of such details, which explains why we cannot draw natural scenes without being taught the tricks to do so. This strategy accelerates decision-making, especially when confronted with only partial information (Snyder *et al.* 2004). It might also accelerate the process of learning because, without grouping information into meaningful packets, the brain is overwhelmed (Seidenberg *et al.* 2002).

(b) Why are all autistic people not savants?

The majority of savants are autistic. Why not all? Autistic spectrum disorders encompass a hugely diverse population. However, it may well be that autistic savants represent autism in its purest form, uncontaminated by learned algorithms and other disorders that are frequently associated with autism. In other words, autistic savants typify an idealized, pure autism, most closely identified with Kanner's (1943) infantile autism—a mind in a protracted state of infancy (Snyder *et al.* 2004), a preconceptual mind that thinks in detail, rather than through concepts. This oversimplifying caricature goes some way to explain why all autistic people are not savants.

(c) Privileged access: a unifying theory of autism?

The label weak coherence (Happé & Frith 2006) and/or lacking theory of mind (Baron-Cohen *et al.* 1985) aptly captures a collection of autistic traits that were first introduced by Kanner (1943)—the *what* of autism—but they do not provide an explanation for the *why* of autism. I suggest that the state of pure (infantile) autism is a failure in the process of concept formation, and its associated top-down inhibition of attributes that comprise concepts, which may offer a mechanism that could unite the present descriptive theories. We have access to models of the world ('mindsets' or mental templates) that embody the familiar. These allow us to manoeuvre rapidly when confronted with only partial information. Concepts order the world internally. Without them, order must be imposed externally, hence the imposition of rigid routines that characterizes infantile autism.

(d) Autistic genius: a consequence of privileged access?

A fundamental bottleneck to creativity is our inability to join the dots up in novel ways. We have a predisposition to impose prior connections (§7.3c above). But, creativity would seem to require that we, at least momentarily, free ourselves of previous interpretations. Such literalness is a consequence of privileged access and thus gives insights into the so-called autistic genius (Snyder 2004) as well as hints to artificially enhance creativity (Snyder *et al.* 2004).

The classical portrait of autism is that of rigid insistence on sameness, rote memory and significant learning disabilities. Even autistic savants are the antithesis of creative, being largely imitative: 'there are no savant geniuses about... Their mental limitations disallow and preclude an awareness of innovative developments'. (Hermelin 2001, p. 177).

Are there instances when privileged access facilitates the creative process? Asperger (1944/1991) spoke of autistic intelligence as being the intelligence of true creativity, adding that it seems that for success in science or art, a dash of autism is essential. And, according to Fitzgerald (2004), a number of intellectual giants had autistic traits.

The fact that genius might fall within the autistic spectrum challenges our deepest notions of creativity. Are there radically different routes to creativity: normal and autistic? The autistic mind builds from the parts to the whole—a strategy ideally suited to working within a closed system of specified rules. By contrast, the 'healthy' mind appears to make unexpected connections between seemingly disparate systems, inventing entire new systems rather than finding novelty within a previously prescribed space (Snyder 2004).

I thank Sophie Ellwood, Roy Roring and Ben Doolan for their insights.

References

Asperger, H. 1944/1991 Die 'Autistischen Psychopathen' im kindesalter. *Arch. Psychiatr. Nervenkr.* **117**, 76–136. (doi:10.1007/BF01837709) [Translated by U. Frith (ed.)*Autism and Asperger's syndrome*, pp. 37–92. Cambridge, UK: Cambridge University Press].

Barnes, R. C. & Earnshaw, S. M. 1995 Problems with the savant syndrome: a brief case study. *Br. J. Learn. Disabil.* **23**, 124–126.

Baron-Cohen, S., Leslie, A. M. & Frith, U. 1985 Does the autistic child have a 'theory of mind'? *Cognition* **21**, 37–46. (doi:10.1016/0010-0277(85)90022-8)

Bartlett, F. C. 1932 *Remembering: a study in experimental and social psychology.* Cambridge, UK: Cambridge University Press.

Beversdorf, D. Q. et al. 2000 Increased discrimination of 'false memories' in autism spectrum disorder. *Proc. Natl Acad Sci. USA* **97**, 8734–8737. (doi:10.1073/pnas.97.15.8734)

Carter, R. 1999 Turn off tune in. *New Sci.* **164**, 30–34.

De Clercq, H. 2003 *Mum, is that a human being or an animal?* Bristol, UK: Lucky Duck Publishing.

Dehaene, S. 1997 *The number sense: how the mind creates mathematics.* Oxford, UK: Oxford University Press.

Edwards, B. 1989 *Drawing on the right side of the brain.* New York, NY: Tarcher/Putnam Press.

Fitzgerald, M. 2004 *Autism and creativity.* Hove, UK: Brunner-Routledge.

Furl, N.J, van Rijsbergen, N. J., Treves, A., Friston, K. J. & Dolan, R. J. 2007 Experience-dependent coding of facial expression in superior temporal sulcus. *Proc. Natl Acad. Sci. USA* **104**, 13485–13489. (doi:10.1073/pnas.0702548104)

Gainotti, G. 2007 Different patterns of famous people recognition disorders in patients with right and left anterior temporal lesions: a systematic review. *Neuropsychologia* **45**, 1591–1607. (doi:10.1016/j.neuropsychologia. 2006.12.013)

Gallate, J., Chi, R., Ellwood, S. & Snyder, A. 2009 Reducing false memories by magnetic pulse stimulation. *Neurosci. Lett.* **449**, 151–154. (doi:10.1016/j.neulet.2008.11.021)

Ginsburg, N. 1976 Effect of item arrangement on perceived numerosity: randomness vs regularity. *Percept. Mot. Skills* **43**, 663–668.

Ginsburg, N. 1991 Numerosity estimation as a function of stimulus organization. *Perception* **20**, 681–686. (doi:10.1068/p200681)

Goel, V., Tierney, M., Sheesley, L., Bartolo, A., Vartanian, O. & Grafman, J. 2007 Hemispheric specialisation in human prefrontal cortex for resolving certain and uncertain inferences. *Cereb. Cortex* **17**, 2245–2250. (doi:10.1093/cercor/bhll32)

Goldberg, E. 2005 *The wisdom paradox.* New York, NY: Gotham.

Gombrich, E. H. 1960 *Art and illusion.* Oxford, UK: Phaidon Press.

Gregory, R. L. 1970 *The intelligent eye.* London, UK: Weidenfeld.

Gregory, R. L. 2004 Illusions. In *The Oxford companion to the mind* (ed. R. L. Gregory), pp. 426–441. Oxford, UK: Oxford University Press.

Happé, F. & Frith, U. 2006 The weak coherence account: detail-focused cognitive style in autism spectrum disorders. *J. Autism Dev. Disord.* **35**, 5–25. (doi:10.1007/S10803-005-0039-0)

Heaton, P., Hermelin, B. & Pring, L. 1998 Autism and pitch processing: a precursor for savant musical ability. *Music Percept.* **15**, 291–305.

Herbert, M. R. et al. 2005 Brain asymmetries in autism and developmental language disorder: a nested whole-brain analysis. *Brain* **128**, 213–226. (doi:10.1093/brain/awh330)

Hermelin, B. 2001 *Bright splinters of the mind: a personal story of research with autistic savants.* London, UK: Jessica Kingsley.

Hilgetag, C.-C, Kotter, R. & Young, M. P. 1999 Chapter 8 Inter-hemispheric competition of sub-cortical structures is a crucial mechanism in paradoxical lesion effects and spatial neglect. *Prog. Brain Res.* **121**, 121–141. (doi:10.1016/S0079-6123(08)63071-X)

Hilgetag, C. C, Theoret, H. & Pascual-Leone, A. 2001 Enhanced visual spatial attention ipsilateral to rTMS-induced 'virtual lesions' of human parietal cortex. *Nat. Neurosci.* **4**, 953–957. (doi:10.1038/nn0901-953)

Hillier, A., Campbell, H., Keillor, J., Phillips, N. & Beversdorf, D. Q. 2007 Decreased false memory for visually presented shapes and symbols among adults on the autism spectrum. *J. Clin. Exp. Neuropsychol.* **29**, 610–616. (doi:10.1080/13803390600878760)

Hoffman, R. E. & Cavus, L. 2002 Slow transcranial stimulation, long-term depotentiation, and brain hyper-excitability disorders. *Am. J. Psychiatry* **159**, 1093–1102. (doi:10.1176/appi.ajp.159.7.1093)

Hou, C., Miller, B. L., Cummings, J. L., Goldberg, M., Mychack, P., Bottino, V. & Benson, D. F. 2000 Artistic savants. *Neuropsychiatry Neuropsychol. Behav. Neurol.* **13**, 29–38.

Humphrey, N. 2002 Comments on shamanism and cognitive evolution. *Camb. Archaeol. J.* **12**, 91–94.

Jevons, S. W. 1871 The power of numerical discrimination. *Nature* **3**, 281–282. (doi:10.1038/003281a0)

Johnson, R. 2005 *Guardian Weekend* 12 February 2005. See http://www.guardian.co.Uk/theguardian/2005/feb/l2/weekend7.weekend2.

Kanner, L. 1943 Autistic disturbances of affective contact. *Nerv. Child* **2**, 217–250.

Kapur, N. 1996 Paradoxical functional facilitation in brain-behaviour research: a critical review. *Brain* **119**, 1775–1790. (doi:10.1093/brain/119.5.1775)

Koshino, H., Carpenter, P. A., Minshew, N. J., Cherkassky, V. L., Keller, T. A. & Just, M. A. 2005 Functional connectivity in an fMRI memory task in high-functioning autism. *Neuroimage* **24**, 810–821. (doi:10.1016/j.neuro-image.2004.09.028)

Krueger, L. E. 1984 Perceived numerosity: a comparison of magnitude production, magnitude estimation and discrimination judgements. *Percept. Psychophys.* **35**, 536–542.

LaFay, L. 1987 That smarts! Accident leaves man with unforgettable gift. *Virginia Pilot*, 31–33.

Loftus, E. 2003 Our changeable memories: legal and social implications. *Nat. Rev. Neurosci.* **3**, 231–234. (doi:10.1038/nrn1054)

Miller, B. L., Cummings, J., Mishkin, F., Boone, K., Prince, F., Ponton, M. & Cotman, C. 1998 Emergence of artistic talent in fronto-temporal dementia. *Neurology* **51**, 978–982.

Miller, B. L., Boone, K., Cummings, J. L., Read, S. L. & Mishkin, F. 2000 Functional correlates of musical and visual ability in frontotemporal dementia. *Br. J. Psychiatry* **176**, 458–463. (doi:10.1192/bjp.176.5.458)

Minshew, N. J. & Hobson, J. A. 2008 Sensory sensitivities and performance on sensory perceptual tasks in high-functioning individuals with autism. *J. Autism Dev. Disord.* **38**, 1485–1498. (doi:10.1007/s10803-007-0528-4)

Mummery, C. J., Patterson, K., Price, C. J., Ashburner, J., Frackowiak, R. S. J. & Hodges, J. R. 2000 A voxel-based morphometry study of semantic dementia: relationship between temporal lobe atrophy and semantic memory. *Ann. Neurol.* **47**, 36–45. (doi:10.1002/1531-8249(200 001) 47:1 < 36::AID-ANA8 > 3.0.CO;2-L)

Noppeney, U., Patterson, K., Tyler, L. K., Moss, H., Stamatakis, E. A., Bright, P., Mummery, C. & Price, C. 2007 Temporal lobe lesions and semantic impairment: a comparison of herpes simplex virus encephalitis and semantic dementia. *Brain* **130**, 1138–1147. (doi:10.1093/brain/aw1344)

O'Connor, N. O. 1989 The performance of the 'idiot-savant'. Implicit and explicit. *Br. J. Disord. Commun.* **24**, 1–20. (doi:10.3109/13682828909011943)

Oliveri, M., Rossini, P. M., Traversa, R., Cicinelli, P., Palmieri, M. G., Pasqualetti, P., Tomaiuolo, F. & Caltagirone, C. 1999 Left frontal transcranial magnetic stimulation reduces contralesional extinction in patients with unilateral right brain damage. *Brain* **122**, 1731–1739. (doi:10.1093/brain/122.9.1731)

Oliveri, M., Romero, L. & Papagno, C. 2004 Left but not right temporal involvement in opaque idiom comprehension: a repetitive transcranial magnetic stimulation study. *J. Cogn. Neurosd.* **16**, 848–855. (doi:10.1162/089892904970717)

Olson, I., Plotzker, A. & Ezzyat, Y. 2007 The enigmatic temporal pole: a review of findings on social and emotional processing. *Brain* **130**, 1718–1731. (doi:10.1093/brain/awm052)

Osborne, L. 2003 Savant for a day. *New York Times Magazine,* 22 June 2003.

Pobric, G., Jeffries, E. & Lambon-Ralph, M. A. 2007 Anterior temporal lobes mediate semantic representation: mimicking semantic dementia by using rTMS in normal participants. *Proc. Natl Acad. Sci. USA* **104**, 20 137–20 141. (doi:10.1073/pnas.0707383104)

Pobric, G., Mashal, N., Faust, M. & Lavidor, M. 2008 The role of the right cerebral hemisphere in processing novel metaphoric expressions: a transcranial magnetic stimulation study. *J. Cogn. Neurosd.* **20**, 170–181. (doi:10.1162/jocn.2008.20005)

Rimland, B. & Fein, D. 1988 Special talents of autistic savants. In *The exceptional brain: neuropsychology of talent and special abilities* (eds L. Obler & D. Fein), pp. 472–492. New York, NY: Guilford Press.

Robertson, E. M., Theoret, H. & Pascual-Leone, A. 2003 Studies in cognition: the problems solved and created by transcranial magnetic stimulation. *J. Cogn. Neurosd.* **15**, 948–960. (doi:10.1162/089892903770007344)

Roediger, H. L. & McDermott, K. B. 1995 Creating false memories: remembering words not presented in lists. *J. Exp. Psychol. Learn.* **21**, 803–814. (doi:10.1037/0278-7393.21.4.803)

Sack, A. T, Camprodon, J. A., Pascual-Leone, A. & Goebel, R. 2005 The dynamics of interhemispheric compensatory processes in mental imagery. *Science* **308**, 702–704. (doi:10.1126/science.1107784)

Sacks, O. 1986 *The man who mistook his wife for a hat.* London, UK: Picador.

Sacks, O. 2007 *Musicophilia: tales of music and the brain.* New York, NY: Knopf Publishing Group.

Schacter, D. & Addis, D. R. 2007 Constructive memory: the ghosts of past and future. *Nature* **445**, 27. (doi:10.1038/445027a)

Scripture, E. W. 1891 Arithmetical prodigies. *Am. J. Psychol.* **4**, 1–59. (doi:10.2307/1411838)

Seidenberg, M. S., MacDonald, M. C. & Saffran, J. C. 2002 Does grammar start where statistics stop? *Science* **298**, 553–554. (doi:10.1126/science.1078094)

Selfe, L. 1977 *Nadia: a case of extraordinary drawing ability in children.* London, UK: Academic Press.

Simons, J. S., Verfaellie, M., Hodges, J. R., Lee, A. C, Graham, K. S., Koutstaal, W., Schacter, D. L. & Budson, A. E. 2005 Failing to get the gist: reduced false recognition of semantic associates in semantic dementia. *Neuropsychology* **19**, 353–361. (doi:10.1037/0894-4105.19.3.353)

Snyder, A., Bahramali, H., Hawker, T. & Mitchell, D. J. 2006 Savant-like numerosity skills revealed in normal people by magnetic pulses. *Perception* **35**, 837–845. (doi:10.1068/p5539)

Snyder, A. W. 2004 Autistic genius. *Nature* **428**, 470–471. (doi:10.1038/428470a)

Snyder, A. W. & Barlow, H. B. 1988 Revealing the artist's touch. *Nature* **331**, 117–118. (doi:10.1038/331117a0)

Snyder, A. W. & Mitchell, D. J. 1999 Is integer arithmetic fundamental to mental processing? The mind's secret arithmetic. *Proc. R. Soc. Lond. B* **266**, 587–592. (doi:10.1098/rspb.1999.0676)

Snyder, A. W. & Thomas, M. 1997 Autistic artists give clues to cognition. *Perception* **26**, 93–96. (doi:10.1068/p260093)

Snyder, A. W., Mulcahy, E., Taylor, J. L., Mitchell, D. J., Sachdev, P. & Gandevia, S. C. 2003 Savant-like skills exposed in normal people by suppressing the left fronto-temporal lobe. *J. Integr. Neurosd.* **2**, 149–158. (doi:10.1142/S0219635203000287)

Snyder, A. W., Bossomaier, T. & Mitchell, D. J. 2004 Concept formation: 'object' attributes dynamically inhibited from conscious awareness. *J. Integr. Neurosd* **3**, 31–46. (doi:10.1142/S0219635204000361)

Steven, M. S. & Pascual-Leone, A. 2006 Transcranial magnetic stimulation and the human brain: an ethical evaluation. In *Neuroethics: defining the issues in theory, practice and policy* (ed. J. Illes), pp. 123–140. Oxford, UK: Oxford University Press.

Summerfield, C, Egner, T, Greene, M., Koechlin, E., Mangels, J. & Hirsch, J. 2006 Predictive codes for forthcoming perception in the frontal cortex. *Science* **314**, 1311–1314. (doi:10.1126/science.1132028)

Tammet, D. 2007 *Born on a blue day.* London, UK: Hodder & Stoughton Ltd.

Tammet, D. 2009 *Embracing the wide sky.* New York, NY: The Free Press.

Theoret, H., Kobayashi, M., Valero-Cabre, A. & Pascual-Leone, A. 2003 Exploring paradoxical functional facilitation with TMS. *Clin. Neurophysiol.* **56**, 211–219.

Thompson, S., Patterson, K. & Hodges, J. 2003 Left/right asymmetry of atrophy in semantic dementia. *Neurology* **61**, 1195–1203.
Treffert, D. A. 2005 The savant syndrome in autistic disorder. In *Recent developments in autism research* (ed. M. F. Casanova), ch. 2, pp. 27–55. New York, NY: Nova Science Publishers, Inc.
Treffert, D. A. 2006 *Extraordinary people: understanding savant syndrome*. New York, NY: Ballantine Books.
Walsh, V. & Cowey, A. 2000 Transcranial magnetic stimulation and cognitive neuroscience. *Nat. Rev. Neurosd* **1**, 73–79. (doi:10.1038/35036239)
Walsh, V., Ellison, A., Battelli, L. & Cowey, A. 1998 Task-specific impairments and enhancements induced by magnetic stimulation of human visual area V5. *Proc. R. Soc. B* **265**, 537–543. (doi:10.1098/rspb.1998.0328)
Wilson, T., Rojas, D., Reite, M., Teale, P. & Rogers, S. 2007 Children and adolescents with autism exhibit reduced MEG steady-state gamma responses. *Biol. Psychiatry* **62**, 192–197. (doi:10.1016/j.biopsych.2006.07.002)
Wiltshire, S. 1987 *Drawings*. London, UK: J. M. Dent & Sons Ltd.
Wolford, G., Miller, M. B. & Gazzaniga, M. 2000 The left hemisphere's role in hypothesis formation. *J. Neurosd.* **20**, RC64.
Young, R., Ridding, M. & Morrell, T. 2004 Switching skills on by turning off part of the brain. *Neurocase* **10**, 215–222. (doi:10.1080/13554790490495140)
Zatorre, R. J. 1989 Intact absolute pitch ability after left temporal lobectomy. *Cortex* **25**, 567–580.

8

Talent in the taxi: a model system for exploring expertise

Katherine Woollett, Hugo J. Spiers and Eleanor A. Maguire

While there is widespread interest in and admiration of individuals with exceptional talents, surprisingly little is known about the cognitive and neural mechanisms underpinning talent, and indeed how talent relates to expertise. Because many talents are first identified and nurtured in childhood, it can be difficult to determine whether talent is innate, can be acquired through extensive practice or can only be acquired in the presence of the developing brain. We sought to address some of these issues by studying healthy adults who acquired expertise in adulthood. We focused on the domain of memory and used licensed London taxi drivers as a model system. Taxi drivers have to learn the layout of 25 000 streets in London and the locations of thousands of places of interest, and pass stringent examinations in order to obtain an operating licence. Using neuropsychological assessment and structural and functional magnetic resonance imaging, we addressed a range of key questions: in the context of a fully developed brain and an average IQ, can people acquire expertise to an exceptional level; what are the neural signatures, both structural and functional, associated with the use of expertise; does expertise change the brain compared with unskilled control participants; does it confer any cognitive advantages, and similarly, does it come at a cost to other functions? By studying retired taxi drivers, we also consider what happens to their brains and behaviour when experts stop using their skill. Finally, we discuss how the expertise of taxi drivers might relate to the issue of talent and innate abilities. We suggest that exploring talent and expertise in this manner could have implications for education, rehabilitation of patients with cognitive impairments, understanding individual differences and possibly conditions such as autism where exceptional abilities can be a feature.

Keywords: taxi; magnetic resonance imaging; neuropsychology; expertise; hippocampus; plasticity

8.1 Introduction

Talent is highly prized in human culture. 'Gifted' musicians, artists, mathematicians, chess grandmasters, the multi-lingual and those with exceptional memories are lauded for their talent. Despite our passion for seeking out and appreciating talent, we still know relatively little about the basis of talent, and, in particular, there is a paucity of knowledge concerning its neural substrates (Kalbfleisch 2004; Ericsson *et al.* 2006; Grafton 2008). Perhaps this is not surprising, given that even defining talent is not straightforward. According to Kalbfleisch (2004), 'Someone exhibits 'talent' when they perform in a certain capacity above the norm'. But is talent innate or can it be acquired? Is it the same as expertise or being highly skilled? For many people talent implies innateness. However, talents are often first identified and nurtured in childhood and thus development and talent are typically conflated, making it difficult to determine whether talent is innate, can be acquired through extensive practice or can only be acquired in the presence of a 'plastic' developing brain. In order to understand whether exceptional ability is innately determined or can be acquired, we suggest that in the first instance it is necessary to eschew development as an influencing factor and establish whether exceptional ability can develop in healthy adults. In this paper, we review a series of experiments where we investigated this issue. In doing so, we use the more general term expertise rather than talent in order to avoid connotations about the origin of exceptional abilities.

In addition to examining expertise acquired in adulthood, we also focused on individuals with average IQs, thus the need for enhanced intellectual capacity as a prerequisite for expertise was removed. The skill we selected for investigation is widely acknowledged to be impressive and, moreover, with each participant being tested in a similar fashion by an independent body, the acquisition of expertise was verifiable. By acquiring cognitive data, and structural and functional magnetic resonance imaging (MRI) scans on these experts, we could address a number of key questions relating to expertise: in the context of fully developed brains and an average IQ, can people acquire expertise to an exceptional level; what are the neural signatures, both structural and functional, associated with the use of expertise; does expertise change the brain compared with unskilled control participants; does it confer any added cognitive advantages, and, similarly, does expertise come at a cost to other functions; and what happens to their brains and behaviour when experts stop using their skills? Knowing the answers to these questions could be beneficial to those of us wishing to become skilled, for educationalists too, and for those involved in rehabilitation of patients with cognitive impairments. Furthermore, the data relating to expertise in average healthy individuals may aid in the interpretation of skills in clinical populations such as autism, where exceptional abilities are known to feature (Treffert 2009).

8.2 Licensed london taxi drivers

We chose to focus on the domain of memory, as we are all aware of the shortcomings of our own memories, covet exceptional memory and fear the devastating effects of pathologies such as Alzheimer's disease. Exceptional memory, sometimes for unusual material (e.g. bus routes, telephone directories—Pring 2008), is also displayed by some autistic savants. We made use of a unique learning situation in London (UK) and used licensed London taxi drivers as a model for exceptional memory. While the expertise of taxi drivers has been studied in Paris (Pailhous 1970, 1984; Peruch *et al.* 1989), Chicago (Chase 1982) and Helsinki (Kalakoski & Saariluoma 2001), only in London is their expertise truly exceptional and clearly defined. Training to become a taxi driver in London can take place only after the age of 21. Trainees undergo extensive training over a period of 2–4 years known as acquiring 'The Knowledge'. This involves the impressive feat of learning the layout of 25 000 streets in the city (figure 8.1) and thousands of places of interest, leading to a stringent set of examinations by the Public Carriage Office in order to obtain an operating licence. That there are 25 000 licensed London taxi drivers registered currently with the Public Carriage Office suggests that many people are able to acquire this expertise and our sampling of this population confirms an average level of IQ (Maguire *et al.* 2006a; Woollett & Maguire in press).

Talent in the taxi: a model system for exploring expertise 91

Figure 8.1 Central London, UK. Reproduced with the permission of Geographers' A–Z Map Co. Ltd. Crown Copyright 2005. All rights reserved. Licence number 100017302.

Key to the taxi drivers' skill is their ability to navigate. A wide body of evidence indicates that navigation is supported by a brain structure called the hippocampus (O'Keefe & Nadel 1978; Andersen *et al.* 2006; Bird & Burgess 2008). Lesions to the hippocampus impair navigation (Morris *et al.* 1982), and neurons within it exhibit location-specific firing creating a cognitive map of the environment (O'Keefe & Dostrovsky 1971; O'Keefe & Nadel 1978). The volume of the hippocampus in some non-human species can vary as a function of the demands placed on spatial memory, with food-caching species having greater hippocampal volume compared with those who do not cache food (Barnea & Nottebohm 1994; Smulders *et al.* 1995; Volman *et al.* 1997; Lee *et al.* 1998; Biegler *et al.* 2001).

In the first instance, we sought to ascertain whether taxi drivers use their hippocampus during navigation. Consequently, we scanned taxi drivers using functional MRI (fMRI) while they navigated in a highly accurate and interactive virtual reality (VR) simulation of central London (figure 8.2). This was developed as the backdrop for a commercial video game but enabled us to assess *in situ* navigation in a controlled manner. 'The Getaway' (Sony Computer Entertainment Europe) has over 110 km (70 miles) of London's driveable roads, accurately recreated from Ordinance Survey map data, covering 50 square kilometres (20 square miles) of the city centre. The one-way systems, working traffic lights, the busy London traffic and an abundance of Londoners going about their business are all included. Conveniently, one can simply navigate freely (with the usual game scenarios suspended) around the city using the game console, with a normal ground-level first-person perspective, in a car of one's choice. A distributed network of brain areas, including the hippocampus, was active in the brains of taxi drivers while they navigated around

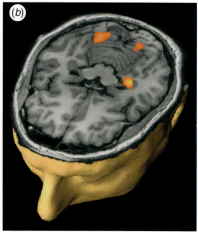

Figure 8.2 Virtual navigation around London, (*a*) An example view at Trafalgar Square from within the video game 'The Getaway' 2002 Sony Computer Entertainment Europe is shown. Image is reproduced with the kind permission of Sony Computer Entertainment Europe, (*b*) Some of the brain areas—including the hippocampus—activated when the taxi drivers navigated around virtual London during fMRI brain scanning are shown (data from Spiers & Maguire 2006).

VR London (Spiers & Maguire 2006, 2007*a,b;* see figure 8.2). The same is true of non-taxi drivers when they imagined navigating between the houses of friends in London (Kumaran & Maguire 2005), and when they navigated around various VR environments (Maguire *et al.* 1998; Hartley *et al.* 2003; Iaria *et al.* 2003). Given that taxi drivers and non-taxi drivers activate the hippocampus during navigation, are there identifiable neural or behavioural correlates of being an expert navigator that differentiate them from non-experts?

8.3 Navigation expertise: positive outcomes

Unsurprisingly, relative to non-experts, taxi drivers have been found to be significantly more knowledgeable about London landmarks and their spatial relationships. This was true even when taxi drivers were compared with another group of navigators, London bus drivers (Maguire *et al.* 2006*a*; Woollett & Maguire 2009; see figure 8.3*a,b*). Bus drivers also spend all day driving among the busy London traffic and dealing with customers, but unlike taxi drivers who navigate widely around the city, bus drivers operate along a constrained set of routes.

While their vastly superior London knowledge distinguished them, an examination of grey matter volume in the brains of taxi drivers revealed further differences. Structural MRI brain scans of taxi drivers and non-taxi driver control participants were analysed using voxel-based morphometry (VBM), a method that permits automatic whole-brain analysis of grey matter volume (Ashburner & Friston 2005; Mechelli *et al.* 2005). Compared with controls, taxi drivers had greater grey matter volume in the posterior hippocampi (Maguire *et al.* 2000). This finding was replicated when taxi drivers were compared with bus drivers (Maguire *et al.* 2006*a*—see figure 8.3*c*; see also Woollett & Maguire 2009). On the basis of these results, we suggested that learning, representing and using

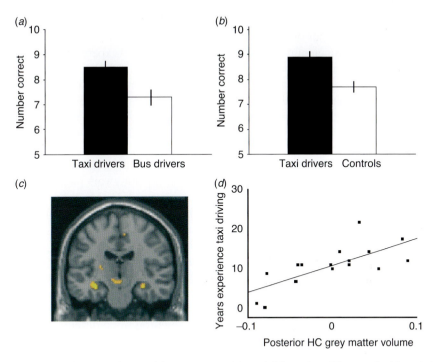

Figure 8.3 Navigation expertise: positive outcomes. (*a*) Taxi drivers (*n* = 18) were significantly better at judging the relative locations of landmarks in London than bus drivers (*n* = 17; mean scores ± 1 s.e., data from Maguire *et al.* 2006*a*). (*b*) This result was replicated in a different cohort of taxi drivers and a control group of non-taxi drivers (*n* = 20 each group; data from Woollett & Maguire 2009). (*c*) Taxi drivers had greater grey matter volume in the posterior hippocampus bilaterally compared with bus drivers (data from Maguire et al. 2006*a*). (*d*) Posterior hippocampal (HC) grey matter volume correlated positively with increasing navigation experience in taxi drivers (data from Maguire *et al.* 2006*a*).

a spatial representation of a highly complex and large-scale environment is a primary function of the posterior hippocampus in humans such that this brain region might adapt structurally to accommodate its elaboration. Evidence that this pattern of grey matter volume was acquired from the experience of learning and using the highly complex mental map of London comes from an additional finding. The number of years of navigation experience correlated with hippocampal grey matter volume only in taxi drivers (and not bus drivers who were matched for number of years navigating in London), with right posterior grey matter volume increasing with more navigation experience (figure 8.3*d*).

While the correlation of time taxing driving and grey matter volume suggests that the brain changes are acquired and not innate, it could still be argued that the difference in hippocampal volume is instead associated with innate navigational expertise, leading to an increased likelihood of becoming a taxi driver. To investigate this possibility, we used VBM to examine a group of non-taxi drivers who navigated in a VR environment (Maguire *et al.* 2003*a*). Despite this group showing a wide range of navigational expertise, there was no association between expertise and posterior hippocampal grey matter volume (or, indeed, grey matter volume throughout the brain). This failure to find an association between hippocampal volume and navigational expertise thus suggests that structural differences in the hippocampus of taxi drivers reflect the detail and/or duration of the use of the spatial representation acquired and not innate navigational expertise *per se.*

Clearly, taxi drivers in London have to learn a vast amount of information. Another question that naturally arises is whether intensive and extensive acquisition of knowledge in domains other than spatial navigation produces the same results (Terrazas & McNaughton 2000). In order to examine this issue, participants were required who were similar to taxi drivers in terms of how their knowledge acquisition occurs, but whose knowledge was less spatial. We focused on medical doctors as an appropriate group to test (Woollett *et al.* 2008). They also acquire their knowledge in adulthood over a number of years of initial intensive medical training. While our previous work has shown that taxi drivers and their control subjects generally have average IQs (Maguire *et al.* 2006*a*; Woollett & Maguire 2009), the medical doctors had above-average IQs. Thus, we compared the medical doctors with control participants matched on IQ, but who had not undergone university education or periods of intense learning. VBM analysis failed to identify any differences in grey matter volume between the groups, including in the hippocampus. Moreover, the amount of medical experience, which ranged from 0.5 to 22.5 years, did not correlate with grey matter volume in the hippocampus or elsewhere in the brain. From this, we conclude that intensively acquiring a large amount of knowledge over many years is not invariably associated with structural brain differences. Instead, it would seem that hippocampal grey matter volume effects are more likely to be observed when the knowledge acquired concerns a complex and detailed large-scale spatial layout.

This is supported by the findings from another group with exceptional memory, namely participants in the World Memory Championships, held in London every year. Their memory skills are wide ranging including the ability to memorize numerous decks of playing cards and long lists of random digits. Exceptional memory in these individuals was not found to be associated with higher IQ or any structural brain differences relative to control participants (Maguire *et al.* 2003*b*). However, fMRI scanning revealed that they activated brain areas associated with navigation, including the hippocampus, more than control participants. The expert memorizers in general used a mnemonic strategy known as the Method of Loci (Yates 1966). With extensive practice, this method is effective at enabling one to remember the order of stimuli by imagining familiar routes and placing the to-be-remembered items along the routes thus promoting deeper encoding of the stimuli with rich associations. Unlike taxi drivers, however, the restricted set of routes they employed was not sufficient to affect structural brain changes. This is concordant with the findings from bus drivers who also learn and use a constrained set of routes and show no structural brain changes (Maguire *et al.* 2006*a*).

Thus, it would seem that intensive learning of a city's spatial layout is possible, and the effective use of mnemonics can facilitate memory for impressive amounts of information. This suggests that becoming an expert in the domain of memory may be attainable by any of us, with a great deal of time and effort as in the case of taxi drivers, and the use of mnemonics as employed by the memory champions. Structural brain changes associated with learning over a time scale of years, however, seem to be restricted to taxi drivers and the acquisition of a large, integrated and complex spatial layout (see Draganski *et al.* (2004, 2006) for effects relating to short time scales). Expertise in other domains has been associated with grey matter volume differences in various parts of the brain relative to control participants, for example in musicians (Munte *et al.* 2002; Sluming *et al.* 2002, 2007; Gaser & Schlaug 2003), mathematicians (Aydin *et al.* 2007) and bilinguals (Mechelli *et al.* 2004). Professional musicians were also found to show enhanced judgements of line orientation and three-dimensional mental rotation ability (Sluming *et al.* 2002, 2007). This was attributed to their musical sight-reading and motor sequencing expertise. However, to our knowledge, there are no reports of adult-acquired expertise in these domains, thus grey matter and neuropsychological differences in these cases may be due to the interaction between practice and brain development.

8.4 Navigation expertise: negative outcomes

Talent and expertise are typically viewed in a positive light. However, we would argue that the potential costs of expertise also warrant consideration. There have been several case reports of individuals whose memories are so good that it actually causes them great distress as they are unable to forget anything (Luria 1987; Parker *et al.* 2006). There can also be devastating effects when one suddenly loses expertise. Using the VR simulation of central London described above, we assessed the navigation ability of a licensed London taxi driver who had sustained bilateral hippocampal damage as a consequence of limbic encephalitis (Maguire *et al.* 2006*b*). In this test, patient TT and matched control taxi drivers drove a virtual London taxi along the streets they had first learned 40 years before. We found that the hippocampus is not required for general orientation in the city, detailed topographical knowledge of landmarks and their spatial relationships, or even for the navigation along some routes, all of which abilities were preserved. However, in his navigation, TT was very reliant on main artery or 'A' roads, and became lost when navigation depended instead on non-A roads (figure 8.4). The hippocampus in humans is therefore necessary for facilitating navigation even when the navigator is an expert of very longstanding. Thus expertise, while taking many years to develop, can be vulnerable to sudden and focal brain insult, leading in this case to a loss of livelihood and independence.

Considered next is the question of whether expertise and its associated neuroanatomy result in broader cognitive costs. Of note, exceptional abilities in autism occur in the context of impairments in social cognition and executive functions (Frith & Happé 2005), and some expert musicians suffer focal dystonia, a loss of control and degradation of skilled hand movements (Munte *et al.* 2002). In taxi drivers, we noted above their enhanced knowledge of London. However, in two separate studies, the performance of taxi drivers was significantly poorer than both bus drivers (Maguire *et al.* 2006*a*) and control participants (Woollett & Maguire 2009) on a widely used test of spatial memory, the delayed recall of the Rey-Osterrieth Complex Figure (Rey 1941; Osterrieth 1944; Corwin & Bylsma 1993; figure 8.5*a,b*). Furthermore, they were also deficient at acquiring and retaining other types of new information. Specifically, they were poorer at learning object-place and word-pair associations. After a delay they also recalled less of this associative information. This pattern of anterograde memory performance was in the context of learning and recognition memory for single items being comparable with control participants, as were retrograde memory for autobiographical and semantic information, executive and perceptual functions, working memory and levels of stress and anxiety.

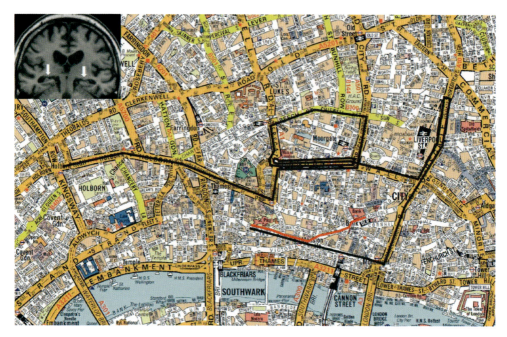

Figure 8.4 The sudden loss of expertise. Patient TT, with bilateral hippocampal lesions (see inset upper left), and control taxi drivers retired for a similar length of time as TT, navigated around the VR London. An example of their navigation performance for a route from St Paul's Cathedral to the Bank of England is shown. All 10 controls performed in an identical manner, shown in red on this map. TT's route is shown in black and was grossly impaired being mainly restricted to the A roads (shown in orange and yellow on the map) and he never reached the required destination (data from Maguire et al. 2006b). Map reproduced with the permission of Geographers' A–Z Map Co. Ltd. Crown Copyright 2005. All rights reserved. Licence number 100017302.

Negative effects of navigation expertise were not only found behaviourally but also structurally in the brain. In comparison with the posterior hippocampus that had greater grey matter volume compared with control participants, the anterior hippocampus had reduced grey matter volume in taxi drivers (Maguire *et al.* 2000, 2006a; Woollett & Maguire 2009; figure 8.5c). Moreover, anterior hippocampal grey matter volume decreased as navigation experience increased in taxi drivers (figure 8.5d). We suggest that the below-average scores observed in taxi drivers on tests of anterograde associative memory could be related to their reduced right anterior hippocampal grey matter volume. This accords with the findings across species that there may be functional differentiation along the anterior-posterior axis of the hippocampus (e.g. Jung *et al.* 1994; Colombo *et al.* 1998; Hock & Bunsey 1998; Moser & Moser 1998; Maguire *et al.* 2000; Bannerman *et al.* 2004; Gogtay *et al.* 2006). In humans, functional neuroimaging studies have linked anterior hippocampal activity with the detection of stimulus novelty and encoding, while the posterior hippocampus has been associated with retrieval and spatial memory (e.g. Lepage *et al.* 1998; Strange & Dolan 2001; Kumaran & Maguire 2005; Spiers & Maguire 2006; but see Small *et al.* 2001).

We have established that navigation expertise is associated with structural brain differences and behavioural consequences, both positive and negative. In particular, the correlations between time taxi driving and hippocampal grey matter volume suggest that

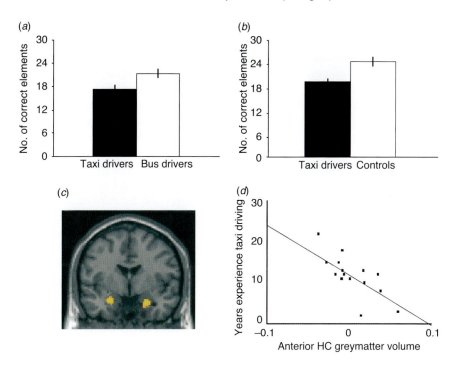

Figure 8.5 Navigation expertise: negative outcomes. (*a*) Taxi drivers (*n* = 18) were significantly worse at recalling elements of the Rey-Osterrieth Complex Figure at delayed recall compared with bus drivers (*n* = 17; mean scores ± 1 s.e., data from Maguire *et al.* 2006*a*). (*b*) This result was replicated in a different cohort of taxi drivers and a control group of non-taxi drivers (*n* = 20 each group; data from Woollett & Maguire 2009). (*c*) Taxi drivers had less grey matter volume in the anterior hippocampus bilaterally compared with bus drivers (data from Maguire *et al.* 2006*a*). (*d*) Anterior hippocampal (HC) grey matter volume correlated negatively with increasing navigation experience in taxi drivers (data from Maguire *et al.* 2006*a*).

experience drives the patterns observed. However, studies to date have been cross-sectional and we acknowledge that in order to categorically conclude this, a within-subject longitudinal study is required, which permits the comparison before and after taxi driver training (such a study is ongoing). This longitudinal approach will also permit the examination of the characteristics of those who succeed at taxi driver training, and whether innate pre-training cognitive factors and/or hippocampal volume are predictive of subsequent successful qualification. This will provide vital information about brain plasticity and navigation expertise, and the factors that might affect or limit the ability to develop such expertise. Even then, further questions will remain, which must be addressed in future studies. Navigational accuracy can be supported by different types of representation, for example remembering individual routes versus a coherent map-like representation (O'Keefe & Nadel 1978; Hartley *et al.* 2003; Iaria *et al.* 2003; Bohbot *et al.* 2007). It may be that some individuals have an innate bias for using one type of representation, with successful taxi drivers perhaps more likely to use map-like strategies. Beyond representational biases, successful qualification might also depend on genetic factors, with perhaps the propensity for hippocampal plasticity more likely in individuals with a certain genetic profile (Egan *et al.* 2003; Hariri *et al.* 2003).

8.5 Use it or lose it?

If, as the cross-sectional studies suggest, navigation expertise results in structural changes to the brain and positive and negative neuropsychological consequences, then what happens if one stops using this expertise? Anecdotally, it is suggested that skills can be lost if not practised—use it or lose it. If expertise and its expression are indeed plastic, then can the effects of expertise be reversed? We have started to examine this issue by comparing retired taxi drivers with taxi drivers who are still working full time. We hypothesized that the full-time taxi drivers would be better at navigation in London than the retired. We tested this by using the VR London navigation test described earlier (figure 8.2). Preliminary data show that the full-timers are indeed significantly better at navigation in London than the retired taxi drivers (figure 8.6*a*). Interestingly, this was also the case for performance on tests of London knowledge, such as making proximity judgements between landmarks. In figure 8.6*b*, it is clear that the still-working taxi drivers perform best while there is very little difference between the retired taxi drivers and a set of retired non-taxi driver control participants.

Consideration of the negative outcomes is particularly interesting. If taxi drivers perform poorly on tests such as the delayed recall of the Rey Complex Figure, does performance improve in retired taxi drivers? Our preliminary data suggest that this may be the case. Figure 8.6*c* shows that, as in our previous studies (Maguire *et al.* 2006*a*, Woollett & Maguire 2009), control non-taxi drivers were significantly better on the delayed recall of the Rey Figure than the full-time taxi drivers. Interestingly, there was no significant difference between the controls and the retired taxi drivers. The intermediate performance of the retired taxi drivers, not as poor as the full-timers, and not as good as controls, is in line with the view that ceasing to use a skill might result in the normalization of expertise-related negative outcomes. On average, the taxi drivers in this preliminary sample had only been retired for 3.6 years. It may be that with a longer period of retirement, performance on tests such as the Rey Figure would normalize entirely.

In line with the pattern of behavioural tests, it seems that the structural brain changes observed in taxi drivers in our previous studies may also reverse in retired taxi drivers. Full-time taxi drivers had significantly greater grey matter volume in the posterior hippocampus than retired taxi drivers, who had greater volume in this region than the non-taxi driver retired control participants (figure 8.6*d*). Clearly, increased numbers of participants are required to confirm these findings. Nevertheless, the possibility of plasticity effects in both directions, i.e. during acquisition and use of expertise, and then again when use of the skill ceases, serves to highlight that expertise and its behavioural consequences may be plastic and, in the case of the hippocampus at least, so are the related structural brain changes. The improvement of performance on tests such as the Rey Figure by the retired taxi drivers is also interesting in that it may indicate that the 'elderly' hippocampus can support memory improvement, in contrast with the more traditional view of age-related memory decline.

8.6 Conclusions

Understanding the cognitive and neural mechanisms underpinning talent and expertise is important for a number of reasons. First, this issue has universal relevance by informing what each of us can hope to achieve, and providing much-needed insights into the basis

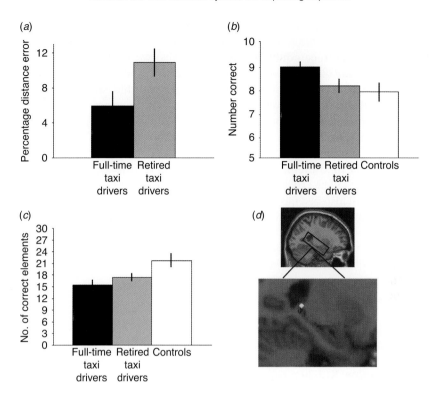

Figure 8.6 Ceasing to use a skill: preliminary data. Mean scores are shown ± 1 s.e. (*a*) The performance of elderly taxi drivers who were still working full-time was compared with retired taxi drivers on the VR London navigation test ($n = 8$ each group). Consistently chosen legal routes were established for each trial, and the ideal minimum length of these routes was computed. The distance each participant drove and the ideal distance for each route were measured and the difference calculated as percentage distance error. The routes of the retired taxi drivers were longer and less ideal than those taxi drivers who were still working. (*b*) A group of elderly still-working taxi drivers, retired taxi drivers and retired control non-taxi drivers were compared on a range of neuropsychological measures. Groups ($n = 10$ each group) were matched for age (mean age 66.1, 69.5, 66 years, respectively) and years experience taxi driving (full-timers 34.2 years, retired 36.2 years). Full-timers were significantly better on tests of London knowledge (landmark proximity judgements). (*c*) The reverse pattern was apparent on tests of new learning, with full-timers significantly worse on the delayed recall of the Rey-Osterrieth Complex Figure. (*d*) Full-time taxi drivers ($n = 10$) had greater grey matter volume in the posterior hippocampus than retired taxi drivers ($n = 9$; voxel of peak difference shown in yellow), while the retired taxi drivers had greater grey matter volume in this region than the retired control participants ($n = 10$; voxel of peak difference shown in red). Data are shown at a threshold of $p < 0.05$ corrected for the volume of the hippocampus.

of individual differences, as well as having relevance in the realm of education. Second, understanding skill acquisition may have implications for patients with cognitive impairments. If we are to approach rehabilitation in a systematic and efficacious way, then it is vital to know, for example, whether the memory system has the propensity for plasticity in adulthood, the limiting factors on such plasticity and the time scales of any plastic change. Third, understanding exceptional abilities in the healthy brain may also offer benchmarks for interpreting talent and expertise in clinical populations, such as those with autism. Here we have focused on one type of expertise in the domain of memory, availing a unique learning situation in London known to engage the hippocampus, and by studying healthy average adults operating in a real-world setting over many years. From this, we conclude that the development of expertise is possible with extensive effort, and that this can be associated with neuropsychological and structural brain consequences. These effects can be positive and negative, with increased expertise and grey matter volume in some brain regions occurring in tandem with decreased performance on other tasks and decreased grey matter volume in neighbouring brain areas. Clearly, more work is required to establish whether the effects we have described here in relation to taxi drivers generalize beyond the domain of memory and the hippocampus. In particular, longitudinal studies will be crucial to explore the nature and consequences of skill acquisition. Finally, it will also be vital to consider whether expertise and its related effects can be expected to develop in any individual or whether they are genetically determined.

This work was supported by the Wellcome Trust.
All participants gave informed written consent to participation in accordance with the local research ethics committee.

References

Andersen, P., Morris, R. G. M., Amaral, D., Bliss, T. & O'Keefe, J. 2006 *The hippocampus book.* Oxford, UK: Oxford University Press.
Ashburner, J. & Friston, K. J. 2005 Unified segmentation. *Neuroimage* 26, 839–851. (doi:10.1016/j.neuroimage.2005.02.018)
Aydin, K., Ucar, A., Oguz, K. K., Okur, O. O., Agayev, A., Unal, Z., Yilmaz, S. & Ozturk, C. 2007 Increased gray matter density in the parietal cortex of mathematicians: a voxel-based morphometry study. *Am. J. Neuroradiol.* 28, 1859–1864. (doi:10.3174/ajnr.A0696)
Bannerman, D. M., Rawlins, J. N., McHugh, S. B., Deacon, R. M., Yee, B. K., Bast, T, Zhang, W. N., Pothuizen, H. H. & Feldon, J. 2004 Regional dissociations within the hippocampus: memory and anxiety. *Neurosci. Biobehav. Rev.* 28, 273–283. (doi:10.1016/j.neubiorev.2004.03.004)
Barnea, A. & Nottebohm, F. 1994 Seasonal recruitment of hippocampal neurons in adult free-ranging black-capped chickadees. *Proc. Natl Acad. Sci. USA* 91, 11 217–11 221. (doi:10.1073/pnas.91.23.11217)
Biegler, R., McGregor, A., Krebs, J. R. & Healy, S. D. 2001 A larger hippocampus is associated with longer-lasting spatial memory. *Proc. Natl Acad. Sci. USA* **98**, 6941–6944. (doi:10.1073/pnas.121034798)
Bird, C. M. & Burgess, N. 2008 The hippocampus and memory: insights from spatial processing. *Nat. Rev. Neurosci.* 9, 82–194. (doi:10.1038/nrn2335)
Bohbot, V. D., Lerch, J., Thorndycraft, B., Iaria, G. & Zijdenbos, A. P. 2007 Gray matter differences correlate with spontaneous strategies in a human virtual navigation task. *J. Neurosci.* **27**, 10 078–10 083. (doi:10.1523/JNEUROSCI.1763-07.2007)
Chase, W. G. 1982 Spatial representations of taxi drivers. In *Acquisition of symbolic skills* (eds D. Rogers & J. A. Sloboda), pp. 391–05. New York, NY: Plenum Press.
Colombo, M., Fernandez, T, Nakamura, K. & Gross, C. G. 1998 Functional differentiation along the anterior-posterior axis of the hippocampus in monkeys. *J. Neurophysiol.* **80**, 1002–1005.
Corwin, J. & Bylsma, F. W. 1993 Translations of excerpts from Andre Rey's psychological examination of traumatic encephalopathy and PA Osterrieth's the complex figure test. *Clin. Neuropsychol.* 7, 15–21. (doi:l0.1080/13854049308401883)
Draganski, B., Gaser, C., Busch, V., Schuierer, G., Bogdahn, U. & May, A. 2004 Neuroplasticity: changes in grey matter induced by training. *Nature* **427**, 311–312. (doi:10.1038/427311a)

Draganski, B., Gaser, C., Kempermann, G., Kuhn, H. G., Winkler, J., Buchel, C. & May, A. 2006 Temporal and spatial dynamics of brain structure changes during extensive learning. *J. Neurosci.* **26**, 6314–6317. (doi:10.1523/JNEUROSCI.4628-05.2006)

Egan, M. F. *et al.* 2003 The BDNF val66met polymorphism affects activity-dependent secretion of BDNF and human memory and hippocampal function. *Cell* **112**, 257–269. (doi:10.1016/S0092-8674(03)00035-7)

Ericsson, K. A., Charness, N., Hoffman, R. R. & Feltovich, P. J. 2006 *The Cambridge handbook of expertise and expert performance.* Cambridge, UK: Cambridge University Press.

Frith, U. & Happé, F. 2005 Autism spectrum disorder. *Curr. Biol.* **15**, R786–R790. (doi:10.1016/j.cub.2005.09.033)

Gaser, C. & Schlaug, G. 2003 Gray matter differences between musicians and nonmusicians. *Ann. NYAcad.* **999**, 514–517. (doi:10.1196/annals.1284.062)

Gogtay, N. *et al.* 2006 Dynamic mapping of normal human hippocampal development. *Hippocampus* **16**, 664–672. (doi:10.1002/hipo.20193)

Grafton, S. 2008 Developing talent: expertise and the brain. In *Your brain on cubs: inside the heads of players and fans* (ed. D. Gordon), pp. 21–42. Washington, DC: Dana Press.

Hariri, A. R., Goldberg, T., Mattay, V. S., Kolachana, B. S., Callicott, J. H., Egan, M. F. & Weinberger, D. R. 2003 Brain-derived neurotrophic factor val66met polymorphism affects human memory-related hippocampal activity and predicts memory performance. *J. Neurosci.* **23**, 6690–6694.

Hartley, T., Maguire, E. A., Spiers, H. J. & Burgess, N. 2003 The well-worn route and the path less traveled: distinct neural bases of route following and wayfinding in humans. *Neuron* **37**, 877–888. (doi:10.1016/S0896-6273(03)00095-3)

Hock Jr, B. J. & Bunsey, M. D. 1998 Differential effects of dorsal and ventral hippocampal lesions. *J. Neurosd.* **18**, 7027–7032.

Iaria, G., Petrides, M., Dagher, A., Pike, B. & Bohbot, V. D. 2003 Cognitive strategies dependent on the hippocampus and caudate nucleus in human navigation: variability and change with practice. *J. Neurosd.* **23**, 5945–5952.

Jung, M. W, Wiener, S. I. & McNaughton, B. L. 1994 Comparison of spatial firing characteristics of units in dorsal and ventral hippocampus of the rat. *J. Neurosd.* **14**, 7347–7356.

Kalakoski, V. & Saariluoma, P. 2001 Taxi drivers' exceptional memory of street names. *Mem. Cogn.* **29**, 634–638.

Kalbfleisch, M. L. 2004 Functional neural anatomy of talent. *Anat. Rec.* **277B**, 21–36. (doi:10.1002/ar.b.20010)

Kumaran, D. & Maguire, E. A. 2005 The human hippocampus: cognitive maps or relational memory? *J. Neurosd* **25**, 7254–7259. (doi:10.1523/JNEUROSCI.1103–05.2005)

Lee, D. W, Miyasato, L. E. & Clayton, N. S. 1998 Neurobiological bases of spatial learning in the natural environment: neurogenesis and growth in the avian and mammalian hippocampus. *Neuroreport* **9**, R15–R27.

Lepage, M., Habib, R. & Tulving, E. 1998 Hippocampal PET activations of memory encoding and retrieval: the HIPER model. *Hippocampus* **8**, 313–322. (doi:10.1002/(SICI)1098-1063(1998)8:4 < 313::AID-HIPO1 > 3. O.CO;2–I)

Luria, A. R. 1987 *The mind of a mnemonist.* New York, NY: Harvard University Press.

Maguire, E. A., Burgess, N., Donnett, J. G., Frackowiak, R. S. J., Frith, C. D. & O'Keefe, J. 1998 Knowing where, and getting there: a human navigation network. *Science* **280**, 921–924. (doi:10.1126/science.280.5365.921)

Maguire, E. A., Gadian, D. G., Johnsrude, I. S., Good, C. D., Ashburner, J., Frackowiak, R. S. & Frith, C. D. 2000 Navigation-related structural change in the hippocampi of taxi drivers. *Proc. Natl Acad. Sci. USA* **97**, 4398–4403. (doi:10.1073/pnas.070039597)

Maguire, E. A., Spiers, H. J., Good, C. D., Hartley, T, Frackowiak, R. S. & Burgess, N. 2003a Navigation expertise and the human hippocampus: a structural brain imaging analysis. *Hippocampus* **13**, 250–259. (doi:10.1002/hipo.10087)

Maguire, E. A., Valentine, E. R., Wilding, J. M. & Kapur, N. 2003b Routes to remembering: the brains behind superior memory. *Nat. Neurosd.* **6**, 90–95. (doi:10.1038/nn988)

Maguire, E. A., Woollett, K. & Spiers, H. J. 2006a London taxi drivers and bus drivers: a structural MRI and neuro-psychological analysis. *Hippocampus* **16**, 1091–1101. (doi:10.1002/hipo.20233)

Maguire, E. A., Nannery, R. & Spiers, H. J. 2006b Navigation around London by a taxi driver with bilateral hippocampal lesions. *Brain* **129**, 2894–2907. (doi:10.1093/brain/awl286)

Mechelli, A., Crinion, J. T, Noppeney, U., O'Doherty, J., Ashburner, J., Frackowiak, R. S. & Price, C. J. 2004 Neurolinguistics: structural plasticity in the bilingual brain. *Nature* **431**, 757. (doi:l0.1038/431757a)

Mechelli, A., Price, C. J., Friston, K. J. & Ashburner, J. 2005 Voxel–based morphometry of the human brain: methods and applications. *Curr. Med. Imaging Rev.* **1**, 105–113. (doi:10.2174/1573405054038726)

Morris, R. G., Garrud, P., Rawlins, J. N. & O'Keefe, J. 1982 Place navigation impaired in rats with hippocampal lesions. *Nature* **297**, 681–683. (doi:10.1038/297681a0)

Moser, M. B. & Moser, E. I. 1998 Functional differentiation in the hippocampus. *Hippocampus* **8**, 608–619. (doi:10.1002/(SICI)1098–1063(1998)8:6 < 608::AID–HIPO3 > 3. 0.CO;2–7)

Munte, T. F., Altenmuller, E. & Jancke, L. 2002 The musician's brain as a model of neuroplasticity. *Nat. Rev. Neurosci* **3**, 473–78. (doi:10.1038/nrm866)

O'Keefe, J. & Dostrovsky, J. 1971 The hippocampus as a spatial map. Preliminary evidence from unit activity in the freely-moving rat. *Brain Res.* **34**, 171–175. (doi:10.1016/0006-8993(71)90358-1)

O'Keefe, J. & Nadel, L. 1978 *The hippocampus as a cognitive map.* Oxford, UK: Oxford University Press.

Osterrieth, P. A. 1944 Le test de copie d'une figure complexe. *Archives de Psychologie* **30**, 206–356.

Pailhous, J. 1970 *La representation de l'espace urbain: L'example du chauffeur de taxi.* Paris, France: Presses Universitaires de France.

Pailhous, J. 1984 The representation of urban space: its development and its role in the organisation of journeys. In *Social representation* (eds R. Farr & S. Moscovici), Cambridge, UK: Cambridge University Press.

Parker, E. S., Cahill, L. & McGaugh, J. L. 2006 A case of unusual autobiographical remembering. *Neurocase* **12**, 35–9. (doi:10.1080/13554790500473680)

Peruch, P., Giraudo, M.-D. & Garling, T. 1989 Distance cognition by taxi drivers and the general public. *J. Environ. Psychol.* **9**, 233–239. (doi:10.1016/S0272-4944(89) 80037-4)

Pring, L. 2008 Memory characteristics in individuals with savant skills. In *Memory in autism: theory and evidence* (eds J. Boucher & D. Bowler), pp. 210–230. Cambridge, UK: Cambridge University Press.

Rey, A. 1941 L'examen psychologique dans les cas d'ence-phalopathie traumatique. *Archives de Psychology* **28**, 286–340.

Sluming, V., Barrick, T., Howard, M., Cezayirli, E., Mayes, A. & Roberts, N. 2002 Voxel-based morphometry reveals increased gray matter density in Broca's area in male symphony orchestra musicians. *Neuroimage* **17**, 1613–1622. (doi:10.1006/nimg.2002.1288)

Sluming, V., Brooks, J., Howard, M., Downes, J. J. & Roberts, N. 2007 Broca's area supports enhanced visuo-spatial cognition in orchestral musicians. *J. Neurosci.* **27**, 3799–3806. (doi:10.1523/JNEUROSCI.0147-07.2007)

Small, S. A., Nava, A. S., Perera, G. M., DeLaPaz, R., Mayeux, R. & Stern, Y. 2001 Circuit mechanisms underlying memory encoding and retrieval in the long axis of the hippocampal formation. *Nat. Neurosci.* **4**, 442–449. (doi:10.1038/86115)

Smulders, T. V., Sasson, A. D. & DeVoogd, T. J. 1995 Seasonal variation in hippocampal volume in a food-storing bird, the black-capped chickadee. *J. Neurobiol.* **27**, 15–25. (doi:10.1002/neu.480270103)

Spiers, H. J. & Maguire, E. A. 2006 Thoughts, behaviour, and brain dynamics during navigation in the real world. *Neuroimage* **31**, 1826–1840. (doi:10.1016/j.neuroimage.2006.01.037)

Spiers, H. J. & Maguire, E. A. 2007a A navigational guidance system in the human brain. *Hippocampus* **17**, 618–626. (doi:10.1002/hipo.20298)

Spiers, H. J. & Maguire, E. A. 2007b The neuroscience of remote spatial memory: a tale of two cities. *Neuroscience* **149**, 7–27. (doi:10.1016/j.neuroscience.2007.06.056)

Strange, B. A. & Dolan, R. J. 2001 Adaptive anterior hippocampal responses to oddball stimuli. *Hippocampus* **11**, 690–698. (doi:10.1002/hipo.l084)

Terrazas, A. & McNaughton, B. L. 2000 Brain growth and the cognitive map. *Proc. Nad Acad. Sci. USA* **97**, 4414–4416. (doi:10.1073/pnas.97.9.4414)

Treffert, D. A. 2009 The savant syndrome: an extraordinary condition. A synopsis: past, present, future. *Phil. Trans. R. Soc. B* **364**, 1351–1357. (doi:10.1098/rstb.2008.0326)

Volman, S. R, Grubb Jr, T. C. & Schuett, K. C. 1997 Relative hippocampal volume in relation to food-storing behavior in four species of woodpeckers. *Brain Behav. Evol.* **49**, 110–120. (doi:10.1159/000112985)

Woollett, K. & Maguire, E. A. In press. The expertise of London taxi drivers compromises anterograde associative memory. *Neuropsychologia*.

Woollett, K., Glensman, J. & Maguire, E. A. 2008 Non-spatial expertise and hippocampal gray matter volume in humans. *Hippocampus* **18**, 981–984. (doi:10.1002/hipo.20465)

Yates, F. A. 1966 *The art of memory*. London, UK: Pimlico.

9

Do calendrical savants use calculation to answer date questions? A functional magnetic resonance imaging study

Richard Cowan and Chris Frith

Calendrical savants can name the weekdays for dates from different years with remarkable speed and accuracy. Whether calculation rather than just memory is involved is disputed. Grounds for doubting whether they can calculate are reviewed and criteria for attributing date calculation skills to them are discussed. At least some calendrical savants possess date calculation skills. A behavioural characteristic observed in many calendrical savants is increased response time for questions about more remote years. This may be because more remote years require more calculation or because closer years are more practised. An experiment is reported that used functional magnetic resonance imaging to attempt to discriminate between these explanations. Only two savants could be scanned and excessive head movement corrupted one savant's mental arithmetic data. Nevertheless, there was increased parietal activation during both mental arithmetic and date questions and this region showed increased activity with more remote dates. These results suggest that the calendrical skills observed in savants result from intensive practice with calculations used in solving mental arithmetic problems. The mystery is not how they solve these problems, but why.

Keywords: arithmetic; savant syndrome; functional magnetic resonance imaging

9.1 Introduction

Calendrical savants are people with pervasive disabilities who can tell you the weekdays corresponding to dates without resorting to external aids such as calendars or computers. Some surveys suggest it is the most common savant skill (e.g. Saloviita *et al.* 2000). It is certainly one of the strangest. These may be linked: so rarely is it reported in typically functioning people that any indication of it is remarkable. In this paper, we use existing research to argue that some calendrical savants have skills that go beyond rote memory. They therefore challenge accounts of savant skills in terms of rote learning just as the originality of savant artists and the inventiveness of savant musicians do (Sloboda *et al.* 1985; O'Connor & Hermelin 1987). Although we shall argue that the skills of several previously studied calendrical savants include date calculation, this does not imply that they calculate to answer every date question. In the second part of the paper, we describe a functional magnetic resonance imaging (fMRI) investigation to determine whether savants take longer to answer questions about more remote dates because these involve additional calculation or more extensive memory search.

Before discussing the grounds for attributing date calculation skills to savants, we consider why some have rejected calculation as a basis for their skill. A principal reason is that calculation draws on cognitive processes that constitute general intelligence. It thus seems paradoxical that people with low measured intelligence should show prowess in a form of calculation that is rarely shown by people with superior levels of cognitive functioning.

The simplest explanation is that the calculations involved are not very demanding. Calendrical skills are not rare in typically functioning people because they are difficult to acquire: Cowan *et al.* (2004) described two typically developing boys who showed calendrical skills at the ages of 5 and 6. Both had developed them without instruction.

It is more likely that calendrical skills are uncommon in the general population because few people are motivated to develop them. Indeed, on following up the boys 2 years later neither had progressed much in calendrical skill. Both had found more conventional domains in which to excel and receive attention and praise. By contrast, calendrical savants may not have opportunities to develop other socially engaging skills.

Among those motivated to develop calendrical skills, the level of intelligence is likely to affect the development of skill: in a set of calendrical savants, there is a relationship between the Wechsler Adult Intelligence Scales Intelligence Quotient (WAIS IQ) and calendrical skill (Hermelin & O'Connor 1986; O'Connor *et al.* 2000). Omnibus intelligence tests such as the WAIS have limitations for assessing people with autism (Happé 1994; Frith 2003). Most of the sample in O'Connor *et al.* (2000) had received diagnoses of autism.

Even stronger relationships might be observed between calendrical skill and intelligence when measured with tests that require less informal knowledge, although this would depend on whether amounts of practice were similar. Although some claim that savant skills do not develop with practice (e.g. Snyder & Mitchell 1999), there is evidence that they do (Scheerer *et al.* 1945; Horwitz *et al.* 1965; Hoffman 1971; Rosen 1981; Cowan & Carney 2006).

The confounding of informal knowledge with computation might also have led to claims that calendrical savants cannot be calculating to solve date questions because they lack even basic arithmetical skills. The WAIS arithmetic subscale features arithmetical problems embedded in verbal contexts. The context may cause difficulty, not the computation. Ho *et al.* (1991) described a calendrical savant who performed poorly on WAIS arithmetic but was very successful on tests that just required calculation.

Cowan *et al.* (2003) also observed differences between WAIS arithmetic scores and a test of mental arithmetic, the graded difficulty arithmetic test (GDA, Jackson & Warrington 1986) in a sample of calendrical savants. In normal adults, performance on the GDA is highly related to WAIS arithmetic. The calendrical savants showed no such association: several showed marked discrepancies between the tests. No savant performed at a superior level on the WAIS arithmetic test and several performed poorly. By contrast, several calendrical savants were at ceiling level on the GDA: they were also more proficient on calendrical tasks.

The GDA just involves addition and subtraction, but algorithms for date calculation typically involve division (e.g. Berlekamp *et al.* 1982; Carroll 1887). However, the suggested process of date calculation by calendrical savants does not involve division. Instead, it involves converting the target year into a known year by addition or subtraction (Cowan & Carney 2006; Thioux *et al.* 2006).

Another feature of calendrical savants that has been considered to argue against calculation is that they are typically unable to give an account of how they solve date questions (O'Connor 1989). Normally, one would expect conscious awareness of calculation.

However, savants may not be able to introspect even when they can be observed counting when solving problems (Scheerer *et al.* 1945). If savants do not mention calculation even when they can be observed to be calculating, then what they do not say about their method is inconclusive about the basis of their skill.

In summary, calculation by calendrical savants has been considered unlikely because of their measured intelligence, their apparent lack of arithmetical skills and their silence about their method. None of these is compelling.

Positive evidence that the skill does not just reflect memory for calendars is provided when savants can answer questions outside the range of calendars that they could have memorized. Just being able to answer questions about dates in the future is not decisive as there are several sources of information about future dates: diaries often give the calendar for years in the near future. Calendars for more remote years can be obtained from reference books such as Whitaker's Almanac and perpetual calendars. The range of years these cover is, however, limited. Reference books and perpetual calendars do not cover more than 400 years in the Gregorian period, as the Gregorian calendar repeats every 400 years. Typically, they cover fewer. So a savant who can answer questions concerning years more than 400 years in the future must calculate to work out the correspondence between a remote year and a closer one. Several reports of savants with very large ranges exist: Tredgold & Soddy (1956) mentioned an inmate of an idiot asylum who could answer questions on any date in the years from 1000 to 2000. George, the more able of the twins studied by Horwitz *et al.* (1969), correctly answered all questions asked concerning years between 4100 and 40 400. O'Connor *et al.* (2000) described three savants who correctly answered questions for years further in the future than 8000: GC, MW and HP.

Systematic errors provide another form of evidence that the skills are not just the product of memorizing calendars. Century years such as 1800, 1900 and 2000 are only leap years in the Gregorian calendar if they are exactly divisible by 400. Some savants respond to date questions as though all century years were leap. They answer questions about dates in the nineteenth century with the day before the correct answer, e.g. claiming that the 14 July 1886 was a Saturday when it was a Sunday. For dates in the eighteenth century, their answers are 2 days before the correct day and for future centuries their answers are days after the correct answer, e.g. claiming that 1 July 2192 will be a Monday rather than a Sunday and that 22 May 2209 will be a Wednesday instead of a Monday. These systematic deviations are inconsistent with a method solely based on remembered calendars. Extrapolation from calendars studied is more likely, but this implies that they have detected regularities to extrapolate from and that they have used these to calculate correspondences between remote and proximal years (O'Connor & Hermelin 1984; Hermelin & O'Connor 1986). Calendrical savants who made such systematic errors have been described by several researchers: Kit (Ho *et al.* 1991), TMK (Hurst & Mulhall 1988), Donny (Thioux *et al.* 2006), DM and JG (O'Connor *et al.* 2000).

The remote past can also provoke systematic errors inconsistent with memorizing. Before adopting the Gregorian calendar, European countries used the Julian calendar in which every year exactly divisible by four is leap. Countries adopted the Gregorian calendar in different years: from 1582 for Italy, France, Spain and Portugal, to 1923 for Greece. Adoption of the Gregorian calendar involved more than just the change to century years: a number of days were dropped in the year of change. When Great Britain adopted the Gregorian calendar in 1752, the days between 3 and 13 September did not happen, a cause of some civil unrest. False extrapolations of the Gregorian calendar to years before

1752 were made by George (Horwitz et al. 1969) and MW (Cowan et al. 2003). GC assumed that 1700 was a leap year but was ignorant of the omission of days in 1752 (Cowan et al. 2003). Donny (Thioux et al. 2006) and DM (Cowan et al. 2003) extrapolated their versions of the calendar across the change date. Only HP (Cowan et al. 2003) responded consistently with the change and knew what dates had been omitted.

Another way of establishing that savants can calculate to solve date problems was derived by analogy with research on children's arithmetic. Dowker (1998) devised a test of children's knowledge of arithmetical principles, which involves first determining the range of problems a child could reliably solve and then presenting them with problems beyond it but with the solution to a problem related to it by an arithmetical principle. So, for example, a child who could solve single-digit addend problems such as 9 + 8 but not two-digit addend problems such as 26 + 72 would be told that 44 + 23 = 67 and asked whether they could solve 23 + 44 (related to it by commutativity). The calendrical analogue involved first establishing the limits of the range of years within which the savant could answer correctly, telling them days for dates outside that range and then asking them to solve date questions related to them by calendrical regularities. Two such regularities are the 1 year, 1 day rule (the same date in adjacent years falls on adjacent days unless there is an intervening 29 February) and the 28 year rule (the same date in 28 years apart in the same century falls on the same day). Answering both types of problem correctly requires knowledge of the principles and discrimination—the correct answer to 1 year, 1 day problems is never the same weekday but it is always for the 28 year rule problems. Savants who answered both types of problem correctly included DK and PE, as well as GC and MW (Cowan et al. 2001).

Any of the above characteristics might be regarded as sufficient evidence that a particular calendrical savant's skills are more than just memory. None, however, are necessary. It would be wrong to conclude that a savant cannot calculate dates just because their range is less than that of a perpetual calendar or because they do not systematically err. An inability to solve related problems outside their range is also inconclusive: it proved beyond the ability of the experimenters to explain the task to some savants (Cowan et al. 2001). So our conclusion is that at least some calendrical savants, and maybe all, can calculate the answers to date questions.

A feature of many calendrical savants, even those with limited ranges, is that they take longer to answer questions concerning years more remote from the present (O'Connor & Hermelin 1984; Dorman 1991; Cowan et al. 2003). This could result from increased calculation for more remote years (O'Connor & Hermelin 1984). It might also result from differential effects of practice. As a result of practising date calculations and studying calendars, savants may develop richer networks of associations between dates and weekdays and stronger associations for more proximal years.

Behavioural data are equivocal about why response times increase with remoteness. Imaging studies can help to resolve the issue. If areas of greater activation when calendrical savants answer date questions overlap with those when they are calculating answers to arithmetical problems, then calculation is the probable basis. If remote years elicit even greater activation of these regions, then these are likely to involve more calculation, as O'Connor & Hermelin (1984) hypothesized.

The neural processing of numbers in the brain involves several different regions. For example, the right fusiform gyrus is implicated in the identification of Arabic numerals (Pinel et al. 2001). However, it is generally agreed that the parietal lobe has the major role

(Dehaene et al. 2003). In particular, the intraparietal sulcus (IPS) is involved in representing quantity in both humans (Pinel et al. 2004) and monkeys (Nieder 2005). Supporting this idea are data from an experiment (Pinel et al. 2001) in which subjects had to decide whether a number was larger or smaller than a memorized reference number (65). There were three categories of target, close (60–64, 66–69), medium (50–59, 70–79) and far (30–49, 80–89). Reaction times for classifier target numbers decreased as the distance of the targets from the reference. These reaction time differences were paralleled by the magnitude of the activity elicited in left and right IPS (–40, –44, 36 and 44, –56, 48). The more difficult the numerical comparison (i.e. the closer the numbers), the longer was the reaction time and the greater was the activity in the IPS.

The study of calendrical savants is problematic for a number of reasons. First, there are too few suitable savants for a group study to be conducted. We originally attempted to scan four, but one was unable to remain in the scanner for long enough. Another was unable to learn to press buttons instead of responding orally. It is therefore necessary to conduct single case studies. Given the very limited power from such studies using fMRI, we chose to restrict our investigation to the parietal lobe and to test the hypothesis that calendrical calculation engages this region in the same manner as mental arithmetic.

The second problem is that it is not possible to scan 'normal' volunteers doing calendrical calculation because their abilities would typically be dramatically inferior. To avoid this problem, we asked our calendrical calculators to perform an established mental arithmetic task (Menon et al. 2000) that could be compared with normal volunteers. We then used conjunction analysis to locate regions in parietal cortex that were activated both by mental arithmetic and by calendrical calculation. Finally, we asked whether these regions also showed a difficulty effect when calendrical calculations were performed on dates that were more or less remote from the present.

9.2 Material and methods

(a) Participants

Two autistic calendrical savants (GC and MW) and a normal adult male participated. GC and MW are examples of classic autism and have WAIS IQs of 97 and 82, respectively. Both GC and MW show evidence of being able to calculate dates by having ranges that transcend those of perpetual calendars, making systematic errors for dates in the remote past and by being able to use calendrical regularities to solve date problems outside their range. GC is left-handed and MW is right-handed. Written consent was obtained from both savants before each occasion on which they were scanned. MW's parents accompanied him and also consented to his participation. The study was approved by the National Hospital research ethics committee. The single normal participant was tested on the mental arithmetic task to check that the results of Menon et al. (2000) could be replicated in a single subject.

(b) Experimental tasks

(i) Arithmetic

We modified Menon et al.'s (2000) verification task slightly to increase the probability of calculation. Initial and final numbers always contained two digits, e.g. '25 – 6 + 8 = 27;

true or false?' The control task presented strings of eight digits and also required both true and false, e.g. '3 4 9 0 5 7 8 6 contains 0; true or false?'

(ii) Calendrical tasks

We used two types of calendrical and control tasks on different occasions. Calendrical I featured dates from the 1940s and 2020s, e.g. '3 March 2025 is a Monday; true or false?' The control task comprised statements about the initial letters of months, e.g. 'July begins with J; true or false?'

The second session calendrical task, calendrical II, featured dates from three periods, varying in remoteness from the late twentieth century. Close dates sampled from the 1970s and 1980s, e.g. '16 July 1981 is a Monday; true or false?' Medium dates sampled the 1940s and 2020s. Remote dates featured the 1910s and 2050s. The control task presented statements such as '8 June 2055 is a June day: true or false?', using dates from all six decades.

Each task involved equal numbers of true and false statements. There were 60 different items for each of the arithmetic, first session calendrical task and control tasks and for each of the periods in the second session calendrical task. All calendrical task items concerned Mondays.

Testing occurred in two sessions for the savants and one for the normal participant. Problems were visually presented. The interval between problems was fixed at 8 s. Participants responded by pressing buttons with their left or right thumb to indicate true or false, respectively, and response times were recorded. Savants were scanned for four blocks in both sessions. In the first session, a block consisted of 30 items from a particular task (arithmetic or calendrical task dates) and 30 items from the corresponding control task. In the second session, a block consisted of 45 calendrical task items, 15 from each period and 15 control items. The normal participant received the two arithmetic blocks. The order of problems within each block was randomized.

(c) Data acquisition

Images were acquired using a 1.5 tesla Siemens Sonata MRI scanner to acquire gradient-echo, T2-weighted echo-planar images with blood oxygenation level-dependent contrast. Each volume comprised 36 axial slices of 2 mm thickness with 1 mm slice gap and 3×3 mm in plane resolution. Volumes were acquired continuously every 3.077 s. Each run began with six 'dummy' volumes discarded for analyses. At the end of each scanning session, a T1-weighted structural image was acquired.

(d) Data analysis

The images were analysed with SPM2 (Wellcome Department of Imaging Neuroscience, London, UK) using an event-related model (Josephs *et al.* 1997). To correct for motion, functional volumes were realigned to the first volume (Friston *et al.* 1995*a*), spatially normalized to a standard template with a resampled voxel size of $3 \times 3 \times 3$ mm and smoothed using a Gaussian kernel with a full width at half maximum of 8 mm. In addition, high-pass temporal filtering with a cut-off of 128 s was applied. After pre-processing, statistical analysis was carried out using the general linear model (Friston *et al.* 1995*b*). The response to each problem was modelled by convolving a 4 s boxcar starting at problem onset with a canonical haemodynamic response function to create regressors for each problem type. Problems that were incorrectly answered were omitted. Residual effects of head motion were corrected by including the six estimated motion parameters for each subject as regressors of no interest. Contrast images (e.g. arithmetic versus control problems) were then calculated by applying appropriate linear contrasts to the parameter estimates for the parametric regressor of each event. Probabilities are corrected for multiple comparisons using false discovery rate (FDR) unless stated otherwise. In session 2, regions where there was a relationship between activity and increasing remoteness of the date were identified by the conjunction of the contrasts (remote–medium) and (medium–close).

9.3 Results

According to an experienced clinical radiologist, inspection of the structural scans of the two savants indicated no structural abnormalities. We also looked for small scale differences in the structure using voxel-based morphometry (Ashburner & Friston 2000), but found no consistent differences in our two subjects in comparison with an age-matched control group. In particular, we found no differences in the parietal lobe.

(a) First session: mental arithmetic and calendrical I

(i) Mental arithmetic
Behavioural data are summarized in table 9.1. In testing GC, but not MW, there were a few invalid trials owing to the failure to press buttons (arithmetic, 7 out of 60; control, 8 out of 60). Table 9.1 shows both savants responded correctly to almost all valid trials and their response times were fast, although not as fast as the control subject.

Table 9.1 Accuracies and mean correct response times for arithmetic and calendrical tasks and corresponding control tasks.

Item type	Person	Period	Task Main Accuracy (%)	Mean response time (s)	s.d.	Control Accuracy (%)	Mean response time (s)	s.d.
arithmetic	GC		96	4.68	1.07	96	1.57	0.64
	MW		97	3.42	0.81	97	1.55	0.45
	control		95	2.86	0.86	97	1.06	0.22
calendrical I	GC		97	3.63	1.24	100	1.71	0.73
	MW		98	2.63	0.91	100	1.30	0.42
calendrical II	GC	close	96	3.51	1.19			
		medium	81	5.06	1.44	95	3.88	1.41
		remote	85	5.18	1.67			
	MW	close	100	2.05	0.59			
		medium	98	2.85	0.86	83	2.65	1.03
		remote	97	3.78	1.13			

Table 9.2 Areas of greater parietal activation during arithmetic reported by Menon et al. (2000) and observed in a control participant and calendrical savant GC. (Data from Menon et al. (2000) are copyright 2000 by Elsevier. Reprinted with permission.)

Location	MNI coordinates			z-values	p-values (FDR corrected)
	x	y	z		
Menon et al. (2000)					
inferior parietal lobe (BA40)	−48	−50	50	9.46	<0.0001
superior parietal lobe (BA7)	−26	−78	42	5.37	<0.0001
superior parietal lobe (BA7)	30	−76	40	5.61	<0.0001
control participant					
inferior parietal lobe (BA40)	−36	−36	42	7.46	<0.0001
superior parietal lobe (BA7)	−30	−60	48	>8.0	<0.0001
superior parietal lobe (BA7)	21	−69	51	>8.0	<0.0001
GC					
inferior parietal lobe (BA40)	−42	−54	42	4.14	<0.003
inferior parietal lobe (BA40)	39	−42	42	4.46	<0.001
superior parietal lobe (BA7)	−24	−60	42	4.48	<0.001
superior parietal lobe (BA7)	33	−60	39	4.78	<0.001

Unfortunately, MW's first session data could not be analysed further owing to the excessive head movement (within session movement more than 7 mm). Table 9.2 shows activation in parietal cortex while performing the mental arithmetic task (versus control) for the group reported by Menon et al. (2000), the control participant and GC. Both the control participant and GC show considerable correspondence with Menon et al.'s data. The only difference is the indication of bilateral activation of the inferior parietal region in GC.

(ii) Calendrical I

Table 9.1 shows the accuracies and response times for the two calendrical savants on the calendrical and control tasks. Accuracy was high on both the calendrical and control tasks and there were no invalid trials.

A conjunction analysis (Friston et al. 2005) was performed on the data for GC to identify regions that were activated by both the mental arithmetic and calendrical tasks. This analysis revealed activations in the same regions of parietal cortex (table 9.3).

Figure 9.1 shows all the activity in common between mental arithmetic and calendrical calculation in GC using the glass brain format. In addition to parietal cortex, activity

Table 9.3 Activity in the parietal lobe observed during mental arithmetic and calendrical I in GC.

Location	MNI coordinates			z-values	p-values (FDR corrected)
	x	y	z		
inferior parietal lobe (BA40)	−40	−56	52	4.48	<0.004
inferior parietal lobe (BA40)	40	−50	50	3.62	<0.041
superior parietal lobe (BA7)	−26	−68	52	3.84	<0.025
superior parietal lobe (BA7)	34	−64	52	4.08	<0.013

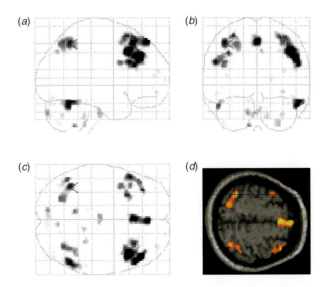

Figure 9.1 (*a–c*) Activity in common between mental arithmetic and calendrical calculation in GC using glass brain format. All voxels reaching a significance level of $p < 0.01$ (uncorrected) are shown. (*d*) The major regions superimposed on a horizontal slice from GC's structural scan.

can be seen in premotor cortex, the supplementary motor area and in left inferior temporal cortex. These areas were also activated by the mental arithmetic tasks in the study of Menon *et al.* (2000). Figure *1d* shows the major regions of activity superimposed on a horizontal slice from the structural scan of GC's brain.

(b) Second session

GC, but not MW, had a few invalid trials (close, 3 out of 60; medium, 6 out of 60; and remote, 7 out of 60). For valid trials, the overall accuracy was high, as table 9.1 shows. GC's accuracy for medium and remote dates was lower than that for close dates, but MW's accuracy did not vary: GC, $\chi^2_{2,164} = 6.45, p < 0.05;$ MW, $\chi^2_{2,180} = 2.03$, *ns*. MW made 10 errors on the task II control problems. All but one were correct answers to the corresponding calendrical question, suggesting that he failed either to recognize them as control items or to inhibit the response to the calendrical question.

Correct response times varied with remoteness of years according to analyses of log response times: GC, $F_{2,141} = 24.22, p < 0.0005, \eta^2 = 0.26$; MW, $F_{2,174} = 67.70, p < 0.0005, \eta^2 = 0.46$. Both answered close questions faster than medium but only MW took longer to answer remote than medium questions, according to *post hoc* Ryan–Einot–Gabriel–Welsch range comparisons (*ps* < 0.05).

Neither savant showed excessive head movement during scanning. For GC, we could predict which regions in parietal cortex should show increasing activity with increasing remoteness on the basis of the first session. For MW, however, we had not been able to identify the relevant regions. As a strict test of the replicability of the results for GC, we used the regions identified for GC in the first session to guide our analysis of the data for MW in the second session. These were the two most significant regions of parietal cortex

Table 9.4 Activity in the parietal cortex associated with increasing distance of dates in calendrical II. Coordinates (used for the plots in Figure 9.2) are of the nearest location to activations in conjunction analysis of arithmetic and calendrical I for GC and peaks in an unconstrained analysis of effects of increasing remoteness of dates.

Savant	Nearest location to conjunction activations			Peaks in unconstrained analysis				
	Coordinates			Coordinates				
	x	y	z	x	y	z	z-values	p-values
GC	−40	−58	48	−42	−54	46	2.91	<0.002[a]
	34	−64	40	30	−56	40	2.95	<0.002[a]
MW	−42	−48	46	−42	−40	40	4.30	<0.004[b]
	30	−70	48	22	−70	52	4.62	<0.002[b]

[a] uncorrected.
[b] FDR corrected

identified from the conjunction analysis of GC's mental arithmetic and calendrical calculation (left parietal cortex (−40, −56, 52), right parietal cortex (34, −64, 52); table 9.3). The nearest locations where there was significant activity (uncorrected) in session 2 were used to plot the data shown in Figure 9.2. In addition, we performed an unconstrained analysis to identify the regions where activity increased with increasing remoteness of dates.

Table 9.4 shows the coordinates so identified. The regions of interest identified from the conjunction analysis of the first session for GC were included in clusters identified by the unconstrained analysis for both GC and MW. Figure 9.2 shows response time and associated activity in the parietal cortex on the same graph, as in Pinel et al. (2001). It reveals a striking correspondence between the increase in response time and neural activity with increasing date distance.

9.4 Discussion

Despite some limitations, we were able to conduct a case study with one savant, GC, and a normal participant and replicate it with a second savant, MW. The results do contribute to our knowledge of savants, and, in particular, understanding why they take longer to answer questions about more remote dates.

When GC was doing mental arithmetic, the peaks of activation were in regions associated with arithmetic in studies of normal people (Menon et al. 2000). The conjunction analysis indicated that it was these regions that were particularly active when solving date problems. Data from the second session showed that it was these regions that increased in activity in both GC and MW when asked questions about more remote years.

For these savants, it seems that the relationship between response time and remoteness from the present reflects increased calculation for remote dates as hypothesized by O'Connor & Hermelin (1984). Whether this is generally true for savants who vary in response time with period is a matter for future research.

More tentatively, the lack of abnormalities revealed by the brain scans of the two savants does not support the proposal that all savants are severely brain damaged

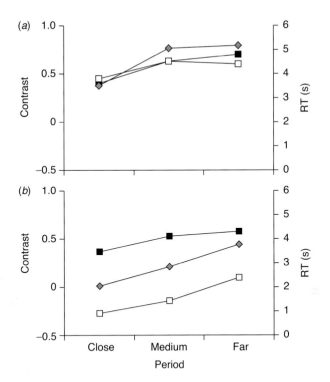

Figure 9.2 Correspondence between brain activation estimates in left (filled squares) and right (open squares) parietal regions and reaction times (RT; diamonds) for each savant with increasing date distance. Activation estimates are in contrast to those for the control task. (*a*) The data for GC in left parietal region (−40, −58, 48) and right parietal region (34, −64, 40) are shown. (*b*) MW's data in left parietal region (−42, −48, 46) and right parietal region (30, −70, 48) are shown.

(Snyder & Mitchell 1999), or that savant skills are achieved by rededication of low-level perceptual systems (Mottron *et al.* 2006).

In summary, the calendrical skills of savants are most plausibly considered to develop from practice and extensive study of calendars. The skills may be unusual but they do not, in these two cases at least, seem to involve any abnormal cognitive processes or depend on fundamentally different brains.

The idea for this study originated in conversations with Neil O'Connor. We are grateful to Dr John Stevens for assessing the scans for structural abnormalities and to Professor Cathy Price for carrying out the voxel-based morphometry.

References

Ashburner, J. & Friston, K. J. 2000 Voxel-based morphometry—the methods. *NewoImage* **11**, 805–821. (doi:10.1006/nimg.2000.0582)
Berlekamp, E. R., Conway, J. H. & Guy, R. K. 1982 *Winning ways.* New York, NY: Academic Press.
Carroll, L. 1887 To find the day of the week for any given date. *Nature* **35**, 517. (doi:10.1038/035517a0)

Cowan, R. & Carney, D. 2006 Calendrical savants: exceptionality and practice. *Cognition* **100**, B1–B9. (doi:10.1016/j.cognition.2005.08.001)

Cowan, R., O'Connor, N. & Samella, K. 2001 Why and how people of limited intelligence become calendrical calculators. *Infancia y Aprendizaje* **93**, 53–65. (doi:10.1174/021037001316899811)

Cowan, R., O'Connor, N. & Samella, K. 2003 The skills and methods of calendrical savants. *Intelligence* **31**, 51–65. (doi:10.1016/S0160-2896(02)00119-8)

Cowan, R., Stainthorp, R., Kapnogianni, S. & Anastasiou, M. 2004 The development of calendrical skills. *Cogn. Dev.* **19**, 169–178. (doi:10.1016/j.cogdev.2003.11.005)

Dehaene, S., Piazza, M., Pinel, P. & Cohen, L. 2003 Three parietal circuits for number processing. *Cogn. Neuro-psychol.* **20**, 487–506. (doi:10.1080/02643290244000239)

Dorman, C. 1991 Exceptional calendar calculation ability after early left hemispherectomy. *Brain Cogn.* **15**, 26–36. (doi:10.1016/0278-2626(91)90013-X)

Dowker, A. 1998 Individual differences in normal arithmetical development. In *The development of mathematical skills* (ed. C. Donlan), pp. 275–302. Hove, UK: Psychology Press.

Friston, K. J., Ashburner, J., Poline, J. P., Frith, C. D., Heather, J. D. & Frackowiak, R. S. 1995a Spatial registration and normalization of images. *Hum. Brain Mapp.* **2**, 165–188. (doi:10.1002/hbm.460030303)

Friston, K. J., Holmes, A. P., Worsley, K. J., Poline, J. P., Frith, C. D. & Frackowiak, R. S. 1995b Statistical parametric maps in functional imaging: a general linear approach. *Hum. Brain Mapp.* **2**, 189–210. (doi:10.1002/hbm.460020402)

Friston, K. J., Penny, W. D. & Glaser, D. E. 2005 Conjunction revisited. *NeuroImage* **25**, 661–667. (doi:10.1016/j.neuroimage.2005.01.013)

Frith, U. 2003 *Autism: explaining the enigma*. Oxford, UK: Blackwell.

Happé, F. G. E. 1994 Wechsler IQ profile and theory of mind in autism: a research note. *J. Child Psychol. Psychiatry* **35**, 1461–1471. (doi:10.1111/j.1469-7610.1994.tb01287.x)

Hermelin, B. & O'Connor, N. 1986 Idiot savant calendrical calculators: rules and regularities. *Psychol. Med.* **16**, 885–893.

Ho, E. D. F., Tsang, A. K. T. & Ho, D. Y. F. 1991 An investigation of the calendar calculation ability of a Chinese calendar savant. *J. Autism Dev. Disord.* **21**, 315–327. (doi:10.1007/BF02207328)

Hoffman, E. 1971 The idiot savant: a case report and review of explanations. *Menu Retard.* **9**, 18–21.

Horwitz, W. A., Kestenbaum, C, Person, E. & Jarvik, L. 1965 Identical twin 'idiot savants'- calendar calculators. *Am. J. Psychiatry* **121**, 1075–1079.

Horwitz, W. A., Deming, W. E. & Winter, R. F. 1969 A further account of the idiots savants, experts with the calendar. *Am. J. Psychiatry* **126**, 412–415.

Hurst, L. C. & Mulhall, D. J. 1988 Another calendar savant. *Br. J. Psychiatry* **152**, 274–277. (doi:10.1192/bjp.152.2.274)

Jackson, M. & Warrington, E. K. 1986 Arithmetic skills in patients with unilateral cerebral lesions. *Cortex* **22**, 611–620.

Josephs, O., Turner, R. & Friston, K. J. 1997 Event-related fMRI. *Hum. Brain Mapp.* **5**, 243–248. (doi:10.1002/(SICI)1097-0193(1997)5:4 < 243::AID-HBM7 > 3.0.CO;2-3)

Menon, V., Rivera, S. M., White, C. D., Glover, G. H. & Reiss, A. L. 2000 Dissociating prefrontal and parietal cortex activation during arithmetic processing. *NeuroImage* **12**, 357–365. (doi:10.1006/nimg.2000.0613)

Mottron, L., Lemmens, K., Gagnon, L. & Seron, X. 2006 Non-algorithmic access to calendar information in a calendar calculator with autism. *J. Autism Dev. Disord.* **36**, 239–247. (doi:10.1007/sl0803-005-0059-9)

Nieder, A. 2005 Counting on neurons: the neurobiology of numerical competence. *Nat. Rev. Neurosci.* **6**, 177–190. (doi:10.1038/nrnl626)

O'Connor, N. 1989 The performance of the 'idiot-savant': implicit and explicit. *Br. J. Disord. Commun.* **24**, 1–20. (doi:10.3109/13682828909011943)

O'Connor, N. & Hermelin, B. 1984 Idiot savant calendrical calculators: maths or memory? *Psychol. Med.* **14**, 801–806.

O'Connor, N. & Hermelin, B. 1987 Visual and graphic abilities of the idiot savant artist. *Psychol. Med.* **17**, 79–90.

O'Connor, N., Cowan, R. & Samella, K. 2000 Calendrical calculation and intelligence. *Intelligence* **28**, 31–48. (doi:10.1016/S0160-2896(99)00028-8)

Pinel, P., Dehaene, S., Riviere, D. & LeBihan, D. 2001 Modulation of parietal activation by semantic distance in a number comparison task. *NeuroImage* **14**, 1013–1026. (doi:10.1006/nimg.2001.0913)

Pinel, P., Piazza, M., Le Bihan, D. & Dehaene, S. 2004 Distributed and overlapping cerebral representations of number, size, and luminance during comparative judgments. *Neuron* **41**, 983–993. (doi:10.1016/S0896-6273(04)00107-2)

Rosen, A. M. 1981 Adult calendar calculators in a psychiatric OPD: a report of two cases and comparative analysis of abilities. *J. Autism Dev. Disord.* **11**, 285–292. (doi:10.1007/BF01531511)

Saloviita, T., Ruusila, L. & Ruusila, U. 2000 Incidence of savant syndrome in Finland. *Percept. Mot. Skills* **91**, 120–122. (doi:10.2466/PMS.91.5.120-122)

Scheerer, M., Rothmann, E. & Goldstein, K. 1945 A case of 'idiot savant': an experimental study of personality organization. *Psychol. Monogr.* **58**, 1–63.

Sloboda, J. A., Hermelin, B. & O'Connor, N. 1985 An exceptional musical memory. *Music Percept.* **3**, 155–170.

Snyder, A. W. & Mitchell, D. J. 1999 Is integer arithmetic fundamental to mental processing?: the mind's secret arithmetic. *Proc. R. Soc. Lond.* B **266**, 587–592. (doi:10.1098/rspb.1999.0676)

Thioux, M., Stark, D. E., Klaiman, C. & Schultz, R. T. 2006 The day of the week when you were born in 700 ms: calendar computation in an Autistic savant. *J. Exp. Psychol. Hum. Percept. Perform.* **32**, 1155–1168. (doi:10.1037/0096-1523.32.5.1155)

Tredgold, R. F. & Soddy, K. 1956 *Tredgold's text-book of mental deficiency.* London, UK: Balliere, Tindall and Cox.

10

A case study of a multiply talented savant with an autism spectrum disorder: neuropsychological functioning and brain morphometry

Gregory L. Wallace, Francesca Happé and Jay N. Giedd

> Neuropsychological functioning and brain morphometry in a savant (case GW) with an autism spectrum disorder (ASD) and both calendar calculation and artistic skills are quantified and compared with small groups of neurotypical controls. Good memory, mental calculation and visuospatial processing, as well as (implicit) knowledge of calendar structure and 'weak' central coherence characterized the cognitive profile of case GW. Possibly reflecting his savant skills, the superior parietal region of GW's cortex was the only area thicker (while areas such as the superior and medial prefrontal, middle temporal and motor cortices were thinner) than that of a neurotypical control group. Taken from the perspective of learning/practice-based models, skills in domains (e.g. calendars, art, music) that capitalize upon strengths often associated with ASD, such as detail-focused processing, are probably further enhanced through over-learning and massive exposure, and reflected in atypical brain structure.
>
> **Keywords:** autism; savant; weak central coherence; implicit learning; neuroanatomy; magnetic resonance imaging

10.1 Introduction

Autism spectrum disorders (ASD) are associated with a remarkable combination of cognitive strengths and difficulties. The same individual may struggle to express or understand speech, while demonstrating amazingly good memory for routes, or fantastic understanding of mechanical systems. In some cases, special abilities are so pronounced that savant skills or 'islands of genius' may be considered to be present. Over the years, there have been many case, and some group, studies of savant skills (for review, see Treffert 1989; Hermelin 2001; Heaton & Wallace 2004). Although there have been reports of multiple skills possessed by a single individual (e.g. performance and memory skills for music; Hermelin *et al.* 1989), there have been limited reports of multiple skills across unrelated domains (e.g. music and maths). Furthermore, cognitive and neural mechanisms underlying savant skill development and expression remain elusive.

The case presented here, involving both neuropsychological assessment and structural neuroimaging, complements and adds to the extant literature, because this savant presents skills in two domains: art and calendar calculations. In addition to the assessment of IQ, calendar calculation, mental calculation, memory and general visuospatial abilities, we tested three broad neuropsychological domains hypothesized to be relevant to savant skill development (Heaton & Wallace 2004): (i) 'weak' central coherence, (ii) implicit learning, and (iii) information processing speed (reviewed below). To assess potential neural correlates of his exceptional calculation and artistic abilities, we examined cortical thickness from a structural magnetic resonance image of his brain.

(a) Weak central coherence

A large body of evidence (for review, see Happé & Frith 2006) suggests that individuals with autism tend to favour local over global processing, opposite to the typical pattern. This bias, termed 'weak central coherence' (WCC), is reflected in, for example, relative strength on the block design subtest of the Wechsler Intelligence Scales, where ability to see a whole design in terms of its parts, and ability to resist the gestalt, is advantageous (Happé, 1994). Similarly, individuals with ASD often outperform controls on the embedded figures test (EFT; Witkin *et al.* 1971), in which a simple shape (e.g. a triangle) must be spotted within a more complex figure (Shah & Frith 1983).

This detail-focused cognitive style may relate to the expression and development of savant skills, including calendar calculation and artistic abilities. For calendar calculation, Heavey *et al.* (1999) suggest that the calendars can be broken down into 'fragments' of dates. Combining the natural tendency to segment large chunks of information with idiosyncratic interest in dates, calendar calculation skills may emerge. Happé & Frith (2006) suggest that stringing together calendar facts in the service of calendar calculation is indicative of 'local' coherence (analogous to processing grammar in language).

Artistic abilities also may rely upon good detail focus. Mottron & Belleville (1993) provided the example of a savant artist who approached his drawings in a piecemeal fashion, while a professional draughtsman who served as a control used outlines in his drawings initially, then progressed to more detailed elements. Furthermore, both savant artists with autism and typically developing artists obtain high scores on the block design task (Pring *et al.* 1995). This shared facility for segmenting patterns in both artists and those with autism suggests that WCC may contribute to the over-representation of savant skills in ASD.

(b) Implicit learning

'Implicit', or unintentional, learning has a number of definitions and associated theoretical accounts. What most share is the notion of an implicit knowledge base developed through non-conscious learning. The notion of implicit learning has particular appeal when explaining some savants' untrained abilities, and may help to explain savants' aptitude for learning relationships in a specific set of domains. Just as for neurotypical individuals participating in implicit learning studies, savants (particularly calendar calculators) cannot tell you how they know the right answer or they will give you false answers when queried. Furthermore, savants' engagement in high levels of training, practice and exposure to domain-specific information may lead to implicit learning of component properties. (see Chapter 3) suggest that reduced awareness of one's own mental states (part of a theory of mind deficit) may increase the likelihood of implicit learning, and reduce interfering attempts at explicit rule extraction, which are known to hamper performance on certain sorts of tasks (e.g. artificial grammars; Reber 1993). 'Systemizing', which includes implicit or explicit rule extraction as applied to predictable and lawful 'systems', is a purported strength in ASD and may be related to savant skill development (see

Baron-Cohen *et al.* 2009). Thus far, the limited evidence suggests intact implicit learning among individuals with ASD (Klinger *et al.* 2006; Barnes *et al.* 2008), although at least one study has found impaired implicit learning (Mostofsky *et al.* 2000).

Although researchers have suggested a role for implicit learning in savant skill development for some time (Treffert 1989; Hermelin 2001), this possibility has not been assessed empirically using traditional tasks. In the most relevant study to date, a musical savant demonstrated outstanding incidental learning of digit-symbol pairs (with no instruction to remember these paired associations) from the coding subtest of the Wechsler Scales (Lucci *et al.* 1988). Even though there was limited opportunity to learn the associations (exposure time was only 90 s) and the savant performed poorly on the coding portion of the task (i.e. number correct), perfect recall of all nine paired associates was accomplished.

(c) Information processing speed

According to some theorists (e.g. Anderson 2001), information processing speed forms the basis of individual differences in IQ. Evidence is derived mostly from correlations (around $r = -0.50$; Grudnik & Kranzler 2001) between measures of general intelligence and inspection time (IT), a method for assessing speed of information processing not reliant on motor speed. IT is measured by establishing the minimum stimulus exposure needed for an individual to accurately discriminate a simple stimulus feature. The IT task design avoids difficulties inherent to reaction time (RT) studies, such as motoric and 'thinking time' confounds especially relevant when an individual is unsure how to respond, possibly resulting in a 'speed/accuracy trade-off'.

IT among individuals with ASD has been reported to be (i) much better than expected, based upon measured IQ, (ii) equal to that of a typically developing group with mean IQ scores 25 points higher, (iii) significantly better than that of a non-ASD intellectually impaired group (Scheuffgen *et al.* 2000) and (iv) uniquely uncorrelated with IQ, unlike for controls (Wallace *et al.* 2009). Scheuffgen *et al.* argue that, if information processing speed is good among individuals with autism, some other aspect(s) of cognition are responsible for the low measured IQ frequently observed in autism—and suggest social insight and socially mediated learning to be responsible.

Rapid processing of stimuli would certainly be advantageous for mastering savant domains. Anderson *et al.* (1998) showed that the IT of a savant prime number calculator with autism was consistent with that of typical university undergraduates, but inconsistent with his own low measured IQ. Based on the findings from these studies, it may be that intact or superior processing speed is one factor contributing to the high rates of savant skills in ASD.

(d) Neural correlates of calculation and artistic abilities

A growing body of research has examined the neural correlates of calculation and to a lesser extent artistic abilities. Most functional neuroimaging studies (see Dehaene *et al.* 2004 for review) indicate a role for the superior parietal lobe, particularly the intra-parietal sulcus (IPS), in the processing of numbers (including Cowan and Frith's study of two calendar calculators, Cowan & Frith (2009)). The IPS also has been linked to calculation difficulties through structural neuroimaging studies. For example, dys-calculic adolescents with a history of very low birth weight and premature birth had grey matter reduction in the left parietal lobe (in the vicinity of the IPS) when compared with other adolescents with similar histories but no current presentation of mathematical difficulties (Isaacs et al. 2001).

Although the neural correlates of artistic ability have not been examined thoroughly, at least one study has examined the neural correlates of drawing behaviour using functional neuroimaging. Makuuchi et al. (2003) consistently observed bilateral (particularly superior) parietal lobe activations across participants when they were asked to 'draw in the air' a contour of an object depicted on a screen. Furthermore, visual mental imagery, a skill potentially relevant to talent in the visual arts, is also associated with activation in the superior parietal lobe (e.g. Guillot et al. 2009). Thus, based on the evidence collected so far, calculation and artistic abilities share mediation within the (particularly superior) parietal lobes.

Savants, particularly those with autism, exhibit circumscribed interests, usually within their skill area (O'Connor & Hermelin 1991), which leads to considerable rehearsal, practice and training. There are several studies now showing measurable structural brain differences after individuals practise various tasks over shorter (e.g. juggling; Draganski et al. 2004) or longer (e.g. the 'Knowledge' learnt by London taxi drivers; Maguire et al. 2000) periods of training. Savants represent a clear case of expertise and over-learning within restricted domains. We therefore used structural neuroimaging to assess possible neural correlates of calculation and artistic expertise, with the prediction of changes in superior parietal regions implicated in both domains.

10.2 Hypotheses

(a) Neuropsychological study

In comparison with age- and IQ-matched neurotypical participants, GW is predicted to exhibit: (i) WCC, (ii) superior implicit learning, and (iii) superior IT. In comparison with the existing norms, it was predicted that GW would exhibit superior recognition memory, spatial reasoning abilities and mental calculation abilities. GW also is expected to demonstrate exceptional calendar calculation and a priming effect resulting in a relative RT gain when consecutive dates from the same calendar template are presented to him.

(b) Neuroimaging study

In comparison with age- and IQ-matched neurotypical controls, GW's cortex is predicted to be relatively thicker in superior parietal regions (areas implicated in both calculation and artistic abilities) but thinner in medial prefrontal and temporal areas (regions associated with social cognition, a domain of impairment in ASD; Frith & Frith 2006).

10.3 Material and methods

(a) Participants

(i) Case GW
GW is a 42-year-old right-handed male diagnosed with Asperger's syndrome as an adult (and meeting screening criteria for an ASD according to the Social Communication Questionnaire), who demonstrates both superior calendar calculation skill and high-level

artistic abilities. Atypically, GW reports he was not very interested in calendars as a child, but instead developed these abilities as an adult. However, GW reports that at age 5 or 6 years, he remembers seeing his grandmother's calendar and 'knowing' dates for 'only a couple of years'. Although he dabbled in young adulthood, GW did not begin calendar calculation over large ranges until he was 32 years old. Similar to other calendar calculators, he cannot tell you precisely how he does it, but he 'just knows' the answer and it usually 'feels right'.

GW reports that he has been drawing 'as long as he can remember' and has always excelled in this endeavour; he was usually considered the best drawer in his class throughout his school years. As a young child, his drawings were usually focused on a single object, but later his subject matter broadened in scope. GW's unique artistic style has changed over time, going from drawings of scenes and buildings during adolescence, to more abstract impressionist style paintings as a young adult and then back again to technical-type drawings of real and/or imaginary machines, for example, although with more stylistic elements included (Figure 10.1). GW's work has attracted interest from galleries across the USA and Europe resulting in numerous exhibitions and requests for commissioned artwork.

Two art judges (one has previously judged art competitions and the other has experience as a judge and also as a curator) were asked to evaluate GW's artwork. Both were highly

Figure 10.1 Example of GW's artwork.

laudatory of GW's work and style and, without hesitation, favourably compared GW's work with that of other contemporary artists who exhibit widely and sell very successfully.

(ii) Comparison groups

Seven neurotypical adult males of approximately the same age and IQ as GW (see table 10.1 for details) were recruited to serve as controls for the neuropsychological study. An additional group of 14 neurotypical adult males, group-matched to GW's age ($M = 36.54 \pm 5.48$; $t = 1.30$, $p = 0.22$) and to his vocabulary score from the Wechsler Scale ($M = 13.54 \pm 1.90$; $t = 0.78$, $p = 0.45$) in 13 out of the 14 (one missing), acted as controls for the neuroimaging study.

Informed consent was obtained from all participants.

(b) Measures

(i) Standardized neuropsychological tasks

Wechsler Adult Intelligence Scale-3rd Edition **(WAIS-III)** is a widely used assessment of intelligence with excellent psychometric properties. Case GW was tested on 11 subtests

Table 10.1 GW's scores from clinical neuropsychological measures. (Note: WAIS-III subtest and GDA scores are presented in scaled score format ($M = 10 \pm 3$) while WAIS-III index and IQ scores as well as WJ-R and WRAT-3 scores are presented in standard score format ($M = 100 \pm 15$).

Measure	GW's score
Wechsler Adult Intelligence Scale-III (WAIS-III)	
vocabulary	12
similarities	4
information	14
verbal comprehension index: (vocabulary + similarities + information)	*100*
arithmetic	11
digit span	9
comprehension	9
verbal IQ	*98*
picture completion	14
block design	11
matrix reasoning	13
perceptual organization index: (picture completion + block design + matrix reasoning)	*116*
digit symbol	7
picture arrangement	8
performance/non-verbal IQ	*104*
full-scale IQ	*100*
Woodcock–Johnson Revised (WJ-R)	
picture recognition	111
spatial relations	113
Wide Range Achievement Test-3 (WRAT-3)	
arithmetic	110
Graded Difficulty Arithmetic Test (GDA)	16

from the WAIS-III. The vocabulary and block design short form of the WAIS-III was administered to estimate full-scale IQ in the control group.

Picture recognition is a subtest from the Woodcock-Johnson-Revised (WJ-R) Cognitive Battery testing visuospatial recognition. The participant views briefly a number of line drawings of everyday objects, and must then choose those previously seen from an array of familiar and distracter images.

Spatial Relations is a subtest of the WJ-R in which participants must select which parts from an array would be needed to form a target whole or complete shape.

Wide Range Achievement Test-3 (WRAT-3) *Arithmetic Subtest* measures basic mathematical skills, requiring solution (using paper and pencil) of simple to complex mathematical problems ranging from basic mechanics to algebraic equations.

Graded Difficulty Arithmetic Test (GDA; Jackson & Warrington 1986) requires participants to answer rapidly (within 10 s) 12 addition and 12 subtraction problems varying from two digit ± one digit numbers to three digit ± three digit numbers, without the use of paper and pencil.

Previously administered to GW, and reported here as relevant, were: the *Wisconsin Card Sorting Test* (WCST) assessing cognitive flexibility; copying and drawing *Rey–Osterrieth Complex Figure* from memory after a 30 min interval; and the *Hooper Visual Organization Test* assessing the ability to identify a whole object from its cut up and rearranged parts.

(ii) Experimental tasks

EFT (Witkin *et al.* 1971) requires participants to find as quickly as possible a simple shape (e.g. a triangle) hidden within a larger, more complex figure. A combination of seven items from the children's and eight items from the standard (adult's) EFT were administered. Scoring is based on per cent correct and time (limit of 60 s per item) needed to locate each embedded figure.

Implicit learning was assessed using a new pattern sequence task combining serial RT/statistical learning methods (Kirkham *et al.* 2002). Participants pressed the green mouse button when they saw a green shape and the yellow mouse button when they saw a yellow shape appear in the centre of the computer display; no button press to be made to any other coloured shape (i.e. blue triangle or pink square). Within the structured condition, the appearance of the pink square predicted perfectly the appearance next of the green circle, while the contingency for all non-predictable shape co-occurrences was equated at 33 per cent. The chance of any of the four possible shapes appearing was equated (i.e. 25% each) across the entire task. In order to document implicit learning, an RT difference score was calculated by subtracting the RT to the green, predictable shape from the RT to the yellow, non-predictable shape with the resulting quotient divided by the participant's RT to the yellow shape, to account for differences in baseline visuo-motor speed. The gain in proportional RT between the first and second halves of the task was used to indicate a 'learning effect'.

IT was measured using a computerized task (Anderson *et al.* 1998), with four blocks of 25 stimulus presentations of a 'space invader' figure with two antennae of either the same or different lengths. The participant was asked to indicate whether the lengths of the antennae were the same or different by pressing one of two buttons. Stimulus duration (followed by a mask) was systematically varied to establish a 70 per cent accuracy level, using a parameter estimation by sequential testing (PEST) procedure (see Scheuffgen *et al.* (2000) for further details).

(iii) Questionnaires

GW and the matched controls were asked to complete the *Folk Physics Test* (Baron-Cohen *et al.* 2001) which is composed of 20 multiple-choice questions designed to assess an individual's understanding of the workings of macro- (e.g. gravity) and micro-level physical systems based on everyday experience with the physical world. The *Systemizing Quotient* (SQ; Baron-Cohen *et al.* 2003), a self-rating scale, was used to assess a participant's tendency to 'systemize' in everyday contexts.

(iv) Savant domain assessment

Calendar Performance Tests (Cowan *et al.* 2003) were given to assess the knowledge of day-date correspondence (accuracy and RT) over a large span of years in the Gregorian calendar (90 items), and later years from the Julian calendar (25 items). Calendar knowledge was also assessed by having GW calculate the day on which two identical dates from different years fell (18 pairs); the dates shared the same calendar template (e.g. 5 April 2005 and 5 April 1994), which should result in faster RT on the second date if (implicit or explicit) knowledge of this template was used as a strategy (Hermelin & O'Connor 1986). Priming was therefore assessed and operationalized through the calculation of a percentage savings score.

(v) Cortical thickness quantification from structural neuroimaging

One hundred and twenty four contiguous 1.5 mm axial slices from T1-weighted magnetic resonance images were obtained with a three-dimensional spoiled gradient recalled echo in the steady state on a 1.5 T General Electric Signa scanner (Milwaukee, WI, USA). Grey and white matter surfaces with over 80 000 polygons, each fitted and nonlinearly aligned, were derived (Robbins *et al.* 2004). Each vertex of the white matter surface corresponds to a grey matter surface counterpart, thereby creating linked polygons on the grey and white matter surfaces. The distance between corresponding vertices of the grey and white matter boundaries is then used to define cortical thickness. A 30 mm surface-based blurring kernel that maximizes statistical power and minimizes false positives (Lerch & Evans 2005) was used. Cortical thickness (CT) was calculated in native space at 40 962 cortical points in each hemisphere for a total of 81 924 cortical points across the entire cortex. Using z-scores ((control group CT mean GW's CT)/control group CT standard deviation), maps were created in which GW's cortex was at least: one standard deviation thinner than the mean of the control group (figure 10.2a) or one standard deviation thicker than the mean of the control group (figure 10.2b) for each of the 81 924 vertices.

10.4 Results

(a) Neuropsychological tasks and questionnaires

Table 10.1 shows GW's scores on the standardized neuropsychological assessments. Note that GW's IQ was in the average range, and neither digit span nor arithmetic was outstanding within the Wechsler Scales, although the GDA did show extremely good skills of mental addition and subtraction.

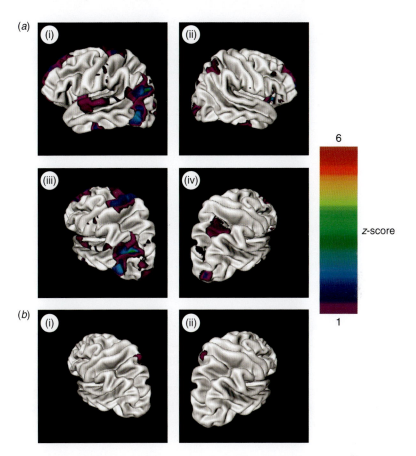

Figure 10.2 Cortical regions (*a*i–iv) thinner and (*b*i,ii) thicker for GW than for controls.

Table 10.2 shows GW's performance, and that of the comparison group, on the experimental tasks, as well as the short-form IQ subtests used for approximate matching. GW showed fast and accurate EFT performance, and IT performance as good as that of the controls, who had slightly higher measured IQ. Group differences (using a modified t-test; Crawford & Howell 1998) did not reach significance; however, a large effect size (Cohen's $d > 0.80$) was noted for EFT speed.

The positive proportional RT scores for both GW and controls indicate that an RT benefit was derived from the predictable sequence of shapes, even after accounting for baseline differences in RT. In other words, implicit learning of shape co-occurrences was demonstrated for case GW and for the group of controls as a whole.

In previous testing (3 years earlier), GW exhibited some difficulty in completing the WCST. He was able to use feedback to shift problem-solving sets, but he sometimes 'lost set' and then became fixated on matching sets by colour. GW adequately copied the Rey–Osterrieth Complex Figure, but when asked to recall the figure approximately 30 min later, his strategy was fragmented leading to a disorganized figure. His performance at recall fell in the bottom 10 per cent of performance on this task for comparably

Table 10.2 Performance on experimental tasks administered to GW and the comparison group, and matching variables: mean ± s.d.

	GW	Control group ($n = 7$)	t	p-value	Cohen's d
Age	42	40.68 ± 7.45	0.17	0.87	0.17
full-scale IQ	100[a]	111.57 ± 11.80	0.92	0.39	0.98
vocabulary	12	12.29 ± 3.40	0.08	0.94	0.09
block design	11	11.71 ± 1.60	0.42	0.69	0.44
EFT					
percentage correct	93	86 ± 10	0.65	0.54	0.70
mean time	9.07	19.59 ± 7.40	1.33	0.23	1.42
implicit learning proportional RT gain: first versus second half	0.10	0.06 ± 0.18	0.20	0.85	0.22
IT (ms)	39	33.43 ± 8.54	0.61	0.56	0.65

[a] Based on all subtests from the WAIS-III, not the two subtest short form (vocabulary and block design) as used for the control group.

aged neurotypical adults. On the Hooper Visual Organization Test, GW excelled at identifying objects based on line drawings of their parts, correctly identifying all 30 items.

On the questionnaire measures, GW's self-rating for systemizing (33) was not significantly higher than the mean for the comparison group (24.9 ± 9.9; $t = 0.76$, $p = 0.47$), but the effect size was large (Cohen's $d = 0.82$). His Folk Physics performance (55%) was below that of the comparison group ($M = 63.57 ± 18.19$), again with no significant difference ($t = 0.44$, $p = 0.67$; Cohen's $d = 0.47$).

(b) Savant domain assessment
Overall calendar performance was excellent, with 92 per cent correct for dates 1828–1836 and 2017–2024, 85 per cent for years 1772–1777 and 2072–2165, and 96 per cent for 2363–8378 in the Gregorian calendar. For dates from the Julian calendar (1591–1751), GW obtained 84 per cent correct.

The priming study showed that GW saved just less than 1 (0.83) second per pair (15 s across 18 pairs). Although this is a small amount, the baseline RTs were very fast: a total of 48 s on initial items and 33 s on the second items in pairs, amounting to a savings of 15/48 = 0.3125 or 31.25 per cent savings, which is a relatively large savings score and evidence of 'priming' based on knowledge of calendar regularities.

(c) Cortical thickness quantification

For GW relative to controls ($z > 1$), thinner cortex was found in bilateral superior frontal gyrus, medial prefrontal cortex (Brodmann area 8), left primary motor/precentral gyrus (Brodmann area 4) and left middle temporal gyrus (Brodmann area 39) among others (figure 10.2*a*), while thicker cortex was limited to bilateral portions of the superior parietal region (Brodmann area 7; figure 10.2*b*).

10.5 Discussion

(a) Neuropsychological study

GW's easily quantifiable skill, calendar calculation, was 'prodigious' (Treffert 1989), even by calendar savant standards. Although GW is not flawless in his calendar calculations, his excellent performance in terms of accuracy and RT did not vary considerably based on temporal distance from the present and his calendar range is practically endless (years tested here ranged from 1591 to 8378). Similarly, the two art judges enthusiastically endorsed GW's artistic abilities as comparable with those of professional artists who regularly exhibit in the community.

Overall GW's general, verbal and non-verbal IQs fell in the average range, but with considerable scatter across the subtests. GW's perceptual organization index was one standard deviation above his verbal comprehension index, but was not exceptional. This relative visuospatial strength was corroborated on the Hooper test and WJ-R visuospatial tasks.

GW scored in the average to above average range on a measure of written arithmetic. However, GW's GDA (mental calculation) total score (correctly answering 21 out of 24 items, each within 10 s) placed him in the 99th centile (Jackson & Warrington 1986). Therefore, it is likely that a significant component to GW's superior calendar calculating ability, especially his extraordinary range, is good, rapid mental calculation ability. Indeed, Cowan *et al.* (2003), also using the GDA, found that 4 out of 10 calendar savants performed at superior levels when compared with the same standardization sample.

Memory has been implicated in calendar calculation and other savant skills although rarely do savants score highly on standardized tasks. GW performed above average on a visuospatial recognition task, roughly commensurate with his overall IQ (as was his digit span). However, there is evidence that GW's memory, especially for numerical information, is excellent, similar to previous reports of superior memory within a savant's area of talent (O'Connor & Hermelin 1989). He recently memorized the exact populations for hundreds, if not thousands, of cities in the USA, based on the latest census data. When informally questioned on approximately 50 randomly chosen cities (population above 30 000), GW incorrectly recalled only a single digit among these population values. Moreover, when asked again eight months later the populations associated with 10 out of these 50 cities, he made no errors.

A difference in speed of calendar calculation, expressed as a savings score, was demonstrated between those (pairing of) items where the same calendar template could be used and those where it could not. This finding not only corroborates indirect documentation of rule use by calendar savants (Hermelin & O'Connor 1986), but also provides evidence of calendar structure knowledge by GW, ruling out the explanation that his calendar skills are nothing more than memory feats. Indeed, taken together with GW's good mental calculation abilities, it is clear that GW, similar to other calendar savants, may rely on both memory and rule use in his calendar calculation, with good calculation abilities serving to extend his calendar range well into the future.

In contrast to GW's flexible approach to art (given the various styles and techniques he has used, unlike many other savant artists), he demonstrated perseveration and an occasional inability to maintain a problem-solving set on the WCST. Also surprising was GW's poor incidental memory for the Rey figure. His reproduction from memory was characterized by a fragmented approach, similar to the graphic savant described by Mottron & Belleville (1993). This might be taken as a sign of detail focus or weak coherence. Also suggestive of this cognitive style is GW's accurate and fast EFT performance, which compared with that of control participants was not significantly different, but was associated with a large effect size.

GW demonstrated intact implicit learning and IT that was comparable with that of the control group. At least one previously studied savant has shown surprisingly good IT, although he also had intellectual impairments, unlike case GW (Anderson *et al.* 1998). In accordance with the trend in findings among those with ASD, GW not only demonstrated implicit learning but his performance was comparable with that of controls. Therefore, it may be that intact, rather than enhanced information processing speed and implicit learning predict assets in ASD.

GW's grasp of intuitive physics did not exceed those of matched neurotypical controls, although his self-rated systemizing tendencies were (non-significantly, but with large effect size) higher and comparable with those of other adults with ASD (Baron-Cohen *et al.* 2003). In summary, findings from studying GW's calendar calculation implicate good memory, superior mental calculation and knowledge of calendar templates as underlying elements for his talent. More generally, GW's neuropsychological profile is consistent with a detail-focused cognitive style, as well as intact implicit learning and IT, all of which may be related to his multiple savant skills.

(b) Neuroimaging study

Consistent with predictions, relative to the mean cortical thickness of the control group, GW's cortex was: (i) thinner in regions associated with social cognition and other domains impaired in ASD (Frith & Frith 2006), but (ii) thicker in a bilateral segment of the superior parietal lobe, which has been connected with drawing and other visuospatial functions (Makuuchi *et al.* 2003; Simon *et al.* 2004) as well as calculation abilities (Dehaene *et al.* 2004). Without longitudinal imaging we cannot establish whether these anatomical differences played a part in the initial selection of GW's talent domains, or are the result of talent development and practice. However, the growing literature on brain changes with expertise development (e.g. Maguire *et al.* 2000; Draganski *et al.* 2004) suggests, perhaps, that GW's increased superior parietal thickness may have been acquired through practice of calendar and drawing skills. Increased cortical thickness in this region does not appear to be part of ASD *per se:* Hadjikhani *et al.* (2006) documented cortical thinning in areas associated with social cognition, similar to those shown here, in a group of adults with ASD (of a similar age to GW) relative to controls. However, these investigators did not identify any regions of cortex that were thicker among adults with ASD relative to controls. Although the cortical thickness findings supported *a priori* predictions, they (particularly thicker superior parietal cortex for the savant) should be considered preliminary (requiring replication) because more conservative criteria, addressing the potential issue of multiple comparisons, might provide different results.

10.6 Conclusions

Consistent with recently delineated models of savant skills (e.g. Heaton & Wallace 2004), good memory, mental calculation, visuospatial processing as well as (implicit) knowledge of calendar structure and WCC characterized the cognitive profile of case GW. Possibly reflecting these assets in visuospatial processing and calculation, the superior parietal region of GW's cortex was the only area thicker than that of the neurotypical control group. By contrast, cortical thinning for GW as compared with neurotypical controls was noted in several regions associated with social cognition (e.g. superior and medial prefrontal cortices). These findings may be best viewed from a learning/practice-based model, in which domains (e.g. calendars, art, music) tapping into existing ASD-related strengths, such as detail-focused processing, are further enhanced through over-learning and reflected in cognitive profiles and brain structure.

G.L.W. (in partial fulfilment of his PhD) and F.H. were supported by the Baily Thomas Charitable Fund for the neuropsychological components of this research, and G.L.W. and J.N.G. were supported by the Intramural Research Program of the NIH and NIMH for the neuroimaging study. The authors would like to thank the study participants, particularly GW, for their time and assistance in completing this research.

References

Anderson, M. 2001 Annotation: conceptions of intelligence. *J. Child Psychol Psychiatry* **42**, 287–298. (doi:10.1017/S0021963001007016)

Anderson, M., O'Connor, N. & Hermelin, B. 1998 A specific calculating ability. *Intelligence* **26**, 383–483. (doi:10.1016/S0160-2896(99)00007-0)

Barnes, K. A., Howard, J. H., Howard, D. V., Gilotty, L., Kenworthy, L., Gaillard, W. D. & Vaidya, C. J. 2008 Intact implicit learning of spatial context and temporal sequences in childhood autism spectrum disorder. *Neuropsychology* **22**, 563–570. (doi:10.1037/0894-4105.22.5.563)

Baron-Cohen, S., Wheelwright, S., Spong, A., Scahill, V. & Lawson, J. 2001 Are intuitive physics and intuitive psychology independent?: a test with children with Asperger syndrome. *J. Dev. Learn. Disord.* **5**, 47–78.

Baron-Cohen, S., Richler, J., Bisarya, D., Gurunathan, N. & Wheelwright, S. 2003 The systemizing quotient: an investigation of adults with Asperger syndrome or high-functioning autism, and normal sex differences. *Phil. Trans. R. Soc. Lond. B* **358**, 361–374. (doi:10.1098/rstb.2002.1206)

Baron-Cohen, S., Ashwin, E., Ashwin, C, Tavassoli, T. & Chakrabarti, B. 2009 Talent in autism: hyper-systemizing, hyper-attention to detail and sensory hypersensitivity. *Phil. Trans. R. Soc. B* **364**, 1377–1383. (doi:10.1098/rstb.2008.0337)

Cowan, R. & Frith, C. 2009 Do calendrical savants use calculation to answer date questions? A functional magnetic resonance imaging study. *Phil. Trans. R. Soc. B* **364**, 1417–1424. (doi:10.1098/rstb.2008.0323)

Cowan, R., O'Connor, N. & Samella, K. 2003 The skills and methods of calendrical savants. *Intelligence* **31**, 51–65. (doi:10.1016/S0160-2896(02)00119-8)

Crawford, J. R. & Howell, D. C. 1998 Comparing an individual's test score against norms derived from small samples. *Clin. Neuropsychol.* **12**, 482–486. (doi:10.1076/clin.12.4.482.7241)

Dehaene, S., Molko, N., Cohen, L. & Wilson, A. J. 2004 Arithmetic and the brain. *Curr. Opin. Neurobiol.* **14**, 218–224. (doi:10.1016/j.conb.2004.03.008)

Draganski, B., Gaser, C., Busch, V., Schuierer, G., Bogdahn, U. & May, A. 2004 Neuroplasticity: changes in grey matter induced by training. *Nature* **427**, 311–312. (doi:10.1038/427311a)

Frith, C. D. & Frith, U. 2006 The neural basis of mentalizing. *Neuron* **50**, 531–534. (doi:10.1016/j.neuron.2006.05.001)

Grudnik, J. L. & Kranzler, J. H. 2001 Meta-analysis of the relationship between intelligence and inspection time. *Intelligence* **29**, 523–535. (doi:10.1016/S0160-2896(01)00078-2)

Guillot, A., Collet, C., Nguyen, V. A., Malouin, F., Richards, C. & Doyon, J. 2009 Brain activity during visual versus kinesthetic imagery. *Hum. Brain Mapp.* **30**, 2157–2172. (doi:10.1002/hbm.20658)

Hadjikhani, N., Joseph, R. M., Snyder, J. & Tager-Flusberg, H. 2006 Anatomical differences in the mirror neuron system and social cognition network in autism. *Cereb. Cortex* **16**, 1276–1282. (doi:10.1093/cercor/bhj069)

Happé, F. G. 1994 Wechsler IQ profile and theory of mind in autism: a research note. *J. Child Psychol. Psychiatry* **35**, 1461–1471. (doi:10.1111/j.1469-7610.1994.tb01287.x)

Happé, F. & Frith, U. 2006 The weak coherence account: detail-focused cognitive style in autism spectrum disorders. *J. Autism Dev. Disord.* **36**, 5–25. (doi:10.1007/S10803-005-0039-0)

Happé, F. & Vital, P. 2009 What aspects of autism predispose to talent? *Phil. Trans. R. Soc. B* **364**, 1369–1375. (doi:10.1098/rstb.2008.0332)

Heaton, P. & Wallace, G. L. 2004 Annotation: the savant syndrome. *J. Child Psychol. Psychiatry* **45**, 899–911. (doi:10.1111/j.1469-7610.2004.t01-1-00284.x)

Heavey, L., Pring, L. & Hermelin, B. 1999 A date to remember: the nature of memory in savant calendrical calculators. *Psychol. Med.* **29**, 145–160. (doi:10.1017/S0033291798007776)

Hermelin, B. 2001 *Bright splinters of the mind: a personal story of research with autistic savants.* London, UK: Jessica Kingsley Press.

Hermelin, B. & O'Connor, N. 1986 Idiot savant calendrical calculators: rules and regularities. *Psychol. Med.* **16**, 885–893.

Hermelin, B., O'Connor, N., Lee, S. & Treffert, D. 1989 Intelligence and musical improvisation. *Psychol. Med.* **19**, 447–457.

Isaacs, E. B., Edmonds, C. J., Lucas, A. & Gadian, D. G. 2001 Calculation difficulties in children of very low birthweight—a neural correlate. *Brain* **124**, 1701–1707. (doi:10.1093/brain/124.9.1701)

Jackson, M. & Warrington, E. K. 1986 Arithmetic skills in patients with unilateral cerebral lesions. *Cortex* **22**, 611–620.

Kirkham, N. Z., Slemmer, J. A. & Johnson, S. P. 2002 Visual statistical learning in infancy: evidence for a domain general learning mechanism. *Cognition* **83**, B35–B42. (doi:10.1016/S0010-0277(02)00004-5)

Klinger, L. G., Klinger, M. R. & Pohlig, R. 2006 Implicit learning impairments in autism spectrum disorders: implications for treatment. In *New research in autism: the future is today* (eds J. M. Perez, P. M. Gonzalez, M. L. Comi & C. Nieto), pp. 76–103. London, UK: Jessica Kingsley Press.

Lerch, J. P. & Evans, A. C. 2005 Cortical thickness analysis examined through power analysis and a population simulation. *Neuroimage* **24**, 163–173. (doi:10.1016/j.neuroimage.2004.07.045)

Lucci, D., Fein, D., Holevas, A. & Kaplan, E. 1988 Paul: a musically gifted autistic boy. In *The exceptional brain: neuropsychology of talent and special abilities* (eds L. K. Obler & D. Fein), New York, NY: Guilford Press.

Maguire, E. A., Gadian, D. G., Johnsrude, I. S., Good, C. D., Ashburner, J., Frackowiak, R. S. & Frith, C. D. 2000 Navigation-related structural change in the hippocampi of taxi drivers. *Proc. Natl Acad. Sci. USA* **97**, 4398–4403. (doi:10.1073/pnas.070039597)

Makuuchi, M., Kaminaga, T. & Sugishita, M. 2003 Both parietal lobes are involved in drawing: a functional MRI study and implications for constructional apraxia. *Cogn. Brain Res.* **16**, 338–347. (doi:10.1016/S0926-6410(02)00302-6)

Mostofsky, S. H., Goldberg, M. C., Landa, R. J. & Denckla, M. B. 2000 Evidence for a deficit in procedural learning in children and adolescents with autism: implications for cerebellar contribution. *J. Int. Neuropsychol. Soc.* **6**, 752–759. (doi:10.1017/S1355617700677020)

Mottron, L. & Belleville, S. 1993 A study of perceptual analysis in a high-level autistic subject with exceptional graphic abilities. *Brain Cogn.* **23**, 279–309. (doi:10.1006/brcg.1993.1060)

O'Connor, N. & Hermelin, B. 1989 The memory structure of autistic idiot-savant mnemonists. *Br. J. Psychol.* **80**, 97–111.

O'Connor, N. & Hermelin, B. 1991 Talents and preoccupations in idiot savants. *Psychol. Med.* **21**, 959–964.

Pring, L., Hermelin, B. & Heavey, L. 1995 Savants, segments, art and autism. *J. Child Psychol. Psychiatry* **36**, 1065–1076. (doi:10.1111/j.l469-7610.1995.tb01351.x)

Reber, A. S. 1993 *Implicit learning and tacit knowledge: an essay on the cognitive unconscious.* Oxford, UK: Oxford University Press.

Robbins, S., Evans, A. C, Collins, D. L. & Whitesides, S. 2004 Tuning and comparing spacial normalization methods. *Med. Image Anal.* **8**, 311–323. (doi:10.1016/j.media.2004.06.009)

Scheuffgen, K., Happé, F., Anderson, M. & Frith, U. 2000 High 'intelligence', low 'IQ'? Speed of processing and measured IQ in children with autism. *Dev. Psychopathol.* **12**, 83–90. (doi:10.1017/S095457940000105X)

Shah, A. & Frith, U. 1983 An islet of ability in autistic children: a research note. *J. Child Psychol. Psychiatry* **24**, 613–620. (doi:10.1111/j.l469-7610.1983.tb00137.x)

Simon, O., Kherif, F., Flandin, G., Poline, J. B., Riviere, D., Mangin, J. F., Le Bihan, D. & Dehaene, S. 2004 Automatized clustering and functional geometry of human parietofrontal networks for language, space, and number. *Neuroimage* **23**, 1192–1202. (doi:10.1016/j.neuroimage.2004.09.023)

Treffert, D. 1989 *Extraordinary people: understanding 'idiot savants.'.* New York, NY: Harper and Row.

Wallace, G. L., Anderson, M. & Happé, F. 2009 Brief report: information processing speed is intact in autism but not correlated with measured intelligence. *J. Autism Dev. Disord.* (doi:10.1007/s10803-008-0684-1)

Witkin, H. A., Oltman, P. K., Raskin, E. & Karp, S. A. 1971 *A manual for the embedded figures test.* Palo Alto, CA: Consulting Psychologists Press.

11

Radial cytoarchitecture and patterns of cortical connectivity in autism

Manuel Casanova and Juan Trippe

To explain the pattern of preserved and superior abilities found in autism spectrum disorders, a hypothesis has emerged, which assumes that there is a developmental bias towards the formation of short-range connections. This would result in excessive activity and over-connectivity within susceptible local networks. These networks might become partially isolated and acquire novel functional properties. In turn, this would affect the formation of long-range circuits and systems governing top-down control and integration. Despite many tantalizing clues, mechanisms relating pathogenesis and altered cell function to the 'disconnection' of integrative and focal activity remain obscure. However, recent *post-mortem* studies of brains of individuals with autism have shown characteristic differences in the morphometry of radial cell minicolumns, which add credence to the connectivity hypothesis.

Keywords: autistic disorder; cortical minicolumn; cytoarchitecture

11.1 Introduction

Autism spectrum disorders (ASDs) comprise a heterogeneous array of conditions with seemingly dissociable phenotypes. In this special issue, the focus is on the phenotype that is characterized by uneven and sometimes superior ability in specific skills. We believe that a recently emerging hypothesis regarding brain organization and its disruption can throw some admittedly speculative light on the development of this phenotype. In recent years, a new perspective has emerged postulating systematic disruption of the control or coordination of specialized networks distributed throughout the cortex (Buxhoeveden & Casanova 2002). This approach assumes that there are hierarchical or distributed circuit and network interactions. In the case of autism, these appear to be disrupted. Thus we might expect to see altered processes of self-organization and integration in cortical networks at multiple levels of function and phases of development. Current biological and genetic research speculatively suggests that autism involves disruptions of synapse development and function. But how is one to imagine the nature of such disruptions? One possibility is that mechanisms susceptible to genetic or epigenetic disruption are affected at early neuroproliferative stages. This disruption would have widely distributed and compounded effects on later development. The integration of affected neurons within local circuits and, in turn, the incorporation of local circuits into larger self-organizing cortical networks, would amplify the effects of perturbed mechanisms. One way to understand the mechanisms involved is to look at the structures that involve multiples of neurons working together in a concerted fashion, so-called minicolumns.

11.2 Autism as a 'minicolumnopathy'

Minicolumns are radially oriented arrangements of cellular elements, which have a stereotypical morphometry and are distributed throughout the cortex. They share common input-output operations mediated by recurrent circuits linking translaminar columns of pyramidal neurons (Mountcastle 1997; Buxhoeveden & Casanova 2002; DeFelipe 2005). These modules have commonly been considered to represent a canonical microcircuit contained within a defined cylindrical volume, and linked by specified patterns of connections within uniform modular arrays distributed throughout all areas of the neocortex.

Recent studies have shown equivalent alignment and spacing in pairwise comparisons between pyramidal cell columns, their associated apical dendrites and myelinated axon bundles, and aligned radial processes of certain interneurons containing the inhibitory neurotransmitter gamma-aminobutyric acid (GABA). These cell elements are grouped in identical arrangements corresponding to minicolumns, which in turn are distributed within arrays that vary by cortical area in their distribution of minicolumns and cell composition (Ballesteros Yanez et al. 2005; DeFelipe 2005).

GABA interneurons are varied in their molecular content, electrophysiological properties, morphology and distribution patterns within cortex, and are organized within circuits that are adapted to dynamically regulate the output of their associated pyramidal cell columns. GABA neurons however can be classified as one of a group of common inhibitory cell types, each defined by a particular combination of these properties (Markram et al. 2004). For example, most GABA neurons are immunoreactive for one of three calcium-binding proteins: parvalbumin (PV); calbindin (CB); or calretinin (CR). CR neurons are widely distributed in supragranular layers, and have processes that may extend radially across several layers and are regularly spaced in a radial columnar cytoarchitecture distributed throughout all cortical areas in monkeys and humans (Gabbott & Bacon 1996; Peters & Sethares 1997; Gabbott 2003; Ballesteros Yánez et al. 2005). PV-positive neurons, by contrast, have predominantly tangentially oriented axonal processes that synapse on cell bodies of projection neurons and whose synchronized fast-spiking activity serves to coordinate the output of local minicolumnar groupings (Galarreta & Hestrin 2001*b*).

The output of local circuits of pyramidal cell columns is regulated by the phasic activity of networks of GABA neurons within minicolumns and across minicolumn networks. GABA neurons are functionally linked within subtype-specific networks or by characteristic patterns of connection with other subtypes of neurons (Gibson et al. 1999; Galarreta & Hestrin 2001*a*). Certain GABA neurons may transition between the phases of oscillatory activity at different frequencies and entrain their activity with networks of other GABA neuron subtypes.

Output in beta (15–30 Hz) and lower frequency bands is associated with longer range interareal transmission, as the long cycle length allows for the integration of a variety of inputs with a broader range of signal timing variation (Kopell et al. 2000). CR+ interneurons were shown to form a coherent oscillatory network in the beta-frequency band, which transiently coupled to gamma-band frequency output of tangential FS basket cell networks in deep layer III/IV (Szabadics et al. 2001; Beierlein et al. 2003). Relevant to the discussion of autism, beta-band activity has been shown to coordinate functional activity across fronto-parietal networks involved in top-down visual attention activity (Schnitzler & Gross 2005) as well as sensory gating (Kisley & Cornwell 2006; Hong et al. 2008).

11.3 Altered minicolumnar morphometry in autism

Minicolumnar cytoarchitecture shows systematic differences in the comparisons of *post-mortem* cortical tissue series of ASD and control cases (Casanova *et al.* 2002a,b, Casanova *et al.* 2006a,b). Minicolumns were found to be narrower in all areas examined with the greatest decrease found in BA 9. No difference was found in the core width of pyramidal cell columns, indicating that reduced minicolumnar width reflected primarily the loss of peripheral neuropil (figure 11.1). The number of minicolumns in each frame was increased. Cell dispersion was greater in the test series, indicating a decrease in the alignment of pyramidal cells along the core axis and possible disorganization of local circuits within the minicolumn core. In addition, the volume density of pyramidal cell bodies measured by the grey level index (GLI) showed an increase in the amplitude difference across axis-to-axis intervals. This suggested to us that there was an increased delimitation of the minicolumnar core periphery and loss of directly adjacent peripheral neuropil, including proximal dendrite segments.

As overall GLI data showed no interaction by group, increased numbers of minicolumns and equivalent cell spacing within minicolumnar cores implied that pyramidal cells within each column must be, in some combination, smaller or fewer in number. These results suggest possible developmental disruptions in the formation of minicolumnar microcircuits. It remains to be seen how these findings might relate to pathophysiological processes underlying ASD pheno-types. Perhaps the reduced volume of peripheral neuropil indicates reductions in the numbers of radially oriented GABA neurons or in the extent of their axonal and dendritic processes.

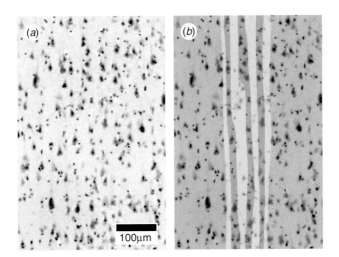

Figure 11.1 The appearance of different compartments of the minicolumns under the microscope is shown. Here a tissue slice (*a*) taken from the inferior orbital gyrus in the human brain and (*b*) Nissl stained and processed with a method known as the grey level index, or GLI (Schlaug *et al.* 1995). Minicolumnar cores (dark bands) comprise mostly pyramidal cells. These are surrounded by peripheral neuropil (light bands), comprising interneurons and also neural processes not visible in Nissl stains.

11.4 Development of area hierarchies

V1 is an area in the occipital part of the brain, which is vital to visual processing. Interposed minicolumn networks in V1 constitute stimulus-response maps, i.e. retinotopic location, frequency, orientation, contrast, direction of motion, etc. Ordered patterns of the activity of various stimulus maps are integrated in associated areas selective for higher order feature representations, including geometric motifs, facial or body features and spatial relationships. Feature extraction is modulated by the coordinate activity in other sense modalities and top-down input providing semantic or contextual, emotional and goal-related information. Interaction of local groups of minicolumns and their intrinsic interconnection by collaterals and interneurons have adapted to be responsive to invariant properties of the environment, which have significance for reproductive success. Thus, wiring patterns are highly constrained between VI and extrastriate areas associated with face recognition (Batardiere et al. 2002; Kennedy et al. 2007).

Disrupted patterns of coordinated oscillatory output in distributed minicolumn networks might be associated with cortical disconnectivity in autism. Likewise, altered oscillatory activity in developing cortical circuits may contribute to impaired development of intra-areal and transcortical connections. Oscillatory output of GABA neurons in the beta-frequency range guides early stage development of radial columnar circuits of pyramidal and radial interneurons. Synchronized GABAergic inhibitory output results in a brief period of increased sub-threshold depolarization during which correlated firing of presynaptic spikes may generate a postsynaptic action potential, thereby strengthening the weights of the participating synapses. This mechanism of spike timing-dependent plasticity results in the strengthening of synapses contributing to selected circuits and the elimination of weaker or discordant synapses. This activity serves to specify and refine both local and long-distance connections according to the oscillatory output frequency generated by specific GABA interneuron circuits.

Conversely, the loss of peripheral neuropil inhibition mediated by GABA neurons that are responsive to CR and somatostatin might alter local as well as longdistance anatomical and functional connectivity (Courchesne & Pierce 2005). Collateral excitation of neighbouring minicolumns would be increased, introducing additional noise into each discrete mini-columnar circuit and degrading the specificity and resolution of activity within differentially activated networks of minicolumns. Excitatory cross-activation among local networks of minicolumns would also sustain and grow intrinsic collateral connections between distributed segments of a feature map as well as between minicolumns in adjoining feature maps. This might possibly provide an enhanced or novel mechanism for local feature binding.

Lack of refinement of feedback connections could be the basis for synaesthesia (Hubbard & Ramachandran 2005). Synaesthesia is relevant to considerations of the savant syndrome. For example, Daniel Tammet relates in his autobiography (Tammet 2006) that his synaesthesia is vital to his ability to remember numbers and to carry out calculations. In an attempt to explain savant talent, Mottron and colleagues suggested that there may be increased local activity in specialized local or grapheme areas owing to environmental access/interest (Mottron et al. 2006). This could perhaps be explained by assuming that critical periods of synaptic plasticity affect adjoining areas (i.e. V4/V8) as a consequence of bias towards the activity of short-range connections. Furthermore, in visual cortex, feedback projections from layer V of visual association areas subtending grapheme processing to isomodal areas such as V4 are shorter than the corresponding feed-forward projections originating from layer II/III (Bannister 2005). It is therefore only to be expected that tones also activate lexical representations (i.e. simple sound to associative lexeme). These cross-modal connections are pre-existing (Pascual-Leone & Hamilton 2001) and could be facilitated by increased activation within adjacent areas. It is plausible that the activity is increased in association areas processing low-level perceptual information including grapheme/lexical information, phonemic, or visual object or feature representations, because access to such information is available during the window of synaptic development of those areas post-natally. Increased functionality of those areas is reinforced through positive feedback from the environment (Mottron et al. 2006). Increased connectivity within minicolumnar microcircuits, and their incorporation into specialized subnetworks within the cortical area, would allow for rapid efficient and discriminative processing of low-level perceptual/semantic representations, i.e. within word categories such as proper names. These subnetworks would be strengthened by increased connections to areas processing elemental features such as phonemes, morphemes or low-level visual features.

In summary, the pathological processes that lead to autism have distributed effects. We speculate that they may reflect a disruption of multiple fundamental processes during the patterning and organization of cortical cytoarchitecture. The effects of these disrupted processes may be manifested widely, yet altered connectivity/structure in early maturing regions will compound developmental disruptions in subsequently developing areas. Atypical or adaptive behaviours associated with these changes may well provide a basis for overtraining of compensatory or developmentally enhanced functions.

References

Ballesteros Yanez, I., Munoz, A., Contreras, J., Gonzalez, J., Rodriguez-Veiga, E. & DeFelipe, J. 2005 Double bouquet cell in the human cerebral cortex and a comparison with other mammals. *J. Comp. Neurol.* **486**, 344–360. (doi:10.1002/cne.20533)

Bannister, A. P. 2005 Inter- and intra-laminar connections of pyramidal cells in the neocortex. *Neurosci. Res.* **53**, 95–103. (doi:10.1016/j.neures.2005.06.019)

Batardiere, A., Barone, P., Knoblauch, K., Giroud, P., Berland, M., Dumas, A.-M. & Kennedy, H. 2002 Early specification of the hierarchical organization of visual cortical areas in the macaque monkey. *Cereb. Cortex* **12**, 453–465. (doi:10.1093/cercor/12.5.453)

Beierlein, M., Gibson, J. R. & Connors, B. W. 2003 Two dynamically distinct inhibitory networks in layer 4 of the neocortex. *J. Neurophysiol.* **90**, 2987–3000. (doi:10.1152/jn.00283.2003)

Buxhoeveden, D. P. & Casanova, M. F. 2002 The minicolumn hypothesis in neuroscience. *Brain* **125**, 935–951. (doi:10.1093/brain/awf110)

Casanova, M. F., Buxhoeveden, D. P., Switala, A. E. & Roy, E. 2002a Minicolumnar pathology in autism. *Neurology* **58**, 428–432.

Casanova, M. F., Buxhoeveden, D. P., Switala, A. E. & Roy, E. 2002b Neuronal density and architecture (gray level index) in the brains of autistic patients. *J. Child Neurol.* **17**, 515–521. (doi:10.1177/088307380201700708)

Casanova, M. F., Van Kooten, I. A. J., Switala, A. E., Van Engeland, H., Heinsen, H., Steinbusch, H. W. M., Hof, P. R. & Schmitz, C. 2006a Abnormalities of cortical minicolumnar organization in the prefrontal lobes of autistic patients. *Clin. Neurosci. Res.* **6**, 127–133. (doi:10.1016/j.cnr.2006.06.003)

Casanova, M. F. et al. 2006b Minicolumnar abnormalities in autism. *Ada Neuropathol.* **112**, 287–303. (doi:10.1007/s00401-006-0085-5)

Courchesne, E. & Pierce, K. 2005 Why the frontal cortex in autism might be talking only to itself: local over-connectivity but long-distance disconnection. *Curr. Opin. Neurobiol.* **15**, 225–230. (doi:10.1016/j.conb.2005.03.001)

DeFelipe, J. 2005 Reflections on the structure of the cortical minicolumn. In *Neocortical modularity and the cell mini-column* (ed. M. F. Casanova), pp. 57–92. New York, NY: Nova Biomedical.

Gabbott, P. L. A. 2003 Radial organisation of neurons and dendrites in human cortical areas 25. *Brain Res.* **992**, 298–304. (doi:10.1016/j.brainres.2003.08.054)

Gabbott, P. L. A. & Bacon, S. J. 1996 Local circuit neurons in the medial prefrontal cortex (areas 24a,b,c, 25 and 32) in the monkey, I: cell morphology and morphometrics. *J. Comp. Neurol.* **364**, 567–608. (doi:10.1002/(SICI)l096–9861(19960122)364:4 < 567::AID-CNE1 > 3.0.CO;2-1)

Galarreta, M. & Hestrin, S. 2001a Electrical synapses between GABA-releasing interneurons. *Nat. Rev. Neurosd.* **2**, 425–433. (doi:10.1038/35077566)

Galarreta, M. & Hestrin, S. 2001b Spike transmission and synchrony detection in networks of GABAergic interneurons. *Science* **292**, 2295–2299. (doi:10.1126/science.1061395)

Gibson, J. R., Beierlein, M. & Connors, B. W. 1999 Two networks of electrically coupled inhibitory neurons in neocortex. *Nature* **402**, 75–79. (doi:10.1038/47035)

Hong, L. E., Summerfelt, A., Mitchell, B. D., McMahon, R. P., Wonodi, I., Buchanan, R. W. & Thaker, G. K. 2008 Sensory gating endophenotype based on its neural oscillatory pattern and heritability estimate. *Arch. Gen. Psychiatry* **65**, 1008–1016. (doi:10.1001/archpsyc.65.9.1008)

Hubbard, E. M. & Ramachandran, V. S. 2005 Neurocogni-tive mechanisms of synesthesia. *Neuron* **48**, 509–520. (doi:10.1016/j.neuron.2005.10.012)

Kennedy, H., Douglas, R. J., Knoblauch, K. & Dehay, C. 2007 Self-organization and pattern formation in primate cortical networks. In *Cortical development: genes and genetic abnormalities* (eds G. Bock & J. Goode), pp. 178–198. Chichester, UK: Wiley.

Kisley, M. A. & Cornwell, Z. M. 2006 Gamma and beta neural activity evoked during a sensory gating paradigm: effects of auditory, somatosensory and cross-modal stimulation. *Clin. Neurophysiol.* **117**, 2549–2563. (doi:10.1016/j.clinph.2006.08.003)

Kopell, N. J., Ermentrout, G. B., Whittington, M. A. & Traub, R. D. 2000 Gamma rhythms and beta rhythms have different synchronization properties. *Proc. NatlAcad. Sd. USA* **91**, 1867–1872. (doi:10.1073/pnas.97.4.1867)

Markram, H., Toledo-Rodriguez, M., Wang, Y., Gupta, A., Silberberg, G. & Wu, C. 2004 Interneurons of the neocortical inhibitory system. *Nat. Rev. Neurosd.* **5**, 793–807. (doi:10.1038/nrnl519)

Mottron, L., Dawson, M., Soulieres, I., Hubert, B. & Burack, J. 2006 Enhanced perceptual functioning in autism: an update, and eight principles of autistic perception. *J. Autism Dev. Disord.* **36**, 27–43. (doi:10.1007/sl0803-005-0040-7)

Mountcastle, V. B. 1997 The columnar organization of the neocortex. *Brain* **120**, 701–722. (doi:10.1093/brain/120.4.701)

Pascual-Leone, A. & Hamilton, R. 2001 The metamodal organization of the brain. In *Vision: from neurons to cognition* (eds C. Casanova & M. Ptito), Amsterdam, UK: Elsevier.

Peters, A. & Sethares, C. 1997 The organization of double bouquet cells in monkey striate cortex. *J. Neurocytol.* **26**, 779–797. (doi:10.1023/A:1018518515982)

Schlaug, G., Schleicher, A. & Zilles, K. 1995 Quantitative analysis of the columnar arrangement of neurons in the human cingulate cortex. *J. Comp. Neurol.* **351**, 441–52. (doi:10.1002/cne.903510310)

Schnitzler, A. & Gross, J. 2005 Normal and pathological oscillatory communication in the brain. *Nat. Rev. Neurosd.* **6**, 285–296. (doi:10.1038/nrnl650)

Szabadics, J., Lorincz, A. & Tamas, G. 2001 ($ and γ frequency synchronization by dendritic gabaergic synapses and gap junctions in a network of cortical interneurons. *J. Neurosd.* **21**, 5824–5831.

Tammet, D. 2006 *Born on a blue day: a memoir of Aspergers and an extraordinary mind*. London, UK: Hodder & Stoughton.

12

How does visual thinking work in the mind of a person with autism? A personal account

Temple Grandin

My mind is similar to an Internet search engine that searches for photographs. I use language to narrate the photo-realistic pictures that pop up in my imagination. When I design equipment for the cattle industry, I can test run it in my imagination similar to a virtual reality computer program. All my thinking is associative and not linear. To form concepts, I sort pictures into categories similar to computer files. To form the concept of orange, I see many different orange objects, such as oranges, pumpkins, orange juice and marmalade. I have observed that there are three different specialized autistic/Asperger cognitive types. They are: (i) visual thinkers such as I who are often poor at algebra, (ii) pattern thinkers such as Daniel Tammet who excel in math and music but may have problems with reading or writing composition, and (iii) verbal specialists who are good at talking and writing but they lack visual skills.

Keywords: visual thinking; imagination; autobiography; photo-realistic memory

12.1 Introduction

My mind works similar to an Internet search engine, set to locate photos. All my thoughts are in photo-realistic pictures, which flash up on the 'computer monitor' in my imagination. Words just narrate the picture. When I design livestock facilities, I can test run the equipment in my imagination similar to a virtual reality computer program. I did not know that this was a special skill until I started interviewing other people about how they think. I was surprised to discover that the other non-autistic equipment designers could not do full motion test runs of equipment in their minds.

My mind is associative and does not think in a linear manner. If you say the word 'butterfly', the first picture I see is butterflies in my childhood backyard. The next image is metal decorative butterflies that people decorate the outside of their houses with and the third image is some butterflies I painted on a piece of plywood when I was in graduate school. Then my mind gets off the subject and I see a butterfly cut of chicken that was served at a fancy restaurant approximately 3 days ago. The memories that come up first tend to be either early childhood or something that happened within the last week. A teacher working with a child with autism may not understand the connection when the child suddenly switches from talking about butterflies to talking about chicken. If the teacher thinks about it visually, a butterfly cut of chicken looks like a butterfly.

12.2 Putting little pieces together

When I design equipment, I take bits and pieces of other equipment I have seen in the past and combine them to create a new system. All my thinking is bottom-up instead of top-down. I find lots of little details and put them together to form concepts and theories.

During the last 5 years, I successfully used this method to fix some of my health problems. Most people have to have a theory first, and then they try to make the data conform to it. My mind works the opposite way. I put lots of little pieces of data together to form a new theory. I read lots of journal papers and I take little pieces of information and put them together as if completing a jigsaw puzzle. Imagine if you had a thousand-piece jigsaw puzzle in a paper bag and you had no idea what the picture on the box is. When you start to put the puzzle together, you will be able to see what the picture is when it is approximately one-third or one-quarter of the way completed. When I solve the problem, it is not top-down and theory driven. Instead, I look at how all the little pieces fit together to form a bigger picture.

When I was in college, I called this *finding the basic principle*. On everything in life, I was overwhelmed with a mass of details and I realized that I had to group them together and try to figure out unifying principles for masses of data.

12.3 Finding a unifying principle in scientific literature

I have recently started to lose my hearing. The ear specialist said that there was nothing I could do. I did not accept this; so I spent two weeks at the computer reading journal papers on sudden sensorial hearing loss, Meniere's disease and other disorders. I had to read hundreds of abstracts and journal papers just to get the background information so that I could find the answer that would save my hearing. I was looking for a unifying principle that would explain all the research results. One study reported that steroids such as Prednisone could save my hearing and another study reported that steroids do not work. How did I sort the data out? The first clue was that many studies were published in arthritis journals instead of ear and nose journals. The reason for this is that arthritis doctors really understand autoimmune disorders where the immune system attacks a person's body. In my mind, I pictured wrecked, deformed arthritic joints. For a treatment to be successful, the drug has to be given *before* the immune system has destroyed the joints. I then had a flash of visual thinking insight. I imagined that the immune system attacking my inner ear was such as a house on fire. This is what I call a *visual symbol picture*. If the fire is put out when it is confined to a waste basket, the house can be saved. If the whole house starts burning, it will be destroyed. The explanation for all the conflicting studies in the medical journals was really simple. Steroid drugs such as Prednisone put out the fire of autoimmune inflammation, but they do not repair the damage. Treatment has to be started before the ear is wrecked. The explanation for all the conflicting scientific studies was a simple basic principle. I had to get a prescription for Prednisone before the autoimmune inflammation destroyed my inner ear. I looked up a second ear specialist in the phone book and he immediately gave me the prescription that saved my hearing.

12.4 Filling up the internet in my mind

The method of bottom-up thinking really works well for me in problem solving where a basic principle has to be determined from masses of conflicting data. One disadvantage of my kind of thinking is that huge amounts of data are required to find the answers. Since my mind works similar to an Internet search engine, my ability to solve problems got better and better as I had more and more experiences and read more and more books and journal papers. This provided lots of images in my memory for the search engine in my mind to search. Many people have told me that my talks have improved between the ages of 40 and 60. My ability to think in a less rigid way keeps getting better as I fill up the Internet in my mind with more and more information. I greatly improved socially in my 40s and 50s compared with my 20s. This was due to having more experiences in my memory that provided guidance on how to behave.

12.5 Door symbols

When I was in high school at age 16, many teachers did not understand why I kept talking about going through little doors and thinking in visual symbols. Since my mind stores information as photo-realistic pictures, I do not have true abstract thinking. To visualize the concept of my future after high school, I had to use door symbols. In fact, the first door symbols were real doors I could practise walking through. Today I no longer think in door symbols because I have a huge database in the Internet inside my head. Instead of visualizing doors, I visualize either real past experiences or events I have read about.

12.6 Categories are the beginning of concept formation

To form a concept from the many specific photo-realistic pictures I have stored in my memory, I sort them into categories. Categorization of my specific visual memories was the beginning of concept formation (Grandin 2000, 2002). When I was a child, I categorized dogs from cats by sorting the animals by size. All the dogs in our neighbourhood were large until our neighbours got a Dachshund. I remember looking at the small dog and trying to figure out why she was not a cat. I had to find a visual feature that she shared with big dogs. I had to create a new category in my mind to differentiate. All dogs, no matter how big or small, have the same nose shape. My concept is sensory based, not word based. Other ways of sensory-based categorization would be sound (barking or meowing) or smell.

Researchers have found that people with autism often have difficulty in forming new categories (Minshew *et al.* 2002). When I was a child, we played lots of games such as Twenty Questions that forced me to get good at thinking in categories. Category formation is a fundamental property of the nervous system. Brains are wired to put visual information into categories (Freedman *etal.* 2001). The hippocampus also has the ability to determine whether or not similar photos of objects are the same or different (Bakker *et al.* 2008). Observations of stroke patients have shown that brain damage can cause them to lose their ability to categorize objects such as tools, but they can still categorize vegetables and animals (e.g. Mummery et al. 1998).

In my case even abstract questions are answered by putting photo-realistic pictures into categories. One time I was asked 'Is capitalism a good system?' To answer this question, I put pictures from countries that had different types of governmental systems into the following categories: (i) capitalistic, (ii) capitalistic/socialistic, (iii) socialistic, (iv) benevolent dictatorship, (v) brutal dictatorship, and (vi) war and chaos. These pictures were taken from my memory and they are from experiences travelling or the news media. My answer was that I absolutely do not want to live in a brutal dictatorship, or war and chaos. Pictures helped me make a choice because in the last two choices I see news photos and TV images of killing and destruction.

My ability to provide a well thought-out answer has greatly improved with age because I have travelled more, and have more pictures both from actual experiences and from reading. They can be sorted into the different categories. When I read, I convert text to images as if watching a movie. The images are then stored in my memory. In college, I photocopied images of my class notes into my brain. When I was a teenager, answering the question about capitalism in an intelligent manner would have been impossible. I simply did not have enough experiences or enough information in my memory to answer it.

12.7 How I developed faster category thinking

In college, the process of sorting out the basic principles from masses of data was much slower and laborious compared with my abilities today at 60. I figured out my ear problem in two weeks. When I was in my 20s, it took me 10 times longer to develop a theory from 100 journal papers.

As an undergraduate, I did an honour's thesis on the subject of sensory interaction. Here the question was how a stimulus to one sense, such as hearing, affects the sensitivity of other senses. I had over 100 journal papers and I numbered each paper. On small pieces of paper, I typed the major findings of each study. I then pinned hundreds of little slips of paper on a bulletin board. I called it my logic board. Since my thinking is totally non-sequential, I had to develop a way so I could see a display of all the information at the same time on the bulletin board. To discover the categories and concepts, I started pinning the slips of paper into different categories. It was very time-consuming. As I gained more experience with sifting through scientific research, I no longer needed the bulletin board. I became better and better at finding unexpected clues, such as many deafness treatment papers being in arthritis journals. From my previous scientific knowledge, I made the association of rheumatoid arthritis to autoimmune, and therefore saw that ear damage would work the same way as joint damage.

When I was young, my thinking process was extremely slow because I was less skilled at finding the *basic principle* from the masses of data. But skills in people on the autism spectrum still develop when they are adults. The more research I did analysing the results of scientific studies, the better I got at it. I always read the methods section of a paper carefully so I can visualize how the experiment was done. Differences in methods often explain conflicting results of scientific studies.

12.8 Different ways of thinking

For many years I thought everybody else thought in pictures the same way as I do. When I wrote *Thinking in pictures*, I started interviewing people about how they think. I was shocked to learn that most people processed information differently to how I did. Most people are able to visualize their own car or visualize walking through their own house. They can do it because they are very familiar with it. I discovered the differences in thinking when I asked other people about objects they were less familiar with. I asked them about an object that everybody sees really often, but it was not visible when I asked the question. I always ask the question in the exact way so I do not bias the answer. 'Access your memory of church steeples. How do they come into your mind?' I was shocked to discover that many people saw a vague generalized steeple and sometimes it was a stick figure. They saw a generalized steeple where I saw only a whole lot of photo-realistic pictures of specific ones that I could identify. Research by Nancy Minshew and her colleagues has shown that in people with autism, word-based tasks are processed in the visual parts of the brain. Functional magnetic resonance imaging scanning indicated that sentences with both high and low visual imageries were processed in the visual parts of the brain in the autistic subjects and that low visual imagery sentences were processed in the language parts of the brain in normal subjects (Kana *et al.* 2006). The sentences with high visual imagery were about animals and plants. One of the low visual imagery sentences was about arithmetic. When I did the experiment, I instantly saw my third-grade teacher writing on the blackboard and explaining borrowing in subtraction.

12.9 Autistic thinking is specialized

When I wrote *Thinking in pictures* (Grandin 1995) I thought everybody on the autism/Asperger spectrum was a *visual* thinker. People with autism and Asperger's are *specialist* thinkers. They are good at one thing and bad at other things. From both books and interviews, I have concluded that there are three principal types of specialist thinking.

(i) *Photo-realistic visual thinkers*—such as I. All my thoughts are in photo-realistic pictures (Grandin & Johnson 2005). My area of weakness is in algebra because there is no way to visualize it. Visual thinkers can do geometry and trigonometry, but not algebra. For my work, visual thinking is very important. I can see everything in my head and then draw it on paper. Figures 12.1 and 12.2 show two of my drawings, done by hand, of livestock handling facilities. They date from the mid-1980s when I did much of my best work.
(ii) *Pattern thinking—music and math mind*. This is a more abstract form of visual thinking. Thoughts are in patterns instead of photo-realistic pictures. Pattern thinkers see patterns and relationships between numbers. Some of the best descriptions are in Daniel Tammet's book *Born on a blue day* (Tammet 2006) and in Jerry Newport's book *Mozart and the whale* (Newport *et al.* 2007) The weak area in pattern thinkers is usually reading and writing composition.
(iii) *Word—fact thinkers*. These individuals have a huge memory for verbal facts on all kinds of things such as film stars and sporting events. They are often poor at drawing and other visual thinking skills.

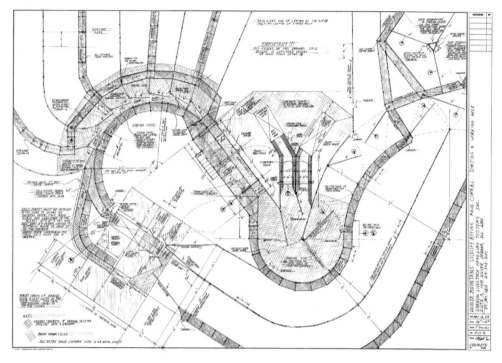

Figure 12.1 Drawings of livestock handling facilities by Temple Grandin dated 13 May 1985.

12.10 Different kinds of brains

Recent research on the white matter in the brain may provide an explanation for the uneven profile of abilities that is found in many individuals with autism. There are defects in the white matter interconnections between different localized brain regions. Courchesne *et al.* (2004) called these connections the 'computer cables' that wire different parts of the brain together. The frontal cortex gets less connections than other parts of the brain, but some local areas in the brain may get extra connections (Minshew & Williams 2007). Casanova and colleagues (2006, 2007; Casanova & Trippe 2009) found that the brain of both famous neuroscientists and people on the autism spectrum have more circuits (minicolumns) per square centimetre of brain. They suggest that this may explain savant-like skills. The disadvantage of this type of brain construction is that these small circuits have fewer long-distance connections between distant brain regions that facilitate complex social behaviours.

There is a wide range of brains that should be considered part of normal variation. A brain can be built with larger fast circuits that facilitate social communication or smaller, slower circuits that improve cognition in a specialized area.

In any information processing system, there are always trade-offs. Brains with high-speed connections to many distant areas will be fast and details will be missed. Research shows that normal brains fail to process details that the autistic person perceives (see Happé & Frith 2009; Chapter 3). My model for visualizing the different types of brains is a large corporate office building. The president (frontal cortex) is located at the

How does visual thinking work in the mind of a person with autism? A personal account   147

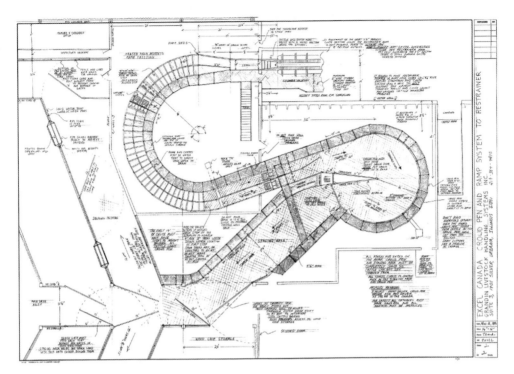

Figure 12.2 Drawings of livestock handling facilities by Temple Grandin dated 02 November 1987.

top and he has telephone and computer connections (white matter) to offices throughout the building. I hypothesize that in a highly social brain, the frontal cortex has high-speed connections that go mainly to the department heads in the building. The network is fast and details are omitted. In the autistic/Asperger brain, the frontal cortex is poorly connected, but the visual and auditory parts of the brain (technical nerd departments) have lots of extra local connections providing better processing of detailed information.

12.11 Autistic intelligence

Michelle Dawson, a woman with autism, has teamed up with Laurent Mottron, a researcher in Canada, to show that autistic intelligence goes beyond just rote memorization. Instead of using just the Wechsler IQ tests, they tested both normal and autistic children with Raven's Progressive Matrices (Dawson *et al.* 2007). In this test, the person is shown complicated patterns and he/she has to choose the pattern that will complete a series of patterns. Dawson and colleagues found that the IQ scores for the autistic children were 30–70 percentile points higher on the Raven's compared with the Wechsler Intelligence Scale for Children (WISC), while normal children have similar IQ scores when given the Raven's and the WISC. Scheuffgen *et al.* (2000) found that children with autism can show fast information processing despite poor measured IQ. These results show that autistic intelligence is truly different.

In 2006, Nancy Minshew and her colleagues performed a method called diffusion tensor imaging on me. They found a huge white fibre tract that runs from deep in my visual cortex up to my frontal cortex. It is located in the brain slice made at the level of my eyes. It is almost twice as large as my sex- and age-matched controls. I used to joke about having a big high-speed Internet line deep in my visual cortex. It has turned out that I really do have one. This may explain my ability to read massive amounts of detailed literature and sort out the details. In my case, abstract thought based on language has been replaced with high-speed handling of hundreds of 'graphics' files. Studies of patients with fronto-temporal dementia show that language-based thinking can cover up detailed visual thinking and music. As the disease destroys the frontal lobe and the language parts of the brain, art and music talent can emerge in people who had no previous interest in art or music (Miller *et al.* 1998, 2000; see also Snyder 2009).

12.12 Harnessing autistic creativity and Asperger's syndrome

I am concerned that people with mild Asperger's syndrome may be held back by the diagnosis because people may perceive them as not capable. Simon Baron-Cohen asks 'is Asperger's syndrome a disability?' (Baron-Cohen 2000; see also Baron-Cohen *et al.* 2009). Many famous musicians, scientists, artists and politicians would probably be diagnosed with Asperger's syndrome if they were children today (Ledgin 2002; Fitzgerald & O'Brien 2007). What would happen to them in today's system? In the USA, the lucky ones get apprenticed into the Silicon Valley technical world by their parents. Many parents in technical fields teach their children their jobs at a young age. The unlucky ones do not have somebody to help them develop their skills. In countries such as China or India, a person with mild Asperger's syndrome would go to engineering or computer science school. I have discussed this with parents from India or East Asia and they stress working with the child from a young age in career-relevant skills. We need to be working to develop the unique abilities of these individuals. I am worried about them getting 'stuck in a rut' and their creative skills will not be used.

References

Bakker, A., Kirwan, C. B., Miller, M. & Stark, C. E. L. 2008 Pattern separation in the human hippocampal CA3 and dentate gyrus. *Science* **319**, 1623–1624. (doi:10.1126/science.1152882)

Baron-Cohen, S. 2000 Is Asperger's syndrome and high functioning autism necessarily a disability? *Dev. Psychopathol.* **12**, 489–500. (doi:10.1017/S0954579400003126)

Baron-Cohen, S., Ashwin, E., Ashwin, C, Tavassoli, T. & Chakrabarti, B. 2009 Talent in autism: hyper-systemizing, hyper-attention to detail and sensory hypersensitivity. *Phil. Trans. R. Soc. B* **364**, 1377–1383. (doi:10.1098/rstb.2008.0337)

Casanova, M. & Trippe, J. 2009 Radial cytoarchitecture and patterns of cortical connectivity in autism. *Phil. Trans. R. Soc. B* **364**, 1433–1436. (doi:10.1098/rstb.2008.0331)

Casanova, M. E. *et al.* 2006 Minicolumnar abnormalities in autism. *Acta Neuropathol.* **112**, 287–303. (doi:10.1007/s00401-006-0085-5)

Casanova, M. E., Switala, A. E., Tripp, J. & Fitzgerald, M. 2007 Comparative minicolumnar morphomery of three distinguished scientists. *Autism* **11**, 557–569. (doi:10.1177/1362361307083261)

Courchesne, E., Redcay, E. & Kennedy, D. 2004 The autistic brain: birth through adulthood. *Curr. Opin. Neurol.* **17**, 489–496. (doi:10.1097/01.wco.0000137542.14610.b4)

Dawson, M., Soulieres, I., Gernsbacher, M. A. & Mottron, L. 2007 The level and nature of autistic intelligence. *Psychol. Sci.* **18**, 657–662. (doi:10.1111/j.1467-9280.2007.01954.x)

Fitzgerald, M. & O'Brien, B. 2007 *Genius genes, how Asperger talents changed the woxrld*. Shawnee Mission, KS: Autism Asperger Publishing Co.

Freedman, D. J., Riesenhubert, M., Poggio, T. & Miller, E. K. 2001 Categorical representation of visual stimuli in the primate prefrontal cortex. *Science* **291**, 312–315. (doi:10.1126/science.291.5502.312)

Grandin, T. 1995 *Thinking in pictures*. New York, NY: Vintage Press Random House. (Expanded version 2006)

Grandin, T. 2000 My mind as a web browser—how people with autism think. *Cerebrum* **9**, 13–22.

Grandin, T. 2002 Do animals and people with autism have true consciousness. *Evol. Cogn.* **8**, 241–248.

Grandin, T. & Johnson, C. 2005 *Animals in translation*. New York, NY: Scribner.

Happé, F. & Frith, U. 2009 The beautiful otherness of the autistic mind. *Phil. Trans. R. Soc. B* **364**, 1345–1350. (doi:10.1098/rstb.2009.0009)

Happé, F. & Vital, P. 2009 What aspects of autism predispose to talent? *Phil. Trans. R. Soc. B* **364**, 1369–1375. (doi:10.1098/rstb.2008.0332)

Kana, R. K., Keller, T. A., Cherkassky, V. L., Minshew, N. J. & Just, M. A. 2006 Sentence comprehension in autism: thinking in pictures with decreased functional connectivity. *Brain* **129**(Pt 9), 2484–2493. (doi:10.1093/brain/awl164)

Ledgin, N. 2002 *Aspergers and self esteem*. Arlington, TX: Future Horizons.

Miller, B. L., Cummings, J., Mishkin, F., Boone, B., Prince,F., Ponton, M. & Cotman, C. 1998 Emergence of artistic talent in frontotemporal dementia. *Neurology* **51**, 978–981.

Miller, B. L., Boone, K., Cummings, J. L., Read, S. L. & Mishkin, F. 2000 Functional correlates of musical and visual ability in fronto-temporal dementia. *Br. J. Psychiatry* **176**, 458–463. (doi:10.1192/bjp.176.5.458)

Minshew, N. J. & Williams, D. L. 2007 The new neurobiology of autism: cortex, connectivity, and neuronal organization. *Arch. Neurol.* **64**, 945–950. (doi:10.1001/archneur.64.7.945)

Minshew, N. J., Meyer, J. & Goldstein, G. 2002 Abstract reasoning in autism—a disassociation between concept formation and concept identification. *Neuropsychology* **16**, 327–334. (doi:10.1037/0894-4105.16.3.327)

Mummery, C. J., Patterson, K., Hodges, J. R. & Price, C. J. 1998 Functional neuroanatomy of the semantic system: divisible by what? *J. Cogn. Neurosci.* **10**, 766–777. (doi:10.1162/089892998 563059)

Newport, J., Newport, M. & Dodd, J. 2007 *Mozart and the whale*. New York, NY: Touchstone.

Scheuffgen, K., Happé, F., Anderson, M. & Frith, U. 2000 High 'intelligence,' low 'IQ'? Speed of processing and measured IQ in children with autism. *Dev. Psychopathol.* **12**, 83–90. (doi:10.1017/S095457940000105X)

Snyder, A. 2009 Explaining and inducing savant skills: privileged access to lower level, less-processed information. *Phil. Trans. R. Soc. B* **364**, 1399–1405. (doi:10.1098/rstb.2008.0290)

Tammet, D. 2006 *Born on a blue day*. New York, NY: Free Press.

13

Assessing musical skills in autistic children who are not savants

Pamela Heaton

> Descriptions of autistic musical savants suggest that they possess extraordinary skills within the domain. However, until recently little was known about the musical skills and potential of individuals with autism who are not savants. The results from these more recent studies investigating music perception, cognition and learning in musically untrained children with autism have revealed a pattern of abilities that are either enhanced or spared. For example, increased sensitivity to musical pitch and timbre is frequently observed, and studies investigating perception of musical structure and emotions have consistently failed to reveal deficits in autism. While the phenomenon of the savant syndrome is of considerable theoretical interest, it may have led to an under-consideration of the potential talents and skills of that vast majority of autistic individuals, who do not meet savant criteria. Data from empirical studies show that many autistic children possess musical potential that can and should be developed.
>
> **Keywords:** autism; music; cognition; perception; savants

13.1 Background

This paper focuses on music perception and cognition in that majority of children with autism who do not possess 'savant talent' as defined by Treffert (1989). Research on this topic was originally motivated by an interest in musical savants and questions about the cognitive characteristics that distinguish savants from autistic people without savant talent. However, findings from studies comparing non-savant autistic participants with age- and intelligence-matched controls revealed an intriguing pattern of enhanced and spared musical abilities. Consequently, this topic became interesting in its own right.

It was not only investigations sparked by the phenomenon of savantism that raised questions about unusual musical cognition in autism. Kanner, who first described autism in 1943, described several instances of extraordinary musical memory in his clinical group. Indeed, case reports of 6 of the 11 individuals described include descriptions of music-related behaviours that are extraordinary given their developmental levels. Particularly remarkable was case 9, who was able to discriminate between 18 symphonies and name their composers by 18 months. While Kanner's description has been hugely influential clinically, the potential functional significance of these children's intense and early preoccupation with music has been little considered. This may have been because their music-related behaviours were characterized as *rote memory* and assumed to be without affective or functional significance.

However, research shows that typical listeners learn about music simply by listening and it is clear that in this respect, the children in Kanner's group were similar to typical children: they learned by listening. Statistical learning, the mechanism that enables individuals to extract and represent higher-order domain-specific structures, from the stimuli to which they are exposed, has been widely implicated in music (e.g. Krumhansl *et al.* 2000), and it seems likely that the extraordinary musical memory abilities noted in Kanner's children were the end product of similar processes.

Nevertheless, while it is plausible to invoke 'typical' learning mechanisms, it also appears that early, atypically focused attention to and perception of music may differentiate at least some children with autism from those with typical development. Indeed, it is difficult to understand how case 9, described by Kanner, could have memorized such a large corpus of musical compositions were this not the case. The weak central coherence (WCC; Frith 1989; Happé 1999; Happé & Frith 2006) and enhanced perceptual functioning (Mottron & Burack 2001; Mottron *et al.* 2006) models of autism both hypothesize domain-general atypical perceptual and cognitive processing, and predictions from these models have been tested in a number of studies comparing music perception and cognition in autism and typical development. The findings from several of these studies have identified superior performance in autism, and these will be outlined in §2.

13.2 Enhanced music perception in non-savant children with autism

The first study to identify superior performance on a musical task in autism was carried out by Applebaum *et al.* (1979). They observed that reproduction of atonal melodies was superior in the autistic child participants, compared with intellectually able typical children who had higher levels of musical experience. The second study to investigate musical pitch processing in autism (Heaton *et al.* 1998) tested the hypothesis that absolute pitch ability (AP), invariably observed in musical savants (Miller 1989), might also be more prevalent in autism. Motivated by Zatorre *et al.*'s (1998) suggestion that AP might reflect the ability to retrieve an arbitrary association between a pitch and a verbal label, children with autism and age- and intelligence-matched comparison children were presented with tones and animal pictures for paired learning. The findings from the study showed superior recall for the tone/animal pairings in the autism group. It was also noted that retrieval scores correlated with scores on the block design test from the Wechsler Intelligence Scales (Wechsler 1992), a test considered to be a marker for WCC (Shah & Frith 1993). It was therefore suggested that a local bias at the perceptual level (Happé 1999) was implicated in AP in autism.

However, while subsequent group and case studies replicated enhanced pitch identification in autism (Heaton *et al.* 1999a, 2008a; Bonnel *et al.* 2003; Heaton 2003), a significant positive correlation between pitch identification and block design scores was not observed, and this brought the positive association between AP and a local bias, as measured by the block design test, into question.

In typical populations, AP, or the ability to associate a pitch and a (usually verbal) label, is associated with the early onset of musical tuition. It is assumed that during early training the child focuses attention on tones and their corresponding note names and stores them in long-term memory (see Takeuchi & Hulse 1993). Increased attention to music, as suggested by Kanner's report, may enable autistic children to represent discrete, but unlabelled pitches in long-term memory. Anecdotal reports of autistic children remembering and reproducing environmental sounds are consistent with this suggestion. However, findings showing that autistic children, without musical training, can associate tones and retrieval labels in long-term memory (Heaton *et al.* 2008*a*) suggests that AP acquisition in autism and typical development is influenced by different processes. The suggestion that AP may be acquired by multiple routes is consistent with findings showing that the changes in functional anatomy (planum temporale) associated with AP in typical groups (e.g. Zatorre *et al.* 1998) are not observed in those with AP and congenital blindness (Hamilton *et al.* 2004). While abnormalities in planum temporale volumes have been observed in adults and children with autism (Rojas *et al.* 2002, 2005), the pattern of asymmetry is unlike that observed in typical AP possessors. As pitch naming skills were not tested in these studies, no conclusions about the neural correlates of AP in autism can be drawn.

If, as has been suggested, increased early attention to music is implicated in enhanced pitch memory in autism, fundamental questions about why such atypical attention is characteristic are worthy of investigation. In a recent study, J. L. Ward (2008, unpublished thesis) attempted to address this. She hypothesized that enhanced sensitivity to the perceptual components of music increases its reward value, thereby motivating increased listening.

Timbre refers to the colouristic aspects of sound. Orchestral music, written for a range of string, wind, brass and percussion instruments, provides an extremely rich palette of sounds. The timbre of a solo cello, violin or clarinet, or of a favourite singer's voice, can increase the listeners' aesthetic and emotional experience. Each instrument has its own particular sound, and Grey's multidimensional scaling model (Grey 1977) formalizes the degree of difference in psycho-acoustic qualities between instruments.

In Ward's study, children with autistic spectrum disorder (ASD) and comparison children were presented with pairs of melodies and asked to say whether they were played by the same or different instruments. Different melody pairs were played by either *timbre-similar* (Bb bass clarinet and saxophone) or *timbre-dissimilar* (cello and soprano saxophone) instruments. The results from the study were analysed using signal detection theory and showed overall enhanced sensitivity to differences in timbre in the ASD group. Their pattern of discrimination performance was also different from that of controls. While controls were significantly better able to discriminate dissimilar from similar instruments, the ASD participants distinguished both types equally well. Thus, the largest between-group difference was observed when children were required to discriminate between instruments closely related in terms of timbre.

The findings from this study support the EPF theory of autism and also provide important clues about why some children with autism might show increased early attention to music. Perceptual information within creative domains, such as music (e.g. timbre) and art (e.g. colour), possesses considerable affective value. As Patel (2008) suggests 'a musical melody is a set of tones that love each other, a linguistic melody is a group of tones that work together to get a job done'. It may then be the case that increased sensitivity to these affectively rich aspects of sound increases listening and promotes enhanced pitch memory skills in some individuals. However, increased motivation to listen also increases the individual's opportunities to learn about other higher-order properties of music. In contrast to studies testing lower-order musical properties and showing enhanced performance in autism, experiments testing perception of higher-order musical properties have largely failed to identify differences between autism and control groups. These experiments will be discussed in the next section.

13.3 Spared music perception in non-savant children with autism

In Frith's original formulation of the WCC theory (1989), she outlined a deficit in global processing. However, several studies directly addressed the question of whether a global deficit would impair music processing, and the findings showed that this is not the case. For example, in one open-ended experiment, where chords could be processed holistically or at the local (tone) level, a typical global bias was observed in the autism group (Heaton 2003). Similarly, when Gestalt preserving changes were made to one of a pair of melodies, participants with autism, like controls, judged that both melodies were the same (Heaton 2005). In a study by Mottron *et al.* (2000), autistic participants were also able to understand that when the second of a pair of melodies was presented in transposition (different notes/key) it was the same melody as the first (Mottron *et al.* 2000). It does not appear that a global deficit, at least as operationalized in these studies, characterizes music processing in autism.

One higher-order component of music that is relatively easy to define is its structure. The study of musical forms, e.g. sonata form and fugue, has long been part of the classical musician's training. However, as interest in music psychology has grown, researchers have turned their attention to questions about how musical structure is represented cognitively. This work has provided important insights into ways in which music perception parallels and differs from perception of other types of auditory stimuli, especially language (see Patel 2008). For example, experimental studies show that listeners' expectancies for upcoming musical events are primed by harmonic contexts at both global and local levels, with the former being most important (Tillman *et al.* 1998). This provides parallels with speech perception, where expectancies are primed by semantic content.

Using an adaptation of the sequential processing paradigm used by Tillman *et al.* (1998), we tested musically untrained children with ASD and typical development, and observed, in both groups, patterns of performance that were very similar to those observed when similar paradigms were tested with musically untrained adults. When individual target chords were preceded by sequences of seven chords to which they were harmonically related at global (chords 1–6) and local (chord 7) levels, our participants thought that they sounded correct. Numbers of 'correct' judgements fell when targets were related to the preceding context at the global level only, although these were still higher than when chords were related at the local level only. Targets were invariably judged to be incorrect when they were unrelated at global or local levels (Heaton *et al.* 2007).

This study showed that children with ASD acquire an understanding of the rules governing Western musical harmony. However, in a replication of this study, in which speed manipulations were carried out on the chord sequences (G. M. Nash 2008, unpublished thesis), some of the children with autism showed a temporal processing deficit. So, while a clear global bias was observed when stimuli were presented at a moderate tempo, this was lost and responses became random when stimuli were presented slowly. It was interesting that in a recent study carried out with high-functioning adults with ASD (Allen et al. 2009), 2 of the 12 participants in the study expressed a dislike for slow music, describing it as 'dirgey' and 'dirge-like'. This suggests that for a subgroup of individuals, temporal processing abnormalities result in a degree of musical impairment. However, the children in Nash's study showed no abnormalities when music was presented at moderate tempo, and the effects of such a difficulty may be limited to influencing a preference for faster music.

Other investigations tested the extent to which children with autism understand music's emotional connotations. The first of these examined perception of musical mode (Heaton et al. 1999b) and showed that children with autism were just as likely to pair fragments of major mode music with happy faces and fragments of minor mode music with sad faces as were age- and intelligence-matched controls.

In an extension of this study (Heaton et al. 2008b) we tested groups of typical 4- to 10-year-old children, musically naive adults, high- and low-functioning children and adolescents with autism and children and adolescents with Down syndrome. The task was to listen to extracts of music drawn from the classical orchestral repertoire and to match them with pictures depicting anger, fear, triumph, tenderness and contemplation. As a control condition, music and pictures depicting movement states (walking, running, gliding, climbing and jumping) were also presented for pairing. Our analysis of the data from the typical children and adults showed higher levels of music/picture matching for the feeling state conditions in comparison with the movement state conditions. Correct performance on the feeling state condition increased significantly from 4 to 6 years and from 6 to 8 years, at which point discrimination did not differ from that of musically untrained adults. The participants with Down syndrome showed poor performance on the task although it was significantly better than chance. The individuals in the ASD group performed well and, similar to typically developing participants, showed better identification of feeling state than of movement stimuli. When a regression analysis was carried out on the data, we found that performance was unaffected by diagnostic category and that verbal mental age explained much of the variance in the study. The results from our music screening questionnaire confirmed that good performance in the ASD group did not reflect increased musical exposure or training.

While sensitivity to music's affective and cultural connotations appears to depend on the extent to which language develops, sensitivity to other aspects of the musical language may be less dependent on language. In the study investigating the perception of musical structure (Heaton et al. 2007), groups were matched for chronological age and non-verbal intelligence, and verbal intelligence scores were not collected. While statistically significant group differences did not emerge in the study it is possible that mean verbal IQ scores were lower for the participants with autism suggesting that performance was enhanced relative to verbal mental age. While this is somewhat speculative, it is consistent with the findings from a recent study testing implicit learning of musical syntax. In this experiment, the autistic children were again matched to controls for chronological age and non-verbal intelligence, but tests of receptive vocabulary and grammar were also administered. The findings showed that the children with autism obtained significantly higher implicit learning test scores than controls even though their scores on the receptive vocabulary and grammar tests were significantly lower (J. L. Ward 2008, unpublished thesis).

13.4 Why are autistic people so drawn to music?

Temple Grandin has suggested that individuals with autism show a strong appreciation for musical structure, and Mottron *et al.* (2009) have provided a convincing account for why this might be the case. However, it should not be assumed that increased sensitivity to musical structure implies decreased sensitivity to music's affective qualities. Musicologists have long been interested in the relationship between the listeners' perception of structure, and his/her experience of emotion in response to this. Indeed, recent work by Huron (2006) suggests that is not really possible to disentangle musical structure and emotion, as the latter arises in direct response to the former. Mottron *et al.* (2009) suggest that pattern-rich, highly structured domains are affectively rewarding for people with autism and this provides a convincing explanation for why, for example, calendar calculating is so much more commonly observed in autism than in typical development.

However, music differs from calendars in important ways and consideration of these differences may provide insights into the question of why autistic people are so motivated to listen to music. First, 'lower level' musical information (e.g. timbre and groups of pitches) possesses rich affective qualities that may serve to 'capture' attention. Once attention is captured, statistical learning processes may come online and enable the individual to learn about music's higher-order characteristics. Although calendars and music share some organizational similarities, music may be distinguished by the extent to which perception of unfolding structure and experiences of emotion are linked (Mayer 1956; Huron 2006). Thus, while perceptual and cognitive accounts of autism continue to contribute much to our understanding of skills and talents in autism, the importance of affect in motivating autistic interests has yet be given full consideration. Recently, Berthoz & Hill (2005) identified type-II alexithymia, a disorder characterized by difficulties in verbally expressing emotions, in autistic adults. This raises interesting questions about how musical preoccupations might relate to difficulties in interpersonal domains.

13.5 The problem of unexploited musical potential in autism

While research into music cognition was originally motivated by an interest in musical savants, findings from studies testing children who do not meet criteria for savant skills suggest that they nevertheless possess considerable, but often unexploited, musical potential. For example, Heaton *et al.* (1999*a*) described the case of an adolescent boy with autism, who had AP and performed at ceiling on a battery of music analysis tasks. This individual had access to several instruments and carried a trumpet around with him but instrumental lessons had been very difficult to organize and his instrumental skills were negligible.

More recent data further address the question of unexploited musical potential in children with autism. In this study (Heaton *et al.* 2008*a*), high- and low-functioning children with autism completed tests of pitch discrimination and memory. The tasks required the children to map learned tones onto a visuospatial format (a staircase) for immediate and delayed retrieval. While the majority of the children with autism performed similarly to controls, scores for a subgroup of three children, comprising approximately 10 per cent of the sample, were between four and five standard deviations higher than those of the remaining autistic and typically developing participants. An analysis of the musical background data confirmed that their unusually accurate discrimination and memory skills did not reflect music lessons or a musically enriched environment. Indeed, their formal and informal opportunities to learn about music had been very limited. However, they all obtained high ratings for parental responses to the question 'How often does your child *choose* to listen to music at home?' and 'How would you rate your child's *reaction* to music?' Unfortunately, none of the children had been provided with the opportunity to learn to play a musical instrument, and the extent to which enhanced pitch analysis skills and increased self-motivated listening, would, if appropriately *scaffolded,* manifest in a talent for musical performance, is not known.

13.6 Future directions

Descriptions of musical savants suggest that they acquire instrumental skills with minimal tuition, and sometimes with relatively limited access to musical instruments (Miller 1989). However, this is very unusual, and it would never be assumed that a typically developing child would develop musical skills without tuition and supported and extensive practice. Teaching music to children with social and communication difficulties poses special challenges for music educators. Nevertheless, there are several compelling reasons why such challenges should be met. First, there is some evidence that music instruction is associated with improvements in spatio-temporal processing (Hetland 2000), in some mathematical skills (Graziano *et al.* 1999) and in reading (Butzlaff 2000). Second, music serves important intra-personal functions (Patel 2008). As one adult autistic participant in the study carried out by Allen *et al.* (2009) said, 'I find that sometimes if you're feeling very sad or something, listening to that kind of music can put you in touch with your feelings, it can help you to access your feelings. You can really feel the feelings instead of their just being there, you can really dwell in that state and deal with it.' Finally, music may convey interpersonal advantages. Children who sing, or play musical instruments, may increase their opportunities for social interactions, for example, by playing music in chamber groups and orchestras and singing in choirs.

Mottron *et al.* (2009) have suggested that there may be a particularly strong fit between the cognitive demands of savant domains and the pattern of strengths displayed by people with autism. The findings from the studies reviewed in this paper are consistent with this view. But it is also clear that for music, such strengths very rarely progress to skilled performance unaided. Children with autism, like typical children, need to be taught. The time therefore seems ripe to focus attention on how best this might be achieved.

References

Allen, R., Hill, E. & Heaton, P. 2009 'Hath charms to soothe...': an exploratory study of how high-functioning adults with ASD experience music. *Autism* **13**, 21–41. (doi:10.1177/1362361307098511)

Applebaum, E., Egel, A. L., Koegel, R. L. & Imhoff, B. 1979 Measuring musical abilities of autistic children. *J. Autism Dev. Disord.* **9**, 279–285. (doi:10.1007/BF01531742)

Berthoz, S. & Hill, E. L. 2005 The validity of using self-reports to assess emotion regulation abilities in adults with autism spectrum disorder. *Eur. Psychiatry* **20**, 291–298. (doi:10.1016/j.eurpsy.2004.06.013)

Bonnel, A., Mottron, L., Peretz, I., Trudel, M., Gallun, E. & Bonnel, A. M. 2003 Enhanced pitch sensitivity in individuals with autism: a signal detection analysis. *J. Cogn. Neurosci.* **15**, 226–235. (doi:10.1162/089892903321208169)

Butzlaff, R. 2000 Can music be used to teach reading? *J. Aesthetic Educ.* **34**, 167–178. (doi:10.2307/3333642)

Frith, U. 1989 *Autism: explaining the enigma.* Oxford, UK: Blackwell.

Graziano, A. B., Peterson, M. & Shaw, G. L. 1999 Enhanced learning of proportional math through music training and spatial-temporal training. *Neurol. Res.* **21**, 139–152.

Grey, J. M. 1977 Multidimensional perceptual scaling of musical timbre. *J. Acoust. Soc. Am.* **61**, 1270–1277. (doi:10.1121/1.381428)

Hamilton, R. H., Pascual-Leone, A. & Schlaug, G. 2004 Absolute pitch in blind musicians. *Neuroreport* **15**, 803–806. (doi:10.1097/00001756-200404090-00012)

Happé, F. 1999 Autism: cognitive deficit or cognitive style? *Trends Cogn. Sci.* **3**, 216–222. (doi:10.1016/S1364-6613(99)01318-2)

Happé, F. & Frith, U. 2006 The weak coherence account: detail-focused cognitive style in autism spectrum disorders. *J. Autism Dev. Disord.* **1**, 1–21. (doi:10.1007/S10803-005-0039-0)

Heaton, P. 2003 Pitch memory, labeling and disembedding in autism. *J. Child Psychol. Psychiatry* **44**, 543–551. (doi:10.1111/1469-7610.00143)

Heaton, P. 2005 Interval and contour processing in autism. *J. Autism Dev. Disord.* **35**, 787–793. (doi:10.1007/sl0803-005-0024-7)

Heaton, P., Hermelin, B. & Pring, L. 1998 Autism and pitch processing: a precursor for savant musical ability? *Music Percept.* **15**, 291–305.

Heaton, P., Pring, L. & Hermelin, B. 1999a A pseudo-savant: a case of exceptional musical splinter skills. *Neurocase* **5**, 503–509. (doi:10.1080/13554799908402745)

Heaton, P., Hermelin, B. & Pring, L. 1999b Can children with autistic spectrum disorders perceive affect in music? An experimental investigation. *Psychol. Med.* **29**, 1405–1410. (doi:10.1017/S0033291799001221)

Heaton, P., Williams, K., Cummins, O. & Happé, F. 2007 Beyond perception: musical representation and on-line processing in autism. *J. Autism Dev. Disord.* **37**, 1355–1360. (doi:10.1007/sl0803-006-0283-y)

Heaton, P., Williams, K., Cummins, O. & Happé, F. 2008a Autism and pitch processing splinter skills: a group and sub-group analysis. *Autism* **12**, 21–37. (doi:10.1177/1362361307085270)

Heaton, P., Allen, R., Williams, K., Cummins, O. & Happé, F. 2008b Do social and cognitive deficits curtail musical understanding? Evidence from autism and Down syndrome. *Br. J. Dev. Psychol.* **26**, 171–182. (doi:10.1348/026151007X206776)

Hetland, L. 2000 Learning to make music enhances spatial reasoning. *J. Aesthetic Educ.* **34**, 179–238. (doi:10.2307/3333643) EJ 658 284

Huron, D. 2006 *Sweet anticipation: music and the psychology of expectation.* Cambridge, MA: MIT Press.

Kanner, L. 1943 Autistic disturbances of affective contact. *Nerv. Child* **2**, 217–250.

Krumhansl, C. L., Toivanen, P., Eerola, T, Toivianen, P., Jarvinen, T. & Louhivuori, J. 2000 Cross-cultural music cognition: cognitive methodology applied to North Sami yoiks. *Cognition* **76**, 13–58. (doi:10.1016/S0010-0277(00)00068-8)

Meyer, L. 1956 *Emotion and meaning in music.* Chicago, IL: University of Chicago Press.

Miller, L. 1989 *Musical savants: exceptional skill in the mentally retarded.* Hillsdale, NJ: Lawrence Erlbaum Associates.

Mottron, L. & Burack, J. 2001 Enhanced perceptual functioning in the development of persons with autism. In *The development of autism* (eds J. A. Burack, T. Charman, N. Yirmiya & P. R. Zalazo), pp. 131–148. Mahwah, NJ: Lawrence Erlbaum Associates.

Mottron, L., Peretz, I. & Menard, E. 2000 Local and global processing of music in high-functioning persons with autism: beyond central coherence? *J. Child Psychol. Psychiatry* **41**, 1057–1065. (doi:10.1111/1469-7610.00693)

Mottron, L., Dawson, M., Soulières, I., Hubert, B. & Burack, J. 2006 Enhanced perceptual functioning in autism: an update, and eight principles of autistic perception. *J. Autism Dev. Disord.* **2**, 1–17. (doi:10.1007/sl0803-005-0048-z)

Mottron, L., Dawson, M. & Soulieres, I. 2009 Enhanced perception in savant syndrome: patterns, structure and creativity. *Phil. Trans. R. Soc. B* **364**, 1385–1391. (doi:10.1098/rstb.2008.0333)

Patel, A. D. 2008 *Music, language, and the brain.* New York, NY: Oxford University Press.

Rojas, D. C, Bawn, S. D., Benkers, T. L., Reite, M. L. & Rogers, S. J. 2002 Smaller left hemisphere planum temporale in adults with autistic disorder. *Neurosci. Lett.* **328**, 237–240. (doi:10.1016/S0304-3940(02)00521-9)

Rojas, D. C, Camou, S. L., Reite, M. L. & Rogers, S. J. 2005 Planum temporale volume in children and adolescents with autism. *J. Autism Dev. Disord.* **35**, 479–486. (doi:10.1007/s10803-005-5038-7) see also 488

Shah, A. & Frith, U. 1993 Why do autistic individuals show superior performance on the block design test? *J. Child Psychol. Psychiatry* **34**, 1351–1364. (doi:10.1111/j.1469-7610.1993.tb02095.x)

Takeuchi, A. H. & Hulse, S. H. 1993 Absolute pitch. *Psychol. Bull.* **113**, 345–361. (doi:10.1037/0033-2909.113.2.345)

Tillman, B., Bigand, E. & Pineau, M. 1998 Effects of local and global context on harmonic expectancy. *Music Percept.* **16**, 99–118.

Treffert, D. 1989 *Extraordinary people: understanding 'idiot savants'.* New York, NY: Harper & Row.

Wechsler, D. 1992 *Wechsler intelligence scales for children,* 3rd edn. London, UK: The Psychological Corporation.

Zatorre, R. J., Perry, D. W, Beckett, C. A., Westbury, C. F. & Evans, A. C. 1998 Functional anatomy of musical processing in listeners with absolute pitch and relative pitch. *Proc. Natl Acad. Sci. USA* **95**, 3172–3177. (doi:10.1073/pnas.95.6.3172)

14

Precocious realists: perceptual and cognitive characteristics associated with drawing talent in non-autistic children

Jennifer E. Drake and Ellen Winner

A local processing bias in the block design task and in drawing strategy has been used to account for realistic drawing skill in individuals with autism. We investigated whether the same kind of local processing bias is seen in typically developing children with unusual skill in realistic graphic representation. Forty-three 5–11-year-olds who drew a still life completed a version of the block design task in both standard and segmented form, were tested for their memory for the block design items, and were given the Kaufmann Brief Intelligence Test-II. Children were classified as gifted, moderately gifted or typical on the basis of the level of realism in their drawings. Similar to autistic individuals, the gifted group showed a local processing bias in the block design task. But unlike autistic individuals, the gifted group showed a global advantage in the visual memory task and did not use a local drawing strategy; in addition, their graphic realism skill was related to verbal IQ. Differences in the extent of local processing bias in autistic and typically developing children with drawing talent are discussed.

Keywords: art; gifted; autism

A realistic drawing does not *copy* information from the world onto paper: even the most highly realistic drawing is an abstraction that differs considerably from the image formed on the retina with a stationary eye (Gombrich 1960; Kennedy 1974; Gibson 1979; Gregory 1997). It is not possible to transfer the infinite gradations in colour and light, or the enormous array of detail in our three-dimensional visual world, onto a two-dimensional surface, and thus much information must be omitted. In addition, the most realistic drawings also must *distort* in order to convey the illusion of realism: a table top drawn with lines that converge is a distortion—an actual table's edges are parallel—and yet the distorted table top conveys the impression of an actual table receding into depth. A viewer-specific rather than object-specific representation must be drawn for the picture to look realistic.

Individuals differ in their ability to draw realistically, and these differences can be seen in very early childhood, prior to any kind of drawing instruction (Golomb 1992; Winner 1996; Milbrath 1998). Children who are gifted in realistic drawing and who are able to create life-like representations (hereafter referred to as precocious realists) create drawings that differ in many respects from the drawings of typical children. Here, we outline some of the most important differences, discuss the role of culture in influencing the type of realistic style adopted, ponder why it is that we see early gifts in realistic representation but not in abstract expressionism, and consider some of the cognitive and perceptual skills associated with precocious realism in typically developing as well as autistic individuals with drawing talent. We argue that the precocious realists and autistic savants are similar in important (though not all) respects.

14.1 Characteristics of drawings by non-autistic precocious realists

(a) Graphic representation, not action representation

While typical children begin to draw recognizable shapes representing objects in the world at around the age of 3 or 4 (Kellogg 1969; Matthews 1984; Golomb 1992), some children produce their first representational drawings at the age of 2. The typical child who made the drawing in figure 14.1 moved the brush in circular motions while labelling his painting an aeroplane: his drawing *represents* an aeroplane, but the representation was in the *action* and the labelling rather than in the final product. Matthews (1984) refers to this kind of drawing as an 'action representation', and contrasts it to a 'graphic representation' (figure 14.2), where it is clear what the drawing represents *after* the process of creating the drawing is complete.

(b) Line as contour or edge

Figure 14.3 is a drawing of two apples by a precocious realist aged 2 years and two months; figure 14.4 is a drawing of two apples by a typical child of precisely the same age. In figure 14.3, the lines stand for the contour of the apples. In figure 14.4, each line stands for an apple, with no regard for the apple's contour. For this child, a line simply stands for 'thingness'.

Figure 14.1 Action representation by a 2-year-old. From Matthews (1984), 'Children Drawing: Are Young Children Really Scribbling' *Early Child Development and Care*, Taylor and Francis, Ltd., http://www.informaworld.com, reprinted with permission from the publisher.

Figure 14.2 Balloons drawn by a precocious realist, age 2. From Winner (1996).

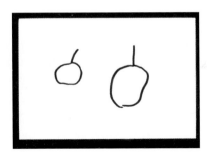

Figure 14.3 Two apples drawn by a precocious realist, age 2.2. From Winner (1996).

Figure 14.4 Age-typical representation of two apples, age 2.2. From Winner (1996).

Figure 14.5 Tadpole human, age 3. From Winner (1996).

(c) Differentiated shape

Figure 14.5 shows the familiar tadpole representation of a human, typical of children at age 3. The head and body are not differentiated, and arms and legs come out of a central circular form. By contrast, figure 14.6 shows a drawing by Grace, a child with an extraordinary ability to draw people realistically as early as age 2. In place of the simple, schematic, flat forms found in typical child art, Grace has produced a differentiated human form suggesting an effort to understand how objects are structured.

Figure 14.6 Dancing figure drawn by Grace, precocious realist, age 3. From Winner (1996). Reprinted with permission from Jennifer and Alan Pekrul.

(d) Proportion

Milbrath (1998) found that artistically gifted children succeed in drawing human figures in proportion between the ages of 4 and 10. The non-gifted children that she studied were still unable to capture proportion by age 14 (which was the oldest age at which she observed their drawings).

(e) Illusion of depth

Typically, children in Western culture do not begin to try to depict volume and depth until middle childhood, and do not use even primitive perspective until adolescence (Willats 1977). But some children invent primitive perspective systems as early as 3 years of age. Figure 14.7 shows a truck drawn by a child aged 3 years and seven months, in which he has represented the third dimension by parallel oblique lines (Golomb 1992). Artistically gifted children begin to make viewer-specific drawings long before ordinary children do so (Milbrath 1998). Their drawings show figures in non-canonical positions (e.g. three-quarter views of faces by age 7, back views, profiles) as well as figures distorted and foreshortened by perspective.

(f) Ease of drawing

Precocious realists draw quickly and with ease (Gordon 1987; Paine 1987; Pariser 1991, 1992/93; Milbrath 1998). They do not labour and erase. The young Picasso could draw anything upon demand, and liked to start a figure from non-canonical places, for instance, by drawing a dog beginning with the ear (Richardson 1991).

Figure 14.7 Truck by Eitan, age 3.7, showing perspective. From Golomb (1992). Reprinted with permission from Claire Golomb.

(g) Realism in juvenilia of great artists

The ability to draw realistically at an earlier than average age also marks the childhoods of those who go on to become established artists, but we only have evidence for this from artists born into a Western artistic tradition. Gordon (1987) studied the childhood works of 31 Israeli artists and found that all stood out for their ability to draw realistically. The desire and ability to draw realistically at an early age also characterized the childhoods of a group of sculptors (Sloane & Sosniak 1985).

Picasso provides a clear example of the ability to draw highly realistically at an early age. He claimed that he bypassed the typical stage of early drawings in which children draw in a fanciful, playful and non-realistic manner. 'I have never done children's drawings. Never' (Richardson 1991, p. 29). When he went to see a show of child art, he noted, 'As a child I would never have been able to participate in a show of this kind: at age 12, I drew like Raphael' (Richardson 1991, p. 29). And he recalled specific examples of this adult-like style: 'Even when I was very small, I remember one of my first drawings. I was perhaps six. In my father's house there was a statue of Hercules with his club in the corridor, and I drew Hercules. But it wasn't a child's drawing. It was a real drawing, representing Hercules with his club' (Richardson 1991, p. 29). At 11, Picasso enrolled in his father's academic drawing class, in which students had to make detailed renderings of plaster casts. While most students considered this drudgery, Picasso loved it.

14.2 The influence of the culture's artistic conventions on drawings by non-autistic precocious realists

A comparison between ink drawings by Yani (figure 14.8), a Chinese child considered a prodigy in painting (Zhensun & Low 1991), and the drawings in figures 14.2, 3 and 6 underscores the role of the culture's artistic conventions (the domain) in shaping the drawings of even very young children gifted in drawing. By the time she was four, Yani had developed a sense of the adult art world, and could make the kind of art valued by the art 'field' in her culture, i.e. the art historians, the museum curators, etc. She used the classical Chinese wash technique: she did not draw outlines around her shapes, and

Figure 14.8 Cat by Yani, age 3. Reprinted with permission from Wang Shiqiang.

she painted in the allusionistic, impressionistic, abbreviated style of Chinese ink paintings. Thus, as Goldsmith (1992) points out, the technical sophistication of her work reveals itself along dimensions different from those of Western children.

We might be tempted to view Grace as the greater realist compared to Yani. However, both child artists mastered the conventions of their culture's art. Grace mastered the use of line as contour or edge, surely a convention, and has conveyed depth through the technique of occlusion (the leg is in front of the skirt and hence part of the skirt is occluded by the leg); Yani mastered the use of thick brush stroke to capture the shape of the cat, with no attempt at creating the illusion of the third dimension.

How can we account for the differences between the drawings of Grace and Yani? We suggest that the differences derive from the pictures these children see. Even 2-year-olds have been exposed to drawings and paintings in the representational style favoured by their culture: children see pictures in magazines, pictures hung on the wall, and pictures in the books that are read to them. Western children are more likely to see realistic drawings and cartoons; Chinese children are more likely to see representational works that are drawn in the allusionistic brush and ink style of Chinese classical art. These two children have an astonishing mimetic ability that enables them to internalize the style of the art to which they were exposed and then to generate paintings in that style. These children were not copying specific drawings; rather they were able to extract the style of the drawings to which they had been exposed. Thus, the domain—the body of works that make up the history of painting in one's culture—exerts as powerful an influence on child prodigies as on adult artists. It is unlikely that either Grace or Yani could have painted as they did without the influence of their respective traditions.

What unites all children with artistic gifts, we argue, is not the ability or proclivity to draw in the style of Western realism, but rather the ability to master one or more of the culture's norms of visual representation at a very early age. At the heart of artistic talent is the ability to master one's culture's representational conventions, whether the convention is Western-style realism in the case of Grace or Eitan, or Chinese-style allusionistic brush painting in the case of Yani. It is a mistake to be blinded by our Western eyes and see Western-style realism as the prime sign of artistic talent, when this style is but one of the many possible representational conventions that artistically gifted children master so early and so independently.

14.3 Why are there no abstract expressionist prodigies?

In 2007, a movie called 'My Kid Could Paint That' was released in the United States. This movie told the story of Marla Olmstead, a 4-year-old whose canvases have been selling for many thousands of dollars. She has been hailed as an abstract expressionist child prodigy. Perhaps people are willing to pay high sums for her paintings because they believe that she is the next Kandinsky or the next de Kooning. Her website http://www.marlaolmstead.com has a painting entitled *Darlene's Bikini* that is superficially similar to a painting by Willem de Kooning (figure 14.9).

Marla is not the only child in the US being touted as an abstract expressionist prodigy. For example, on the website of Dante Lamb, http://www.dantelambart.com/about.html, we read that Dante is the Guinness World Record holder for the 'youngest professional artist'. He began painting at the age of 2 and sold his first painting when he was just 3 years old.

Figure 14.9 Painting by Willem de Kooning. Reprinted with permission from The Willem de Kooning Foundation/Artists Rights Society.

Since then, he has exhibited his work in several galleries in Georgia and Florida. He paints in the form of abstract expressionism. Figure 14.10 shows one of his paintings. Marla Olmstead was given excellent paints to use, and canvas to paint on. One reason why her work may have passed for adult abstract expressionism could be that these superior materials lent her paintings a professional appearance. If one looks through the materials to the forms, it becomes clear that her works as well as those of Dante Lamb are not different in any interesting respect from the works of 'typical' pre-schoolers.

Figure 14.10 Painting by Dante Lamb. Reprinted with permission from Aimee Lamb.

Some of the works by Marla seem more sophisticated and complex but there is a strong suspicion, developed in the movie, that someone else (perhaps her father) fraudulently completed Marla's painting.

The confusion between the abstract works of 3- and 4-year-olds who draw and paint at an age-typical level and the works of abstract expressionists derives from a misunderstanding of abstract art, and from the all too common view that 'anyone can do this'. The confusion is also played upon by the desire of parents to make their children famous and rich.

Why do we not find true abstract expressionist prodigies? Every domain in which child prodigies have been noted has been a fairly formal, structured, rule-governed domain, whether this be classical music, mathematics or realistic drawing. We do not see prodigies in philosophy or in novel writing, and we do not find them in the domain of abstract art. It appears that the kinds of domains that attract young prodigies are those with a formal set of rules to master. Perhaps it is more difficult to master (and to master well) an ill-defined domain such as abstract art with no rules to learn, rules such as geometric perspective, shading, colour mixing, etc.

14.4 Do artistic savants with autism share characteristics with non-autistic precocious realists?

It is striking that all of the characteristics summarized above that we see in the drawings of non-autistic precocious realists have also been noted in the drawings of artistic savants with autism (Selfe 1977, 1983; O'Connor & Hermelin 1987, 1988, 1990; Wiltshire 1987, 1989, 1991; Mottron & Belleville 1993, 1995; Pring & Hermelin 1993; Pring et al. 1995). Artistic savants draw realistically, no abstract expressionist savants have been reported, and culture influences the realistic style of artistic savants, as can be seen in the drawing by a Japanese savant painted in the allusionistic style of Japanese brush paintings (Morishima & Brown 1977). Figure 14.11 shows an extremely realistic and precise drawing by a Western savant artist with autism, E.C., studied by Mottron & Belleville (1993), and figure 14.12 shows an ink drawing of a frog by the Japanese adult savant with autism. The shape of the frog is accurately captured, but there are no lines around its edges, and

Figure 14.11 Drawing by savant, E.C. From Mottron & Belleville (1993). Reprinted with permission from Laurent Mottron.

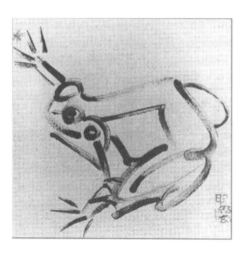

Figure 14.12 Ink drawing of a frog by a Japanese adult savant. From Morishima & Brown (1977). Reprinted with permission from the American Association on Intellectual and Developmental Disabilities.

no attempt to show depth. The drawing by the Japanese savant has more in common with the drawing by Yani than with the drawings of Western savants, and this shows the powerful influence of cultural models, even for savants whose skills exist independent of any kind of general intelligence. The parallels in the drawings of non-autistic and autistic individuals with artistic giftedness strongly suggest that what we see in autistic savants' drawings is primarily a function of their talent rather than their diagnosis.

In what follows, we examine the cognitive characteristics of non-autistic precocious realists in order to determine whether these characteristics are similar to those seen in individuals with autism.

14.5 Cognitive skills associated with precocious realism in non-autistic children

Autistic savant artists have below average IQ, allowing us to conclude that their talent in drawing is IQ independent (Selfe 1977, 1983; O'Connor & Hermelin 1987, 1988, 1990; Wiltshire 1987, 1989, 1991; Pring & Hermelin 1993; Pring et al. 1995). They also use a local drawing strategy, focusing on details rather than the overall shapes and layout of shapes on a page (Mottron & Belleville 1993; Mottron et al. 1999). In the study that we report below, we investigated whether these two characteristics can be seen in non-autistic precocious realists (Drake et al. submitted). We predicted that precocious realism in non-autistic individuals would be IQ independent, and that they would use a more local drawing strategy than children not selected for realistic drawing talent.

Autistic individuals (not selected for drawing talent but instead selected for block design talent) have been shown to excel in mental segmentation (analysing a global whole into its constituent parts and doing this mentally), and in their ability to recall patterns that are not organized into a gestalt (Caron et al. 2006). Autistic individuals with drawing talent have also been shown to excel in mental segmentation (Pring et al. 1995). We investigated whether these two characteristics can be seen in non-autistic precocious realists. Given that artists excel on the hidden figures task, in which one must focus on details and overlook the whole (Getzels & Csikszentmihalyi 1976), we predicted that our non-autistic precocious realists would excel in mental segmentation and in memory for non-wholistically organized visual designs.

We asked 43 children in the age range of 5–11 to sketch a still life containing two complex objects: a vase made up of six connected transparent cylinders and a corkscrew. We videotaped the drawings as they were produced and then classified the drawings in terms of level of realism using a detailed coding scheme. Fifteen children were classified as gifted in realism, 13 as moderately gifted and 15 as age-typical, and the realism scores of these three groups differed significantly from one another. See figures 14.13–15 for a sample drawing from each group. Table 14.1 presents the characteristics of the three groups of participants.

(a) IQ

Drawing savants have low IQs, demonstrating the independence of drawing skill and IQ. Do precocious realists also show no advantage in IQ? To answer this question we administered the verbal and non-verbal sections of the Kaufman Brief Intelligence Test-II (Kaufman & Kaufman 2004). Table 14.2 presents the means and standard deviations for verbal and nonverbal IQ by group.

Not surprisingly, the gifted group was distinguished by their non-verbal IQ, scoring significantly higher than both of the other two groups. The gifted group also scored significantly higher than both of the other groups on verbal IQ. Thus, the relationship between the drawing ability in typically developing gifted children does not obey the same relationship with crystallized intelligence as it does for autistic draughtsmen, in whom realistic drawing talent flourishes alongside below average IQ.

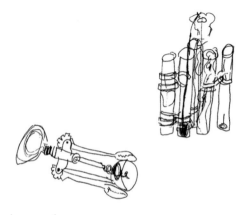

Figure 14.13 Gifted drawing, age 6.

Figure 14.14 Moderately gifted drawing, age 6.

(b) Visual analysis

The block design task assesses the ability to analyse a design into its parts: a design must be copied using blocks, each one of which is a component of the design. Autistic individuals perform well on this test (Lockyer & Rutter 1970; Ohta 1987; Venter *et al.* 1992; Shah & Frith 1993) and benefit less than non-autistic individuals from the presentation of the block design task in a form in which the units are spatially segmented from one another (Shah & Frith 1993). From this finding, it has been concluded that autistic individuals have the ability to spontaneously mentally segment a gestalt into its constituent parts, and that they are characterized by weak central coherence, with the whole less salient for them than the parts.

Similar findings were reported by Caron *et al.* (2006) in a study comparing autistic and typically developing individuals with and without a talent for block design. Caron *et al.* administered a version of the block design task the items of which varied in the level of perceptual cohesiveness. In those with minimal perceptual cohesiveness, the boundary between red and white always co-occurred with the edge separating two blocks, making

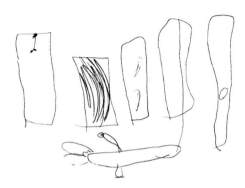

Figure 14.15 Typical drawing, age 6.

Table 14.1 Descriptive characteristics (means (standard deviations)) of each group of children.

	Gifted	Moderately gifted	Typical
n	15	13	15
age	9;2 (1;5)	8;8 (1;3)	8;11 (1;8)
realism score			
6- to 8-year-olds	0.55 (0.12)	0.30 (0.05)	0.04 (0.05)
n	6	5	5
9- to 10-year-olds	0.74 (0.10)	0.46 (0.08)	0.27 (0.09)
n	9	8	10

Table 14.2 Mean IQ (and standard deviations) for each group of children.

	Gifted	Moderately gifted	Typical
n	15	13	15
verbal IQ	120.7 (11.2)	112.8 (10.3)	113.6 (13.7)
non-verbal IQ	133.9 (12.9)	116.9 (13.5)	110.9 (13.9)

it easy to see each block as a unit (figure 14.16). Minimally cohesive items are easily solvable using a local strategy, matching each square to a block, and do not require the ability to analyse a whole into its parts since the parts are given. In those with maximal perceptual cohesiveness, the boundary between red and white never co-occurred with the edge separating two blocks, making it difficult to see each block as a unit (figure 14.17). Maximally cohesive items require analysis of a whole into its parts by mental segmentation (dividing the design mentally into its units of blocks) since the edges do not provide segmentation information. Those intermediate in perceptual cohesiveness had an intermediate number of same coloured adjacencies.

This task was presented in two forms, following Caron *et al.* (2006)—first in unsegmented form, and then in segmented form with the blocks separated from one another by one-third

Figure 14.16 Minimally cohesive item. Reprinted with permission from Laurent Mottron.

Figure 14.17 Maximally cohesive item. Reprinted with permission from Laurent Mottron.

of the width of each block, as in Shah & Frith (1993) (figures 14.17 and 18). Perceptual cohesiveness and segmentation interact: greater perceptual cohesiveness increases task difficulty due to the lack of edge cues; segmentation eliminates this difficulty by providing edge cues through spatial separation. Thus, the items requiring the greatest level of visual analysis were those presented in unsegmented form with maximal perceptual cohesiveness. Skill in visual analysis is demonstrated if individuals do as well on the unsegmented as the segmented version, particularly for the items with maximum perceptual cohesiveness.

Caron *et al.* (2006) present a graph showing that both the autistic and typically developing individuals with a talent for block design were slowed minimally or not at all when perceptual cohesiveness of the designs in the unsegmented condition was increased. This was in contrast to the autistic and typical individuals with no block design talent, for whom the increased cohesiveness slowed their performance. Caron *et al.*'s graph also shows that their typically developing individuals were slowed more by the presentation of the task in unsegmented form than were the autistic individuals. These findings show

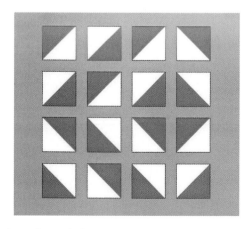

Figure 14.18 Segmented version of figure 14.17. Reprinted with permission from Laurent Mottron.

that skill in visual analysis is not dependent on diagnosis but rather on visual-spatial talent.

We sought to replicate this finding by administering Caron *et al.*'s block design task to our three groups of non-autistic children.

(i) No benefit from segmentation
We found a three-way interaction (group × segmentation × item type): segmentation did not render the tasks easier for any of the groups when the items were minimally cohesive or intermediate in cohesiveness. But for the most difficult items—the maximally cohesive ones—segmentation rendered the task easier for the typical and the moderately gifted group, but had *no* effect on the performance of the gifted group. As hypothesized, the gifted group performed as well on the unsegmented maximally cohesive items as they did on the segmented maximally cohesive items. They were able to mentally analyse/segment the cohesive items and did not need the help of external segmentation. They performed like the autistic individuals with a talent for block design reported by Caron *et al.* (2006).

(ii) No decrement from increasing perceptual cohesiveness
On unsegmented items, our gifted group performed equally well on items of all three levels of cohesiveness; for the other two groups, each level of cohesiveness depressed performance (figure 14.19). Thus, increasing perceptual cohesiveness did not interfere with the visual analysis abilities of the gifted group. Again, our gifted group performed like the autistic individuals with a talent for block design reported by Caron *et al.* (2006).

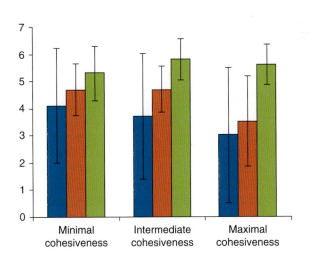

Figure 14.19 Accuracy scores on unsegmented version of the block design task for each group as a function of the level of perceptual cohesiveness. Minimal cohesive items: gifted > typical, $p = 029$; intermediate and maximal cohesive items: gifted > typical and moderately gifted. Minimal cohesive items > maximal cohesive items for the typical and moderately gifted; intermediate cohesive items > maximal cohesive items for the moderately gifted; minimal = intermediate = maximal cohesive items for the gifted group (blue, typical; red, moderately gifted; green, gifted).

(c) Visual memory

Several previous studies have demonstrated an association between the heightened visual memory skill and artistic ability, both instructed visual memory in adult artists (Winner & Casey 1993), and incidental visual memory in children gifted in realism (Rosenblatt & Winner 1988). Caron et al. (2006) assessed incidental visual memory for the block design items to determine whether their autistic sample showed the global advantage in memory seen in typical individuals—recalling the cohesive items better than the fragmented ones. A finding of a diminished global memory advantage in individuals with autism would provide support for the weak central coherence theory of autism; skill in recalling both the cohesive and fragmented designs would provide support for Caron et al.'s view that autistic individuals have enhanced perceptual processing at both the local and global levels. Results showed that both autistic and typically developing individuals had a global advantage—they remembered the more cohesive designs better than the fragmented ones. But the global advantage in memory was weaker for both the autistic and typical individuals with block design talent. With block design skill came the ability to remember the most difficult items—difficult because they were fragmented, not global.

We attempted to replicate this finding in our sample, using Caron et al.'s visual memory test, administered 30 min after completion of the block design test. Children were presented with 36 designs on a computer, one at a time, and were asked to indicate by a key press whether they had seen the design picture before. Half of the designs were from the block design test they had taken; half were distractors (matched to non-distractors in perceptual cohesiveness and size).

Giftedness scores predicted memory for the maximally cohesive items, but not for those low in perceptual cohesiveness. Thus, we conclude that our precocious realists showed superior visual memory. However, they behaved differently from the autistic and non-autistic individuals with block design talent studied by Caron et al. (2006). While Caron et al. found that the global advantage in memory was weaker for both the autistic and typical individuals with block design talent, our gifted sample did not show a weaker global advantage compared with the other two groups. It is possible that their lack of superior performance on the difficult fragmented designs is due to the fact that our participants were children, and the autistic and non-autistic individuals studied by Caron et al. were adults.

(d) Drawing strategy

We examined whether precocious realists show the kind of local drawing strategy described by Mottron & Belleville (1993) in their analysis of the realistic drawing savant, E.C. E.C. used a drawing strategy referred to as 'construction by local progression' (Mottron & Belleville 1993, p. 29). E.C. did not draw the global shape of a figure first but instead began his drawings with a detail, adding contiguous elements, and often moving on to an adjacent part before completing a part already begun. Each new line was in spatial contiguity with the preceding one—as if he were drawing shapes such as tracing a pattern, without reference to the representational meaning of what he was drawing. Such a focus on detail rather than global organization would be consistent with the kind of realistic detail observed in E.C.'s drawings. A similar focus on detail rather than the global form was reported by Mottron et al. (1999) with a sample of 10 autistic individuals.

Mottron found that this strategy was specific to E.C. and did not extend to gifted artists who were not savants. We attempted to replicate these findings, testing whether non-savant children gifted in realistic drawing ever use E.C.'s local strategy. No child in any group used the kind of contiguity strategy shown by E.C. Some children sketched in all six cylinders before adding the details on each cylinder, while others drew each cylinder in all its detail before moving on to the next. But in no case did a child ever move from an uncompleted detail on one cylinder to a part of another cylinder connected by proximity. A local strategy may thus be specific to savant realists. We are now extending our study to autistic children to determine whether this strategy characterizes autistic children in general, or only those with skill in realism.

14.6 Concluding thoughts

While the children in our study were sampled from those taking after-school art classes, they were by no means all gifted child artists. Parents enrol their children in sports, music, and art lessons simply to enrich their children's education. Based on our scoring system, only one-third of the children we sampled were gifted in realistic drawing and 34 percent scored as typical or non-gifted. While a random sample of the population would likely have yielded a smaller percentage of gifted children, the important point to note is that we were able to find a group of non-gifted children to use for comparison purposes.

Our findings show that precocious realists are in some ways unlike artistic savants, and in other respects very similar. One way in which our precocious realists were unlike drawing savants was that their talent is not independent of verbal IQ: the gifted group scored significantly higher in verbal IQ than did the other groups. While one might conclude therefore that verbal IQ differences can explain the superiority of the gifted group, four of the children in the gifted group had only average verbal IQs (ranging from 101 to 113). Thus, an above average verbal IQ is not *necessary* for above average realistic drawing skill in typically developing children.

Our precocious realists were also entirely unlike artistic savants in their drawing strategy. Not one child classified as gifted in drawing, and not one in the other two groups, used a local proximity strategy. Thus, we conclude that a local proximity strategy is used by drawing savants but not by typical children with a gift for realistic drawing. While Mottron *et al.* (1999) found that autistic individuals without drawing talent used the local proximity strategy, we do not know whether there are differences in drawing strategies between those autistic individuals with and without drawing talent. Whether this strategy characterizes autistic individuals in general, irrespective of the realistic drawing talent, is now under investigation in our laboratory.

Our precocious realists showed the same kind of heightened visual analysis skill (as evidenced by their mental segmentation skill) as did the autistic individuals with a block design peak studied by Caron *et al.* (2006), as well as the same kind of heightened visual memory. They did not, however, show the enhanced visual memory for the fragmented items showed by Caron *et al.*'s (2006) participants. We conclude that skill in visual analysis and visual memory both appear to underlie a talent for realism in drawing, with visual analysis perhaps the stronger of these two skills.

It might be considered surprising that a talent for realism predicts superior ability in the block design task. Matching a two-dimensional picture with a two-dimensional pattern of blocks is quite different from translating from a three-dimensional still life to a two-dimensional surface representation (as was required by the still life drawing task). However, both tasks require that one look carefully at the model and analyse it into its component parts. Apparently, children gifted in using their visual analysis skills to build a two-dimensional representation of a two-dimensional model are also gifted in using these skills to construct a two-dimensional representation of a three-dimensional model.

Taken together, these findings demonstrate that heightened visual analysis and visual memory are associated with—and may be causally implicated in—precocious drawing ability. However, unlike autistic individuals, precocious realists do not store fragmented designs in memory at a superior level, they do not use a local drawing strategy, and they do not have below average IQs. Our future work will examine the generality of these findings to a large sample of autistic individuals with and without a talent for realistic graphic representation.

References

Caron, M. J., Mottron, L., Berthiaume, C. & Dawson, M. 2006 Cognitive mechanisms, specificity and neural underpinnings of visuospatial peaks in autism. *Brain J. Neurol.* **129**, 1789–1802. (doi:10.1093/brain/awl072)

Drake, J. E., Redash, A., Coleman, K., Haimson J. & Winner, E. Submitted. *'Autistic' Local Processing Bias Also Found in Children Gifted in Realistic Drawing*.

Getzels, J. W. & Csikszentmihalyi, M. 1976 *The creative vision: a longitudinal study of problem finding in art*. New York, NY: Wiley.

Gibson, J. J. 1979 *The ecological approach to visual perception*. Boston, MA: Houghton Mifflin.

Goldsmith, L. 1992 Stylistic development of a Chinese painting prodigy. *Creativity Res. J.* **5**, 281–293.

Golomb, C. 1992 *The child's creation of a pictorial world*. Berkeley, CA: University of California Press.

Gombrich, E. H. 1960 *Art andillusion*. London, UK: Phaidon Press.

Gordon, A. 1987 Childhood works of artists. *Isr. Mus. J.* **6**, 75–82.

Gregory, R. 1997 *Eye and brain*. Princeton, NJ: Princeton University Press.

Kaufman, A. S. & Kaufman, N. L. 2004 *Kaufman brief intelligence test*, 2nd Circle Pines, MN: American Guidance Service.

Kellogg, R. 1969 *Analyzing children's art*. Palo Alto, CA: National Press Books.

Kennedy, J. M. 1974 Perception, pictures and the et cetera principle. In *Perception: essays in honor of J.J. Gibson* (eds R. B. MacLeod & H. Pick), pp. 209–226. Ithaca, NY: Cornell University Press.

Lockyer, L. & Rutter, M. 1970 A five- to fifteen-year follow-up study of infantile psychosis: IV. Patterns of cognitive ability. *Br. J. Soc. Clin. Psychol.* **9**, 152–163.

Matthews, J. 1984 Children drawing: are young children really scribbling? *Early Child Dev. Care* **18**, 1–39. (doi:10.1080/0300443840180101)

Milbrath, C. 1998 *Patterns of artistic development in children:comparative studies of talent*. Cambridge, UK: Cambridge University Press.

Morishima, A. & Brown, L. 1977 A case report on the artistic talent of an autistic idiot savant. *Ment. Retard.* **15**, 33–36.

Mottron, L. & Belleville, S. 1993 A study of perceptual analysis in a high-level autistic subject with exceptional graphic abilities. *Brain Cogn.* **23**, 279–309. (doi:10.1006/brcg.1993.1060)

Mottron, L. & Belleville, S. 1995 Perspective production in a savant autistic draughtsman. *Psychol. Med.* **25**, 639–648.

Mottron, L., Belleville, S. & Menard, E. 1999 Local bias in autistic subjects as evidenced by graphic tasks: perceptual hierarchization or working memory deficit? *J. Child Psychol. Psychiatry* **40**, 743–755. (doi:10.1111/1469-7610.00490)
O'Connor, N. & Hermelin, B. 1987 Visual and graphic abilities of the idiot savant artist. *Psychol. Med.* **17**, 79–90.
O'Connor, N. & Hermelin, B. 1988 Low intelligence and special abilities. *J. Child Psychol. Psychiatry* **39**, 391–396. (doi:10.1111/j.l469-7610.1988.tb00732.x)
O'Connor, N. & Hermelin, B. 1990 The recognition failure and graphic success of idiot-savant artists. *J. Child Psychol. Psychiatry* **31**, 203–215. (doi:10.1111/j.1469-7610.1990.tb01562.x)
Ohta, M. 1987 Cognitive disorders of infantile autism: a study employing the WISC, spatial relationships, conceptualization, and gesture imitations. *J. Autism Dev. Disord.* **17**, 45–62. (doi:10.1007/BF01487259)
Paine, S. (ed.) 1987 *Six children draw* New York, NY: Academic Press.
Pariser, D. 1991 Normal and unusual aspects of juvenile artistic development in Klee, Lautrec, and Picasso.*Creativity Res. J.* **4**, 457–472.
Pariser, D. 1992/93 The artistically precocious child in different cultural contexts: Wang Yani and Toulouse-Lautrec. *J. Multicult. Cross Cult. Res. Art Educ.* **10/11**, 49–72.
Pring, L. & Hermelin, B. 1993 Bottle, tulip and wineglass: semantic and structural picture processing by savant artists. *J. Child Psychol. Psychiatry* **34**, 1365–1385. (doi:10.1111/j.l469-7610.1993.tb02096.x)
Pring, L., Hermelin, B. & Heavey, L. 1995 Savants, segments, art and autism. *J. Child Psychol. Psychiatry* **36**, 1065–1076. (doi:10.1111/j.l469-7610.1995.tb01351.x)
Richardson, J. 1991 *A life of Picasso*. New York, NY: Random House.
Rosenblatt, E. & Winner, E. 1988 Is superior visual memory a component of superior drawing ability? In *The exceptional brain: neuropsychology of talent and superior abilities* (eds L. Obler & D. Fein), pp. 341–363. New York, NY: Guilford.
Selfe, L. 1977 *Nadia: a case of extraordinary drawing ability in an autistic child*. New York, NY: Academic Press.
Selfe, L. 1983 *Normal and anomalous representational drawing ability in children*. London, UK: Academic Press.
Shah, A. & Frith, U. 1993 Why do autistic individuals show superior performance on the block design task? *J. Child Psychol. Psychiatry* **34**, 1351–1364. (doi:10.1111/j.l469-7610.1993.tb02095.x)
Sloane, K. & Sosniak, L. 1985 The development of accomplished sculptors. In *Developing talent in young people* (ed. B. Bloom), pp. 90–138. New York, NY: Ballantine Books.
Venter, A., Lord, C. & Schopler, E. 1992 A follow-up study of high-functioning autistic children. *J. Child Psychol. Psychiatry* **33**, 489–507. (doi:10.1111/j.1469-7610.1992.tb00887.x)
Willats, J. 1977 How children learn to represent three-dimensional space in drawings. In *The child's representation of the world* (ed. G. Butterworth). New York, NY: Plenum Press.
Wiltshire, S. 1987 *Drawings*. London, UK: Dent.
Wiltshire, S. 1989 *Cities*. London, UK: Dent.
Wiltshire, S. 1991 *Floating cities*. Washington, DC: Summit Books.
Winner, E. 1996 *Gifted children: myths and realities*. New York, NY: BasicBooks.
Winner, E. & Casey, M. 1993 Cognitive profiles of artists. In *Emerging visions: contemporary approaches to the aesthetic process* (eds G. Cupchik & J. Laszlo), Cambridge, UK: Cambridge University Press.
Zhensun, A. & Low, A. 1991 *A young painter: the life and paintings of Wang Yani—China's extraordinary young artist*. New York, NY: Scholastic, Inc.

15

Outsider Art and the autistic creator

Roger Cardinal

> Outsider Art (*art brut*) is defined as a mode of original artistic expression which thrives on its independence, shunning the public sphere and the art market. Such art can be highly idiosyncratic and secretive, and reflects the individual creator's attempt to construct a coherent, albeit strange, private world. Certain practitioners of what may be termed autistic art are examined in the light of this definition; their work is considered as evidence not of a medical condition but of an expressive intentionality entirely worthy of the interest of those drawn to the aesthetic experience.
>
> **Keywords:** Outsider Art; *art brut*; autistic art; strangeness; intentionality; private world

15.1 Defining outsider art

It so happens that certain practitioners of what has become known as Outsider Art have occasionally been referred to as 'autistic'. Applied loosely by non-medical commentators, the term reflects an attempt to identify a certain quality of secretiveness about the artist's manner and his or her seeming reluctance to communicate in a direct fashion. This non-specialist use of a key clinical concept may seem inappropriate to those concerned to explain the condition of autism proper. Nonetheless, it does raise the possibility of a congruity between two separate spheres of creativity, one which I feel to be worth investigating.

Let me first explain my own technical term. 'Outsider Art' constitutes an internationally recognized category of self-taught art. Its ambit of use rests on the notion that art making is a widespread human activity reaching far beyond the world of public galleries, teaching institutions and culturally marked art production. Yet it would be wrong to suppose that the term means nothing more than casual doodling or amateurish fumbling. Instead, it refers confidently to an actual fund of original work produced by untutored creators of talent whose expressions convey a strong sense of individuality.

I am in part responsible for launching the concept of Outsider Art in so far as the coinage appeared some years ago as the title of my book (Cardinal 1972). Recent surveys of this field include Peiry (1997), Rhodes (2000a) and Danchin (2006). In fact, *Outsider Art* had been conceived strictly as a study of *art brut* and was largely based upon the private art collection of the French artist and theorist Jean Dubuffet, now established as a public museum in Switzerland. (The Collection de l'Art brut is housed in the Château de Beaulieu, Avenue des Bergières, Lausanne, Switzerland. Other significant European collections devoted to Outsider Art are the Aracine Collection at the Musée d'art moderne Lille Métropole in Villeneuve d'Ascq, Lille, France; the Musgrave-Kinley Outsider Art

Collection, currently housed at the Irish Museum of Modern Art, Dublin, Ireland; the former De Stadshof Collection, housed at the Museum Dr Guislain in Ghent, Belgium; and the Museum im Lagerhaus at St Gallen, Switzerland.) Fearful that *art brut* might not go down well with an anglophone readership, my editor proposed that the English term be printed on the title page and the cover, despite the fact that the text proper refers exclusively to *art brut*. Since 1972, the term Outsider Art has led a life of its own and has been used and abused in a variety of ways, which have often compromised its usefulness as a technical term. I am simply being consistent with my original intention in continuing to use it as a handy anglophone equivalent for *art brut*.

One of the other key references in my book was the Prinzhorn Collection, the pioneering collection of psychotic art assembled in the early years of the twentieth century by the German psychiatrist Hans Prinzhorn, who worked at the University Clinic in Heidelberg. Prinzhorn was also an art historian and something of a philosopher, and his 1922 book *Bildnerei der Geisteskranken* (Artistry of the Mentally Ill) is a classic account of the art making of persons diagnosed as psychotic (Prinzhorn 1968). The characteristic styles of such creators are eccentric and diverse, yet all tend to embody a *Fremdheitsgefuhl* ('a sense of strangeness'), as Prinzhorn puts it, which could be construed as congruent with one of the recognized features of autism. My book also invoked some inflammatory writings by the Viennese artist Arnulf Rainer, a fervent collector of *art brut* since the 1960s, who speaks of the lunatic artist as one whose expressive acts take place in a notional 'autistic theatre', cut off from the normal world of understanding by virtue of its hermeticism and indifference to an outside audience.

I should point out that the criteria for Outsider Art (*art brut*) are sufficiently flexible to embrace not only art arising within the context of extreme mental dysfunction, but also art produced by individuals who are quite capable of handling their social lives but who recoil, consciously or unconsciously, from the notion of art being necessarily a publicly defined activity with communally recognized standards. Certain commentators have insisted that true Outsider Art can only be produced by people whose mental lives are at odds with the norm, or who have been physically afflicted in some deeply disturbing way, or again whose social status is pitiful and lacking in all comforts. Thus, there has been a tendency to envisage Outsider Art solely in terms of its makers' aberrant biographies, and to insist that its producers be eccentrics, misfits, recalcitrants, lunatics, convicts, hermits and so forth. But I must insist that, despite the signs that certain unconventional lifestyles and deviant beliefs do contribute to the nourishing of an outsider approach to art, there is a better way of handling the issue of definition: namely, by underlining the anti-conventional nature of the art making itself, its idiosyncrasy, its often unworldly distance from artistic norms, as well as from commonplace experience. I insist that Outsider Art earns its name not because of an association with a lurid case history or a sensational biography, but because it offers its audience a thrilling visual experience. Outsider Art is an art of unexpected and often bewildering distinctiveness, and its outstanding exemplars tend to conjure up imagined private worlds, completely satisfying to their creator yet so remote from our normal experience as to appear alien and rebarbative. Thus, the tireless pen drawings produced by the London housewife and medium Madge Gill (1882–1961) establish an other-worldly environment of flickering patterns out of which peer anxious female faces (figure 15.1); while the Polish schizophrenic Edmund Monsiel (1897–1962)

Figure 15.1 Madge Gill, untitled pen drawing (female face). Courtesy Roger Cardinal.

crams his sheets with hundreds of faces within faces to produce a bemusing prospect of boundless proliferation (figure 15.2).

A central element in the definition of Outsider Art, and one particularly cherished by its first theorist Jean Dubuffet, himself a renegade artist, is that it diverges radically from our shared cultural expectation as to what art ought to look like and how it ought to be fashioned (Dubuffet's arguments for an *art brut* immune to cultural influence are set out in the combative essays; see Dubuffet (1973)). As a mode of independent art making, Outsider Art ignores tradition and academic criteria. Instead, it reflects a strong creative impulse, running free of the communicative conventions to which we are accustomed. At the extreme, such independence can produce styles of expression which may be said to be autistic in the loose, non-clinical sense, i.e. Outsider Art often tends to be secretive, wrapped about, apparently insulated from or indifferent to a potential audience (This line of argument was first essayed in my paper '*Ars sub rosa*. Thoughts on the disposition to secrecy in the work of certain autistic artists'; see Cardinal (1987)).

Now, it is a fact that certain clinically diagnosed autistic persons have distinguished themselves as creators of significant artworks, and thus as exponents of what, for convenience sake, I shall call autistic art. I want to make it clear that it is by no means my wish to enforce a facile equation between Outsider Art and autistic art; yet, what I do want to propose is that it makes sense to situate certain autistic creators within the field of Outsider Art. All the same, if some autists can be deemed to be artists, some only of that number should be counted as Outsider artists.

The exceptional psychic confinement imposed by the autistic condition upon the individual could prompt the untrained enquirer to anticipate finding next to no trace of creativity within the autistic personality. Our cruder ideas about the artistic temperament have been coloured by images of nineteenth- and twentieth-century rebels such as Van Gogh, Munch, Kirchner, Egon Schiele, Francis Bacon, Arnulf Rainer and Georg Baselitz, and have given rise to the stereotype of the bohemian rebel whose creativity leads to noisy

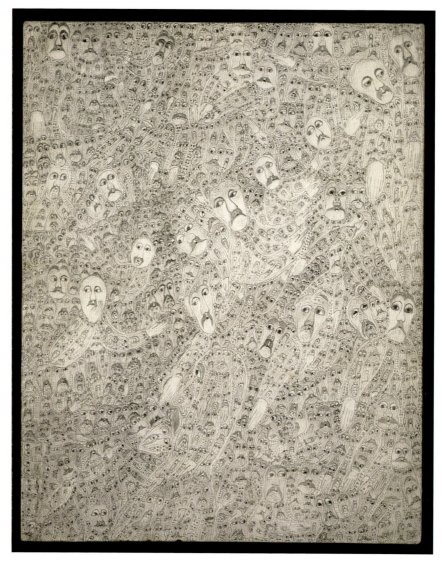

Figure 15.2 Edmund Monsiel, untitled pencil drawing (proliferating faces). Courtesy Henry Boxer Gallery, Richmond, London.

gesturing and a rhetorical emphasis that cannot be dissociated from the impulse to create a public spectacle, one not much different from a public nuisance. Art consistent with what is essentially an *expressionistic* model can be wild, loud and difficult to ignore. Yet, art does not have to be that way, and what I am interested in considering here is the possibility of a quieter, less bombastic idiom arising in conditions of psychological and emotional withdrawal that apparently inhibit normal modes of communication. Such art making can be oddly moving, precisely because it contradicts the stereotype of the noisy hooligan and because it cultivates a characteristic repertoire of marks and signs, creating as it were a peaceful realm of its own, an intimate and vulnerable private world.

I should make it clear that, as a species of art historian or writer about art, I am seeking to open up a perspective onto autistic artmaking, which is, in principle, distinct from the one familiar to the clinical specialist. I am effectively more interested in the autistic drawing as *artwork* than as *scientific document*, and the following discussion will doubtless seem inappropriate or futile to those who are used to pursuing unmistakable signals of disease or psychic distortion. I am by no means seeking to disqualify the scientific reading of the semiotics of autism, but I do hope to offer some perceptions of the strange beauty of the art produced within the autistic context. It is a fresh angle on the mystery, perhaps, but it could be that artistic appreciation will shed some light.

15.2 Six autistic artists

In a well-known case study, the psychologist Lorna Selfe addresses the artistic output of an autistic child called Nadia (b. 1967), who had begun to produce remarkable drawings at the very early age of 3.5 (Selfe 1977; see also Cardinal (1979)). Humphrey (1998) offers an interesting comparison with the cave drawings of the Upper Palaeolithic). One of Nadia's inspirations was the conventional and rather cloying imagery found in the *Ladybird* series of illustrated children's books: she apparently sought to copy a picture of a crowing rooster and another of a horseman blowing his bugle, but her efforts to reproduce the original seem to have gone radically awry, the upshot being a set of scrawled ensembles done with a biro pen, which, at first glance, are hard to construe. We might want to dismiss such work as incompetent and unlovely, were it not that a certain tenacity of manner and consistency of vision do come across. I submit that these ungainly and fantastical images cannot be judged as totally arbitrary and meaningless. There is a sense of an underlying intentionality, a drive towards articulation (even if we might discern an impairment in communication to others). Later on, at the age of 6, Nadia did some sketches of the lower bodies of nurses and women helpers, simply reproducing what, as an infant, she saw in front of her. These sketches have a surprising warmth about them, as if the child meant to convey her affection, a response to the care she was being shown. Within a year or so, as part of a well-meaning attempt to lead the child forward into a positive relation to the social world, Nadia was being taught to read and write, and to do sums; and the process of insistent acculturation seems to have speedily blighted her talent. Her subsequent artwork was stereotyped and normalized, completely losing its fantastical and visionary verve.

The standard of fidelity to the visual has long been a given of Western culture: we tend to feel comfortable with pictures that strongly resemble the world we inhabit. Whether we speak of realism, of naturalism, or of mimeticism, we can find throughout history examples of work the aesthetic virtue of which is judged inseparable from its documentary accuracy. The case of the young autistic artist Stephen Wiltshire (b. 1974) is instructive in this context (see Sacks' (1995) essay on Stephen Wiltshire). Wiltshire had begun drawing at the age of approximately six and impressed his family and teachers by his spontaneous control and meticulous accuracy. The boy's favourite subject matter was architecture. He was able to produce an amazingly faithful representation after no more than a glance at the motif: thus, a day out in London could furnish dozens of (quasi-eidetic) images, which he would subsequently transcribe at speed and with a certain graceful nonchalance. The fact that Sir Hugh Casson, a renowned architect and one-time president of the Royal Academy, became a sponsor of the boy's talent meant that there arose a specific public identification of Wiltshire as an architectural artist. This has led to a prolific output of publications containing drawings of famous cities across the world, to which Wiltshire has been systematically transported. I am impressed by the technical competence of these drawings, but have reservations about their coolness and stylistic sameness. These may be the outcome of external pressure to conform to the expectations of others, or else are simply the result of a particularly well-tuned copying mechanism. At all events, it could be argued that Wiltshire's marked preference for drawing actual buildings distances his pictorial world from that of the imaginative Outsider artist, who creates a coherent and original world of his own. (A useful contrast could be drawn between Wiltshire's art and that of another talented autistic creator, Gilles Trehin, who, in the course of some 20 years, has produced dozens of drawings to illustrate his fantasy of an island metropolis called Urville. These drawings constitute an accomplished pictorial guide to an entirely chimerical, yet seductively coherent, private world. Accompanied by the artist's own architectural, cultural and pseudo-historical notes, they have seen print as Tréhin (2006).)

James Castle (1900–1977), who lived for much of his life on a lonely farm in rural Idaho, seems never to have been fully examined by the medical profession, although a diagnosis of autism has been ventured *a posteriori* (Yau 2002; Trusky 2008). His drawings are remarkable, not least in terms of their material constitution, for he favoured a pigment made of soot scraped from a wood stove, mixed with water or saliva and applied to paper or cardboard, usually with a sharpened piece of wood (figure 15.3). This primitivism of means carries its own pathos and tends to appeal to the Outsider Art connoisseur as confirmation of creative independence. It also represents an involuntary crossover with certain manifestations of twentieth-century avant-gardism whereby minimal marks produced with unsuitable materials have come to be prized within an aesthetic of minimalism.

Figure 15.3 James Castle, untitled drawing in soot and saliva (artist's workplace). Courtesy J. Crist Gallery, Boise, Idaho.

(I am thinking especially of *Arte povera*, the Italian movement, which delighted in rough surfaces and clumsy scrawls, and of the graffiti-like work of contemporary artists such as Cy Twombly).

Castle's achievements as a draughtsman are especially noteworthy given the severe constraints on his sensibility. He was thought to have been born deaf (though no proper test was made during his early years), and was deemed to be retarded by many who knew him. As a teenager, he attended the Idaho School for the Deaf and the Blind, but failed to acquire any communication skills and was finally sent home as 'uneducable'. Thereafter he spent practically all his days loitering about the family farm, never undertaking any work. He might have emerged as a mere idiot observer of circumstance were it not that his images of agricultural buildings and farm paraphernalia possess a conviction, even an aura, that lifts them above the level of crude delineation. Castle seems to be making a deliberate statement about his environment, and his drawings do establish a distinct and recognizable locale. Within it, he seems to have discerned some half-defined quality—something one might love—a quality of recognizable realness, which equally partakes of the unreal, even the surreal. Perhaps it is also the *tininess* of his work which seduces us; for the drawings are small, almost negligible, and too modestly presented to be assertive. In fact, they were virtually never 'presented' to an audience beyond the immediate family. Such discreetness can be compared to the widespread secretiveness of Outsider artists, who often produce prolific work without anyone knowing.

Further aspects of Castle's output reveal considerable inventiveness in both materials and themes. There are hundreds of small 'artist's books'—pattern books, scrapbooks, stamp albums with home-made stamps, calendars, an illustrated autobiography, codebooks full of secret writing (much of it purely nonsensical, since Castle could barely read), not to mention loose collections of matchboxes and cigarette packs. The model he presents of the restless discoverer and inventor echoes that of such Outsiders as the Swiss schizophrenic Adolf Wölfli (1864–1930), who used collage and drawing to construct a multilayered and preposterous autobiography in image and text; or of another schizophrenic patient, Jean Mar (1831–1911), who penned his gnomic thoughts and unexplained drawings on tiny slips of paper that he hid in small containers.

Roy Wenzel (b. 1959) is a Dutch artist (see Rhodes 2000*b*). Since the age of 25, he has lived at home in a southern town in Holland, cared for by his brother and sister. He suffered from severe eczema throughout his childhood and was diagnosed as autistic at the age of approximately 11. During therapy sessions in hospital, he began drawing and apparently achieved some remarkable results. Although this early output has not been saved, his adult work has long since entered the art market and been shown in commercial galleries as well as at international exhibitions of Outsider Art. (He was runner-up in the competitive section of the international triennale of Outsider & Naive Art held at the Slovak National Gallery in Bratislava in 2004.) Wenzel's images are highly assertive and gestural. His pictorial scheme tends to imply a traditional perspectival space, albeit his semi-transparent figures are often set across the background in an overlaying technique which suggests an undivided interest both in what is close to and what is far off. The scenes are mainly urban, with rows of houses with rooftops and repetitive rows of windows; we also see buses, cars, trains and ships. The dominant human figure is a large female whose high-heeled boots, huge crimson lips and ample bosom relay a powerful erotic fixation. This figure would easily win an ugliness contest, so that we may choose to celebrate Wenzel as an artist of excess, perhaps placing him in a Netherlandish tradition of Bosch-like grotesquerie.

Jeroen Pomp (b. 1985) is another Dutch creator (see Gronert 2008). He makes his pictures in an art workshop located in Rotterdam: the Atelier Heren-plaats. Many similar organizations have arisen in the past couple of decades which are dedicated to the fostering of creativity among persons who are physically challenged or have learning difficulties: some of these tend to coax the individual into producing artwork of standard prettiness, following a therapeutic ethos whereby a satisfying picture is the one which deviates the least from a certain norm, never precisely defined yet clearly involving some notion of a desirable standard of technical competence and visual appeal. Pomp, by contrast, operates in an institution whose ethos is radically opposed to any restriction on inspiration. I am told there is neither advice nor tutoring at the Herenplaats, its policy resting on the argument that creativity can only acquire a therapeutic dimension if it is allowed the fullest freedom. Left to his own devices, Pomp has developed an astonishingly colourful style in which objects such as plants and animals proliferate immeasurably (figure 15.4). (I gather that he is keen on botany and can point out dozens of different plants in some of his pictures.) It must be said, however, that our immediate impression of the work is likely to be one of illegibility. Yet to treat his images purely as puzzles in which clear outlines have been perversely obliterated is to miss the point. It seems to me that there is a palpable zestfulness about the teeming spaces Pomp brings to life. Here is physical and emotional energy made visible: we are looking into a vivid interior reality. And I would argue that the surest sign of an Outsider artist working at full stretch is that we are affected by the bustling dynamism and coherence of a visual (perhaps even a visionary) system, orchestrated by the individual performer. Pomp's private realm may not always be easily legible, but its splendour and wilful momentum are sufficient to induce a positive response—we are privileged to contemplate a strange and thrilling beauty.

Figure 15.4 Jeroen Pomp, untitled painting (zoo). Courtesy Hamer Gallery, Amsterdam.

The American artist Gregory Blackstock (b. 1946) has a highly strung personality that keeps him permanently on the *qui vive*. He was first diagnosed as suffering from paranoid schizophrenia, but this was later amended to autism; today he is situated on the spectrum as a savant. He is reported to be able to speak a dozen languages, and can play from memory on the accordion hundreds of tunes picked up from records. He has prodigious powers of recollection and can cite the names of all the children from his schooldays. One of his party tricks is to inform you of the correct time in Vladivostok or Beijing. He has led quite an unexceptional life, having worked for 25 years as a dishwasher at an athletics club in Seattle; latterly, he has developed a secondary career as a performing musician. Above all, he is a fanatical draughtsman.

Blackstock had his first exhibition in a Seattle gallery at the age of 58. His artistic production began with sketches for the club newsletter, and expanded in relation to his obsessive interest in inventories and taxonomies. He is a great reader of encyclopedias and also visits hardware shops to do sketches of utensils and tools. His work culminated in a published book called *Blackstock's Collections* and subtitled *The Drawings of an Artistic Savant* (Blackstock 2006; See also Harmon 2007). Here, we can glimpse something of the man's prodigious appetite for detail and delight in precision and completeness. The individual drawings are diagrammatic, each item being presented plain and simple as the variant of a general type: thus, four dozen kinds of saw are squeezed into a single page, catering to a desire for symmetry as well as completeness. Blackstock's collections include displays of industrial tools (drills, files, saws and trowels), animal life (crows, eagles, ants, owls, wasps and bees, and 'monsters of the deep'), plant life (berries and tropical fruits), types of vehicle (freight trains and automobiles), buildings (barns, castles and jailhouses), not to mention stringed instruments and mariners' knots (figure 15.5).

Here we confront the reproduction of objects that bear witness not so much to the proliferation of things in the actual world, as to the artist's alertness in noticing and documenting all the aspects of difference that distinguish them. This is in fact an instance of autistic repetition in the subtler mode of infinite differentiation. As a species of virtual or theoretical collector, Blackstock is a keen encyclopedist, an ardent completist. His work represents a kind of stocktaking, the reflection of a yearning for order and perhaps ultimately of a longing for mastery over the unthinkable subtleties of our shared world—a desire for supremacy as chief overseer of reality's infinite variations.

Another autistic artist, George Widener (b. 1962), rounds off my brief survey (see Cardinal 2005). Here is another case of amazing savant 'high functioning', for Widener can provide swift answers to arithmetical calculations of great complexity. I have listened to him reciting the doubling sequence '1-2-4-8-16-32-64-128-256-512...' at remarkable speed. His party piece is to ask for a person's birthdate and then, within a few seconds, to come up with the day of the week when it fell.

Widener's case history follows a familiar pattern of misdiagnosis—for some time he was thought to be a depressive schizophrenic—and many wretched years of non-alignment with social norms. He was in his thirties when he was admitted to a special university education programme and diagnosed as suffering from Asperger's syndrome. Widener is now classed as a savant. His adaptation to external life is hampered by a certain sluggishness, yet his mental life is hyperactive. Having by now been tested, interviewed and filmed a good many times, he has settled into a routine in which he will trot out a well-rehearsed statement about his early life, his mental condition and the range of his talents: his ease with others is notably at odds with the customary expectations of autism.

Figure 15.5 Gregory Blackstock, cover of his book *Blackstock's Collections* (2006). Courtesy Princeton Architectural Press, New York.

Widener's passions include numerals and specific historical dates, usually those of catastrophic events, such as the sinking of the Titanic. His passion is for making up calendars which foreground the coincidences arising between various dates and days across history. These home-made time charts represent a form of conceptual art making, based on calculations, symbols and ciphers and incorporating rigorous listings and diagrams. Widener's calendars conform to patterns of association too complex for others to follow, but are seemingly in keeping with a fundamental faith in the efficacy of the numerical system. He is particularly fond of magic squares. I suspect that it is the numerals that give Widener access to a vision of the chaotic prolixity of experience, and numerals again, which allow him to measure and contain that chaos.

Whereas Widener's numerical and taxonomic obsessions are, in effect, extrapolations from objective data (albeit envisaged from a subjective perspective), his pictures of giant cities spring from a more obviously creative area of mental activity. His imagining of a vast and unreal megalopolis must surely be counted an original invention, the summoning-up of a distinctive 'world', one which is in perfect accord with the autonomous worlds or cosmologies of Outsider artistry. His compositions often stretch to a metre and more in width, a dramatic scale which seems to belie any idea of secrecy or privacy: I think Widener really does want us to gaze into his personal world. His carefully inscribed marks appear to confirm a network of highly regulated structures, including streets, buildings, towers, bridges and canals. We might note that no people are to be seen in this unreal city, although incessant activity seems implicit. A number of vessels lie at anchor, as if to intimate that his megalopolis lies at the heart of a wider network of ports and unseen continents. I think it is a visionary achievement of considerable finesse and imaginative daring (figure 15.6).

15.3 The overlap between autistic art and outsider art

Of course, the apparently spontaneous inventions of the untrained creators I have introduced here might serve as objects of medical analysis, in so far as they are construed as direct traces of the autistic condition itself, i.e. they could be read as *symptoms*. Perhaps we might even envisage them as metaphorical *descriptions* of autism—attempts at showing, by virtue of a sort of projection from within, what it feels like to be autistic, or again how the world appears when one views it through the autistic window. (There exists, by the way, a rich literature on the forms of psychopathological art, seen as symptomatic of mental disease. And there have been attempts to tie recurrent stylistic traits to specific mental aberrations (see for instance Rennert 1966; Kraft 2005)).

Figure 15.6 George Widener, *Megalopolis 21*, mixed media drawing. Courtesy Henry Boxer Gallery, Richmond, London.

Alternatively—I contend—these works deserve respect as meaningful and intentional artistic compositions. They may not appear communicative, yet they do articulate something, and that something may well be saturated with hidden affect. They are also formal constructs whose properties are sufficiently inventive and engaging as to widen our aesthetic experience in interesting ways. How are we to appreciate and respond to such work?

Let us consider the potential value of a drawing which happens to show us something we recognize as part of the world we inhabit, such as one of Stephen Wiltshire's sketches of County Hall in London or Gregory Blackstock's rendering of a European Hooded Crow. I would suggest that our sense of recognition is in itself a pretty undeveloped or minimal reaction. The approximation of an appearance is not necessarily the highest aim of the creative act, and a skilful copier of reality is arguably somewhat less than an inspired and imaginative artist. In considering the art of autistic persons, we might wish to find something more dramatic or more poignant than the mechanical replication of visual impressions. We would like to find more in the way of emotional or spiritual substance within the image—not just an inert snapshot of the real but an elaboration upon impressions both objective and subjective, an exploration and an extrapolation that go beyond the mimetic minimum.

Since I have no objective proof that autistic persons at large are more creative than other socially or psychologically defined groups, I would not hazard the claim that autism directly encourages inventive drawing. Nevertheless, I do find striking qualities in the work of the autistic creators I have chosen, enough to embolden me to suggest that a special form of aesthetic pleasure might ensue if we attend carefully to their artistry. One of the criteria for the identification of Outsider Art is the sense of its strangeness, its idiosyncrasy; and I have hinted that this strangeness is nothing less than the mark of a coherent private world conjured up in the sweep of imagery of an individual creator. Provided we as viewers can entertain the fantasy of travelling into that world—in the same way that we might travel into a foreign country with no knowledge of its language or customs—we are in a position to savour the extreme experience of otherness, in the form of a seductive exoticism that produces an inarticulate yet intense pleasure. Such a pleasure may be judged strictly irrelevant to any medical concerns, and might even seem to have something of selfish hedonism about it. Nevertheless, I suggest that the images I have invoked do not deserve to be treated simply as confirmations of a diagnosis (one which is in any case confirmed by other behavioural data); and that they implicitly ask us to treat them as intentional statements worthy of serious and responsible consideration.

Here is where autistic artistry may be said to coincide with Outsider artistry. As I have said, not all autistic persons can be Outsiders, but those who merit inclusion in the latter category will exercise the same fascination and stimulate the same level of excitement in the responsive viewer. It is all a matter of comparative intensity and richness. Similar to Outsider Art, autistic art can exercise a magnetism which transcends the simple communication of an appearance or an idea. In the end, it is not that Gregory Blackstock is saying 'folks, here is a Straight Double-Edge Pruning Saw', as if that were the priority; but that he is communicating the fact of difference, and the wider fact of the continuum of diversity in the world. Similarly, Nadia's horseman transcends the simple stage of being recognized as a man on horseback and becomes an utterly poignant icon steeped in non-verbalized emotion. James Castle's painstaking reproduction of scenes on his farm— I'm tempted to compare them to the painfully long exposures of the early years of photography—conveys not just a disposition of inanimate roofs, fences and telegraph poles, but an intimate relationship, an act of recognition and homage on the part of an individual who is asserting his links to the narrow domain of the homestead—or rather the wider domain of his imagination. Jeroen Pomp's crammed locales may well be derived from some similar cramming within his invisible inner life, and we can inch closer to appreciating them by first digesting the very fact of our bemusement or claustrophobia. Might our hesitancy about interpreting such pictures be analogous to the hesitancies of classic autism as a state of distrust and confusion regarding the outer world? As for Asperger's and its bewildering communicative excesses, there is again an opportunity for us to move beyond the ticking-off of simple facts and to engage with the dynamic thrust of mental systems unlike our own, in an effort to participate in that alien enthusiasm. At some point, we might catch a glimpse of the inner joy of a Gregory Blackstock or a George Widener when the one completes a particular bout of categorial collecting or the other sees a magic square emerging from an abstruse and extended computation in one of his calendars. Their self-engrossed pleasure in their own mastery can become our secondary pleasure as witnesses thereof, and encourage us to attempt further acts of empathetic response. These should lead us beyond selfish indulgence, for in due course we will find that aesthetic pleasure has begun to coincide with our poignant engagement with another sensibility, another personality; at which point art appreciation is revealed not as a peripheral supplement to human experience but as a privileged medium of human contact itself.

References

Blackstock, G. L. 2006 *Blackstock's collections. The drawings of an artistic savant*. New York, NY: Princeton Architectural Press.
Cardinal, R. 1972 *Outsider Art*. London, UK: Studio Vista; New York, NY: Praeger.
Cardinal, R. 1979 Drawing without words: the case of Nadia.*Comparison* **10**, 3–21.
Cardinal, R. 1987 Ars sub rosa. In *The Champernowne Trust. Papers presented at the Annual Forum*. Axbridge, UK: The Axbridge Bookshop, pp. 22–28.
Cardinal, R. 2005 The calendars of George Widener. *RawVision* **51**, 42–7.
Danchin, L. 2006 *Art brut. L'Instinct createur*. Paris, France: Gallimard.
Dubuffet, J. 1973 *L'Homme du commun a l'ouvrage*. Paris, France: Gallimard.
Gronert, F. 2008 Jeroen Pomp. In *Stendhal Syndrome. Art that makes you go crazy*. Rotterdam, The Netherlands: Atelier Herenplaats, pp. 255–277.
Harmon, K. 2007 The taxonomist: Gregory L. Blackstock. *Folk Art* **XXXII**, 68–75.
Humphrey, N. 1998 Cave art, autism, and the evolution of the human mind. *Camb. Archaeol. J.* **VIII**, 165–191. (doi:10.1017/S0959774300001827)
Kraft, H. 2005 *Grenzgänger zwischen Kunst und Psychiatrie*. ologne, Germany: Deutscher Arzte-Verlag. [1986], 3rd evised and expanded edn.
Peiry, L. 1997 *L'Art brut* (transl. *Art brut. The origins of outsider art*, Flammarion, Paris, 2001). Paris, France: Flammarion.
Prinzhorn, H. 1968 *Bildnerei der Geisteskranken. Ein Beitrag zur Psychologie und Psychopathologie der Gestaltung [1922]* (transl. by E. von Brockdorff (1972) as *Artistry of the entally ill*, Springer, New York, NY). Berlin/Heidelberg,Germany; New York, NY: Springer.
Rennert, H. 1966 *Die Merkmale schizophrener Malerei*. Jena, Germany: G. Fischer. [1962], 2nd expanded edition.
Rhodes, C. 2000*a* *Outsider Art. Spontaneous alternatives*. London, UK; New York, NY: Thames & Hudson.
Rhodes, C. 2000*b* *Roy Wenzel. Works on paper*. Zwolle, The Netherlands: De Stadshof.

Sacks, O. 1995 Stephen Wiltshire, 'Prodigies'. In *An anthropologist on Mars. Seven paradoxical tales*, pp. 179–232. London, UK: Picador.
Selfe, L. 1977 *Nadia. A case of extraordinary drawing ability in an autistic child*. London, UK: Academic Press.
Trehin, G. 2006 *Urville*. London, UK; Philadelphia, PA: Jesssica Kingsley Publishers.
Trusky, T. 2008 *James Castle. His life and art*. Boise, Idaho: Boise State University. [2004] 2nd revised edition.
Yau, J. 2002 *James Castle. The common place*. New York, NY: Knoedler & Co.

16

Autistic autobiography

Ian Hacking

Autism narratives are not just stories or histories, describing a given reality. They are creating the language in which to describe the experience of autism, and hence helping to forge the concepts in which to think autism. This paper focuses on a series of autobiographies that began with Grandin's *Emergence*. These are often said to show us autism from the 'inside'. The paper proposes that instead they are developing ways to describe experience for which there is little preexisting language. Wittgenstein has many well-known aphorisms about how we understand other people directly, without inference. They condense what he had found in Wolfgang Köhler's *Gestalt Psychology*. These phenomena of direct understanding what other people are doing are, Köhler wrote, 'the common property and practice of mankind'. They are not the common property and practice of people with autism. Ordinary language is rich in age-old ways to describe what others are thinking, feeling and so forth. Köhler's phenomena are the bedrock on which such language rests. There is no such discourse for autism, because Köhler's phenomena are absent. But a new discourse is being made up right now, i.e. ways of talking for which the autobiographies serve as working prototypes.

Keywords: Köhler; Wittgenstein; Grandin; Donna Williams; Mukhopadhyay; Tammet

16.1 Introduction

We now watch, hear and read a great deal about what it is like to be autistic—in autobiography, biography and fiction. Autism narrative is a new genre: not expert reports by clinicians or reflections by theorists, but stories about people with autism, told by the people themselves, or their families, or by novelists, or by writers of stories for children.

Since this is a new genre, it is multimedia. Its richest habitat is the blogosphere. Chat rooms are awash with autists chatting. I shall unfashionably stick to print, and will mainly refer to four well-known autobiographies, those by Grandin (1986, 1995, 2005), Williams (1992, 1994), Mukhopadhyay (2000, 2008) and Tammet (2006). The authors are more than 'talented', as are for example Nazeer (2006) and Mór (2007). As might be expected, they are not all uniformly 'high-functioning'; Mukhopadhyay is brilliant in the use of words, but needs help in many other aspects of life. I use these four to explore how talented autistic individuals are affecting our understanding of autism.

I shall not use this occasion to quote much of what they say. Let them speak for themselves. I offer instead a suggestion about their role in the ongoing social and cultural evolution of the autistic spectrum. I take for granted that underneath the spectrum is a family of definite biological conditions, be they neurological or genetic or whatever, but that in an important sense the spectrum itself is a 'moving target' that has evolved dramatically (Hacking 2007).

16.2 Some questions

Our instinct is to treat the words of the autobiographies as literal descriptions, albeit tinged with metaphor and coloured by art. That is to that they are true (or false) according to some pre-existing criteria for describing experiences and sensibilities. I wonder whether they are not instead helping to create a language for talking about what was hitherto unknown. Yet even that is not right, for it implies that there was a continent there to know, but not yet explored.

(i) Are the autobiographies and other stories less telling what it is like to be autistic than constituting it, both for those who inhabit the autistic spectrum, and for those who do not?

Despite my few examples, we are concerned with the entire multimedia genre. Different kinds of item influence each other in complex ways. Novelists study autobiographies, whose authors learn from theorists. Parents pick up ideas from novels when they are thinking about their children. We all watch movies and documentaries. A 'thick' kind of human being is coming into being, where once there was only a 'thin' one. The autistic thin man of yore, or rather the thin child, when not having a tantrum, was a silent self-absorbed creature, alone with bizarre habits.

Our four autobiographers clearly have personalities that are thick, dense or rich, whatever adjectives you please. Can they teach anything about other people with autism, and, in particular, more severely impaired people?

(ii) Do the autobiographies provide prototypes for describing and thinking of all autistic people? Or is that exactly the wrong way to go, because it suits only the 'high functioning', and creates too many false expectations about others?

Oliver Sacks wrote his own engaging account of Grandin, under the title, *'An anthropologist on Mars'*. Grandin had said to him after dinner, 'Much of the time I feel like an anthropologist on Mars'. (Sacks 1993, p. 259; 1995.) That phrase invites the all too suggestive trope of the alien, which some in the autistic communities favour and some resent. Wittgenstein (2001, p. 190e) thought that: 'If a lion could talk, we could not understand him'. If a Martian spoke, would we understand it? Only if we shared or came to share some 'forms of life', some ways of living together with lions. That is precisely a problem for a person with severe autism. But the evocative phrase, form of life, is never more than a pointer; we shall need to be more specific about what is missing. Some observations by Wittgenstein and by Wolfgang Köhler, the best-remembered pioneer of Gestalt psychology, are unexpectedly helpful in this respect.

16.3 Texts not people

The people who write autobiographies will not concern us here, only their texts. This has several corollaries. First, it does not matter that in some cases the autist is not the sole author of the final words of the text. Not only have editors had their roles, but also for example Grandin's first volume of autobiography, *Emergence*, was written 'with' a professional co-writer. Mukhopadhyay's recent title, *How Can I Talk if My Lips Don't Move? Inside my Autistic Mind* (2008), was made up by someone in Arcade Publishing Inc.

That is irrelevant. It does not matter for present purposes who contributed what to the final print form of the text.

Second, in my lowbrow sense of the word 'text', the outside of a book is part of the book. The cover with its puffs and blurbs will be more impressed on most people who read the book than the middle 100 pages.

Third, we are not concerned with diagnosis. I use the label 'autism' in a deliberately ill-informed way, to refer to individuals with some sort of autistic spectrum disorder. Mukhopadhyay is the only one out of our four authors diagnosed as autistic at an early age, a diagnosis confirmed by a thorough examination in childhood by British experts. Although sometimes these four individuals are often taken to be aspergic as opposed to autistic, they themselves regularly use the word autism and are heard by the non-discriminating public as speaking about autism. The UK title of Tammet (2006) uses 'Asperger's' where the USA one has 'autistic'.

Suppose, however, that we were to answer question (ii) in the negative, and hold that the autobiographers are speaking only for the high-functioning end of the spectrum. Then it would be essential to attend to the distinctions along the spectrum that I am deliberately ignoring.

Fourth, our concern is not that of neurologists who may hope to decipher from the words of the autobiographers' clues to what is going on their brains, or the biological causes of their condition. My preoccupation is quite different and far less fundamental. I am concerned with what these words are doing to the public understanding of autism.

16.4 The tension between high functioning and severe

Alison Singer, vice-president of *Autism Speaks*, expresses one side of a tension that has bedevilled relationships between parents of autistic children. She contrasts her daughter Jodie, who 'has classic autism, which falls on the other end of the autism spectrum from Asperger syndrome', and another girl and friend of the family, Haley.

> Many days it is hard to believe that the challenges Haley faces with regard to her Asperger syndrome and those Jodie struggles with are related under the same DSM-IV diagnosis.
> At one end of the autism spectrum, we often find lower functioning persons like my daughter who cannot speak, have violent tantrums and can be self injurious, while at the other end we have persons who struggle with very significant, but very different, predominantly social issues.
> (Singer, no date)

Singer is one of the two major participants in the video *Autism Every Day*.[1] She went so far as to say, on screen, that sometimes she wanted to end it all by driving her car, with herself and her daughter in it, over the Brooklyn Bridge. For this, she has been much vilified, even to the extent of some critics saying that her child should be taken away from her.

Singer is, then, an activist who speaks for the family-shattering impact of severe autism, and wants to insist that this is a problem quite distinct from that at the other end of the spectrum. I presume she would say that our four autobiographers speak for high-functioning autists, but not for her daughter. I fully respect her point of view, which

---

[1] *Autism Every Day*, produced by Lauren Thierry of October Group and Eric Solomon of Milestone Video. There is a 13 min version, http://www.autismspeaks.org/sponsoredevents/autism_every_ day.php, and a 44 min one that was shown at the Sundance Festival, 2006.

is shared by myriad mothers on the front lines. I am exploring the alternative possibility, that the spectrum may evolve in such a way that there is thought to be more of a continuum in the descriptions of experience, than there has been. It is not a question, in my opinion, of finding out that there is a continuum, so much as trying to smooth over the contrasts urged on us, and experienced by Alison Singer. Note also that a few children begin as extremely impaired, and somehow grow out of it, to function well, so that a continuum can appear in a single life.

Singer's assertions are of grave practical importance. There is a growing wing of the autistic community that rejects the idea of looking for a cure. That makes sense, Singer implies, for Asperger's people who have a thick if unusual life. It is not fine for her daughter. Likewise Moore, author of *George and Sam* (2004), the remarkable book about her two severely autistic sons, is very much against integrating her children in regular schools, with the assistance of aides qualified in special education. That may be excellent for children further along the spectrum, but not for her older sons.

16.5 Autism narrative

Autism stories thrive on stage, radio, TV, cinema and above all on the Internet. Texting is an ideal mode of communication for many autists. Even when we stick to print, there is a vast publishing world of autism narrative beyond autobiography. Moreover, there are many more than a handful of autobiographies. Williams herself has published two more such volumes as well as other books. There is a host of parental biographies.

The most copious domain of printed autism narrative is fiction. Haddon's (2003) *The curious incident of the dog in the night-time* is only the tip of a book mountain. Reviewing the book, Charlotte Moore wrote that 'Autistic people are not easy subjects for novelists. Their interests are prescribed, their experiences static, their interaction with others limited.' (Moore 2003.) In my loaded terminology, these words imply that George and Sam were thin boys, destined to grow up into thin men. This is in no way intended as a criticism of her parenting; instead, it should serve as a reality check.

In an interview a year after Moore's review, Haddon (2004) implied complete agreement, but ironically reversed its connotations. The lives of autistic people are so boring on the face of it, he said, that he modelled himself on Jane Austen, describing the lives of equally boring people, and making them fascinating. He thereby turns some preconceptions upside down. Little could he have known about the amazing subgenre of retroactive autism narrative that was waiting in the wings. No fewer than eight characters of *Pride and Prejudice* have now been diagnosed, with proud Darcy the prime person with Asperger's or high-functioning autism (Bottomer 2007).

Jane Austen's personages are truly thick, yet, as Haddon playfully insists, most of us would be bored stiff in their socially assigned roles. There is a tension here, for his character Chris is much more high-functioning than George and Sam were said to be. This leads back to question (ii): Should we conceive of George and Sam as living far more complex and indeed more 'interesting' lives than we get on first impression after reading Moore's book? I am deliberately using that book here, because it is the parental biography that I, personally, most admire and am most affected by. Thus I am posing here a question that I find both hard and uncomfortable.

Haddon's tale has become a staple textbook in teacher-training courses, in the unit dedicated to working with children with special needs. Thus the well-informed model furnished by an established writer of young adult fiction is transmitted to a generation of teachers and in turn to their charges. The children may then learn that that is how it is to be autistic. Draaisma (2008) has an important analysis of related phenomena, using Haddon's *The curious incident of the dog in the night-time* among others as a key example.

My own list of autistic fictions has approximately 200 books, and counting. Especially important are the stories for children, some for autistic children, some for non-autistic children and some for all children. They take great pains to describe behaviour and thereby serve as role models. The young adult category is also influential in determining what autism is like and in some sense should be like. They illustrate 'the norm' and thereby help stabilize what the norm should be. Detective stories, spy thrillers, science fiction, gothic horror and Harlequin romances all help to reinforce a way of talking about autism.

The story-tellers learn from autobiographies how to tell their tales. But that is a two-way street. Temple Grandin's *Emergence* was written before the genre got underway, so her self-descriptions are unaffected. Today's autistic child, brought up on children's stories about autistic children, and who in later years goes on to write an autobiography, will give accounts that are textured by the early exposure to role models.

16.6 'Inside' autism

In his foreword to Grandin (2005), Oliver Sacks wrote that her previous book, *Emergence*, was

> Unprecedented because there had never before been an 'inside narrative' of autism; unthinkable because it had been medical dogma for forty years or more that there *was* no 'inside', no inner life, in the autistic.
>
> (Sacks, foreword in Grandin 2005, p. 11)

Even before we dip into these books, we find that word 'inside' over and over again—on their covers. On the back cover of a current paperback of Grandin's (2005) *Emergence*:

> A remarkable story... uniquely valuable in helping us to see autism from the 'inside'.

A quotation from *People* magazine on a paperback of Williams' *Nobody Nowhere*:

> By turns fascinating and harrowing... a riveting autobiography that describes how autism feels like from the inside.

The subtitle of Mukhopadhyay's (2008) is:

> *Inside my Autistic Mind.*

The subtitle of the American edition of Tammet (2006) is:

> *Inside the Extraordinary Mind of an Autistic Savant.*

These examples can be repeated many times without even opening books.

16.7 Unexceptionable uses of the inside metaphor

Sacks put quotation marks—which I take to be 'scare quotes'—around 'inside narrative', and, a line later on, around 'inside'. His point was that Grandin's first book was astonishing, because no one familiar with autistic people expected such a text. It is an 'inside story' in the simple sense that it is an autistic person telling her own story, and not a clinician or parent writing about her. Sacks also meant that before Grandin, someone who had come across autism in only a casual way might have thought that autistic people had nothing like we would countenance as a thick mental life.

In a puff for Mukhopadhyay's (2003) Sacks said that the book,

> is indeed amazing, shocking too, for it has usually been assumed that deeply autistic people are scarcely capable of introspection or deep thought, let alone of poetic or metaphoric leaps of the imagination [.].

To use a phrase of Sacks in the same blurb, Mukhopadhyay 'gives the lie' to the doctrine that autistic thinking is necessarily literal, and that it resists metaphor. Moreover, at an early age, he seems to have had a great aptitude for storytelling and imaginative play. A primary item in Lorna Wing's 'triad' is impairment of imagination. At the age of 5, he is making up stories, starting with one about a lost goat (2003, p. 36). By the age of 8, he well conceptualizes imagination and fantasy. Referring to a time after his grandfather died when he was 4 years old, he wrote: 'Imagination took shape to lead his mind to a world of fantasies' (2003, p. 19).

16.8 'Inside the mind'

When 'inside' connotes written or spoken by a person with autism, and 'outside' connotes written or spoken by an observer, parent, clinician or friend, then the metaphor is benign. But it is also, once the point has been made, rather banal, and hardly worth the constant repetition we have encountered.

Aside from such benign uses, I am cautious about 'inside the mind', for reasons presented in Wittgenstein's *Philosophical Investigations*. This is not the occasion to argue the case or even sketch what is at issue, but it does motivate my approach. It is certainly not a hankering after behaviourism.

A first danger of the 'inside' metaphor needs only to be stated to be scotched. It is the idea of 'a unique insight into *the* autistic mind': as if 'the autistic mind' were a species of mind. Our four autists have very different minds! Grandin describes herself as thinking in pictures. Mukhopadhyay is dominated by sounds. Tammet sees abstract objects in colour. Hence Williams' (2005) metaphor of autistic spectrum 'fruit salads'. To quote a common adage: 'If you know one autistic person, you know *one* autistic person'.

Talk of getting inside the mind of another is apt in its place, but unreflective use out of context often suggests a misleading picture of mental life. It suggests that looking inside is much like looking outside, in the way that looking inside a cardboard box after opening it is no different from looking at it from the outside, except for a change in point of view. This goes along with the sense that our own minds are transparent to us (subject to Freudian reservations). We look inside them all the time. That generates the question of how we ever know what is going on in the mind of another person.

This 'Problem of Other Minds' has been a topic in English-language philosophy for well over a century. It is proposed that we know what other people are feeling and thinking (etc.) by analogy with our own case. Or we postulate a mind similar to ours as the best possible explanation of the actions of another person. In any event, we must always *infer* what someone else is thinking (etc.) from their behaviour. That is nonsense. We often know what someone thinks *via*, or thanks to, their behaviour, but without any need to go through some process of inference. In fact, the emphasis on thinking is misleading; we should think first of knowing what another person is doing, i.e. of immediate recognition of intentions.

Of course sometimes we do have to infer what another person must feel, hope, want, detest, or whatever, from their actions. There are innumerable occasions when we are completely baffled as to what someone else is doing. We have to figure out their intentions and their hidden worries. There are also situations where inference is required, for example the famous false belief tests of Wimmer & Perner (1983).

There can always arise *particular* difficulties in understanding another person. But the puff writers who talk of getting into the mind of an autistic person do not, for a moment, think that there is the same *general* question for most people, as there is for autists. I cannot recall an 'inside the mind' (or variant thereof) being written on the cover of any non-autistic autobiography that I have examined lately. It could certainly occur, of course, in connection with a biography. 'Finally we have got inside the inscrutable mind of Vladimir Putin.' But that is not the norm.

The 'Theory of Mind' approach to the ability to understand what other people believe, hope for and are doing has the great advantage, over philosophers' theories of 'Other Minds', that it does not imagine that we infer, for example, by analogy, that other people have minds. But it is still preoccupied by inference, thanks to ties with the false belief tests. I cannot 'see' that Sally will think the box has Smarties in it, not pencils; I have to infer it from knowledge about what she knows and does not know. That is not a core case of interpersonal relationships. Theory of Mind approaches to autism, driven by false belief tests, focus on complex situations that are parasitic on the bedrock cases of simply knowing what someone else is doing (which may include thinking, feeling, plotting and so forth).

The very label 'Theory' has the unfortunate connotation of always getting to the destination by reasoning. More importantly, it does not easily distinguish between, on the one hand, seeing what someone is doing right off and, on the other, inferring or working it out from clues. To say that there is a distinction is not to quarrel with someone who insists that there is always a 'computation' leading up to knowledge; it is only to conjecture that, within that paradigm, different types of computation must be involved. Two earlier writers thought that such a distinction was profoundly important.

16.9 Wittgenstein and Gestalt Psychology[2]

Wittgenstein's aphorism (2001, p. 152e) captures an important fact about other minds:

> The human body is the best picture of the human soul.

This and related remarks were foreshadowed in the first edition of Köhler's *Gestalt Psychology* (1929). Wittgenstein devoted some of his classes to matters arising from that book. They bore fruit in Part II of the *Philosophical Investigations*. For example, one of

---

[2] I owe these reflections on Köhler and Wittgenstein entirely to a recent PhD dissertation (Dinishak 2008).

Köhler's observations (p. 250) anticipates the aphorism just quoted. It explicitly takes us back to the inner:

> [...] not only the so-called expressive movements but also the practical behavior of human beings is a good picture of their inner life, in a great many cases.

Both the philosopher and the psychologist use the metaphor of a picture. We usually *see* what a picture is *of*, and do not infer it. I look (for example) at Goya's etching, titled *The pitcher's broken*. I *see* a child howling; he is close to a broken jug, and he is being ruthlessly spanked with a slipper by a woman who had been hanging out her laundry.[3] I *infer* from the ironic caption that the child broke the pitcher and that this is Goya's protest against routine cruelty to children, under the guise of fair punishment. But I do not infer what the etching is a picture of.

Likewise I usually just see that a man is in bad humour (Wittgenstein 2001, p. 153e). I note it, and do not infer it. (Of course there are cases when I do have to infer it! But those are parasitic upon cases where I do not.) A kindly boss is upset because he has to reprimand an employee: 'Viewed from without the official's activity is a picture of his inner perturbation' (Köhler, p. 254). We see that he is upset. We do not infer it, in the common case, from the way he looks and acts. (Which is not to deny that sometimes we have to infer, guess or divine that he is upset.) Köhler has many more illustrations. They include that of following a person's gaze (p. 250f):

> If my attention is attracted by a strange object, a snake for instance, I feel directed toward it and at the same time a feeling of tension is experienced. A friend, even if he has not recognized the snake, will see me and especially my face and eyes directed toward it; in the tension of my face he will have a visual picture of my inner tension, as in its direction he has a direct picture of the direction which I experience.

Wittgenstein was also much interested in pointing and less explicit ways of directing attention.

Another example from both Köhler (p. 252) and Wittgenstein (1980, § 1066) is that of a child, reaching out to touch an animal, but not daring to do so. We see what the child wants to do, and also see that that's a bit too scary. The example originates with Watson's (1926, p. 52) experiment with a child and a white rat, to show something about the transfer of fear reactions. The child becomes scared of anything woolly. Köhler cites but refers only to an 'animal', not saying what kind. That made Wittgenstein think of a child and a dog.

Köhler admitted at once, in 1929, that his account 'gives us neither an altogether new nor an altogether perfect key to another person's inner life; it tries only to describe so far as it can that kind of understanding which is *the common property and practice of mankind*' (p. 266, italics added). He hoped for future work 'when the simpler facts described in this chapter will have found more general acknowledgement' (p. 267). Enthusiasts for Theory of Mind may be inclined to say that Köhler was describing, in naive terms, just what it is to have a Theory of Mind. In fact, 'naive' is a word that Köhler often uses himself with cautious approval, as something more true to experience than what psychologists of his day were saying. Whether or not one should repeat that comparison with today's psychologists, I find it a virtue that his descriptions are not at the level of propositional knowledge that so often comes to the fore in cognitive science. Curiously, both Köhler's

---

[3] Francisco Goya, *Si quebró el Canatano*, *Capricho* 25.

approach to these phenomena, and Theory of Mind, originated in studies of the great apes.[4]

16.10 Köhler's phenomena, and their absence

Köhler pointed to a wide range of phenomena in which we see and do not infer what a person is doing. Among these are the examples cited: seeing that the child wants to touch the dog, but does not dare; seeing that the friend is startled by something; seeing where that something must be; and seeing that a man is upset by a disagreeable task. Let us call these *Köhler's phenomena*. You can think of innumerable examples.

Perhaps the future work, for which Köhler hoped, explaining his phenomena, will prove to be research on mirror neurons. They certainly do provide an explanation sketch of how his phenomena might be possible. And yet it is somehow too tidy. A sceptic could suggest that causation runs the opposite way. Electrical impulses reach the mirror neurons precisely because the person has seen that a man is upset, rather than the person seeing that the man is upset because a mirror neuron has been activated.

I shall stick to the phenomena. They are familiar to most people, but are precisely what are *not* familiar, 'automatic', 'immediate' or 'instinctive' for most autistic people. They are not 'the common property and practice' of that part of mankind that is autistic. Expert observers report that autistic children do not see that someone is in a bad humour; they do not follow the direction of a startled person's gaze; they do not readily understand what another person is doing, i.e. they do not easily recognize intentions.

Conversely, most people cannot see, *via* the behaviour of severely autistic people, what they feel, want or are thinking. Even more disturbing is an inability to see what they are doing: their intentions make no sense. With the severely autistic, it may seem as if they do not even *have* many intentions. They are taken to be, to repeat my metaphor, thin children who grow up to be thin men and women, lacking a thick emotional life. Or so it has seemed to most people, including many parents and many clinicians. Since Köhler's phenomena do not take place, when most people are in the company of a severely autistic person, we have to compensate for their absence. This is what autism narrative helps to do.

There is a partial symmetry between the autistic and the non-autistic. Neither can see what the other is doing. The symmetry is only partial because we have an age-old language for describing what the non-autistic are feeling, thinking and so on, but are only creating one for the autistic.

Precisely because autistic children do not share in Köhler's phenomena, it is now common practice to try to teach them how to *infer* the feelings and intentions of other children and adults from their behaviour, from their gestures, from their tone of voice. There are indeed a number of books, posters and videos intended to teach what many people look like when they are happy or sad.

Conversely, ordinary people cannot see what an autistic boy is doing when, to take a banal example, he is furiously flapping his hands. What on Earth is hand flapping? The parent or other outsider knows vaguely that there must be some kind of agitation, yet the

---

[4] Köhler traces his approach back to 'a great many instance of this type' to be found in his book, *The Mentality of Apes* (original Köhler 1921); see Köhler 1929 p. 252. Theory of Mind is usually traced back to the classic paper on chimpanzees, Premack & Woodruff (1978).

child seems so tranquil when hand flapping. Autobiographies tell us how calming it is. So we are now able to infer a bit of what's going on.

Autistic narrative thus comes to our aid. It is striking that although we are told that it takes us into the mind of the autist, in fact autobiographers usually begin with their behaviour, reaching back to childhood. Grandin begins with herself as a 3-year old, having a tantrum and thereby causing her mother to total the car in which they were driving. Then we are told that Temple hated the horrid hat she was required to wear. Thus actions and behaviour are put together not only with common words for emotions, often of fear, shock, assault by the senses, but also with a feeling of peace, of getting to a quiet place. All this works by using ordinary language. Yet at the same time, the autobiographers have to retool linguistic materials made in an age-long community. Köhler's phenomena are the bedrock upon which rests the common understanding of those words. But the phenomena are lacking when we try to empathize with the autistic author. So Grandin and her successors tell stories to help us infer from autistic behaviour the words she would now use to say what is going on.

16.11 Hypersensitivity

Our autobiographers insist that certain sensations cause huge distress to the author. They give examples to demonstrate they are sensitive to the point of anguish by too bright a light, too loud a sound, too scratchy a surface or other touch; when sensations become overwhelming, this leads to virtual collapse, screams, etc. The too much is 'painful'. These accounts are strikingly consistent and backed by parental observation. Possibly they are connected to remarkable sensory acuity, such as 'eagle-eyed' vision and the like now being studied in the laboratory as reported by Baron-Cohen *et al.* (2009).

'Acuity' sounds neutral, but too much sensation is, for many autists, unbearable, and seems to fit into the category of pain. But the fit is loose; we do not know quite what the words should be. We should listen carefully to the ordinary language of pain, and then note how people with autism try to adapt it to their own experience. In this respect, it may be useful to take seriously Wittgenstein's remarks on the public language of pain in order to cast away the stereotypical—I want to say mechanical—conceptions of pain that so often blind theory to experience. We want something subtler than thresholds, acuity and so forth.

16.12 A role for autism narrative

Autism autobiography, and autism narrative more generally, is thus playing a remarkable role in the evolution of the autistic spectrum. It is enabling us to try to compensate for the lack of Köhler's phenomena in our interaction with autistic people. The various regimes that help autistic people learn to understand most other people compensate in one direction. They enable the autist to infer from neurotypical behaviour. The narratives teach many of us how to compensate in the other. That is, they suggest what to infer from autistic behaviour which on the face of it means nothing to us.

I suggested at the outset, in connection with question (i), that the autobiographies do not so much describe the mental life of their autistic authors, as constitute it by choosing words from ordinary language to be applied in connection with their behaviour. This is important for question (ii). If the autobiographies are straight descriptions, true or false according to the existing criteria, then it is a plain matter of fact whether those descriptions apply to less high-functioning people. But if we think of the descriptions as constituting autistic experience, it is less a question of fact than of the ways in which we will come to understand the less able.

16.13 Concluding query on language

There is no space here to do the real job, to look in detail at the ways in which our authors recall and describe their past and present. I invite you to read these texts not as describing well-defined experience, but as creating ways in which to express experiences. I shall end with a puzzle taken from one set of texts. It bears on another question, namely how human speech can be acquired by individuals who have little grasp of the ordinary community of speakers, and then be later used by them to describe their condition before they entered the community.

Our autobiographers imply and sometimes state that they understood what was said around them, long before they could speak. Grandin writes of herself at the age of 3,

> Although I could understand everything people said, my responses were limited.
> (Grandin 2005, p. 22)

Mukhopadhyay communicates in the way developed by his mother and himself. He does not speak. Yet he too reports detailed understanding of what was said around him when he was only 3 years old. He was being interviewed by a psychologist in the presence of his mother. He was diagnosed as autistic. The expert explained that the child was so withdrawn he could not understand what is going on around him. The boy was listening, and a few years later he reported:

> 'I understand very well', said the spirit in the boy.
> (Mukhopadhyay 2003, p. 23)

This does not sound at all like the reading of Frith and Happé in their paper, 'What is it like to be autistic?' Their central thesis is that articulate autists 'appear to arrive at an explicit theory of mind by a slow and painstaking learning process, just as they appear to arrive at self-consciousness by a long and tortuous route'. (1999, p. 2).

If we take the words of Mukhopadhyay and Grandin as straight descriptions of matters of fact, we have to ask whether the memories were reliable. We might then suppose something like them is true, but only at a later age. We would still have to ask how it is possible for these children to acquire a remarkable understanding of language without yet having participated in dialogue, in babble, and in trial and error.

But suppose we are less concerned with whether as a matter of fact the child did understand, than with a form of words that represents how the autist felt, or seems to remember feeling. If we took this point of view, we might come to judge that less gifted autistic children and adults, who communicate very little, also understand, in a quite specific way, far more than is evident to the outsider. If we were to take this route, it would be a shift, perhaps a radical one, in our conceptions of and relationships to individuals on the spectrum.

References

Baron-Cohen, S., Ashwin, E., Ashwin, C, Tavassoli, T. & Chakrabarti, B. 2009 Talent in autism: hyper-systemizing, hyper-attention to detail and sensory hypersensitivity. *Phil. Trans. R. Soc. B* **364**, 1377–1383. (doi:10.1098/rstb.2008.0337)

Bottomer, P. F. 2007 *So odd a mixture: along the autistic spectrum in 'Pride and Prejudice'*. London, UK: Jessica Kingsley.

Dinishak, J. 2008 Wittgenstein and Köhler on seeing and seeing aspects. PhD thesis, University of Toronto, Toronto, Canada.

Draaisma, D. 2008 Who owns Asperger's syndrome? *Sartoniana* **21**, 23–48.

Frith, U. & Happé, F. 1999 Theory of mind and self-consciousness: what is it like to be autistic? *Mind Lang.* **14**, 1–22.

Grandin, T. 1986 *Emergence: labeled autistic*. Novato, CA: Arena Press.

Grandin, T 1995 *Thinking in pictures: and other reports from my life with autism*. New York, NY: Doubleday.

Grandin, T. 2005 *Emergence: labeled autistic, a true story*, with a supplement, 'Looking back 2005'. New York, NY: Grand Central Publishing.

Hacking, I. 2007 Kinds of people: moving targets. *Proc. Br. Acad* **151**, 285–318.

Haddon, M. 2003 *The curious incident of the dog in the nighttime*. London, UK: Jonathan Cape.

Haddon, M. 2004 B is for Bestseller. *The Observer*, 11 April.

Köhler, W 1921 *Intelligenzprüfungen an Menschenaffen*, 2nd revised edn. Berlin, Germany: Springer. (*The mentality of apes*, London, UK: Paul, Trench and Trubner, 1924, first English edition.)

Köhler, W 1929 *Gestalt psychology*. New York, NY: Horace Liveright.

Moore, C. 2003 Just the facts, ma'am, Review of Haddon 2003. *The Guardian*, **24** May.

Moore, C. 2004 *George and Sam: two boys, one family, and autism*. London, UK: Viking.

Mór, C. 2007 *A blessing and curse: autism and me*. London, UK: Jessica Kingsley.

Mukhopadhyay, T. R. 2000 *Beyond the silence: my life, the world and autism*. London, UK: National Autistic Society.

Mukhopadhyay, T. R. 2003 *The mind tree: an extraordinary child breaks the silence of autism*. New York, NY: Arcade.(Extended U.S. v. of Mukhopadhyay 2000.)

Mukhopadhyay, T. R. 2008 *How Can I Talk If My Lips Don't Move? Inside My Autistic Mind*. New York, NY: Arcade.

Nazeer, K. 2006 *Send in the Idiots: or how we grew to understand the world*. London, UK: Bloomsbury.

Premack, D. G. & Woodruff, G. 1978 Does the chimpanzee have a theory of mind? *Behav. Brain Sci.* 1, 515–526.

Sacks, O. 1993 An anthropologist on Mars. *The New Yorker*, **27** December.

Sacks, O. 1995 *An anthropologist on Mars: seven paradoxical tales*. New York, NY: Knopf.

Singer, A. No date. 'Cure' is not a four letter word. See http://www.autismspeaks.org/whatisit/singer_commentary.php.

Tammet, D. 2006 *Born on a blue day: a memoir of Asperger's and an extraordinary mind*. London, UK: Hodder and Stoughton. (US edition: *Born on a blue day: inside the extraordinary mind of an autistic savant. A Memoir*. New York, NY: Free Press.)

Watson, J. B. 1926 Experimental studies on the growth of the emotions. In *Psychologies of 1925: Powell lectures in psychological theory* (ed. C. Murchison). Worcester, MA: Clark University Press.

Williams, D. 1992 *Nobody nowhere: the extraordinary autobiography of an autistic*. New York, NY: Times Books.

Williams, D. 1994 *Somebody somewhere: breaking free from the world of autism*. New York, NY: Times Books.

Williams, D. 2005 *The Jumbled Jigsaw: an insider's approach to the treatment of autistic spectrum 'Fruit Salads'*. London,UK: Jessica Kingsley.

Wimmer, H. & Perner, J. 1983 Beliefs about beliefs: representation and constraining function of wrong beliefs in young children's understanding of deception. *Cognition* **13**, 103–128. (doi:10.1016/0010-0277(83)90004-5)

Wittgenstein, L. 1980 *Remarks on the philosophy of psychology I.* Oxford, UK: Blackwell.

Wittgenstein, L. [1953] 2001 *Philosophical investigations.* Third revised translation, Oxford, UK: Blackwell.

# 17

Stereotypes of autism

Douwe Draaisma

In their landmark papers, both Kanner and Asperger employed a series of case histories to shape clinical insight into autistic disorders. This way of introducing, assessing and representing disorders has disappeared from today's psychiatric practice, yet it offers a convincing model of the way stereotypes may build up as a result of representations of autism. Considering that much of what society at large learns on disorders on the autism spectrum is produced by representations of autism in novels, TV-series, movies or autobiographies, it will be of vital importance to scrutinize these representations and to check whether or not they are, in fact, misrepresenting autism. In quite a few cases, media representations of talent and special abilities can be said to have contributed to a harmful divergence between the general image of autism and the clinical reality of the autistic condition.

Keywords: brain; autism; talent

17.1 Introduction

In the original publication on the syndrome that was to bear his name, Asperger (1944) introduced his case histories with a series of reflections on the proper methodology of classifying and diagnosing psychiatric disorders. In these pages Asperger grappled with issues that are still very much with us, issues of labelling, description and stereotyping. Some of his considerations on diagnosing and describing autism may help us reflect on the professional and media representations of autism. Specifically, it will be argued that Asperger's Gestalt-like assessment and description of autism, even if it is officially denounced in modern psychiatric practice, offers a convincing model of the way stereotypes may build up as a result of representations of autism. Considering that much of what society at large learns on disorders on the autism spectrum is produced by representations of autism in novels, TV-series, movies or autobiographies, it will be of vital importance to scrutinize these representations and to check whether or not they are, in fact, misrepresenting autism. In quite a few cases, media representations of talent and special abilities can be said to have contributed to a harmful divergence between the general image of autism and the clinical reality of the autistic condition.

17.2 Hans Asperger: the power of case description

Asperger wrote his case histories at a time when Gestalt psychology had become a formidable force of influence in the German-speaking world (Ash 1995). It certainly shaped his somewhat holistic view on the proper way of classifying and diagnosing psychiatric disorders. Each human being, Asperger argued, must be understood as an alloy of traits, as a unique blend of capacities and inclinations. To be a good diagnostician, one will have to develop a sensitivity for what he called the 'Zusammenklang' (p. 78) or Gestalt of the child—his voice, face, body language, intonation, gestures, gaze, expression and diction. The true art of clinical observation was being open towards just anything the other person brings into the diagnostic situation. This Gestalt-like orientation precluded the description of syndromes, in terms of lists or assemblies of atomistic traits. Asperger, consequently, did not scale the boys in his case histories along a single polarity, nor did he articulate a single essence, supposedly shared by all the boys.

This was different in the case of Leo Kanner, who did distil an essence of autism with his evocative descriptions of autistic aloneness, insistence on sameness and islets of ability. But in Kanner's landmark article too, it was the case descriptions themselves that shaped clinical insight.

Asperger introduced his readers to three boys who helped to shape a Gestalt-like stereotype of the autistic condition. The first case history, on 6-year-old Fritz V. presents a lengthy description of his looks, his aggressive behaviour on the ward, his resistance against being tested, his thin, high-pitched voice, his adult-like choice of words, his clumsiness, his irritated reactions to any show of affection, his vacant gaze, his nonsense answers to questions, his precociousness in arithmetic and his abrupt mood swings. The second case history, on 8-year-old Harro L., is considerably shorter. He too is clumsy and aggressive, has the same vacant expression, the smile that no one understands, the strange answers, the precociousness in doing sums, the lack of contact with other children and the adult-like speech. After Fritz and Harro, the case of 7-year-old Ernst K. is even shorter. He cannot tolerate other children, looks straight past objects and people, has a high nasal voice and makes a scene if things are not in the same place as he is used to. Ernst also does sums according to his own methods. There is a fourth case history, on Hellmuth L., but this case is only there to demonstrate that brain damage may result in behavioural symptoms that overlap with those of autism, but in fact should be differentiated from the autism diagnosis.

Asperger's description of Fritz is an implicit invitation to his readers to join him in the act of clinical observation and to note the traits that are part of the Gestalt. Perhaps, trusting that his readers will begin to form some sort of mental image of the Gestalt, the second case history is shorter and the third one is still shorter. Each of these three boys is a unique person, yet they share a profile that sets up a new psychiatric category. What Asperger was aiming at was the construction of a compound image or profile. Once this profile has been pointed out to you, Asperger claimed, you will recognize it at first sight, as soon as the boy enters and as soon as he starts talking.

In a psychiatric practice that has become a discipline of protocols and lists of criteria, Asperger's Gestalt-like method has an antiquated ring to it. But from what is known on the role of prototypes and exemplars in psychological studies of categorization, ever since the work of Rosch (1978), one may infer that it is still a fair description of what a diagnostician experiences as he or she feels the routine in diagnosing autism building up. One gets a sensitivity for the *type* of boy or girl on the autism spectrum and this sensitivity is fed not just by test results and the five-out-of-eight on a list, but also by the wider domain of traits and behaviours mentioned by Asperger. The stereotype that builds up will be largely implicit, but it partially guides the diagnostic process, as it does the initiation of novice diagnosticians. Along the same lines one may infer that it is a convincing description of the way media representations contribute to the construction of autism stereotypes in a larger audience of lay persons.

17.3 The proliferation of autism stereotypes

Much has changed since Asperger drew up his case histories in the 1940s. For one thing, among the two-hundred children he had seen and who shared this profile, there were no girls. In his view it was an exclusively male disorder. It no longer is. But by and large, Asperger's clinical picture of autism at the more able end of the spectrum still stands. That is, even if the case histories are over 60 years old, these three boys are recognizably members of the family of autism; they clearly fit the image of what experts today view as a 'normal' autistic person. Even if there has been a controversy on *where* exactly on the autism spectrum they should be positioned, due to idiosyncrasies of the *DSM* (Miller & Ozonoff 1997), there is no doubt they are *on* the spectrum. In this sense, much of the stereotype constructed by Asperger is still valid—that is *among experts*.

Outside, to use a dangerous term, it is a different story. The past 20 years or so have seen a considerable proliferation of autism stereotypes—so much so that one may pause to think whether it is still useful to talk of stereotypes at all. There are now autistic persons as characters in novels and movies, as the subject of biographies or autobiographies, as vignettes in introductory courses, as exemplars in marital guidance books and as cases in books on special education or as patients in retrospective diagnoses, sometimes as far back as medieval times. It is not just that there are many more persons diagnosed as on the spectrum compared with the situation 20 or even 10 years ago, the spectrum itself seems to have exploded. How did this happen?

In an inspiring series of historical and conceptual analyses, Ian Hacking has identified much of the clockwork behind psychiatric classification (Hacking 1995, 2007). Terms such as the 'looping effect' and 'moving target' are simple names for subtle concepts; they are ways of thinking, analysing and looking. Much as Asperger and Kanner made it easier to recognize autistic disorders once they had articulated what to look for, Hacking specified the processes that cause psychiatric categories to be such shifty things. The very act of labelling initiates a complex interaction between the label and the perception and understanding of the person so labelled. Autism is no exception. Labels such as autism, Asperger Syndrome or PDD-NOS carry connotations and consequences, and these will influence pedagogical and educational practices. This interaction takes shape in a world in which psychiatry is not the only, perhaps not even the most important, force of influence. Today, the processes that shape the general understanding of Asperger syndrome and autism have come to be distributed over persons and institutions, literature and film, education and media. A better understanding of the autistic condition and the talents that may come with it demands that we should carefully observe the intricate interaction between the 'expert' view of autism and the general perception of autism as it manifests itself in the way autistic persons are represented in novels, biographies, autobiographies and movies. That there is such a thing as a general perception of autism, perhaps best thought of as a *set* of stereotypes, is graphically brought out by what movies need or need not show to explain the autistic condition.

Up until 6 or 7 years ago, many movies featuring autistic characters had a scene in it in which an expert, usually a psychiatrist, explained about autism and savant skills. We all remember the white-coat scene in *Rain Man*. There is not such a scene in the movie *Snow Cake*, released in 2006. Alex, the character played by Alan Rickman, comes to spend a few days with Linda, an autistic woman, played by Sigourney Weaver. He is puzzled by Linda's bizarre behaviour and at some point halfway through the movie, when they are in the backyard, Linda jumping up and down on a trampoline, her neighbour confides to him, behind the back of her hand: 'Autistic, but very verbal'. Alex answers with a nod of understanding. That is all. She is autistic and apparently he does not need more information, and neither do we. We understand why Linda is carefully aligning shoes in the hallway, for we all know that autistic people hate it when things are in disarray. We understand why she is fascinated by the spinning of a shiny coin. We understand why she throws a temper tantrum when people try to touch her. There is a scene in which one of the neighbours offers her condolences, saying 'I'm sorry you lost your daughter'. Linda answers: 'She's not lost, she's dead'—autistic people are terribly literal. We do not need a doctor to explain all this. The very fact that the topical white-coat scene was silently dropped from autism movies testifies to the proliferation of autism stereotypes.

17.4 Autism and savant skills

In each of Asperger's three cases, there was mention of some special talent or ability, a *Sonderinteresse* (p. 90). Fritz, Harro and Ernst all did sums in a precocious way, two of them with methods of their own device. With other boys Asperger had seen calendar calculating, memorizing tram schedules and one boy with a gift for mathematics who went on to study mathematics and wrote a dissertation on a calculation error in the work of Newton. Asperger emphasized that whatever there are in terms of special abilities may help social integration. But it is important to note that among the family traits of autism, version Asperger, savantism was not included. Most experts would agree that this is still the case. Even if savantism mostly comes with autism, the majority of cases of autism do not have savantism.

In movies, however, there are hardly any autistic characters *not* having savant skills. In the opening scene of *Mozart and the Whale* (2005), Donald, one of the leading characters, is driving a cab. Less than two minutes have passed when you have seen four things that will strike you as odd. He starts talking to his two passengers and keeps on talking even when it is clear they do not listen because they are having a conversation among themselves. Then, after a mere glance on his watch, he calculates to the minute how long it has been since he is employed: 'Seven days, nine hours and thirty-seven minutes'. He goes on to explain that he can see the entire fleet of cabs and their relative distances before his mind's eye ('The trouble is, I just can't *not* see it'.), and finally, when he hits a car parked in front of him, he just walks away from the scene and leaves his passengers to themselves, saying he has a meeting scheduled. All of this is intended to introduce him as a person with Asperger's syndrome: two out of four clues have to do with savant skills.

Later on in the movie Donald explains to the other members of his autism support group: 'By the time I was two years old, my parents basically got the drill: I wasn't exactly what they were looking for in a child. I wasn't normal'. Then the movie cuts to a childhood scene that shows just in what way young Donald was not normal. A couple of kids ask him how much is 5589 burgers times 3972 divided by 17 and he instantly produces the correct, 10-digit answer. Other members of the support group have savant skills as well. One boy remembers all kinds of trivia on any day you care to mention: temperature, humidity and so on. *Mozart and the Whale* is a love story. It is in no way essential to the plot that Donald or anyone else should have savant skills. In movies, savantism has become the quick way of pointing out that autistic people are being dealt with.

The action thriller *Mercury Rising* (1998) is another case in point. The plot hinges on the savantism of Simon, a 9-year-old autistic boy. His almost supernatural pattern-recognition skills allow him to crack even the most sophisticated cryptographic code, including a new two-billion dollar encryption code called Mercury, developed by the American government. This makes Simon a liability. He becomes the boy who knows too much. To protect the lives of thousands of secret agents all over the world, it is decided to have him eliminated.

In one of the pivotal scenes, the head of the encryption project calls in the two cryptographers responsible for leaking the code. It turns out that they had run 'a standard validation protocol', including 'double sets of paired Cray supercomputers, fricking velociraptor machines chewing at Mercury 24 hours a day'. But they wanted to do one final test, to make sure that the code was 'geek proof' too. So they slipped a message in 'one of those egghead word games' in a 'geek magazine' called *Puzzle-line*, a message readable only for someone who is able to decipher Mercury. When they explain this to their chief, he says that apparently this is exactly what has happened: a 9-year-old kid from Chicago has cracked the code. And then he yells: 'Not only is he nine years old, he is handicapped! He is autistic!' One of the cryptographers replies: 'Yes, that explains it!' This infuriates the chief even further:

— 'So our two-billion dollar code is an open book to people of diminished capacity?'
— 'Oh no sir, autism isn't synonymous with diminished capacity. Autistic people., they're shut off. But it is not unusual for an autistic person to be a savant'.
— 'Ah, savant!', says his fellow-cryptographer, as if this explains everything.

The tenor of the scene is quite simple. There are two options for an autistic person: either he is mentally handicapped, an egghead reading geek magazines, or he is a savant with mental powers exceeding those of two Cray supercomputers spinning numbers 24 hours a day. It is either diminished capacity or superhuman capacity, but nothing in between.

Perhaps we would like to think that perpetuating the autistic savant stereotype is something movie-makers do and experts warn against. However, this is not the case. Publicity campaigns for movies often feature experts as advisors. In *Mercury Rising* there are several allusions to science backing up the theme of autism. In an early scene, Simon is in the Chicago Neuropsychiatric Learning Center, a name that is kept in view for about 3 s. This may not seem a long time, but in movie-language it means: 'Watch out! Important clue!' In the 'extras' on the DVD, director Harold Becker says how fortunate he was that the head of Pediatric Psychiatry at the University of Chicago, a world renowned authority, was willing to act as an advisor. The advisor then talks about the way he coached and supported Miko, the young actor playing the Simon character, and how he let him spend time with autistic children in a school for special education. It is clear that he wanted to help Miko to play the autistic character as convincingly as possible. There is nothing actually wrong with what he has to say about autism, the problem is, rather, in what he is *not* saying, and perhaps should have been saying, namely that savantism is rare among autistic persons. As a rule, movie-makers seem to have no trouble finding scientific authorities who are willing to endorse rather than correct the Hollywood stereotype of the autistic savant.

In general, there is a strange discrepancy between the research that directors, script writers and actors put in when they make a film featuring autistic persons and the actual characters they come up with. Actors insist that they invest months of preparation to study the movements and reactions of autistic persons, script writers read scientific articles on autism, directors call on consultants, they all want an *absolutely* sincere and truthful rendition of autism; what they come up with is an autistic character with freak-like savant skills, unlike anything resembling a normal autistic person. The stereotype of autistic persons being savants is without doubt one of the most striking discrepancies between the expert's view and the general view of autism.

Is there any harm in that? It is often mentioned that the stereotype of the autistic savant raises expectations to an unrealistic level, causing disappointment and frustration for the many autistic persons not so gifted. In a subtle analysis of movies featuring autism, Stuart Murray, father of an autistic son, makes it clear that it is mostly the savantism that constitutes the 'worth' of autistic characters. Without their savant skills there would not be much of a plot, or social life for them either (Murray 2008). Anthony Baker, who is also father of an autistic son, pointed out that when he tells people that his son is autistic, they usually ask whether he is a savant as well. When he answers that he is 'just' autistic, it is as if people think that his son is doubly challenged (Baker 2008). Baker also argues that ever since *Rain Man*, movies on autistic savants propose 'a computational, non-human model of the autistic brain' (p. 236), as if autistic thought processes are machine-like. This robotic view of autistic persons—remember Simon's performance surpassing the combined efforts of two Cray supercomputers—may reinforce the myth of autistic persons having no true feelings.

17.5 Differently gifted or not so different after all

Quite a few novels and movies suggest that autistic people may teach the non-autistic a wise lesson. Often these lessons are said to follow from the condition itself, for instance by suggesting that the lack of social skills also eliminates much that is artificial, phoney or plainly dishonest in normal social communication. The archetypical example, again, is *Rain Man* (1988). Initially, Charlie Babbitt, played by Tom Cruise, is a selfish, egocentric character, who takes the death of his father without any signs of sorrow and only pays attention to messages that are relevant to his business of importing fancy sports cars. At the end of the movie he has established a loving relationship with his lost brother and has learned to listen to other people. A more recent example would be the lesson that Christopher, the protagonist of *The curious incident of the dog in the night-time* (2003), is teaching us. Mark Haddon provided his inner world with little more than a few primary emotions, such as sadness or happiness. With these poor instruments Haddon lets him navigate among people who fine-tune their behaviour to the feelings and expectations of other people, or at least have the ability to do so. Such a world, you will find, empathizing with Christopher, is confusing. You come to understand why he hates lies and fantasies; his world is complicated enough as it is; he has little use for alternative versions of reality.

Your empathy quickly changes into sympathy and pity, because it turns out that he has been told many a lie by people who *can* operate with alternative versions of reality—if that suits them better. In this respect, *The curious incident* is really a novel on the deficits in non-autistic lives. The movie *Snow Cake* holds a similar lesson, for instance, when autistic Linda looks with disgust at her neighbours socializing after the funeral of her daughter.

Sometimes this line of reasoning is taken one step further. In the extras on the DVD of *Snow Cake*, Sigourney Weaver talks about Linda's character, saying that she is 'refreshingly frank', 'straightforward', 'upfront about her feelings about things' and that she 'doesn't waste time on social rubbish'. She hints at Linda's moral superiority, even if some would feel that these are behaviours that follow from the condition and that there may not be much of a choice in it. If people do not lie because they can not, they are not on a moral spectrum.

The idea of autistic persons teaching wise lessons is often presented to imply that we should stop viewing autism as a set of deficits or even as a condition at all. This may take the shape of portraying autistic persons as simply having a *different* set of talents, equally valuable as normal talents. And sometimes autistic persons are presented as being not so different from us, after all, or, to say the same that we are all in a sense autistic. Clearly, these are two contrasting views; still, one often finds them in blissful harmony, sometimes on the same page, in the same scene. This is what Alan Rickman says about how he thinks Linda's autistic behaviour is related to normal behaviour: 'I think the thing is we're all on a graph of autism. Frankly, I recognize things in the rules of autism which are things that I do, you know, any kind of little obsessive behaviour, or repetitious things, or, you know, if you rearrange all the things on top of a piece of furniture, make them line up, that's pretty autistic.' In stereotypes such as these, the characteristics of autism blur into normal behaviours, contributing to the 'fuzziness' of the concept of autism.

17.6 The value of limits and leeway

Both the 'freak' savant stereotype and the 'in a sense we're all autistic' stereotype misrepresent autism, but they do so in opposite directions. The former stereotype draws autism in the realm of the exceptional and the spectacular. The latter stereotype suggests that autism is largely co-extensive with normal, non-pathological behaviour and is perhaps not even a disorder at all. What both stereotypes have in common, though, is that they tend to complicate the efforts to delineate autism as a psychiatric category with more or less specific limits and diagnostic criteria.

A further complication may result from representations of autism in the work of persons who are themselves autistic. A case in point is Daniel Tammet's autobiography *Born on a blue day* (2006). Tammet, diagnosed with Asperger's syndrome, describes the rigid obsessions, the ritualistic acts and compulsions, the intense fascination with simple movements such as a spinning coin, the peculiar preference for lists of facts, such as the capitals of the world, and many more of the traits that ever since the work of Asperger have shaped the Gestalt of this syndrome. What are especially touching in his book are the examples of ways of thinking that one ordinarily finds in the professional literature only in the shape of test results. Lacking a 'theory of mind', children with Asperger's syndrome find it difficult to handle 'false belief situations (Baron-Cohen *et al.* 1985), usually brought out in Sally Anne type of tests. Tammet relates a well-known Russian folktale, 'Stone Soup', which was completely incomprehensible to him as a child: 'I found the story very puzzling at the time because I had no concept of deception and did not understand that the soldier was pretending to make a soup from a stone in order to trick the villagers into contributing to it. Only many years later did I finally understand what the story was about'. (Tammet 2006, pp. 64–65).

This is a layered passage. It is a convincing demonstration of the difficulties a child with Asperger's will have understanding what is going on in other people's minds. On the other hand, the reader might wonder whether without such a 'theory of mind', Tammet would have been able to write about his failure to understand the story as a child, or about his present interpretation of his earlier lack of understanding. This is a wonderful instance of the looping effect: a scientific hypothesis on a central deficit in the mental functioning of a person with Asperger's explains to Tammet why he did not understand the gist of the story as a child. Tammet's autobiography clearly demonstrates why Asperger's syndrome is such an evasive concept. The very fact that limits may shift as a consequence of looping effects characterizes this syndrome as the type of diagnosis with uncertain boundaries.

In some cases the diffuseness of limits may be a blessing in disguise. It is partly due to the dedication of his parents and teachers that Daniel Tammet has been able to expand some of the limits of his condition. In his book he uses metaphors, he makes jokes, he analyses his inner life—he does all kinds of things a person with Asperger's is not supposed to be able to do. This is the inspiring, uplifting consequence of limits that are not nailed down in a standard: they invite patients, parents and teachers to test whether these limits are really permanent, whether deficits can be eliminated, compensated or outgrown and whether special talents may be a key to social integration. The persons diagnosed with autism and their loved ones may try to push these limits, transforming the disorder in the process.

At the same time, talents and abilities may introduce conceptual complications, especially on matters such as definition, labelling and classification. This may sound like a philosopher's concern, with little bearing on the practicalities of living with autistic persons—or being an autistic person—but that would be a mistake. Talents are part and parcel of the processes that shape the various labels of autism. In a chapter called 'Mark Haddon's popularity and other curious incidents in my life as an autistic'—some strange loops are definitely there—Burks-Abbott writes that the *Curious incident* has become the new *Rain Man*. When he tells people that he is autistic, 'the first question they ask is, 'Have you read *The curious incident of the dog in the nighttime?*' as if that were the best example of a book written about autism' (Burks-Abbott 2008, p. 295). He adds that by now there are dozens of books on the autistic condition written by autistic authors, but that lay audiences seem to prefer fiction by a non-autistic over the non-fiction by an autistic. This goes to show that the images and stereotypes constructed by novels and movies may eclipse those of experts, be they psychiatrists, paediatricians or autistics.

We have seen that these stereotypes are very diverse and in the manner of all stereotypes misleading, as far as a particular individual's behaviour is concerned. In cases where they do seem to offer a fair and reliable reflection of the autistic condition, such as Daniel Tammet's representation of Asperger's syndrome, stereotypes may still contribute to the lack of specificity in the description and diagnosis of autism. This is a consequence that should not be taken lightly. Putting disorders on a spectrum is always a reassuring thing to do, it allows for leeway, margins, fine-tuning and revision in the light of later developments. But there are also persons who live outside this happy universe of sliding scales and gradients. These are the people who are forced to make dichotomous decisions, often in a professional setting. Should this child be admitted to special education, yes or no? Should I employ this person, yes or no? In The Netherlands, the past 5 years have seen a quick rise of forensic cases where the defence pleaded for milder sentences, arguing that the criminal act was in some way a consequence of a disorder in the autism spectrum. This happened in a great variety of crimes, ranging from fire-setting, stalking and sexual abuse to manslaughter, and an equally great variety of adduced causal links (Draaisma 2008). Even if it is doubtful whether these links really exist, the relevant fact here is that they *were* introduced in pleas and that the judge will pass sentence partly on expert's reports and partly on what he thinks he knows about autism based on general stereotypes and perceptions of autism. That is why it is vital to scrutinize media representations of autism and to see to it that we do not allow these stereotypes to stray too far from the clinical reality of autism. The unrealistic stereotype of autistic savants having supercomputers for brains, to mention but one example, may create the myth of autistic persons having no feelings. In the realm of talent this may have no harmful implications, but in the realm of forensics this myth could have grave consequences. What is meant here has a name. It is called the Thomas Theorem. It says: 'If men define situations as real, they are real in their consequences'. (Thomas & Thomas 1928, pp. 571–572).

References

Ash, M. G. 1995 *Gestalt psychology in German culture, 1890–1967: holism and the quest for objectivity*. Cambridge, UK: Cambridge University Press.
Asperger, H. 1944 Die 'autistischen Psychopathen' im Kindesalter. *Archiv fur Psychiatrie und Nervenkrankheiten* **117**, 76–136. (doi:10.1007/BF01837709)
Baker, A. D. 2008 Recognizing Jake: contending with formulaic and spectacularized representations of autism in film. In *Autism and representation* (ed. M. Osteen), pp. 229–243. New York, NY/London, UK: Taylor & Francis.
Baron-Cohen, S., Leslie, A. M. & Frith, U. 1985 Does the autistic child have a 'theory of mind'? *Cognition* **21**, 37–46. (doi:10.1016/0010-0277(85)90022-8)
Burks-Abbott, G. 2008 Mark Haddon's popularity and other curious incidents in my life as an autistic. In *Autism and representation* (ed. M. Osteen), pp. 289–296. New York, NY/London, UK: Taylor & Francis.
Draaisma, D. 2008 Who owns Asperger's syndrome? *Sartoniana* **21**, 23–48.
Hacking, I. 1995 *Rewriting the soul*. Princeton, NJ: Princeton University Press.
Hacking, I. 2007 Kinds of people: moving targets. *Proc. Br.Acad.* **151**, 285–318.
Haddon, M. 2003 *The curious incident of the dog in the nighttime*. London, UK: Jonathan Cape.
Miller, J. N. & Ozonoff, S. 1997 Did Asperger's cases have Asperger disorder? A research note. *J. Child Psychol. Psychiatry* **38**, 247–251.
Murray, S. 2008 *Representing autism. Culture, narrative, fascination*. Liverpool, UK: Liverpool University Press.
Rosch, E. 1978 *Cognition and categorization*. Hillsdale, NJ: Lawrence Erlbaum.
Tammet, D. 2006 *Born on a blue day. A memoir of Asperger's and an extraordinary mind*. London, UK: Hodder and Stoughton.
Thomas, W. I. & Thomas, D. S. 1928 *The child in America*. New York, NY: Knopf.

Movies

Mercury Rising. 1998. Dir. H. Becker.
Mozart and the Whale. 2005. Dir. P. Næss.
Rain Man. 1988. Dir. B. Levinson.
Snow Cake. 2006. Dir. M. Evans.

Index

absolute pitch 33, 34, 47, 152–3
abstract expressionists 167–9
acquired savant skills 6, 77
action representation 162
affect *see* emotion
alexithymia 156
art brut, *see* Outsider Art
artistic skills 4, 123–4
   abstract expressionists 167–9
   detailed-focused cognitive style 33, 120
   examples of autistic artists 185–91
   induced 77–8
   neural correlates 122
   Outsider Art xiii, 181–5, 191–3
   precocious realists xiii, 161–7, 169–77
Asperger, Hans 209–10, 211, 212
Asperger's syndrome
   harnessing talent 148
   systemizing 44, 45, 46
association 141
auditory processing 47, 48–9;
   see also pitch processing
autism narrative 195, 198–9, 203, 204
autistic triad 30
autobiographies 141–8, 195–8,
   199–200, 203–5, 215–16

behaviour, repetitive xvii, 15, 21, 22–3, 33, 60
beta-band activity 136, 138
Blackstock, Gregory 189
block design 14, 18, 22, 33, 34, 44, 45,
   66, 120, 172–5, 176, 177–8
Born on a blue day (Tammet) 215–16
bottom-up thinking 142, 143
brain imaging 9, 110–14, 122, 126, 128, 130, 148
brain plasticity xvi, 10
bus drivers 92, 94

calbindin 136
   calretinin 136
calculation, number processing 108–9, 121–2
calendrical savants 4, 33, 105–17, 120,
   123, 126, 128, 129
case description 209–11

Castle, James 186–7
categorization 143–4
central coherence 32;
   see also weak central coherence
cinema portrayals of autism 211–14, 215
classification xv, 46
cognitive accounts of autism 30–3
cognitive flexibility 32
cognitive skills 15, 17–18, 170–7;
   see also detailed-focused cognitive style
composition 7
concept formation 45–6, 143
cortical rededication 30
cortical thickness 126, 128, 130
creativity 7, 58–9
crime, defence of autism 217
cross-modal connections 139
culture, artistic conventions 166–7
curious incident of the dog
   in the night-time, *The* (Haddon)
   198–9, 214–15

detailed-focused cognitive style xii, xv, xvii,
   32–3, 35, 36, 41, 43–4, 120
diagnostic triad 30
door symbols 143
dorsal visual stream 69–70
Down, J. Langdon 2, 3
drawing, *see* artistic skills

education
   hyper-systemizing 45–6
   special schools 8
embedded figures test (EFT) 66, 120, 125
emotion 59–60, 155, 156
enhanced perceptual
   functioning (EPF) 53–4, 66, 152, 153
executive dysfunction 32, 46–7
expertise effects 60
explore/exploit xvii–xviii

false memory 80
feature binding 138
female savants 2, 23

fictional accounts of autism 198–9, 214–15, 216
film portrayals of autism 211–14, 215
flow 31
fostering talent xvi–xvii
fractionable triad 30
frequency effect 60
frontal cortex 146, 147
frontal function 32
fronto-parietal networks 136
fronto-temporal dementia 6, 7, 77, 80, 148
functional imaging 9, 110–14
fusiform gyrus 30, 108

gamma-aminobutyric acid (GABA) neurons 136, 138
generalization xv, 58, 59, 66
generativity 32
genetics xv, 14, 36
Gestalt-like method 210
Gestalt psychology 201–2
Gill, Madge 182
global processing 33, 66–9, 120, 154
Grandin, Temple 8–9, 141–8, 196
graphic representation 162
grey matter 92–3, 94–5, 96, 98
grouping 56, 66–9

hearing 47, 48–9; *see also* pitch processing
hemispheric competition 76, 81
hippocampus xv, 91–4, 95, 96, 98, 143
human codes 54, 55
hyperconnectivity xvi, 49
hyperlexia xiv, 61
hypersensitivity xii, 42, 47–9, 204
hyper-systemizing, *see* systemizing

idiot savant, coining of term 2
imagery 122
imaging studies 9, 110–14, 122, 126, 128, 130, 148
implicit learning 31, 120–1, 125, 130, 155
improvisation 7
inference 202–3
inferior parietal lobe 112
inferior temporal cortex 113
information completion 57–8
information processing speed 121, 130
inhibition of savant skills 82
inner state awareness 31
'inside' autism 199–201
inspection time 121, 125, 130
intelligence (IQ) 15, 17–18, 20, 147–8, 171
intentionality 185

interference 60
intraparietal sulcus 109, 121–2
inverse theories 66, 69
isomorphism 55

Kanner, Leo 210
Köhler, W. 201–3
koniocells 70

Lamb, Dante 167–8
language 204–5
latent savant skills 76–7, 82
left anterior temporal lobe (LATL) 76, 77, 78, 80–1
left brain dysfunction 76
left temporal cortex 7, 113
lifelong learning xvi
local drawing strategy 176–7
local feature binding 138
local processing xii–xiii, 33, 44, 120, 152
logic board 144
London bus drivers 92, 94
London taxi drivers xv, 90–4, 95–7, 98
low level processing 47, 54, 66, 69, 75–6, 77, 80
luminance contrast 70–1

magnocellular pathway 69–70, 71
mappings 56
Mar, Jean 187
mathematics 4–5
mechanical skills 5
memory xii, 5–6, 129
    artistic skills 176
    calendrical savants 107–8, 129
    expertise 89–100
    false memory 80
    musical skills 153
    working memory superiority 32
mental imagery 122
mental segmentation 170–1, 172–5
Mercury Rising 213
Method of Loci 94
mind-blindness 30–1
minicolumns xvi, 135–7, 138, 139, 146
mirror neurons 203
mnemonics 94
Monsiel, Edmund 182–3
motion coherence 69
motivation xvii
movie portrayals of autism 211–14, 215
Mozart and the Whale 212–13

multiple skills xv–xvi, 5, 119
musical skills xiv, 4, 7, 33, 151–9

navigation xv, 91–4, 95–7, 98
neural hyperconnectivity xvi, 49
neuroimaging 9, 110–14, 122, 126, 128, 130, 148
novelty xvii–xviii
number processing 108–9, 121–2
numerosity 78–80

olfaction 47–8
Olmstead, Marla 167, 168–9
originality 31
Outsider Art xiii, 181–5, 191–3
overconnectivity xvi, 48

pain sensation 48, 204
parental reports 18–19
parietal lobe 108–9, 112, 113–14, 121–2, 128, 130
parvalbumin 136
parvocells 70–1
pattern completion 57–8
pattern recognition xii, 42, 54–7
pattern thinking 145
peaks of ability 60
perception
    abnormalities in autism 69–71
    enhanced perceptual functioning
      (EPF) 53–4, 66, 152, 153
perceptual cohesiveness 172–5
perceptual grouping 56, 66–9
perceptual peaks 60
phenomenal resemblance 55
photo-realistic visual thinking 141, 143, 144, 145
Picasso, Pablo 165, 166
pitch processing 33, 34, 47, 152–3
planum temporale 153
plasticity xvi, 10
Polaroid camera test 43
Pomp, Jeroen 188
posterior inferior temporal sulcus 61
practice xiv–xv, xvii, 122
precocious realists xiii, 161–7, 169–77
precocious talent xvi–xvii
predisposition to talent 34
premotor cortex 113
prevalence of savant skills xii, 4, 29
prime numbers xi
private world 182, 183, 186, 192
privileged access hypothesis xiv, 54, 66,
    75–6, 82, 83

prodigious savants xii, 5
proofreading 78
pyramidal cells 136, 137

Rain Man 214
Raven's Progressive Matrices 147
redintegration 57
relatives of savants, special skills 6
repetitive behaviour xvii, 15, 21, 22–3, 30, 60
repetitive transcranial magnetic
    stimulation (rTMS) xiv, 77–9, 81
restricted interests 15, 22–3, 33–4, 58–9
reward learning xviii
right posterior inferior temporal sulcus 61
ritualistic behaviours 15, 21, 22–3, 33
Rubik's cube 42–3, 44–5
rule recognition 42

sameness, preference for xvii–xviii
savant skills
    acquired 6, 77
    artificial induction 77–80
    definition 13–14
    inhibition 82
    latent 76–7, 82
    loss of 6–7
    multiple xv–xvi, 5, 119
    prevalence xii, 4, 29
    progression of 7
    sex differences 2, 4, 14, 20–1, 23
    specific areas 4–5, 14
    spectrum 5
schools, *see* education
self-awareness 31
sensory hypersensitivity xii, 42, 47–9, 204
sex differences 2, 4, 14, 20–1, 23
skin sensitivity 48
Snow Cake 212, 215
social interest 31
sound sensitivity 49
spatial skills 5
special interests 15, 22–3, 33–4, 58–9
specialist thinkers 145
special schools 8
speech 205
splinter skills xii, 5
statistical learning 152
stereotyped behaviours 15, 21, 22–3, 33
stereotypes of autism 209–18
stimming 47
structure 54–5, 59–60

superior parietal lobe 112, 121–2, 128, 130
supplementary motor area 113
synaesthesia 77, 138
synaptic function 135
systemizing xv, 41, 42–7, 120–1

tactile discrimination 47
talent, *see* savant skills
talented savants xii, 5
taxi drivers xv, 90–4, 95–7, 98
temporal lobe 7, 76, 77, 78, 80–1, 113
"The Knowledge" xv, 90
theory of mind 201, 202
timbre 153
touch 47
train the talent 8–9
transcranial magnetic stimulation (rTMS) xiv, 77–9, 81
Trehin, Gilles 186
Twins Early Development Study (TEDS) 34

unifying principle 142

V1 138
V5 69
veridical mapping xii, xiv, 56, 58
vision 47, 48
visual attention 136
visual cortex 69, 138, 139, 148
visual memory 176
visual mental imagery 122
visual search 65
visual symbol picture 142
visual thinking 141, 143, 144, 145

weak central coherence (WCC) xii, 32–3, 66, 120, 152, 154
  systemizing 43–5
weight estimation 56
Wenzel, Roy 187
white matter 146
Widener, George 189–91
Wiltshire, Stephen 185–6
Wittgenstein, L. 201–2
Wölfii, Adolf 187
word–fact thinking 145
working memory 32